CHILTON'S REPAIR & TUNE-UP GUIDE
OMNI HORIZON 1978-80

Dodge Omni and 024 • Plymouth Horizon and TC3

Managing Editor KERRY A. FREEMAN, S.A.E.
Senior Editor RICHARD J. RIVELE

President WILLIAM A. BARBOUR
Executive Vice President RICHARD H. GROVES
Vice President and General Manager JOHN P. KUSHNERICK

CHILTON BOOK COMPANY
Radnor, Pennsylvania
19089

Copyright © 1979 by Chilton Book Company
All Rights Reserved
Published in Radnor, Pa., by Chilton Book Company
and simultaneously in Ontario, Canada
by Thomas Nelson & Sons, Ltd.

Manufactured in the United States of America

234567890   876543210

Chilton's Repair & Tune-Up Guide: Omni and Horizon
1978–80
ISBN 0-8019-6845-3 pbk.

Library of Congress Catalog Card No. 78-20257

TL
215
.D66
C47
1979

The Chilton Book Company expresses its appreciation to the Chrysler Corporation, Dodge and Plymouth Divisions, Detroit, Michigan for their generous assistance.

Although the information in this guide is based on industry sources and is as complete as possible at the time of publication, the possibility exists that the manufacturer made later changes which could not be included here. While striving for total accuracy, Chilton Book Company cannot assume responsibility for any errors, changes, or omissions that may occur in the compilation of this data.

Part numbers listed in this book are not recommendations by Chilton for any product by brand name. They are references that can be used with interchange manuals and aftermarket supplier catalogs to locate each brand supplier's discrete part number.

SAFETY NOTICE

Proper service and repair procedures are vital to the safe, reliable operation of all motor vehicles, as well as the personal safety of those performing repairs. This book outlines procedures for servicing and repairing vehicles using safe, effective methods. The procedures contain many NOTES, CAUTIONS and WARNINGS which should be followed along with standard safety procedures to eliminate the possibility of personal injury or improper service which could damage the vehicle or compromise its safety.

It is important to note that repair procedures and techniques, tools and parts for servicing motor vehicles, as well as the skill and experience of the individual performing the work vary widely. It is not possible to anticipate all of the conceivable ways or conditions under which vehicles may be serviced, or to provide cautions as to all of the possible hazards that may result. Standard and accepted safety precautions and equipment should be used when handling toxic or flammable fluids, and safety goggles or other protection should be used during cutting, grinding, chiseling, prying, or any other process that can cause material removal or projectiles.

Some procedures require the use of tools specially designed for a specific purpose. Before substituting another tool or procedure, you must be completely satisfied that neither your personal safety, nor the performance of the vehicle will be endangered.

Contents

1 General Information and Maintenance 1

How to use this book, 1
Tools and Equipment, 2
Routine Maintenance and Lubrication, 11

2 Tune-Up and Troubleshooting 43

Tune-Up Procedures and Specifications, 43
Troubleshooting, 52

3 Engine and Engine Rebuilding 68

Engine Electrical System and Specifications, 68
Engine Service Procedures and Specifications, 83
Engine Rebuilding, 103

4 Fuel System and Emission Controls 121

Emission Control System and Service, 121
Fuel System and Carburetor Adjustments, 132

5 Chassis Electrical 142

Heater, Radio, Windshield Wipers, Instrument Panel, Light Bulbs and Fuses, 144

6 Clutch and Transmission 156

Manual Transaxle, 156
Clutch, 158
Automatic Transaxle, 160

7 Suspension and Steering 164

Front Suspension, 164
Rear Suspension, 173
Steering, 175

8 Brakes 178

Brake System Service and Specifications, 178

9 Body 191

Aligning Hoods and Doors, 191
Repairing Scratches, Dents, and Rust Holes, 193

Appendix 202

Index 206

25 Ways to Improve Fuel Economy 209

Quick Reference Specifications

For quick and easy reference, complete this page with the most commonly used specifications for your vehicle. The specifications can be found in Chapters 1 through 3 or on the tune-up decal under the hood of the vehicle.

TUNE-UP

Firing Order _____

Spark Plugs:

    Type _____

    Gap (in.) _____

Point Gap (in.) _____

Dwell Angle (°) _____

Ignition Timing (°) _____

    Vacuum (Connected/Disconnected) _____

Valve Clearance (in.)

    Intake _____ **Exhaust** _____

CAPACITIES

Engine Oil (qts)

    With Filter Change _____

    Without Filter Change _____

Cooling System (qts) _____

Manual Transmission (pts) _____

    Type _____

Automatic Transmission (pts) _____

    Type _____

Differential (pts) _____

    Type _____

COMMONLY FORGOTTEN PART NUMBERS

Use these spaces to record the part numbers of frequently replaced parts.

PCV VALVE	OIL FILTER	AIR FILTER
Manufacturer _____	Manufacturer _____	Manufacturer _____
Part No. _____	Part No. _____	Part No. _____

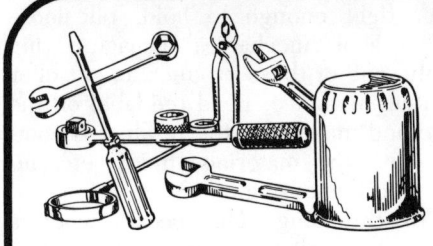

General Information and Maintenance

HOW TO USE THIS BOOK

Chilton's Repair & Tune-Up Guide for the Dodge Omni/Plymouth Horizon is intended to help you learn more about the inner workings of your vehicle and save you money on its upkeep and operation.

The first two chapters will be the most used, since they contain maintenance and tune-up information and procedures. Studies have shown that a properly tuned and maintained car can get at least 10% better gas milage than an out-of-tune car. The other chapters deal with the more complex systems of your car. Operating systems from engine through brakes are covered to the extent that the average do-it-yourselfer becomes mechanically involved. This book will not explain such things as rebuilding the differential for the simple reason that the expertise required and the investment in special tools make this task uneconomical. It will give you detailed instructions to help you change your own brake pads and shoes, replace points and plugs, and do many more jobs that will save you money, give you personal satisfaction, and help you avoid expensive problems.

A secondary purpose of this book is a reference for owners who want to understand their car and/or their mechanics better. In this case, no tools at all are required.

Before removing any bolts, read through the entire procedure. This will give you the overall view of what tools and supplies will be required. There is nothing more frustrating than having to walk to the bus stop on Monday morning because you were short one bolt on Sunday afternoon. So read ahead and plan ahead. Each operation should be approached logically and all procedures thoroughly understood before attempting any work.

All chapters contain adjustments, maintenance, removal and installation procedures, and repair or overhaul procedures. When repair is not considered practical, we tell you how to remove the part and then how to install the new or rebuilt replacement. In this way, you at least save the labor costs. Backyard repair of such components as the alternator is just not practical.

Two basic mechanic's rules should be mentioned here. One, whenever the left side of the car or engine is referred to, it is meant to specify the driver's side of the car. Conversely, the right side of the car means the passenger's side. Secondly, most screws and bolts are removed by turning counterclockwise, and tightened by turning clockwise.

Safety is always the most important rule. Constantly be aware of the dangers involved in working on an automobile and taking the proper precautions. (See the section in this chapter "Servicing Your Vehicle Safely" and the SAFETY NOTICE on the acknowledgement page.)

Pay attention to the instructions provided. There are 3 common mistakes in mechanical work:

1. Incorrect order of assembly, disassembly or adjustment. When taking something apart or putting it together, doing things in the wrong order usually just costs you extra time; however, it CAN break something. Read the entire procedure before beginning disassembly. Do everything in the order in which the instructions say you should do it, even if you can't immediately see a reason for it. When you're taking apart something that is very intricate (for example, a carburetor), you might want to draw a picture of how it looks when assembled at one point in order to make sure you get everything back in its proper position. (We will supply exploded views whenever possible.) When making adjustments, especially tune-up adjustments, do them in order; often, one adjustment affects another, and you cannot expect even satisfactory results unless each adjustment is made only when it cannot be changed by any other.

2. Overtorquing (or undertorquing). While it is more common for overtorquing to cause damage, undertorquing can cause a fastener to vibrate loose causing serious damage. Especially when dealing with aluminum parts, pay attention to torque specifications and utilize a torque wrench in assembly. If a torque figure is not available, remember that if you are using the right tool to do the job, you will probably not have to strain yourself to get a fastener tight enough. The pitch of most threads is so slight that the tension you put on the wrench will be multiplied many, many times in actual force on what you are tightening. A good example of how critical torque is can be seen in the case of spark plug installation, especially where you are putting the plug into an aluminum cylinder head. Too little torque can fail to crush the gasket, causing leakage of combustion gases and consequent overheating of the plug and engine parts. Too much torque can damage the threads, or distort the plug, which changes the spark gap.

There are many commercial products available for ensuring that fasteners won't come loose, even if they are not torqued just right (a very common brand is "Loctite®"). If you're worried about getting something together tight enough to hold, but loose enough to avoid mechanical damage during assembly, one of these products might offer substantial insurance. Read the label on the package and make sure the product is compatible with the materials, fluids, etc. involved before choosing one.

3. Crossthreading. This occurs when a part such as a bolt is screwed into a nut or casting at the wrong angle and forced. Crossthreading is more likely to occur if access is difficult. It helps to clean and lubricate fasteners, and to start threading with the part to be installed going straight in. Then, start the bolt, spark plug, etc. with your fingers. If you encounter resistance, unscrew the part and start over again at a different angle until it can be inserted and turned several turns without much effort. Keep in mind that many parts, especially spark plugs, use tapered threads so that gentle turning will automatically bring the part you're threading to the proper angle if you don't force it or resist a change in angle. Don't put a wrench on the part until it's been turned a couple of turns by hand. If you suddenly encounter resistance, and the part has not seated fully, don't force it. Pull it back out and make sure it's clean and threading properly.

Always take your time and be patient; once you have some experience, working on your car will become an enjoyable hobby.

TOOLS AND EQUIPMENT

Naturally, without the proper tools and equipment it is impossible to properly service your vehicle. It would be impossible to catalog each tool that you would need to perform each or any operation in this book. It would also be unwise for the amateur to rush out and buy an expensive set of tools on the theory that he may need one or more of them at sometime.

The best approach is to proceed slowly, gathering together a good quality set of those tools that are used most frequently. Don't be misled by the low cost of bargain tools. It is far better to spend a little more for better quality. Forged wrenches, 10 or 12 point sockets and fine tooth ratchets are by far preferable to their less expensive counterparts. As any good mechanic can tell you, there are few worse experiences than trying to work on a car or truck with bad tools. Your monetary

GENERAL INFORMATION AND MAINTENANCE

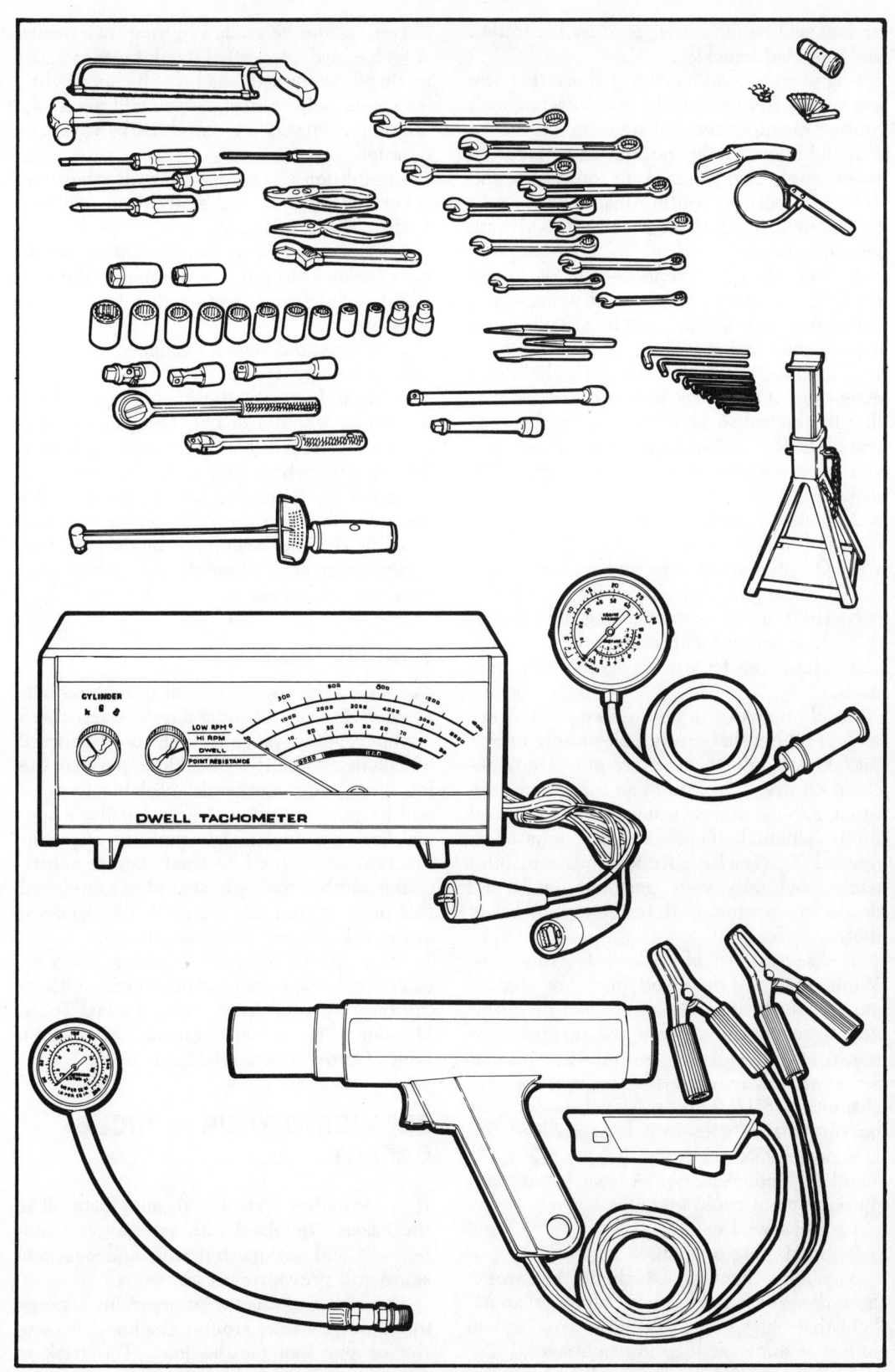

The majority of automotive service can be handled with these tools

GENERAL INFORMATION AND MAINTENANCE

savings will be far outweighed by frustration and mangled knuckles.

Begin accumulating those tools that are used most frequently; those associated with routine maintenance and tune-up.

In addition to the normal assortment of screwdrivers and pliers you should have the following tools for routine maintenance jobs (your Omni or Horizon uses both SAE and metric fasteners):

1. SAE/Metric wrenches—sockets and combination open end/box end wrenches in sizes from 1/8 in. (3 mm) to 3/4 in. (19 mm); and a spark plug socket (13/16).

If possible, buy various length socket drive extensions. One break in this department is that the metric sockets available in the U.S. will all fit the ratchet handles and extensions you may already have (1/4, 3/8, and 1/2 in. drive).

2. Jackstands—for support;
3. Oil filter wrench;
4. Oil filler spout—for pouring oil;
5. Grease gun—for chassis lubrication;
6. Hydrometer—for checking the battery;
7. A container for draining oil;
8. Many rags for wiping up the inevitable mess.

In addition to the above items there are several others that are not absolutely necessary, but handy to have around. These include oil dry, a transmission funnel and the usual supply of lubricants, antifreeze and fluids, although these can be purchased as needed. This is a basic list for routine maintenance, but only your personal needs and desire can accurately determine your list of tools.

The second list of tools is for tune-ups. While the tools involved here are slightly more sophisticated, they need not be outrageously expensive. There are several inexpensive tach/dwell meters on the market that are every bit as good for the average mechanic as a $100.00 professional model. Just be sure that it goes to a least 1,200–1,500 rpm on the tach scale and that it works on 4, 6 and 8 cylinder engines. A basic list of tune-up equipment could include:

1. Tach-dwell meter;
2. Spark plug wrench;
3. Timing light (a DC light that works from the car's battery is best, although an AC light that plugs into 110V house current will suffice at some sacrifice in brightness);
4. Wire spark plug gauge/adjusting tools;
5. Set of feeler blades.

Here again, be guided by your own needs. A feeler blade will set the point gap as easily as dwell meter will read dwell, but slightly less accurately. And since you will need a tachometer anyway . . . well, make your own decision.

In addition to these basic tools, there are several other tools and gauges you may find useful. These include:

1. A compression gauge. The screw-in type is slower to use, but eliminates the possibility of a faulty reading due to escaping pressure;
2. A manifold vacuum gauge;
3. A test light;
4. An induction meter. This is used for determining whether or not there is current in a wire. These are handy for use if a wire is broken somewhere in a wiring harness.

As a final note, you will probably find a torque wrench necessary for all but the most basic work. The beam type models are perfectly adequate, although the newer click type are more precise.

Special Tools

Normally, the use of special factory tools is avoided for repair procedures, since these are not readily available for the do-it-yourself mechanic. When it is possible to perform the job with more commonly available tools, it will be pointed out, but occasionally, a special tool was designed to perform a specific function and should be used. Before substituting another tool, you should be convinced that neither your safety nor the performance of the vehicle will be compromised.

Some special tools are available commercially from major tool manufacturers. Others can be purchased from Miller Special Tools; Division of Utica Tool Company, 32615 Park Lane, Garden City, Michigan 48135.

SERVICING YOUR VEHICLE SAFELY

It is virtually impossible to anticipate all of the hazards involved with automotive maintenance and service but care and common sense will prevent most accidents.

The rules of safety for mechanics range from "don't smoke around gasoline," to "use the proper tool for the job." The trick to avoiding injuries is to develop safe work habits and take every possible precaution.

GENERAL INFORMATION AND MAINTENANCE

Dos

• Do keep a fire extinguisher and first aid kit within easy reach.

• Do wear safety glasses or goggles when cutting, drilling, grinding or prying, even if you have 20-20 vision. If you wear glasses for the sake of vision, then they should be made of hardened glass that can serve also as safety glasses, or wear safety goggles over your regular glasses.

• Do shield your eyes whenever you work around the battery. Batteries contain sulphuric acid; in case of contact with the eyes or skin, flush the area with water or a mixture of water and baking soda and get medical attention immediately.

• Do use safety stands for any undercar service. Jacks are for raising vehicles; safety stands are for making sure the vehicle stays raised until you want it to come down. Whenever the vehicle is raised, block the wheels remaining on the ground and set the parking brake.

• Do use adequate ventilation when working with any chemicals. Like carbon monoxide, the asbestos dust resulting from brake lining wear can be poisonous in sufficient quantities.

• Do disconnect the negative battery cable when working on the electrical system. The primary ignition system can contain up to 40,000 volts.

• Do follow manufacturer's directions whenever working with potentially hazardous materials. Both brake fluid and antifreeze are poisonous if taken internally.

• Do properly maintain your tools. Loose hammerheads, mushroomed punches and chisels, frayed or poorly grounded electrical cords, excessively worn screwdrivers, spread wrenches (open end), cracked sockets, slipping ratchets, or faulty droplight sockets can cause accidents.

• Do use the proper size and type of tool for the job being done.

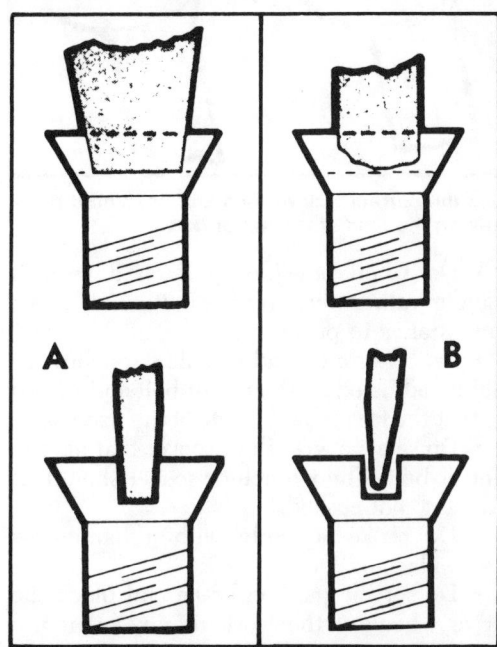

Screwdrivers should be kept in good condition to prevent injury

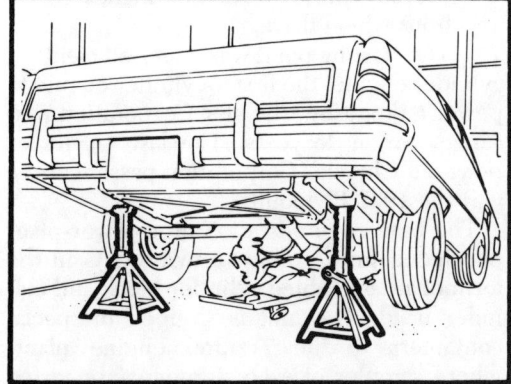

Always use jackstands when working under the car

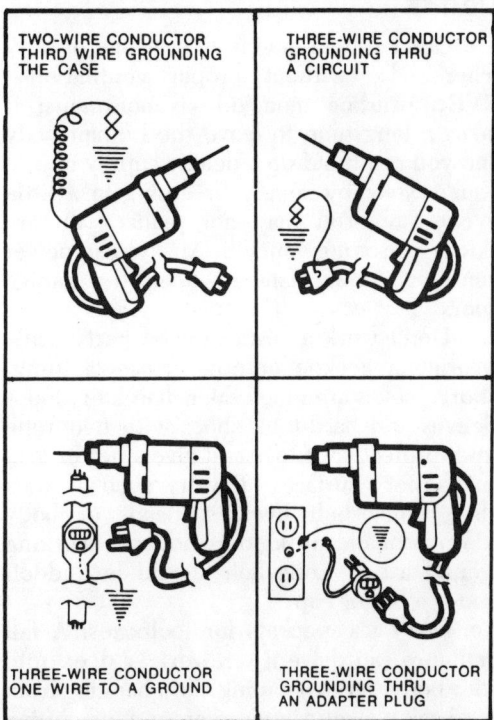

Power tools should always be properly grounded

GENERAL INFORMATION AND MAINTENANCE

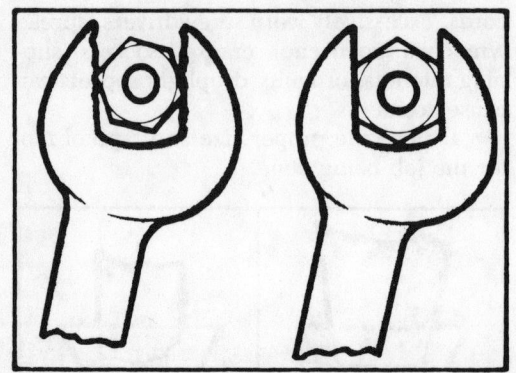

Use the correct size wrench and position it properly on the flats of the nut or bolt

• Do when possible, pull on a wrench handle rather than push on it, and adjust your stance to prevent a fall.
• Do be sure that adjustable wrenches are tightly adjusted on the nut or bolt and pulled so that the face is on the side of the fixed jaw.
• Do select a wrench or socket that fits the nut or bolt. The wrench or socket should sit straight, not cocked.
• Do strike squarely with a hammer—avoid glancing blows.
• Do set the parking brake and block the drive wheels if the work requires that the engine be running.

Don'ts

• Don't run an engine in a garage or anywhere else without proper ventilation—EVER! Carbon monoxide is poisonous; it takes a long time to leave the human body and you can build up a deadly supply of it in your system by simply breathing in a little every day. You may not realize you are slowly poisoning yourself. Always use power vents, windows, fans or open the garage doors.
• Don't work around moving parts while wearing a necktie or other loose clothing. Short sleeves are much safer than long, loose sleeves and hard-toed shoes with neoprene soles protect your toes and give a better grip on slippery surfaces. Jewelry such as watches, fancy belt buckles, beads or body adornment of any kind is not safe working around a car. Long hair should be hidden under a hat or cap.
• Don't use pockets for toolboxes. A fall or bump can drive a screwdriver deep into your body. Even a wiping cloth hanging from the back pocket can wrap around a spinning shaft or fan.
• Don't smoke when working around gasoline, cleaning solvent or other flammable material.
• Don't smoke when working around the battery. When the battery is being charged, it gives off explosive hydrogen gas.
• Don't use gasoline to wash your hands; there are excellent soaps available. Gasoline may contain lead, and lead can enter the body through a cut, accumulating in the body until you are very ill. Gasoline also removes all the natural oils from the skin so that bone dry hands will suck up oil and grease.
• Don't service the air conditioning system unless you are equipped with the necessary tools and training. The refrigerant, R-12, is extremely cold and when exposed to the air, will instantly freeze any surface it comes in contact with, including your eyes. Although the refrigerant is normally non-toxic, R-12 becomes a deadly poisonous gas in the presence of an open flame. One good whiff of the vapors from burning refrigerant can be fatal.

HISTORY

In designing the Omni and Horizon models, Chrysler didn't replace a car as much as design a brand new, efficiency-sized car for the U.S. market. The goal was to design a car with outstanding roominess, good handling characteristics, good fuel economy and flexibility of use.

According to chassis and body development studies the new car would be based on these criteria:
—a fuel-efficient 4-cylinder engine
—base weight less than 2,100 pounds
—overall length less than 165 inches
—overall width less than 66 inches
—front wheel drive.

The starting point was a fuel-efficient, 4-cylinder engine, the first 4-cylinder engine to power a domestic Chrysler Corporation passenger car in 45 years. The last 4-cylinder powered Chrysler Corporation passenger car was the 1932 Plymouth.

The base engine is a 1.7 liter power-plant purchased from Volkswagenwerk AG in the form of an assembled cylinder block and cylinder head. The unit is shipped in special containers to the Trenton engine plant, where samples of each shipment are tested on a dynomometer and completely torn down during a complete quality control in-

GENERAL INFORMATION AND MAINTENANCE

spection. The other components—intake and exhaust manifolds, fuel pump, carburetor and controls, emission controls, alternator, power steering pump, clutch, air cleaner, ignition system—are all obtained from U.S. suppliers and installed at the engine plant. Since the Omni and Horizon models are Chrysler's first metric designed models built in the U.S., the cylinder block, head and crankshaft are built to metric measurements. Other components, mostly those obtained from domestic suppliers, such as the power steering pump or alternator retain inch-size dimensions.

Early in the design stages, Chrysler engineers realized that even with their design parameters, the luggage carrying needs of people hadn't changed that much. Front wheel drive offered the dimensional advantages to obtain the desired front and rear legroom with a superior luggage carrying capacity, and still stay within the design criteria. The lower floor, made possible by front wheel drive eliminating the driveshaft "tunnel", resulted in extra inches that could be devoted to a luggage area.

Front wheel drive also gave advantages in handling. The car was more stable and didn't drift during cornering; directional stability was increased and traction was improved due to more weight over the driving wheels. The front wheel drive transaxle allowed the car to be bigger on the inside and smaller on the outside, to achieve the overall length and width parameters.

Emphasis was also put on minimal weight coupled with a solid, substantial look, to appeal to those who were used to larger cars. The solid, stable look was achieved through the use of a wider "stance," and careful choice of line and form, the proper degree of curvature to the door and the proportion of body panels. Extensive use of strong, but lightweight, components allowed the final product to weigh in at slightly over 2000 pounds, just under the 2100 pound goal.

A strut-type front suspension was chosen to keep weight to a minimum yet provide the best possible handling and ride qualities. The objective was to eliminate the harsh, choppy ride often associated with small cars, through the use of anti-sway bar, soft oval rubber pivot bushings, non-concentric coil springs and well balanced front and rear systems.

The actual design of the cars began in April of 1975, after preliminary planning had settled the issues of length, width, wheel base and configuration. More than 16 different exterior concepts were wind tunnel tested to determine their aerodynamic behavior. The results refined the 4-door hatchback configuration to obtain the minimum aerodynamic drag. Design improvements were translated in half-scale, plastic models before producing a total of 84 prototypes that would log over 6,000,000 test miles. The final result, "Job Number One", rolled off the Belvidere assembly line on November 21, 1977.

Popularity of Dodge Omni and Plymouth Horizon in their first full year in the marketplace, achieved a new production record for Chrysler Corporation's Belvidere assembly plant. In calender year 1978, 288,236 cars were built and sold. Demand was so great that the plant capacity was increased from the initial 960 cars per day to the present rate of almost 1,200 per day.

In 1979 the Plymouth Horizon TC3 and Dodge Omni 024 were introduced. The sporty, 2-door hatchback design had all the basic ingredients that made the 4-door version a success, in addition to a low profile, 2 + 2 sport look. The aerodynamically styled 024 and TC3 are about 8 inches longer and almost 2½ inches lower than their sedan counterparts. The 024 and TC3 are currently accounting for almost ½ of the Omni and Horizon sales.

SERIAL NUMBER IDENTIFICATION

Vehicle (VIN)

The vehicle identification number (VIN) is located on a plate attached to the upper left-hand corner of the instrument panel visible through the windshield. The complete VIN is also on the Safety Certification label located on the rear facing of the driver's door. An abbreviated form of the VIN is also stamped on a pad on the engine and on the transaxle housing.

All VIN's contain 13 digits coded to reveal the following information:
 1st digit—Car line
 2nd digit—Series
 3rd & 4th digit—Body type
 5th digit—Engine displacement
 6th digit—Model year
 7th digit—Assembly plant
 Last 6 digits—Sequential vehicle serial number

8 GENERAL INFORMATION AND MAINTENANCE

4-door Dodge Omni sedan

2-door Dodge Omni 024 Sports Coupe

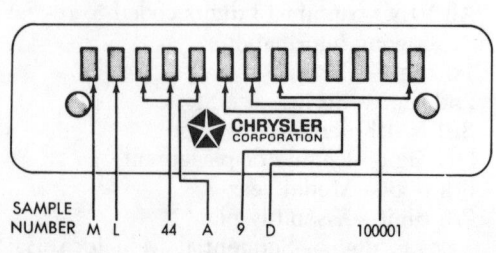

Sample VIN plate (visible through windshield)

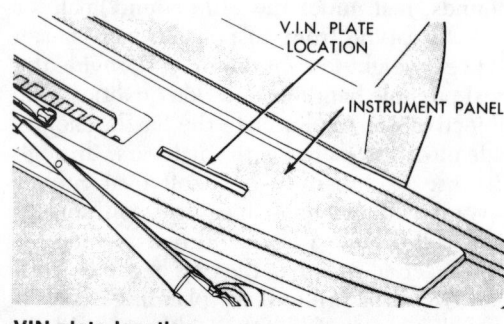

VIN plate location

GENERAL INFORMATION AND MAINTENANCE

4-door Plymouth Horizon sedan

2-door Plymouth Horizon TC3 Sport Coupe

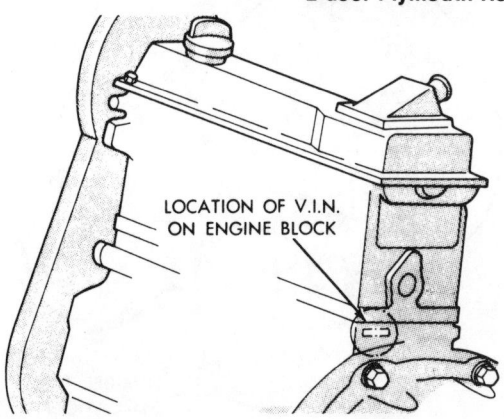

The VIN can also be found on the engine

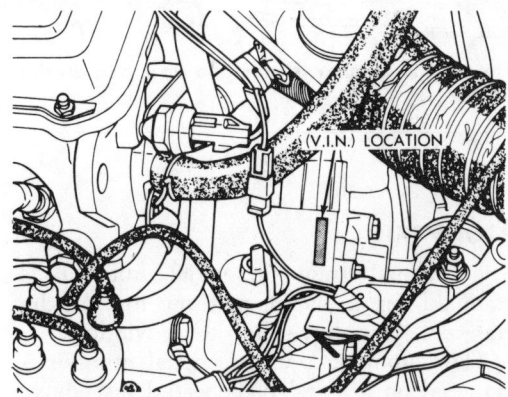

The VIN can also be found on the transaxle

10 GENERAL INFORMATION AND MAINTENANCE

Vehicle Identification Plate Interpretation

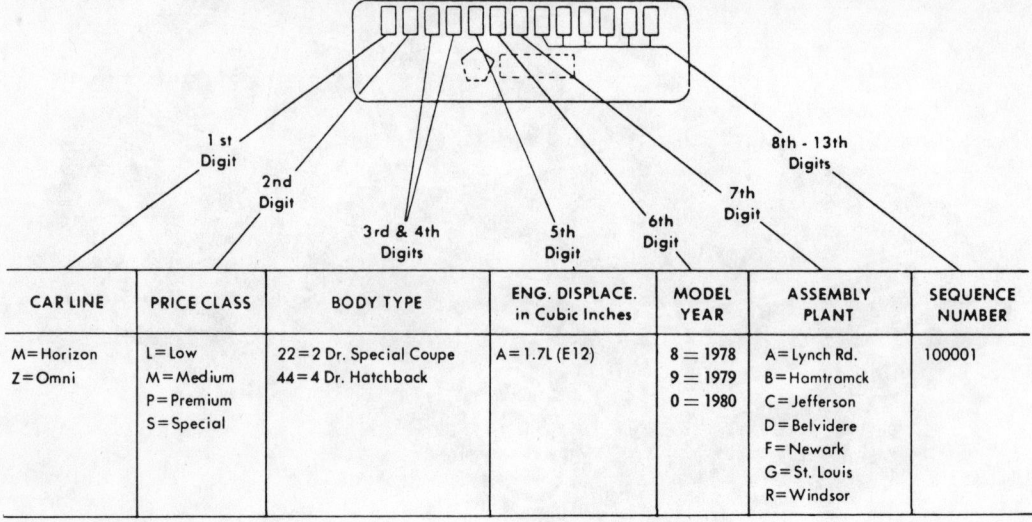

CAR LINE	PRICE CLASS	BODY TYPE	ENG. DISPLACE. in Cubic Inches	MODEL YEAR	ASSEMBLY PLANT	SEQUENCE NUMBER
M = Horizon Z = Omni	L = Low M = Medium P = Premium S = Special	22 = 2 Dr. Special Coupe 44 = 4 Dr. Hatchback	A = 1.7L (E12)	8 = 1978 9 = 1979 0 = 1980	A = Lynch Rd. B = Hamtramck C = Jefferson D = Belvidere F = Newark G = St. Louis R = Windsor	100001

NOTE: A derivative of the Vehicle Identification Number is also stamped on all Production Installed Engines and Transmissions; e.g.:

8 — Model Year
A — Assembly Plant
100001 — Vehicle Sequence Number

Engine

The engine number is stamped on a pad, located just above the fuel pump.

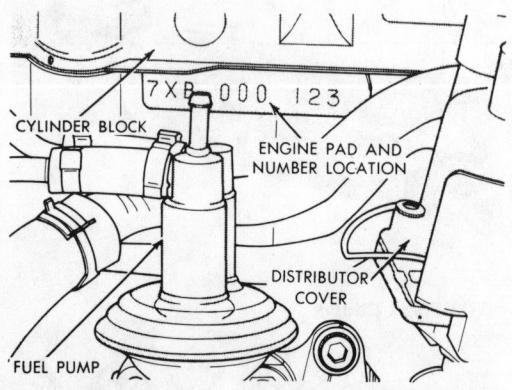

The engine number is stamped on a pad on the engine

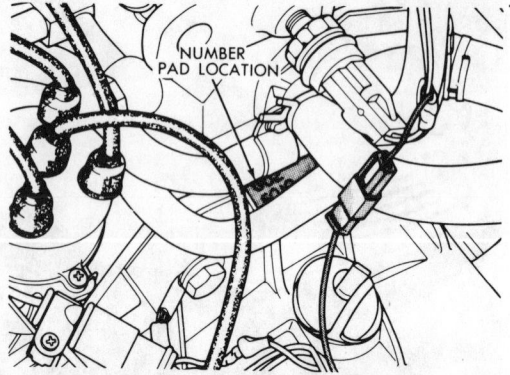

The manual transaxle number is stamped on a pad

Transaxle

The manual transaxle serial number is stamped on a metal pad on top of the transaxle, just above the timing window.

The automatic transaxle serial number is stamped on a metal pad located just above the oil pan at the rear of the transaxle.

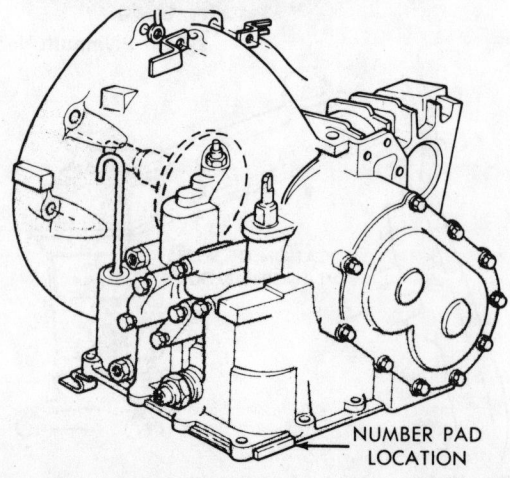

Location of the automatic transaxle number pad

GENERAL INFORMATION AND MAINTENANCE

Body Code Plate Interpretation

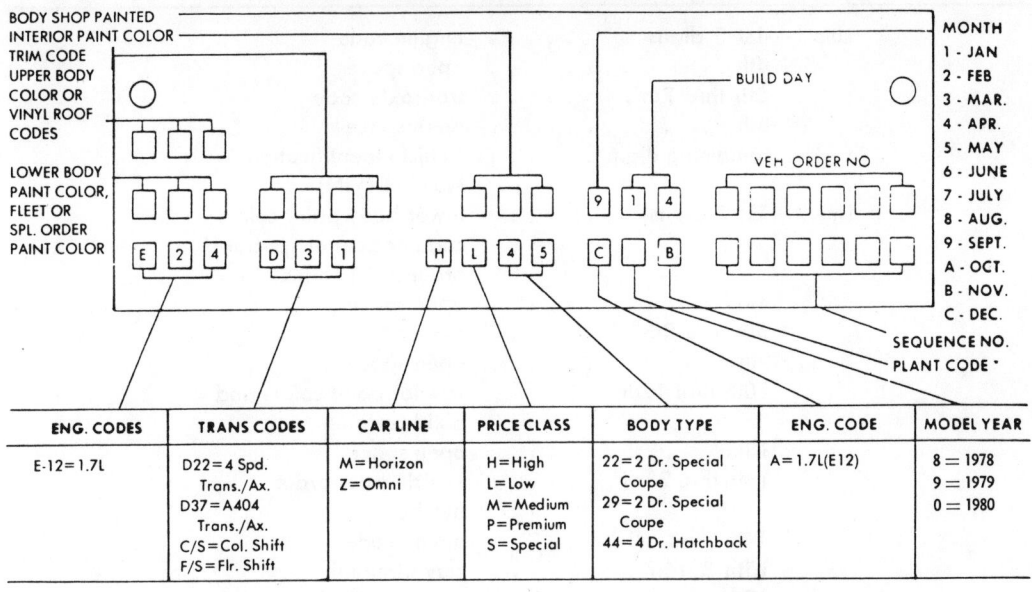

Body Code Plate

The body code plate contains important information about your particular car which is usually needed for any correspondence with the factory. The plate is located on the left front fender side shield, on the left side of the upper radiator support or on the wheel housing.

The information on the plate is coded in 6 rows of digits and is read from left to right. The information can be interpreted using the chart on page 12, beginning with Line 1 (bottom line).

ROUTINE MAINTENANCE

Air Cleaner

The carburetor air cleaner should be replaced every 30,000 miles under normal use. If the car is driven continuously in extremely dirty, dusty or sandy areas, the interval should be cut in half.

1. Remove the 2 wing nuts and unsnap the retaining clips.
2. Remove the air cleaner cover with the filter attached.
3. If the hoses come off, note their location for reinstallation.
4. Unscrew the wing nut on the bottom of the filter element and remove the filter.

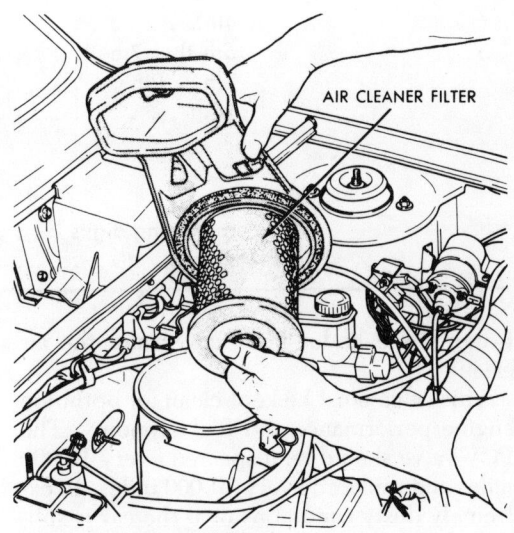

Replacing the air cleaner

5. Install a new filter and replace the wing nut.
6. Reinstall the cover and hand-tighten the wing nuts.
7. Snap the retaining clips into place.

PCV Valve

Omnis and Horizons are equipped with a closed crankcase ventilation system. The PCV valve is located in a line running be-

GENERAL INFORMATION AND MAINTENANCE

Line	Digit	Interpretation
Line 1—	1st 3 digits	engine code
	4th	open space
	5th thru 7th	transaxle code
	8th	open space
	remaining digits	Vehicle Identification Number (VIN)
Line 2—	1st 3 digits	lower body paint color code or fleet or special order paint codes
	4th	open space
	5th thru 8th	trim code
	9th	open space
	10th thru 12th	interior paint colors and build code
	13th	open space
	14th thru 23rd	vehicle sales order number
	14th digit	month code
	15th & 16th	day of month
	17th	open space
	18th thru 23rd	vehicle order number
Line 3—	1st 3 digits	upper body color code or two tone color code
	4th	open space
	5th thru 7th	vinyl roof code
	8th & 9th	open space
	10th	order code: U = U.S. C = Canada I = International
	remaining digits	open spaces
Lines 4 thru 6		For factory use only

tween the cylinder head cover and the air cleaner.

This valve must be kept clean for optimum engine performance and fuel economy. The PCV valve should be inspected every 15,000 miles and replaced every 30,000 miles. In extremely dusty conditions or if the car is subjected to extensive idling or short trip operation, the interval should be halved.

PCV VALVE INSPECTION

There are 2 ways to check the PCV valve. If a valve fails either test, replace it with a new one.

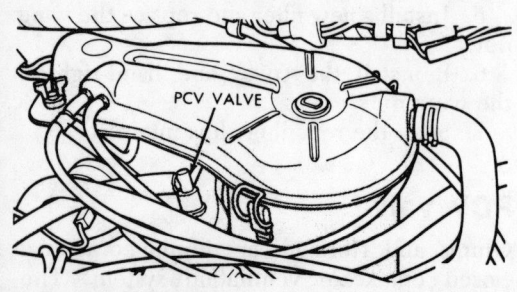

Location of PCV Valve

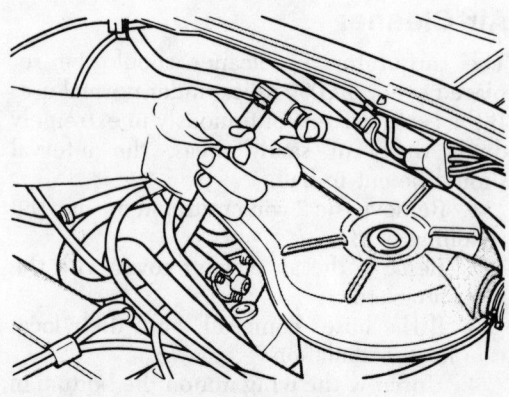

Checking for vacuum at PCV Valve

GENERAL INFORMATION AND MAINTENANCE

Maintenance Intervals

GENERAL MAINTENANCE

			Miles—in thousands					
		7.5	15	22.5	30	37.5	45
Brake Linings	Inspect front brakes				•	•	•
	Inspect rear brakes				•		
* Cooling System	First drain, flush and refill at 24 months or						
	Subsequent drain, flush and refill every 12 months or		•				•
	Check and service system every 12 months or				•		
* Drive Belts	Check tension and condition	•	•	•	•	•	•
* Engine Oil	Change every 12 months or	•	•	•	•	•	•
* Engine Oil Filter	Change every 12 months or	•		•	•	•	•
Rear Wheel Bearings	Inspect				•		
Clutch Pedal Free Play	Adjust every 6 months or	•	•	•	•	•	•
Steering Linkage Tie Rod Ends	Lubricate every 6 months or		•		•		•

* Also an emission control service.

GENERAL INFORMATION AND MAINTENANCE

EMISSION CONTROL SYSTEM MAINTENANCE

		Miles—in thousands
		7.5 / 15 / 22.5 / 30 / 37.5 / 45
Automatic Choke	Check and adjust	• at 15, 30, 45
Carburetor Choke Shaft	Apply solvent every six months	or • at 7.5, 15, 22.5, 30, 37.5, 45
Carburetor Air Filter	Replace	at 7.5
Fast Idle Cam and Pivot Pin	Apply solvent every six months	or • at 7.5, 15, 22.5
Fuel Filter	Replace	at 7.5
Idle Speed & Air-Fuel Mixture	Check and adjust	at • 15, 30, 45
Ignition Cables	Check and replace as required at time of spark plug replacement	
Ignition Timing	Check and adjust if necessary	• 7.5, 15, 30, 45
PCV Valve	Check and adjust if necessary	• 7.5, 15
PCV Valve	Replace	• 30
Spark Plugs	Replace	• 15, 45
Valve Lash	Check and adjust if necessary	at • 15, 45
Underhood Rubber & Plastic Components (Emission Hoses)	Inspect and replace	at • 15, 45

Inspection and Service should also be performed any time a malfunction is observed or suspected.

SEVERE SERVICE MAINTENANCE *

		3	6	9	12	15	18	21	24	27	30	33	36	39	42	45	48
									Miles—in thousands								
Brake Linings	Inspect — Front	•			•		•		•		•		•		•		•
	Rear			•			•		•		•		•		•		•
Engine Oil	Change every 3 months or	•	•	•	•	•	•	•	•	•	•	•	•	•	•	•	•
Engine Oil Filter	Change at initial oil change and every second oil change thereafter																
Rear Wheel Bearings	Inspect and relubricate whenever drums are removed to inspect or service brakes or every								•				•				•
Front Suspension Ball Joints	Inspect at every oil change																
Steering Linkage Tie Rod Ends	Lubricate every 18 months or						•									•	
Transmission Fluid "Automatic"	Change						•				•					•	
Constant Velocity Universal Joints	Inspect at every oil change																

* Driving under any of the following operating conditions: Stop and go driving, driving in dusty conditions, extensive idling, frequent short trips, operating at sustained high speeds during hot weather (above +90°F, +32°C).

16 GENERAL INFORMATION AND MAINTENANCE

Engine Idling

1. Remove the PCV valve from the rubber grommet in the cylinder head cover.
2. If the valve is not plugged, a hissing noise will be heard and a strong vacuum will be felt when you cover the valve with your finger.

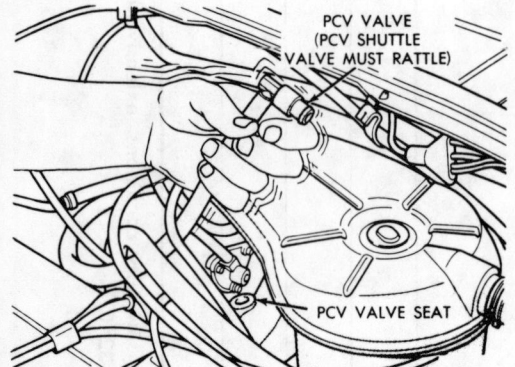

To be considered serviceable, the PCV valve must rattle when shaken

Engine Stopped

1. Remove the PCV valve from the rubber grommet in the cylinder head cover.
2. Shake the valve; a clicking noise should be plainly audible if the valve is free.

PCV VALVE CONNECTING LINE INSPECTION

After a new PCV valve is installed, perform the test under "Engine Idling." If a strong vacuum is not felt, replace or clean the ventilation line and clean the passage in the lower part of the carburetor. The carburetor does not have to be disassembled.

1. Remove the connecting line and either replace it or clean the line in combustion chamber conditioner or a similar solvent. The hose should not remain in solvent more than ½ hour and should be allowed to air dry until thoroughly dry.
2. Remove the carburetor. Turn a ¼ in. drill through the passage by hand to dislodge any solid particles, then blow the passage clean. If necessary, use a smaller drill so that no metal is dislodged.
3. Reinstall the carburetor, connect the line and PCV valve and repeat the PCV valve test under "Engine Idling."

Evaporative Canister

The charcoal canister is a feature on all models to store fuel vapors that evaporate from

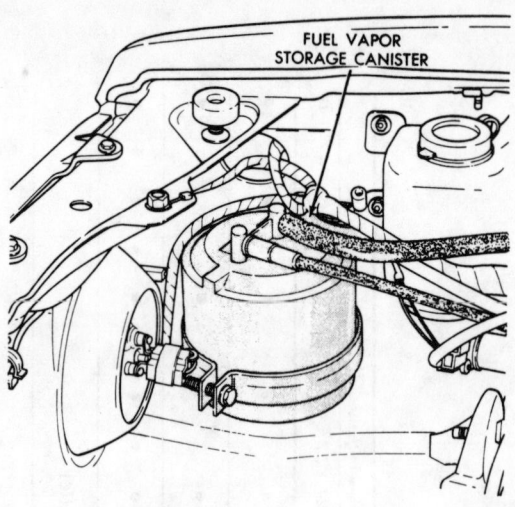

Fuel vapor storage canister

the fuel tank and carburetor bowl. Note that on some fuel bowls, the vent to the evaporative canister is capped since the fuel bowl is vented internally.

The only service is to replace the canister filter every 30,000 miles, if the car is driven in particularly dusty areas. Otherwise, no service is necessary.

All hoses used with this system should be inspected periodically and replaced if cracked or leaking. These hoses are of special fuel resistant material and must be replaced with the same type and quality. The OEM (Original Equipment Manufactured) clamps are "Keystone" type and will be destroyed when they are removed. Replacement types should be aircraft type screw clamps if the original equipment is not available (spring

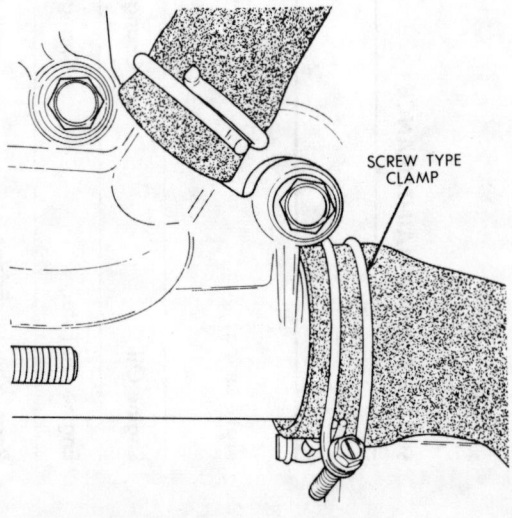

Spring and screw type hose clamps

GENERAL INFORMATION AND MAINTENANCE

type clamps are not recommended). Position the clamps so that no sharp edges contact adjacent hoses.

Battery

Loose, dirty, or corroded battery terminals ae a major cause of "no-start." Every 3 months or so, remove the battery terminals and clean them, giving them a light coating of petroleum jelly when you are finished. This will help to retard corrosion.

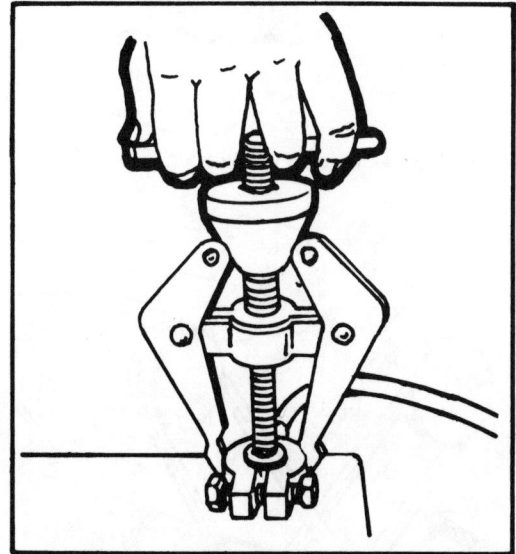

A small puller will easily remove the cable from the terminals

Check the battery cables for signs of wear or chafing and replace any cable or terminal that looks marginal. Battery terminals can be easily cleaned and inexpensive terminal cleaning tools are an excellent investment that will pay for themselves many times over. They can usually be purchased from any well-equipped auto store or parts department. The accumulated white powder and corrosion can be cleaned from the top of the battery with an old toothbrush and a solution of baking soda and water.

Unless you have a "maintenance-free" battery, check the electrolyte level (see Battery under Fluid Level Checks in this chapter) and check the specific gravity of each cell. Be sure that the vent holes in each cell cap are not blocked by grease or dirt. The vent holes allow hydrogen gas, formed by the chemical reaction in the battery, to escape safely.

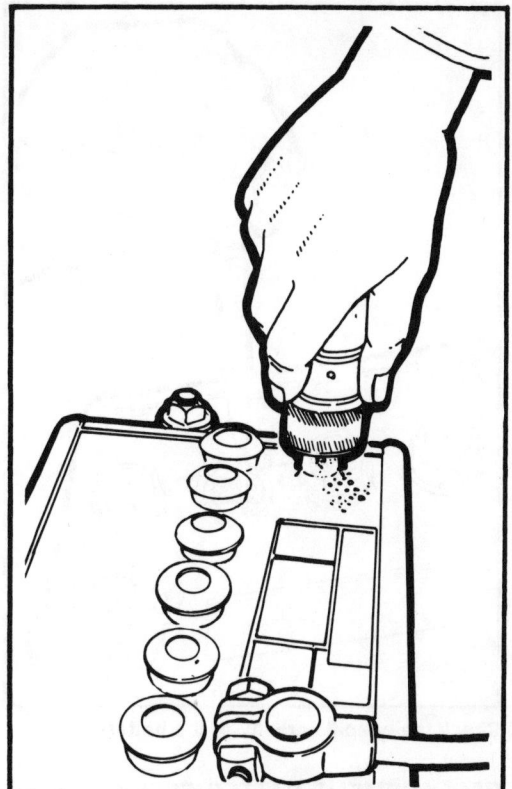

An inexpensive tool easily cleans the battery terminals

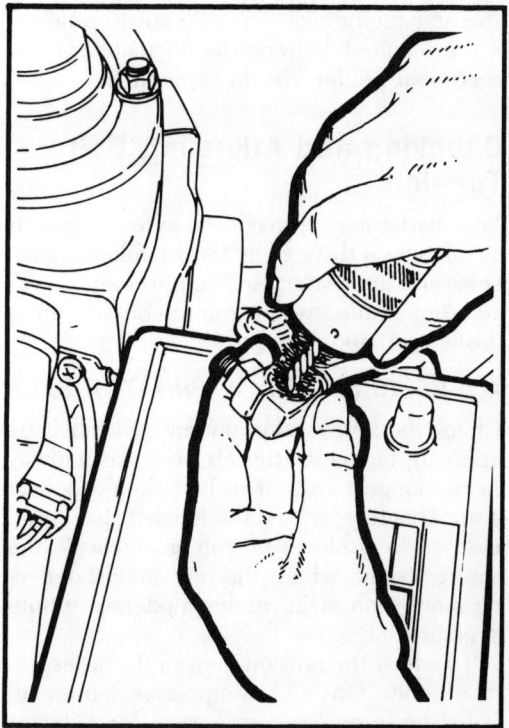

Clean the inside of the terminal clamp

18 GENERAL INFORMATION AND MAINTENANCE

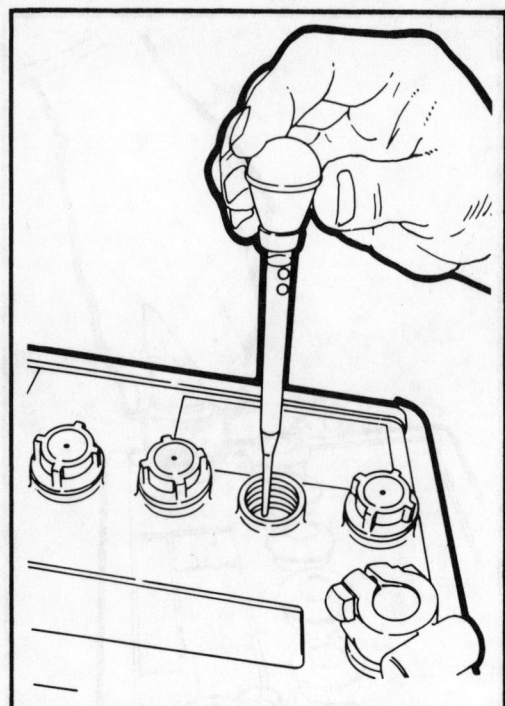

Check the specific gravity of the battery

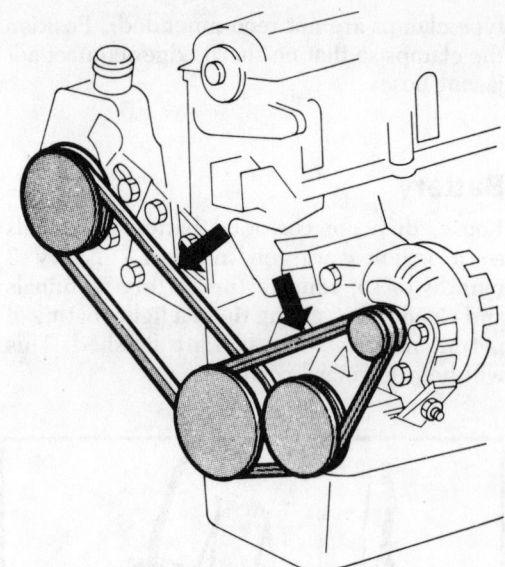

Checking belt tension without A/C

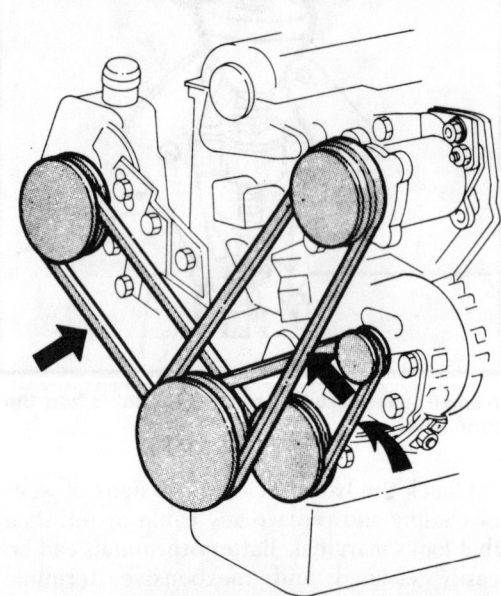

Checking belt tension with A/C

REPLACEMENT BATTERIES

The cold power rating of a battery measures battery starting performance and provides an approximate relationship between battery size and engine size. The cold power rating of a replacement battery should match or exceed your engine size in cubic inches.

Checking and Adjusting Belt Tension

Your particular car may have as few as one or as many as 4 drive belts for the following accessories: alternator, A/C compressor, power steering pump, water pump, or air pump (California models only).

ALL BELTS EXCEPT ALTERNATOR BELT

Check the belt tension on any given belt by applying moderate thumb pressure midway in the longest span. The belt should deflect approximately ½ in. If the longest span is not easily accessible, you can also check the shortest span, where the belt should deflect no more than ¼ in. under moderate thumb pressure.

To adjust the tension, loosen the accessory pivot bolt. On A/C compressor loosen all bolts shown on the compressor decal. Insert a ½ in. breaker bar in the accessory tensioning lug and move the accessory until the belt is properly tensioned. Tighten the pivot bolt.

ALTERNATOR BELT

Proper belt tension on the alternator belt is critical to proper alternator operation. For ease of adjusting alternator belt tension, a special tool has been developed that is easily fabricated or available from the tool company at about $10. The tool, when used with a torque wrench, assures proper belt tension with greater accessibility. Do not use the thumb pressure method on these belts.

GENERAL INFORMATION AND MAINTENANCE

HOW TO SPOT WORN V-BELTS

V-Belts are vital to efficient engine operation—they drive the fan, water pump and other accessories. They require little maintenance (occasional tightening) but they will not last forever. Slipping or failure of the V-belt will lead to overheating. If your V-belt looks like any of these, it should be replaced.

Cracking or weathering

This belt has deep cracks, which cause it to flex. Too much flexing leads to heat build-up and premature failure. These cracks can be caused by using the belt on a pulley that is too small. Notched belts are available for small diameter pulleys.

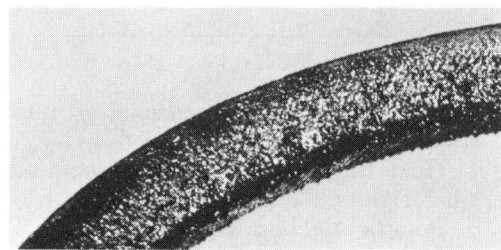

Softening (grease and oil)

Oil and grease on a belt can cause the belt's rubber compounds to soften and separate from the reinforcing cords that hold the belt together. The belt will first slip, then finally fail altogether.

Glazing

Glazing is caused by a belt that is slipping. A slipping belt can cause a run-down battery, erratic power steering, overheating or poor accessory performance. The more the belt slips, the more glazing will be built up on the surface of the belt. The more the belt is glazed, the more it will slip. If the glazing is light, tighten the belt.

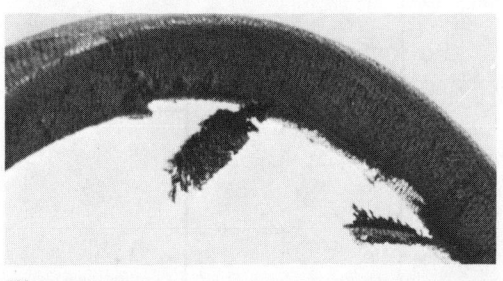

Worn cover

The cover of this belt is worn off and is peeling away. The reinforcing cords will begin to wear and the belt will shortly break. When the belt cover wears in spots or has a rough jagged appearance, check the pulley grooves for roughness.

Separation

This belt is on the verge of breaking and leaving you stranded. The layers of the belt are separating and the reinforcing cords are exposed. It's just a matter of time before it breaks completely.

GENERAL INFORMATION AND MAINTENANCE

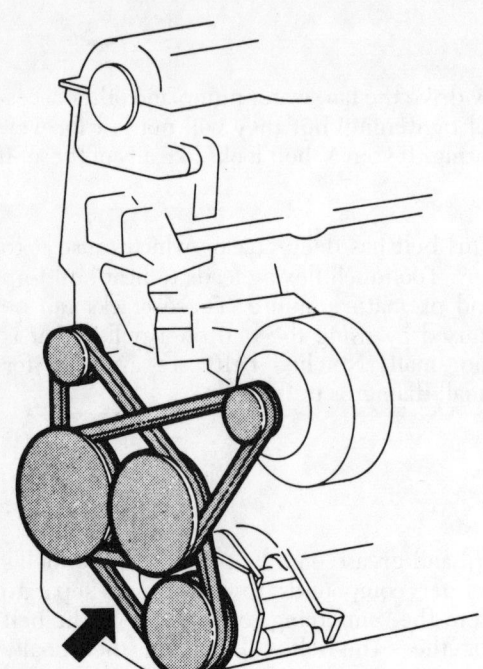

Checking belt tension with AIR pump

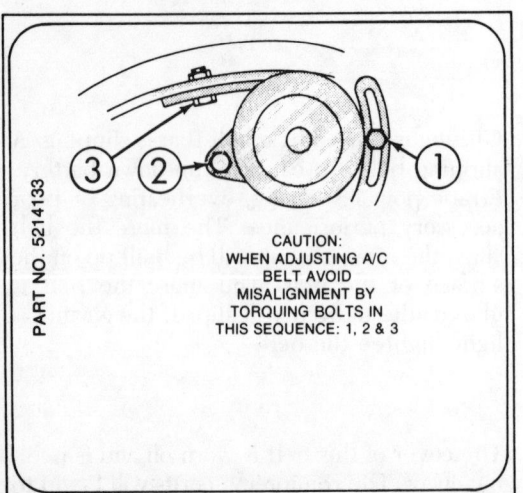

A/C compressor bolt tightening sequence

It is essential that belt adjustment be performed from below the vehicle. The splash shield must be removed and on California models with an air pump, removing the horn will ease access to the adjustment bolt.

1. From underneath the vehicle, install a ½ in. drive torque wrench in the adjusting tool. Position the adjusting tool.
2. Loosen the alternator pivot bolt. If you don't do this, you'll break the alternator housing.
3. Adjust the belt tension to 70 ft lbs (new belt) or 50 ft lbs (used belt).

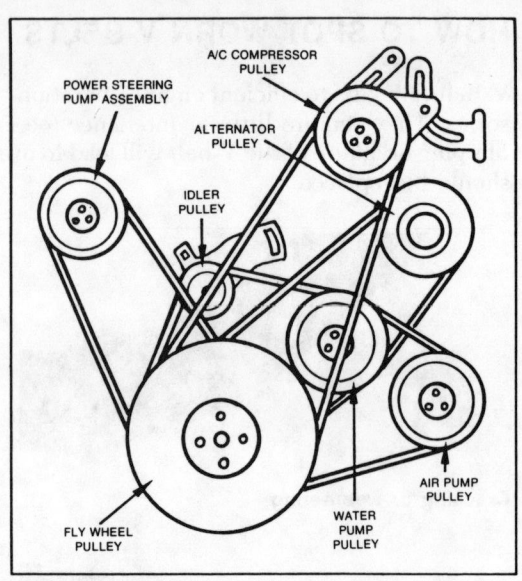

Accessory drive belts

NOTE: *A belt is considered used after 15 minutes of running.*

4. Hold the alternator at the required torque. Tighten the adjusting bolt.
5. Reinstall the horn and splash shield.

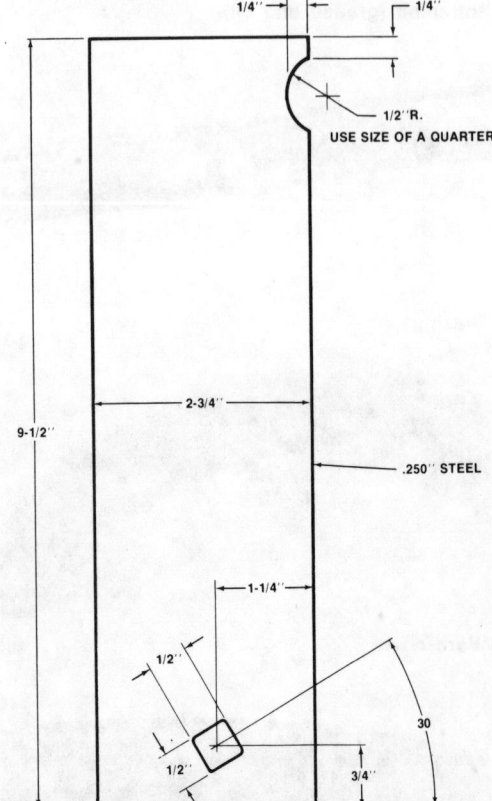

Fabricated special tool for adjusting alternator belt tension

GENERAL INFORMATION AND MAINTENANCE

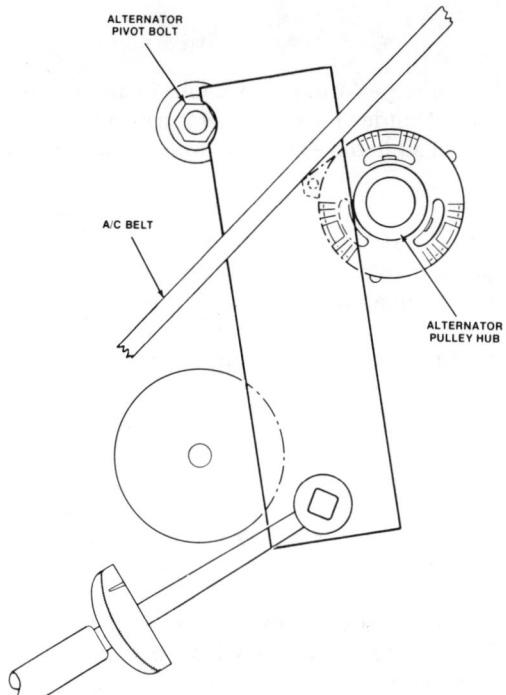

Using special tool to adjust alternator belt tension

Belt Replacement

In most cases the car must be raised and supported, the splash shield removed and the horn removed from cars with air pumps.

1. The A/C compressor drive belt is removed first. Loosen the adjusting nut at the slotted bracket and push the compressor to its lowest position.
2. The alternator belt is removed second. Loosen the tension on the belt and use a ½ in. socket to remove the 3 bolts holding the water pump pulley. Remove the pulley.

NOTE: *The air pump idler pulley is located behind the water pump pulley.*

3. The air pump drive belt is removed next. To remove this belt, the A/C compressor and the alternator belts MUST be removed.
4. The power steering pump drive belt is removed last. It is necessary to remove all other belts, loosen the pump pivot bolt in the slotted bracket and move the pump to its lowest position.
5. New belts are installed in the reverse order. Tension all belts as outlined previously. New belts will usually stretch, so they should be checked after an hour's use.

Hoses

Hoses can be removed or installed with pliers or a screwdriver. Some cars use spring type clamps while others use screw type clamps. If spring type clamps are used, it is recommended to remove these with hose clamp pliers to avoid pinching your fingers.

1. Drain the radiator. If the coolant is less than a year old it can be saved and reused.

NOTE: *Before opening the radiator drain cock to drain the radiator, spray some penetrating solvent around the drain cock to be sure it will open with ease.*

2. Remove the hose clamps.
3. Pull the hose off the fittings on the radiator and engine.
4. Install a new hose. A small amount of soapy water on the inside of the hose end will ease installation.

NOTE: *Radiator hoses should be routed with no kinks and routed as the original. Use of molded hoses is not recommended.*

5. Refill the cooling system and check the level.

Cooling System

The cooling system should be inspected, flushed, and refilled with fresh coolant at the end of the first 2 years and every year thereafter. If the coolant is left in the system too long, it loses its ability to prevent rust and corrosion; if the coolant has too much water, it won't protect against freezing.

The pressure cap should be looked at for signs of age or deterioration. Fan belt and other drive belts should be inspected and adjusted to the proper tension. (See Checking Belt Tension).

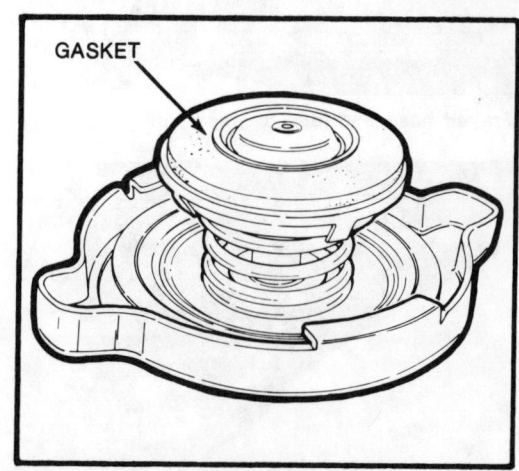

Check the radiator cap gasket

22 GENERAL INFORMATION AND MAINTENANCE

HOW TO SPOT BAD HOSES

Both the upper and lower radiator hoses are called upon to perform difficult jobs in an inhospitable environment. They are subject to nearly 18 psi at under hood temperatures often over 280°F., and must circulate nearly 7500 gallons of coolant an hour—3 good reasons to have good hoses.

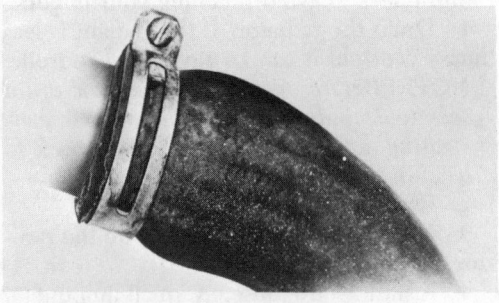
Swollen hose

A good test for any hose is to feel it for soft or spongy spots. Frequently these will appear as swollen areas of the hose. The most likely cause is oil soaking. This hose could burst at any time, when hot or under pressure.

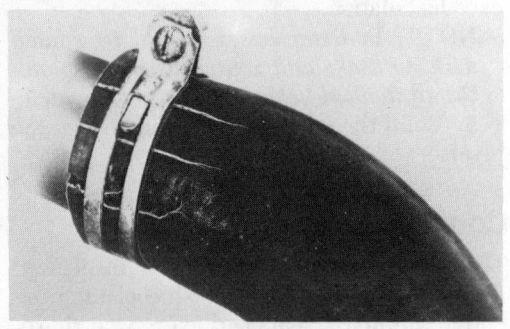
Cracked hose

Cracked hoses can usually be seen but feel the hoses to be sure they have not hardened; a prime cause of cracking. This hose has cracked down to the reinforcing cords and could split at any of the cracks.

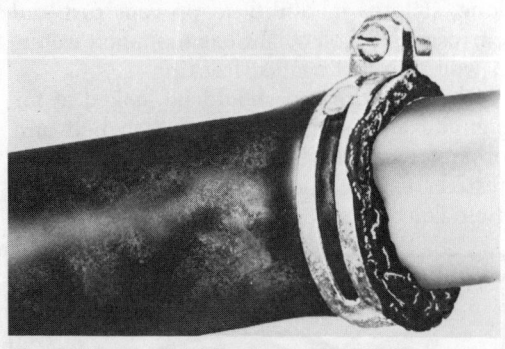
Frayed hose end (due to weak clamp)

Weakened clamps frequently are the cause of hose and cooling system failure. The connection between the pipe and hose has deteriorated enough to allow coolant to escape when the engine is hot.

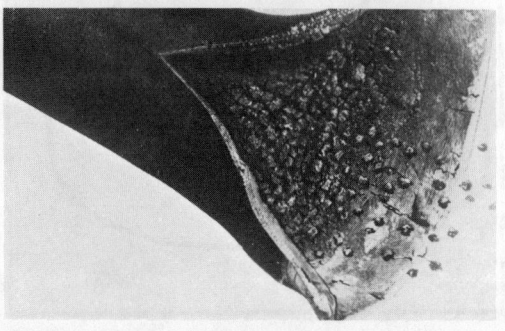
Debris in cooling system

Debris, rust and scale in the cooling system can cuase the inside of a hose to weaken. This can usually be felt on the outside of the hose as soft or thinner areas.

GENERAL INFORMATION AND MAINTENANCE

Hose clamps should be tightened, and soft or cracked hoses replaced. Damp spots, or accumulations of rust or dye near hoses, water pump or other areas, indicate possible leakage, which must be corrected before filling the system with fresh coolant.

CHECK THE RADIATOR CAP

While you are checking the coolant level, check the radiator cap for a worn or cracked gasket. If the cap doesn't seal properly, fluid will be lost and the engine will overheat.

Worn caps should be replaced with a new one.

CLEAN RADIATOR OF DEBRIS

Periodically clean any debris—leaves, paper, insects, etc.—from the radiator fins. Pick the large pieces off by hand. The smaller pieces can be washed away with water pressure from a hose.

Carefully straighten any bent radiator fins with a pair of needle nosed pliers. Be careful—the fins are very soft. Don't wiggle the fins back and forth too much. Straighten them once and try not to move them again.

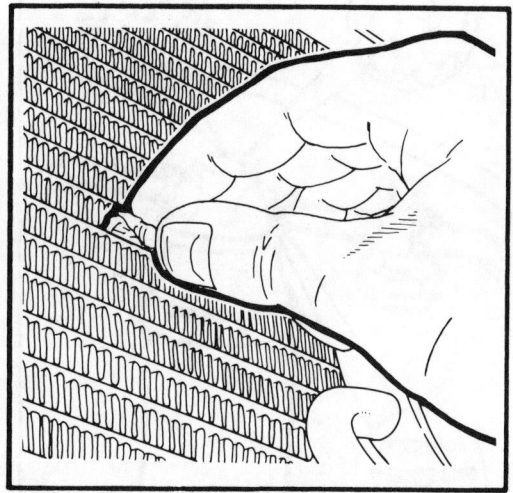
Remove debris from the radiator cooling fins

DRAIN AND REFILL THE COOLING SYSTEM

Completely draining and refilling the cooling system every year at least will remove accumulated rust, scale and other deposits. Coolant should be at least a 50/50 mixture of ethylene glycol and water for year round use. Use a good quality antifreeze with water pump lubricants, rust inhibitors and other corrosion inhibitors along with acid neutralizers.

1. Drain the existing antifreeze and coolant. Open the radiator and engine drain petcocks, or disconnect the bottom radiator hose, at the radiator outlet.

NOTE: *Before opening the radiator petcock, spray it with some penetrating lubricant.*

2. Close the petcock or re-connect the lower hose and fill the system with water.
3. Add a can of quality radiator flush.
4. Idle the engine until the upper radiator hose gets hot.
5. Drain the system again.
6. Repeat this process until the drained water is clear and free of scale.
7. Close all petcocks and connect all the hoses.
8. If equipped with a coolant recovery system, flush the reservoir with water and leave empty.
9. Determine the capacity of your cooling system (see Capacities specifications). Add a 50/50 mix of quality antifreeze (ethylene glycol) and water to provide the desired protection.

NOTE: *Use a minimum of 50% ethylene glycol anti-freeze and water. This is necessary to provide adequate corrosion protection with aluminum parts.*

10. Run the engine to operating temperature.
11. Stop the engine and check the coolant level.
12. Check the level of protection with an anti-freeze tester, replace the cap and check for leaks.

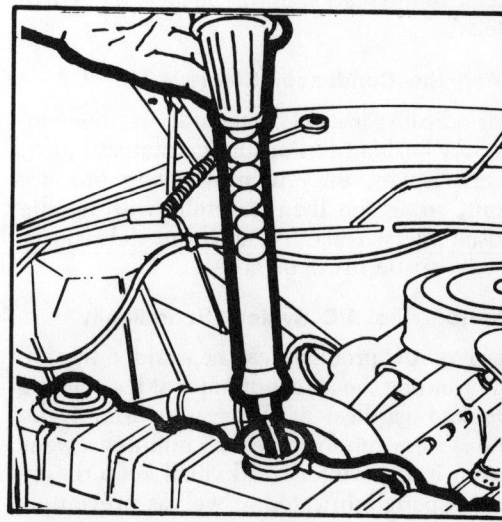
Check the anti-freeze protection

24 GENERAL INFORMATION AND MAINTENANCE

AIR-CONDITIONING SAFETY PRECAUTIONS

There are two particular hazards associated with air conditioning systems and they both relate to the refrigerant gas.

First, the refrigerant gas is an extremely cold substance. When exposed to air, it will instantly freeze any surface it comes in contact with, including your eyes. The other hazard relates to fire. Although normally non-toxic, refrigerant gas becomes highly poisonous in the presence of an open flame. One good whiff of the vapor formed by burning refrigerant can be fatal. Keep all forms of fire (including cigarettes) well clear of the air-conditioning system.

Any repair work to an air conditioning system should be left to a professional. Do not, under any circumstances, attempt to loosen or tighten any fittings or perform any work other than that outlined here.

Checking for Oil Leaks

Refrigerant leaks show up as oily areas on the various components because the compressor oil is transported around the entire system along with the refrigerant. Look for oily spots on all the hoses and lines, and especially on the hose and tubing connections. If there are oily deposits, the system may have a leak, and you should have it checked by a qualified repairman.

NOTE: *A small area of oil on the front of the compressor is normal and no cause for alarm.*

Check the Compressor Belt

Refer to the section in this chapter on "Drive Belts".

Keep the Condenser Clear

Periodically inspect the front of the condenser for bent fins or foreign material (dirt, bugs, leaves, etc.) If any cooling fins are bent, straighten them carefully with needle nosed pliers. You can remove any debris with a stiff bristle brush or hose.

Operate the A/C System Periodically

A lot of A/C problems can be avoided by simply running the air conditioner at least once a week, regardless of the season. Simply let the system run for at least 5 minutes a week (even in the winter), and you'll keep the internal parts lubricated as well as preventing the hoses from hardening.

Refrigerant Level Check

The first order of business when checking the sight glass is to find the sight glass. It is located in the head of the receiver/drier. Once you've found it, wipe it clean and proceed as follows:

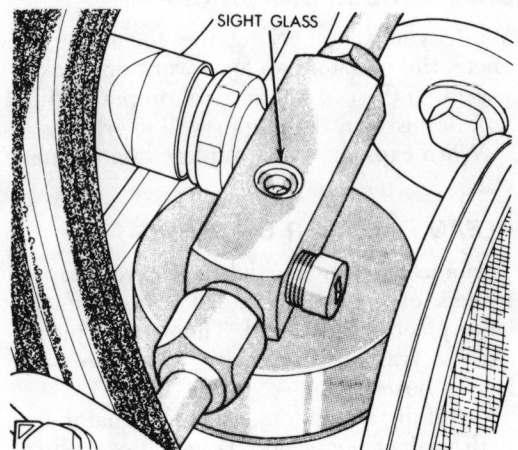

A/C sight glass in the top of the receiver/drier

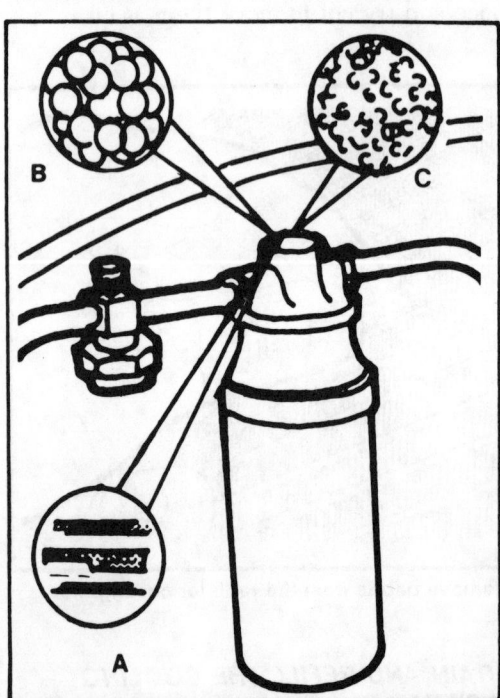

Oil streaks (A), constant bubbles (B) or foam (C) indicate there is not enough refrigerant in the system. Occasional bubbles during initial operation is normal. A clear sight glass indicates a proper charge of refrigerant or no refrigerant at all, which can be determined by the presence of cold air at the outlets in the car. If the glass is clouded with a milky white substance, have the receiver/drier checked professionally

GENERAL INFORMATION AND MAINTENANCE

1. With the engine and the air conditioning system running, look for the flow of refrigerant through the sight glass. If the air conditioner is working properly, you'll be able to see a continuous flow of clear refrigerant through the sight glass, with perhaps an occasional bubble at very high temperatures.

2. Cycle the air conditioner on and off to make sure what you are seeing is clear refrigerant. Since the refrigerant is clear, it is possible to mistake a completely discharged system for one that is fully charged. Turn the system off and watch the sight glass. If there is refrigerant in the system, you'll see bubbles during the off cycle. If you observe no bubbles when the system is running, and the air flow from the unit in the car is delivering cold air, everything is OK.

3. If you observe bubbles in the sight glass while the system is operating, the system is low on refrigerant. Have it checked by a professional.

4. Oil streaks in the sight glass are an indication of trouble. Most of the time, if you see oil in the sight glass, it will appear as a series of streaks, although occasionally it may be a solid stream of oil. In either case, it means that part of the charge has been lost.

Windshield Wipers

Intense heat from the sun, snow and ice, road oils and the chemicals used in windshield washer solvents combine to deteriorate the rubber wiper refills. The refills should be replaced about twice a year or whenever the blades begin to streak or chatter.

WIPER REFILL REPLACEMENT

Normally, if the wipers are not cleaning the windshield properly, only the refill has to be replaced. The blade and arm usually require replacement only in the event of damage. It is not necessary (except on new Tridon refills) to remove the arm or the blade to replace the refill (rubber part), though you may have to position the arm higher on the glass. You can do this turning the ignition switch on and operating the wipers. When they are positioned where they are accessible, turn the ignition switch off.

There are several types of refills and your vehicle could have any kind, since aftermarket blades and arms may not use exactly the same type refill as the original equipment.

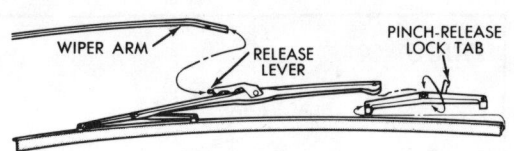

Removing original equipment wiper blade and refill

The original equipment wiper elements can be replaced as follows:

1. Lift the wiper arm off the glass.
2. Depress the release lever on the center bridge and remove the blade from the arm.
3. Lift the tab and pinch the end bridge to release it from the center bridge.
4. Slide the end bridge from the wiper blade and the wiper blade from the opposite end bridge.
5. Install a new element and be sure the tab on the end bridge is down to lock the element in place. Check each release point for positive engagement.

Most Trico styles uses a release button that is pushed down to allow the refill to slide out of the yoke jaws. The new refill slides in and locks in place. Some Trico refills are removed by locating where the metal backing strip or the refill is wider. Insert a small screwdriver blade between the frame and metal backing strip. Press down to release the refill from the retaining tab.

The Anco style is unlocked at one end by squeezing 2 metal tabs, and the refill is slid out of the frame jaws. When the new refill is installed, the tabs will click into place, locking the refill.

The polycarbonate type is held in place by a locking lever that is pushed downward out of the groove in the arm to free the refill. When the new refill is installed, it will lock in place automatically.

The Tridon refill has a plastic backing strip with a notch about an inch from the end. Hold the blade (frame) on a hard surface so that the frame is tightly bowed. Grip the tip of the backing strip and pull up while twisting counterclockwise. The backing strip will snap out of the retaining tab. Do this for the remaining tabs until the refill is free of the arm. The length of these refills is molded into the end and they should be replaced with identical types.

No matter which type of refill you use, be sure that all of the frame claws engage the refill. Before operating the wipers, be sure that no part of the metal frame is contacting the windshield.

26 GENERAL INFORMATION AND MAINTENANCE

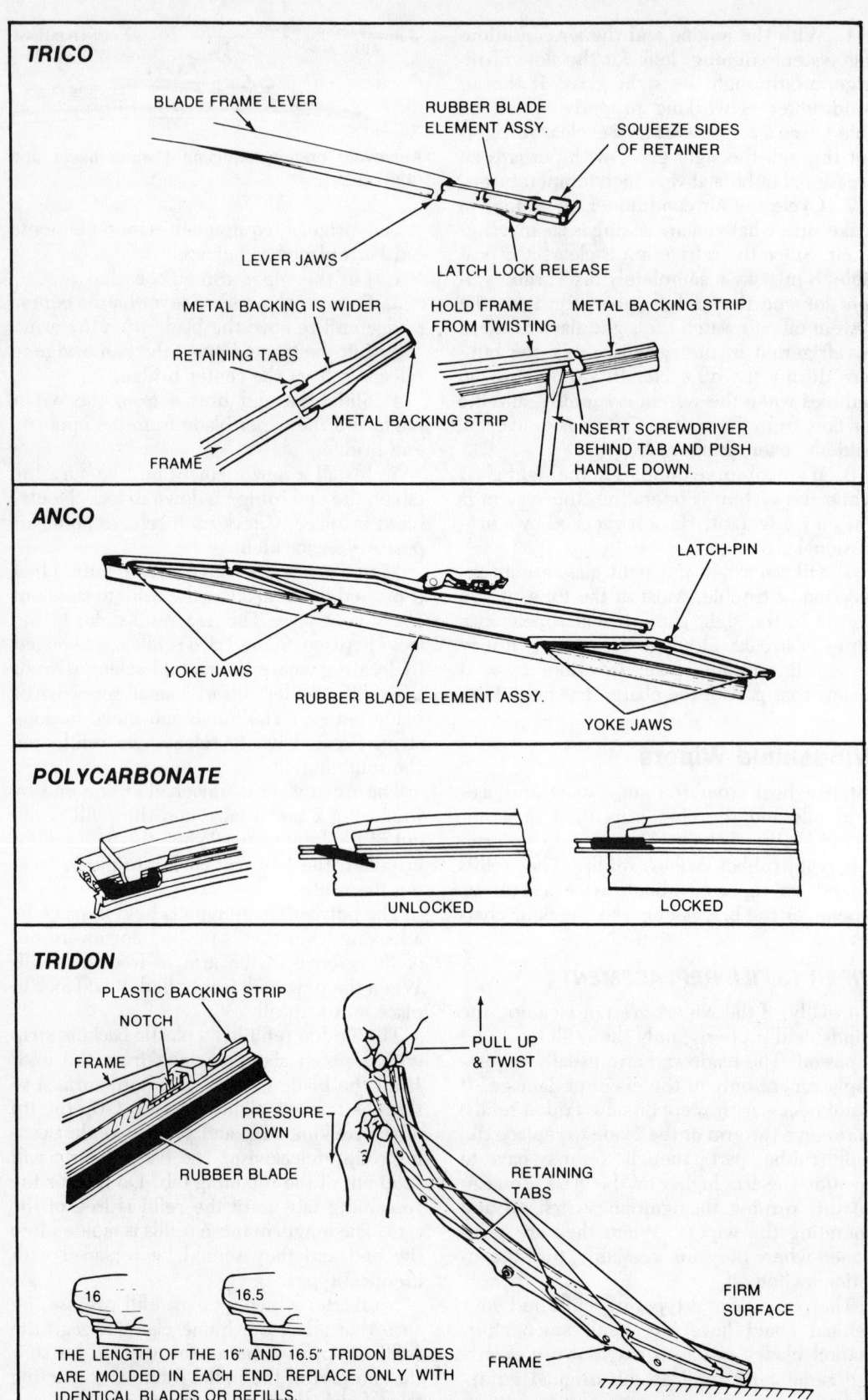

Replacing popular styles of wiper refills

GENERAL INFORMATION AND MAINTENANCE

Fluid Level Checks

ENGINE OIL

The engine oil dipstick is located on the radiator side of the engine. Engine oil level should be checked weekly as a matter of course. Always check the oil with the car on level ground and after the engine has been shut off for about five minutes.

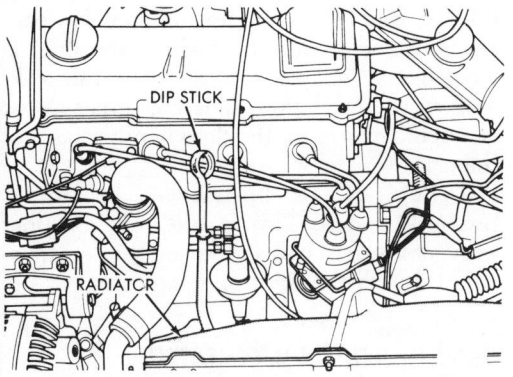

Engine oil dipstick location

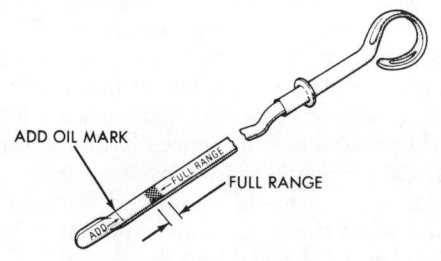

Engine oil dipstick markings

Add oil through the capped opening

The oil level may read at the top of the Full range after the car has been standing for several hours. When the engine is started, the level will drop, due to oil passages filling, but the level should never be allowed to remain below the ADD mark.

1. Remove the dipstick and wipe it clean.
2. Reinsert the dipstick.
3. Remove the dipstick again. The oil level should be between the two marks. The difference between the marks is one quart.
4. Add oil through the capped opening on the top of the valve cover. Select oil of the proper viscosity from the chart later in this chapter.

MANUAL TRANSAXLE

The fluid level in the manual transaxle should be checked twice a year. Maintain the fluid level at the bottom of the filler plug opening.

To check the fluid level, position the car on a level surface and clean the dirt from around the transaxle filler plug. Remove the filler plug. The level should at least reach the bottom of the hole. You can check the level with your finger or a piece of bent wire.

If necessary, replenish the lubricant with MOPAR Hypoid lubricant or a similar lubricant meeting API GL-4 classification standards.

NOTE: *Fluids classified GL-5 by the API are not recommended for this transaxle.*

The recommended SAE grade should be selected from the chart.

Anticipated Temperature Range	Recommended SAE Grade
Above — 10° F.	90, 80W–90, 85W–90
As low as — 30° F.	80W, 80W–90, 85W–90
Below — 30° F.	75W

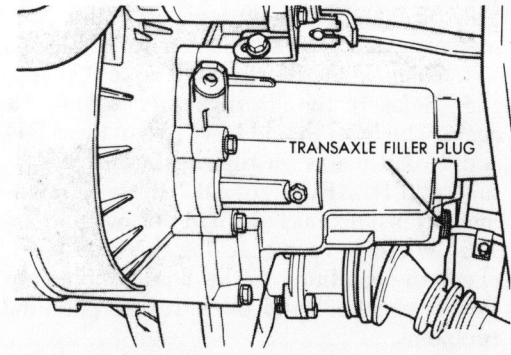

Check the manual transaxle fluid level

28 GENERAL INFORMATION AND MAINTENANCE

AUTOMATIC TRANSAXLE

The automatic transaxle and differential are contained in the same housing, but the units are sealed from each other. The transmission does not have a conventional filler tube, but is filled through a die-cast opening in the case. The filler hole is plugged during operation by the transmission dipstick.

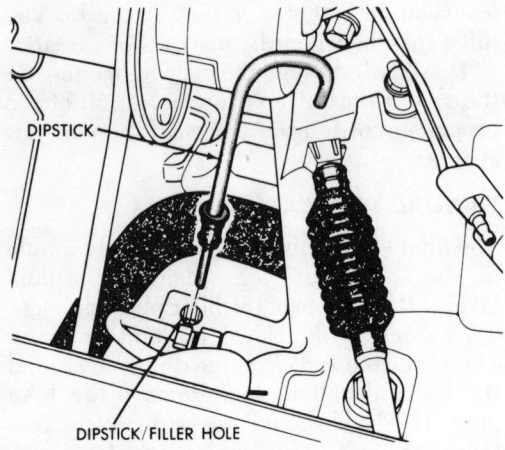
Automatic transaxle dipstick location

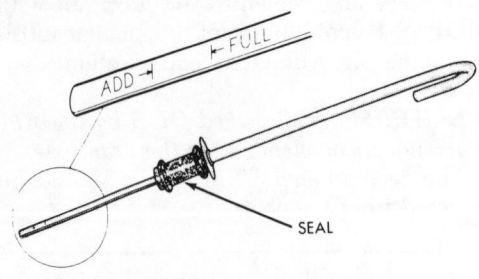
Automatic transaxle dipstick markings

The fluid level should be checked every 6 months when the engine and transmission fluid are warmed to normal operating temperature.

1. Position the car on a level surface.
2. Idle the engage and engage with parking brake.
3. Shift the lever through each gear momentarily and return the lever to PARK.
4. Remove the dipstick and wipe it clean.
5. Reinsert the dipstick and remove it again. The level should be between the ADD and FULL marks on the dipstick. If necessary, add DEXRON® or DEXRON II® automatic transmission fluid. Do not overfill.
6. While you are checking the fluid level, check the condition of the fluid. The condition of the fluid will often reveal potential problems.
7. If the fluid level is consistently low, suspect a leak. The easiest way is to slip a piece of clean newspaper under the car overnight, but this is not always an accurate indication, since some leaks will occur only when the transmission is operating.

Other leaks can be located by driving the car. Wipe the underside of the transmission clean and drive the car for several miles to bring the fluid temperature to normal. Stop the car, shut off the engine and look for leakage, but remember, that where the fluid is located may not be the source of the leak. Airflow around the transmission while the car is moving may carry the fluid to other parts of the car.

8. Reinsert the dipstick and be sure it properly seated. This is the only seal that prevents water or dirt entering the transmission through the filler opening.

DIFFERENTIAL (AUTOMATIC TRANSAXLE)

Automatic transaxles have 2 separate reservoirs that require filling separately. Most models have a drain and fill plug in the differential cover; some models will have only a fill plug. Should it become necessary to drain the differential and the cover has only a fill plug, simply remove the cover to drain. A service gasket, should be formed from RTV sealant when the cover is installed. Use a $1/16$ in. bead of RTV sealant on the cover.

To check the fluid level, remove the filler plug. The level should be at the bottom of

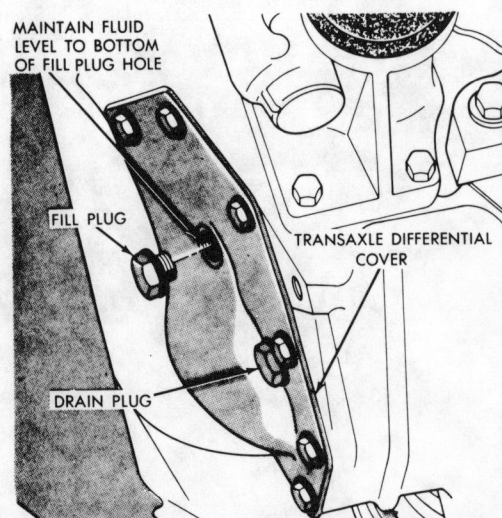
Automatic transaxle differential drain and fill plugs

GENERAL INFORMATION AND MAINTENANCE

Transmission Fluid Indications

The appearance and odor of the transmission fluid can give valuable clues to the overall condition of the transmission. Always note the appearance of the fluid when you check the fluid level or change the fluid. Rub a small amount of fluid between your fingers to feel for grit and smell the fluid on the dipstick.

If the fluid appears:	It indicates:
Clear and red colored	• Normal operation
Discolored (extremely dark red or brownish) or smells burned	• Band or clutch pack failure, usually caused by an overheated transmission. Hauling very heavy loads with insufficient power or failure to change the fluid, often result in overheating. Do not confuse this appearance with newer fluids that have a darker red color and a strong odor (though not a burned odor).
Foamy or aerated (light in color and full of bubbles	• The level is too high (gear train is churning oil). • An internal air leak (air is mixing with the fluid). Have the transmission checked professionally.
Solid residue in the fluid	• Defective bands, clutch pack or bearings. Bits of band material or metal abrasives are clinging to the dipstick. Have the transmission checked professionally.
Varnish coating on the dipstick	• The transmission fluid is overheating.

the hole, which can be checked with your finger or a piece of bent wire.

If fluid is needed, use only Dexron® or Dexron II®.

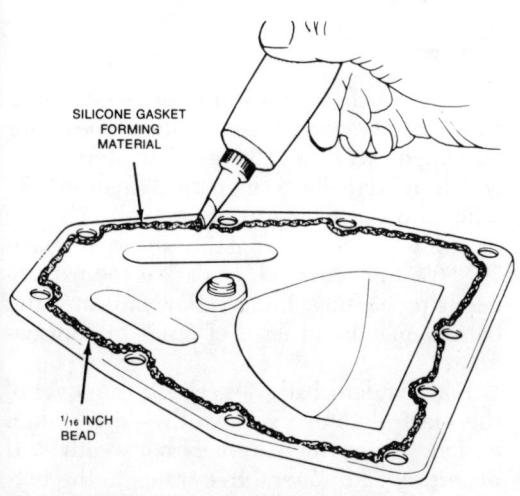

BRAKE MASTER CYLINDER

The brake fluid level should be checked every 6 months.

1. Wipe the area around the master cylinder clean.

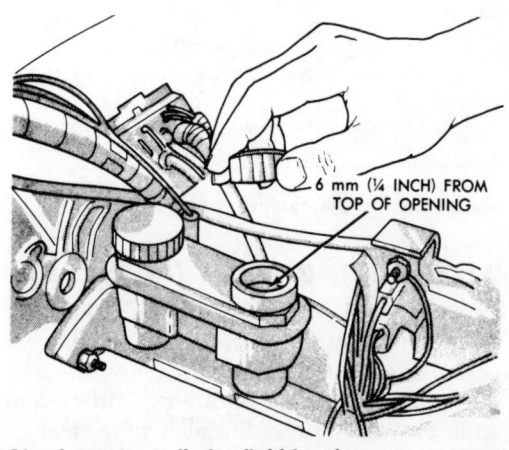

Form a silicone gasket as shown

Check master cylinder fluid level

30 GENERAL INFORMATION AND MAINTENANCE

2. Remove the master cylinder cap. The fluid level should be within ¼ in. of the top of the reservoir.

3. If necessary, add brake fluid identified on the container as conforming to DOT 3 specifications.

COOLANT

The coolant reserve system provides a quick and easy way to verify proper coolant level. With the engine idling and at normal operating temperature, observe the level of the coolant in the plastic see-through tank. It should be between the minimum and maximum marks.

If additional coolant is needed, remove the cap from the reserve tank. DO NOT REMOVE THE RADIATOR CAP. Add a 50/50 mix of ethylene glycol coolant and water.

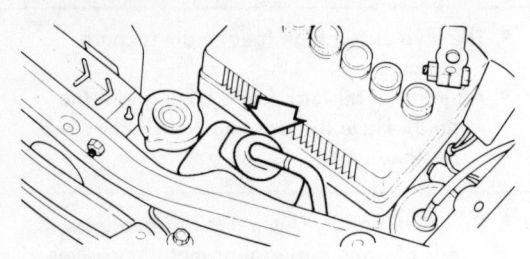

Coolant reserve bottle location

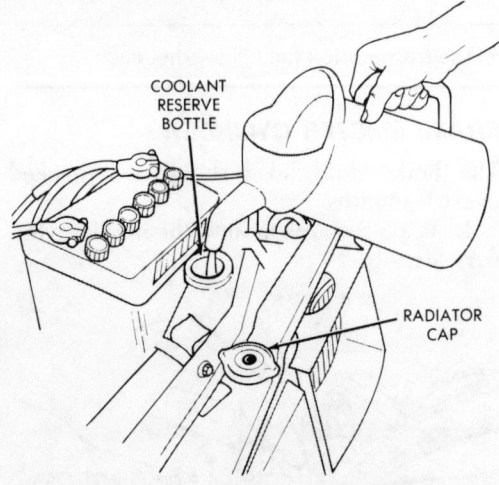

Add coolant to the coolant reserve bottle

DIFFERENTIAL (MANUAL TRANSAXLE)

Under normal conditions, the fluid does not need replacing, but the level should be checked every 6 months.

1. Position the car on a level surface and wipe the area around the filler plug clean.
2. Remove the filler plug.

3. The fluid level should be even with the bottom of the fill plug.

4. If it is necessary to add fluid, use only designated as hypoid lubricant.

5. Replace the filler plug and tighten it.

POWER STEERING RESERVOIR

The power steering reservoir fluid level should be checked with the engine OFF to prevent accidents. Check the level every 6 months.

1. Position the car on a level surface.
2. Wipe the area around the power steering reservoir cap clean and remove the cap.
3. The power steering pump cap has a dipstick attached. Fluid level should be kept at the level indicated on the dipstick.
4. If it is necessary to add fluid, use only MOPAR Power Steering Fluid or the equivalent. DO NOT USE AUTOMATIC TRANSMISSION FLUID.
5. Replace the cap and tighten in place.

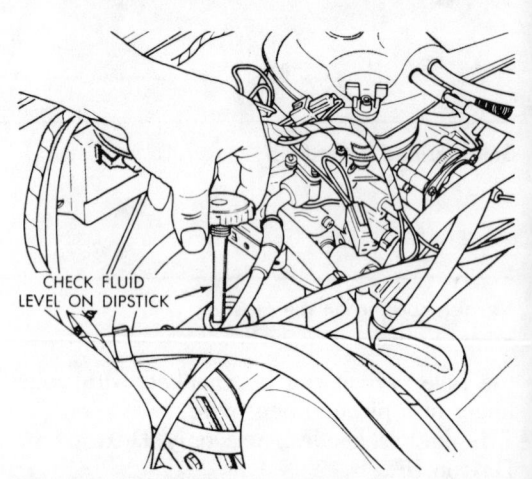

Checking power steering fluid level

BATTERY

Two types of batteries are used—Standard and Maintenance-Free. Both types are equipped with a Charge-Test Indicator, which is actually a miniature hydrometer built into the filler cap of one cell. The indicator will show green if the battery is above 75–80% fully charged, or dark if the battery needs recharging. Light yellow indicates the battery may be in need of water or replacement.

For standard batteries, check the level of the electrolyte every 2 months—more often on long trips or in extremely hot weather. If necessary add mineral free water to the bottom of the filler well.

GENERAL INFORMATION AND MAINTENANCE

Capacities

Year	Model	Engine Displacement	ENGINE CRANKCASE (qts) With Filter	ENGINE CRANKCASE (qts) Without Filter	TRANSMISSION (pts) Manual 4-spd	TRANSMISSION (pts) Manual 5-spd	TRANSMISSION (pts) Automatic	Drive Axle (pts)	Gasoline Tank (gals)	Cooling System (qts) W/ AC	Cooling System (qts) W/O AC
1978	All	104.7	4	4	2.65	—	2.5①	—	13	6.5	8.0
1979	All	104.7	4	4	2.65	—	2.5①	—	13	6.0	6.0
1980	All	104.7	4	4	2.65	—	2.5①	—	13	6.0	6.0

— Not Applicable
① Replacement volume. Unit holds 6.5 qts but torque converter is not equipped with drain plug.

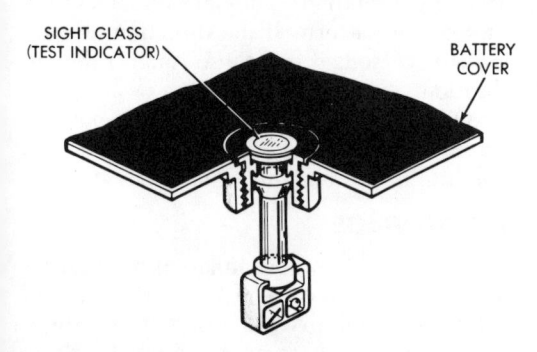

Test indicator on maintenance free battery

At least once a year, check the specific gravity of a standard battery. For other battery maintenance (cables, etc.) see Battery under Routine Maintenance earlier in this chapter.

Tires

INFLATION PRESSURE

Tire inflation is the most ignored item of auto maintenance. Gasoline mileage can drop as much as .8% for every 1 pound per square inch (psi) of under inflation.

Two items should be a permanent fixture in every glove compartment; a tire pressure gauge and a tread depth gauge. Check the tire air pressure (including the spare) regularly with a pocket type gauge. Kicking the tires won't tell you a thing, and the gauge on the service station air hose is notoriously inaccurate.

The tire pressures recommended for your car are usually found on the door post or in the owner's manual. Ideally, inflation pressure should be checked when the tires are cool. When the air becomes heated it expands and the pressure increases. Every 10° rise (or drop) in temperature means a difference of 1 psi, which also explains why the tire appears to lose air on a very cold night. When it is impossible to check the tires "cold," allow for pressure build-up due to heat. If the "hot" pressure exceeds the "cold" pressure by more than 15 psi, reduce your speed, load or both. Otherwise internal heat is created in the tire. When the heat approaches the temperature at which the tire was cured, during manufacture, the tread can separate from the body.

CAUTION: *Never counteract excessive pressure build-up by bleeding off air pressure (letting some air out). This will only further raise the tire operating temperature.*

Before starting a long trip with lots of luggage, you can add about 2–4 psi to the tires to make them run cooler, but never exceed the maximum inflation pressure on the side of the tire.

TREAD DEPTH

All tires made since 1968, have 8 built-in tread wear indicator bars that show up as ½" wide smooth bands across the tire when 1/16" of tread remains. The appearance of tread wear indicators means that the tires should be replaced. In fact, many states have laws prohibiting the use of tires with less than 1/16" tread.

You can check your own tread depth with an inexpensive gauge or by using a Lincoln head penny. Slip the Lincoln penny into several tread grooves. If you can see the top of Lincoln's head in 2 adjacent grooves, the tires have less than 1/16" tread left and should be replaced. You can measure snow tires in

GENERAL INFORMATION AND MAINTENANCE

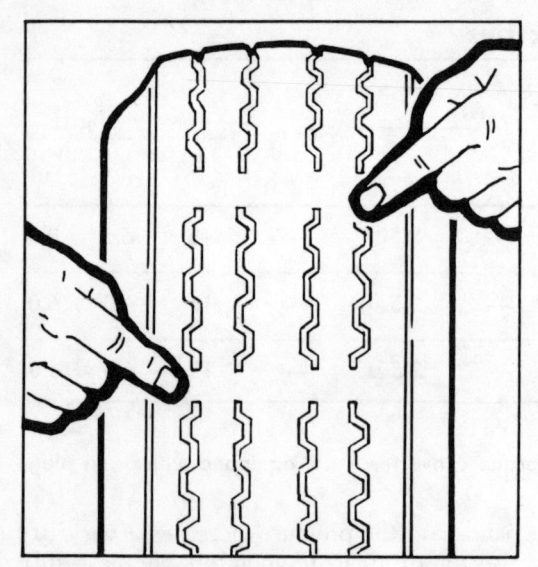

Tire wear indicators appear as 1/2" wide bands when tread is less than 1/16"

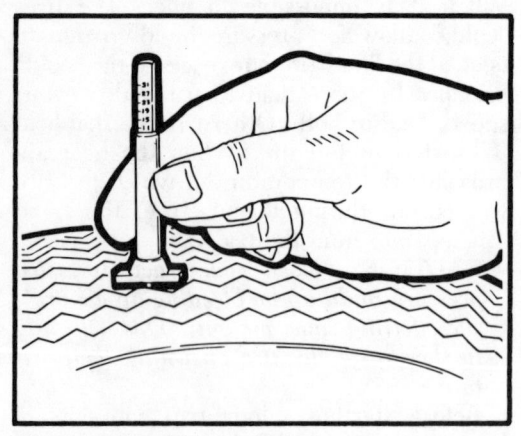

Check tire tread depth with an inexpensive gauge

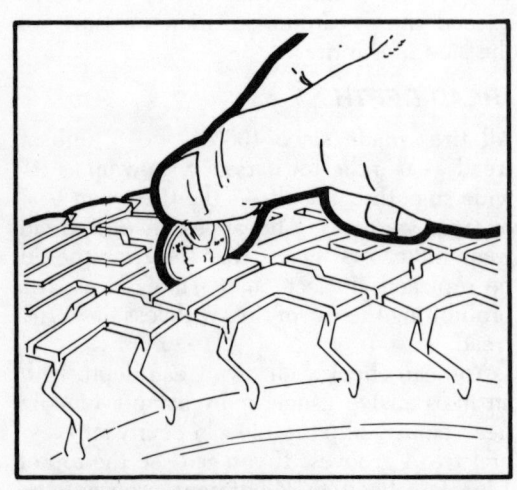

Tread depth can also be roughly checked with a Lincoln head penny. If the top of Lincoln's head is visible, replace the tires

the same manner by using the "tails" side of the Lincoln penny. If you can see the top of the Lincoln memorial, it's time to replace the snow tires.

TIRE ROTATION

Tire wear can be equalized by switching the position of the tires about every 6000 miles. Including a conventional spare in the rotation pattern can give up to 20% more tire life.

CAUTION: *Do not include the new "Spacesaver®" rotation pattern.*

There are certain exceptions to tire rotation, however. Studded snow tires should not be rotated, and radials should be kept on the same side of the car (maintain the same direction of rotation). The belts on radial tires get set in a pattern. If the direction of rotation is reversed, it can cause rough ride and vibration.

NOTE: *When radials or studded snows are taken off the car, mark them, so you can maintain the same direction of rotation.*

TIRE STORAGE

Store the tires at proper inflation pressures if they are mounted on wheels. All tires should be kept in a cool, dry place. If they are stored in the garage or basement, do not let them stand on a concrete floor; set them on strips of wood.

Fuel Filter

The fuel filter is located behind the fuel inlet of the carburetor. Under normal operating conditions, the filter should be replaced after the first 7500 miles and every 15,000 miles thereafter.

1. Remove the clamp from the rubber hose.
2. Spread some dry rags under the fuel fitting to absorb the inevitable gasoline spillage.
3. Unscrew the fitting and remove the filter.
4. Install a new filter.
5. Install and tighten the fitting.

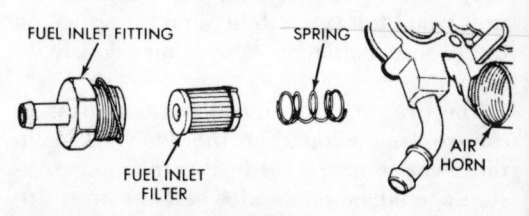

Fuel filter, spring and fitting

GENERAL INFORMATION AND MAINTENANCE

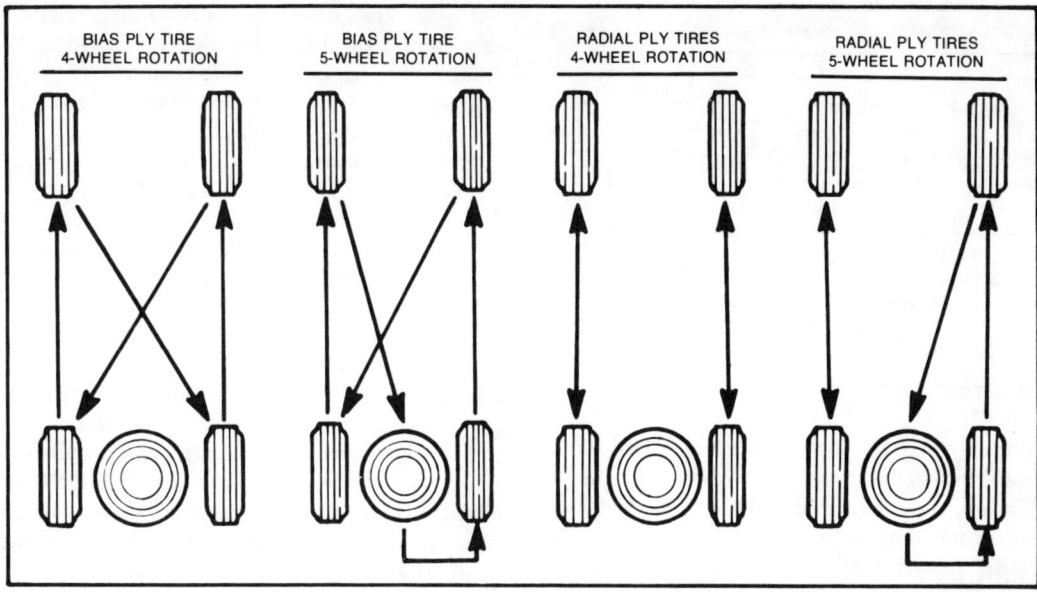

Tire rotation patterns

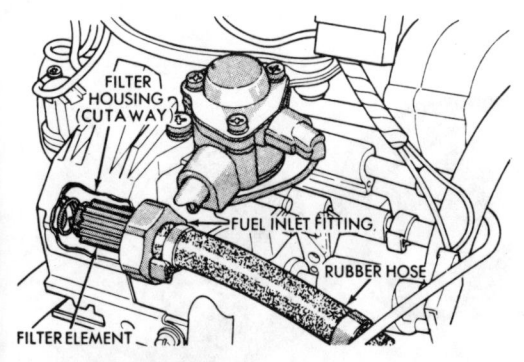

Fuel filter location

6. Connect the fuel line. You may want to use a new screw type clamp that will make future filter replacement easier.

7. Run the engine and check for any leaks.

LUBRICATION

Oil and Fuel Recommendations

Oils and lubricants are classified and graded according to standards established by the Society of Automotive Engineers (SAE), American Petroleum Institute (API), and the National Lubricating Grease Institute (NLGI).

ENGINE OIL

Oils are classified by the SAE and API designations, found on the top of the oil can. The SAE grade number indicates the viscosity of engine oils. SAE 10W-40, for example, is a good all-temperature motor oil suitable for use in winter.

The API classification system defines oil

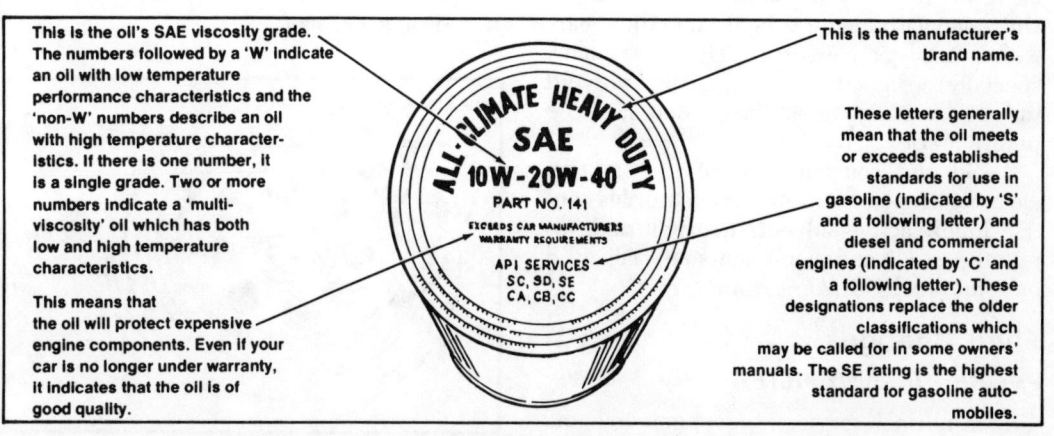

This is the oil's SAE viscosity grade. The numbers followed by a 'W' indicate an oil with low temperature performance characteristics and the 'non-W' numbers describe an oil with high temperature characteristics. If there is one number, it is a single grade. Two or more numbers indicate a 'multi-viscosity' oil which has both low and high temperature characteristics.

This means that the oil will protect expensive engine components. Even if your car is no longer under warranty, it indicates that the oil is of good quality.

This is the manufacturer's brand name.

These letters generally mean that the oil meets or exceeds established standards for use in gasoline (indicated by 'S' and a following letter) and diesel and commercial engines (indicated by 'C' and a following letter). These designations replace the older classifications which may be called for in some owners' manuals. The SE rating is the highest standard for gasoline automobiles.

The top of the oil can will tell you all you need to know about the oil

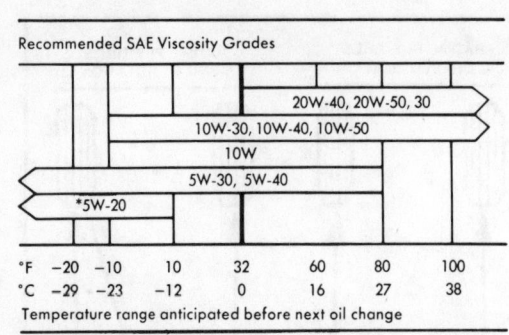

34 GENERAL INFORMATION AND MAINTENANCE

Recommended SAE Viscosity Grades

Grade	Temperature range
20W-40, 20W-50, 30	
10W-30, 10W-40, 10W-50	
10W	
5W-30, 5W-40	
*5W-20	

°F −20 −10 10 32 60 80 100
°C −29 −23 −12 0 16 27 38

Temperature range anticipated before next oil change

*SAE 5W-20 Not recommended for sustained high speed vehicle operation.

Oil viscosity chart

performance in terms of usage. Only oils designed for service "SE" should be used. These oils provide sufficient additives to give maximum engine protection.

GEAR LUBRICANTS

Gear lubricants are graded by the SAE according to viscosity. Chrysler recommends hypoid gear lubricant for manual transaxles, and the proper viscosity according to ambient temperature can be found under Checking the Transaxle Fluid level in this chapter.

The API also grades gear lubricants according to use. Gear lubricants conforming to API GL-4 specifications should be used.

LUBRICANTS AND GREASES

Semi-solid lubricants bear an NLGI designation and are classified as grades 0, 1, 2, 3 or 4. Whenever chassis lubricant is specified, Multi-Purpose grease, NLGI grade 2, EP (Extreme Pressure) is recommended.

FUEL

Only gasolines with a 91 Research Octane Number (RON) or an octane value of 87 if using the (R+M)/2 method, should be used. Unleaded gasoline must be used in those cars with a catalytic converter. These cars have specially designed filler necks that prevent the direct insertion of the leaded gasoline pump nozzle.

Avoid the constant use of fuel system cleaning agents. Many of these materials contain highly active solvents that will deteriorate the gasket and diaphragm materials used on Omni and Horizon carburetors.

Fluid Changes

ENGINE OIL AND FILTER

Under normal service, the engine oil and filter should be changed every 12 months or 7500 miles, whichever comes first.

Under the following conditions, change the engine oil and filter every 3 months or 3000 miles, whichever comes first:
  Frequent driving in dusty conditions
  Frequent trailer pulling
  Extensive idling
  Frequent short trip driving (less than 10 miles)
  More than 50% operation at sustained high speeds (over 70 mph).

NOTE: *Drain the engine oil when the engine is at normal operating temperature.*

To change the oil, the vehicle should be on a level surface at normal operating temperature. This ensures that you will drain away the foreign matter in the oil, which will not happen if the engine is cold. Oil which is slightly dirty when drained is a good sign. This means that the contaminants are being drained away and not being left behind to form sludge.

You should have available some means to support the car, a 13 mm wrench, a filter

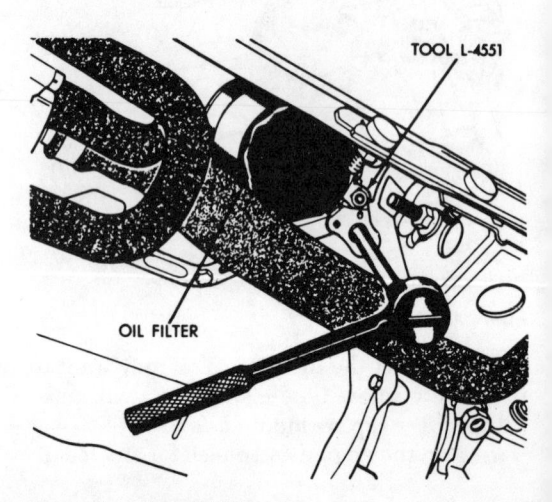

Removing the oil filter

Lubricate the gasket on a new filter with clean engine oil

GENERAL INFORMATION AND MAINTENANCE

You'll need these tools to replace the oil filter

wrench, 4 quarts of oil, a drain pan and some rags.

1. Jack up the front of the car and support it.
2. Position the drain pan under the drain plug, which is located at the rear of the oil pan.
3. Loosen, but do not remove the drain plug. Cover your hand with a heavy rag and slowly unscrew the drain plug. Pushing the plug against the threads in the oil pan will prevent hot oil from running down your arm. As the drain plug comes to the end of the threads, quickly pull it away and allow all of the oil to drain into the pan.
4. When all of the oil has drained, replace the drain plug and tighten it.
   NOTE: *Be sure to dispose of the old oil in an environmentally safe manner.*
5. Remove the oil filter. It can only be removed with the tools shown, from below the car. Once the filter is loose, cover your hand with a thick rag and spin it off by hand.
   NOTE: *On May 29, 1979, the assembly plant began installing 4" diameter oil filters in place of the previously used 3" diameter filters. The 4" filters are the same as those used on other Chrysler vehicles and should be used for service.*
6. Coat the rubber gasket on a new filter with clean engine oil and install the new filter. Tighten it by hand until the gasket contacts the mounting base and then ¾–1 turn further.
7. Refill the engine with 4 quarts of fresh oil of the proper viscosity according to the anticipated temperatures before the next oil change.

NOTE: *It requires 4 quarts of oil to fill the engine regardless of whether the filter was changed or not.*

8. Run the engine for a few minutes and check the oil level.

MANUAL TRANSAXLE

Under normal conditions, the manual transaxle fluid will never need changing. Rare circumstances, such as the fluid becoming contaminated with water will necessitate fluid replacement.

It is relatively easy to change your own gear oil. The only equipment required is a drain pan, a wrench to fit the filler and drain plugs, and an oil suction gun. Gear oil can be purchased in gallon cans at automotive supply stores.

To change the oil:

1. Jack up the front of the car and support it safely on stands.
2. Slide drain pan under the transaxle.
3. Remove the filler plug and then the drain plug.
4. When the oil has been completely drained, install the drain plug. Tighten to 18 ft lbs.
5. Using the suction gun, refill the gearbox or rear axle up to the level of the filler plug. Use an SAE 80 or 90 gear oil.
6. Install and tighten the filler plug.

AUTOMATIC TRANSAXLE

NOTE: *RTV silicone sealer is used in place of a pan gasket.*

36 GENERAL INFORMATION AND MAINTENANCE

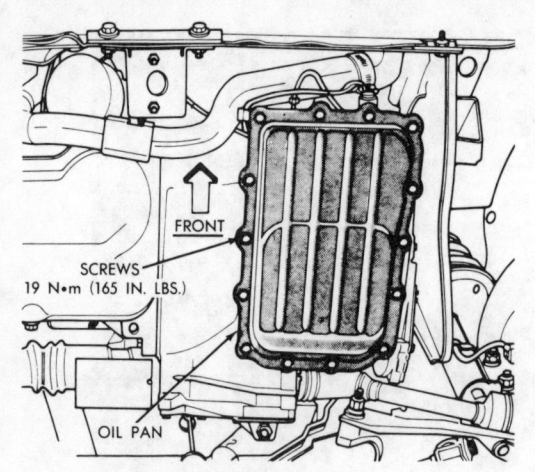

Automatic transaxle oil pan

Chrysler recommends no fluid or filter changes during the normal service life of the car. Severe usage requires a fluid and filter change every 15,000 miles. Severe usage is defined as:

  a. more than 50% heavy city traffic during 90° F weather.
  b. police, taxi or commercial operation or trailer towing.

When changing the fluid, only Dexron or Dexron II fluid should be used. A filter change should be performed at every fluid change.

1. Raise the vehicle and support it on jackstands.
2. Place a large container under the pan, loosen the pan bolts and tap at one corner to break it loose. Drain the fluid.
3. When the fluid is drained remove the pan bolts.
4. Remove the retaining screws and replace the filter. Tighten the screws to 35 inch pounds.
5. Clean the fluid pan, peel off the old RTV silicone sealer and install the pan, using a ⅛ inch bead of new RTV sealer. Always run the sealer bead inside the bolt holes. Tighten the pan bolts to 10–12 ft lb.
6. Pour four quarts of Dexron or Dexron II fluid through the filler tube.
7. Start the engine and idle it for at least 2 minutes. Set the parking brake and move the selector through each position, ending in Park.
8. Add sufficient fluid to bring the level to the FULL mark on the dipstick. The level should be checked in Park, with the engine idling at normal operating temperature.

COOLANT

See Draining and Refilling the Cooling System under Routine Maintenance in this chapter.

Chassis Greasing

TIE-ROD ENDS

There are only 2 points on the car that require periodic greasing. The tie-rod end ball joints are semi-permanently lubricated and should be lubricated every 3 years or 30,000 miles, whichever occurs first. These joints should also be inspected whenever the car is serviced for other reasons. Damaged seals should be replaced.

To lubricate the tie-rod end ball joints:

1. Clean the accumulated dirt and grease from the outside of the seal area to permit a close inspection.
2. Clean the grease fitting and surrounding area.
3. Using a grease gun fill the joint with fresh grease.
4. Stop filling when the grease begins to flow freely from the areas at the base of the seal or when the seal begins to balloon.
5. Wipe off the excess grease.

STEERING SHAFT SEAL

The steering shaft seal where the steering shaft passes through the dash is lubricated at manufacture. If the seal becomes noisy when the steering shaft is turned, it should be relubricated with multi-purpose chassis grease, NLGI Grade 2 EP.

FRONT SUSPENSION BALL JOINTS

The 2 lower front suspension ball joints are permanently lubricated at the factory. In-

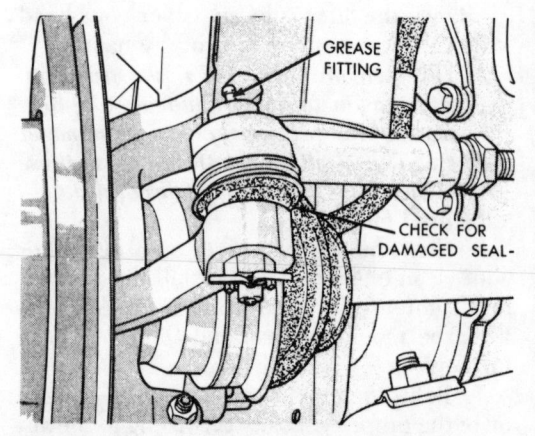

Check the tie-rod end ball joint seals

GENERAL INFORMATION AND MAINTENANCE

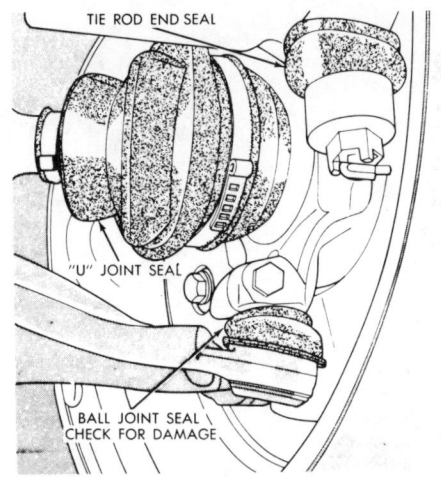

Check ball joints for damaged seals

spect the joints whenever the car is serviced for other reasons. Damaged seals should be replaced to prevent leakage of grease.

CLUTCH CABLE

If the clutch cable begins to make odd noises or if the effort to depress the clutch becomes excessive, lubricate the clutch cable ball end with multi-purpose chassis grease NLGI Grade 2 EP.

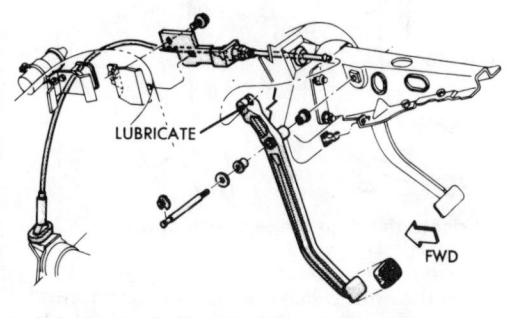

Lubricate the ball end of the clutch cable

FLOORSHIFT CONTROL LINKAGE

The gearshift control linkage should be lubricated whenever the shifting effort becomes excessive or if the linkage exhibits a rattling noise. Use a multi-purpose chassis grease NLGI Grade 2 EP. Remove the unit and lubricate the spherical balls, metal caps and shaft and lubricate each plastic grommet or bushing.

DRIVESHAFT U-JOINTS

The car has 4 constant velocity U-joints. No periodic lubrication is required, but the joint seals should be inspected for damage or leakage whenever the car is serviced. If damage

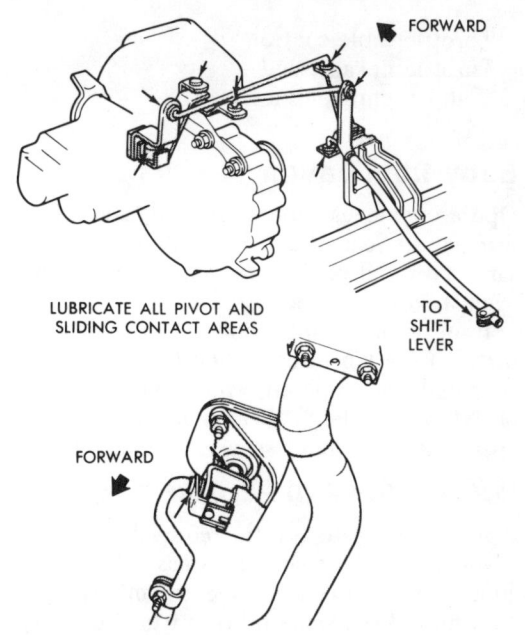

Lubricate the floor shift linkage

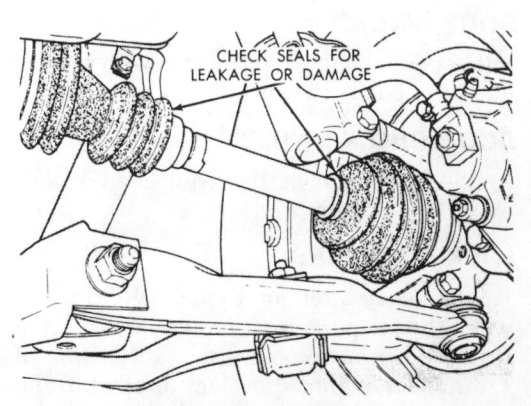

Inspect U-joint seals for leakage

is found, replace the U-joint boot and seal and fill with fresh grease immediately. Failure to do so will eventually require complete replacement of the constant velocity joint.

PARTS REQUIRING NO LUBRICATION

Some components are permanently lubricated. Some parts will be adversely affected by lubricants. In particular, rubber bushings should not be lubricated, since it will destroy their frictional characteristics. Parts that should not be lubricated are?
  Alternator bearings,
  Drive belts,
  Fan idler belt pulley,
  Front wheel bearings,
  Rubber bushings,
  Starter bearings,
  Suspension strut bearing,

38 GENERAL INFORMATION AND MAINTENANCE

Throttle cable control,
Throttle linkage, and
Water pump bearings.

Body Lubrication

Operating mechanisms of the body should be inspected, cleaned and lubricated as necessary. This will provide maximum protection against rust and wear.

Prior to lubricating, wipe the parts clean of dirt and old lubricant. When Lubriplate® is specified, use a smooth, white body lubricant of NLGI Grade 1. When Door-Ease® is specified, use a stainless, wax-type lubricant.

HOOD LATCH AND RELEASE

Apply Lubriplate, or the equivalent to all pivot and sliding contact areas. Work the lubricant into the lock mechanism. Apply a thin film of the same lubricant to the safety catch.

BODY HINGES

These parts should be lubricated with engine oil at the points shown.

DOOR CHECK STRAPS

Apply Lubriplate or the equivalent whenever the car is serviced.

LOCK CYLINDERS

Pay particular attention to the lock cylinders when the temperature is around the freezing mark. When necessary, apply a thin film of Lubriplate, or the equivalent directly to the key and insert the key in the lock. Work the lock several times and wipe the key dry.

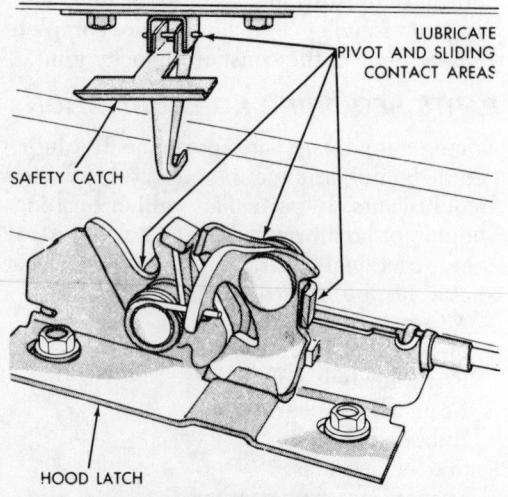

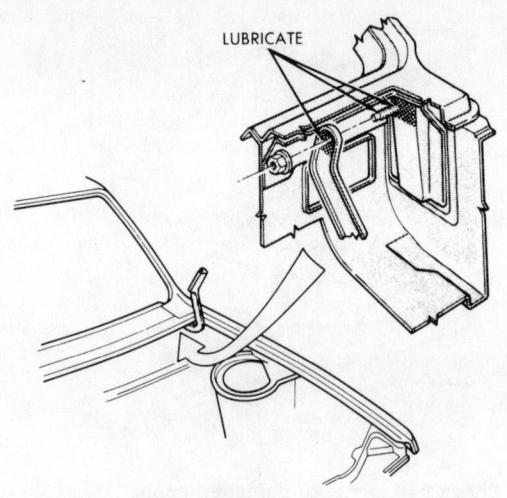

Lubricate the hood hinges

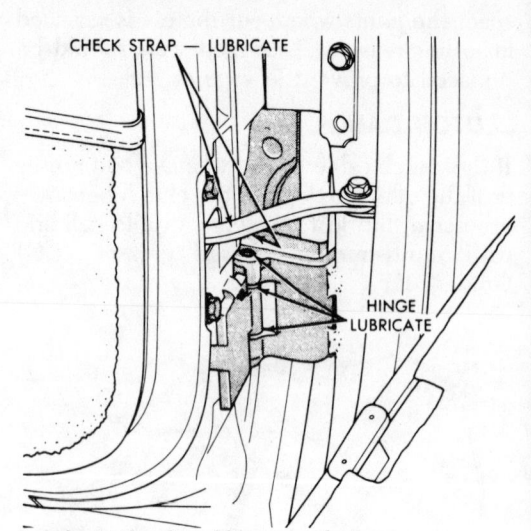

Lubricate the door hinge check strap

Lubricate the hood latch release

Another alternative is to use a commercial spray that is sprayed directly into the lock to prevent freezing.

LIFTGATE PROP PIVOTS AND LATCH

Lubricate these points with Lubriplate or the equivalent.

DOOR LATCH, LOCK CONTROL LINKAGE AND WINDOW REGULATOR

To lubricate these parts it is necessary to remove the trim panel. Lubricate all pivot and sliding contact areas with Lubriplate or the equivalent.

PARKING BRAKE MECHANISM

Lubricate all parking brake sliding and pivot contact areas with Lubriplate or the equivalent.

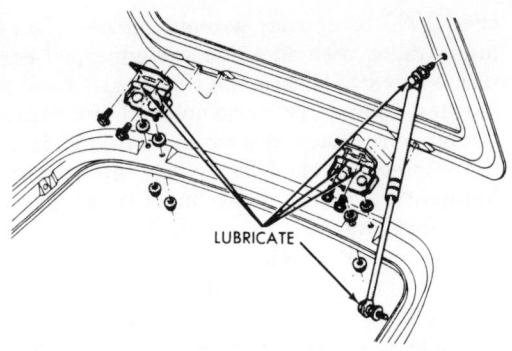

GENERAL INFORMATION AND MAINTENANCE

Lubricate the liftgate hinges and prop pivots

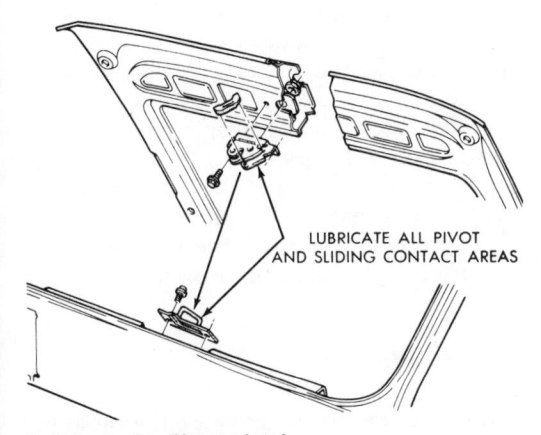

Lubricate the liftgate latch

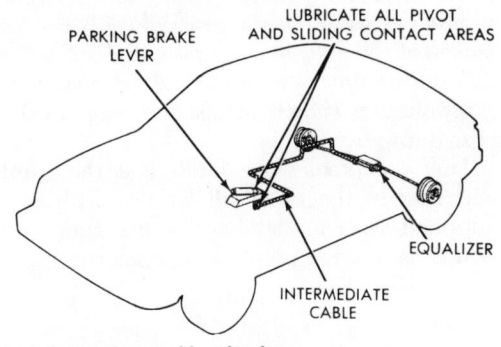

Lubricate the parking brake

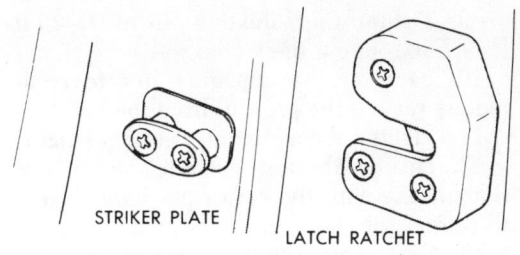

Lubricate the door latches

DOOR LATCH AND STRIKER PLATE

Lubriplate the striker plate contact area and the ratchet pivot areas with a stainless, wax-type lubricant such as Door Ease.

FRONT WHEEL BEARINGS

The front wheel bearings are permanently sealed and require no periodic lubrication.

REAR WHEEL BEARINGS

The rear wheel bearings should be inspected and relubricated whenever the rear brakes are serviced or at least every 30,000 miles.

Repack the bearings with high temperature multi-purpose grease.

Check the lubricant to see if it is contaminated. If it contains dirt or has a milky appearance indicating the presence of water, the bearings should be cleaned and repacked.

Clean the bearings in kerosene, mineral spirits or other suitable cleaning fluid. Do not dry them by spinning the bearings. Allow them to air dry.

1. Raise and support the car with the rear wheels off the floor.
2. Remove the wheel grease cap, cotter pin, nut-lock and bearing adjusting nut.
3. Remove the thrust washer and bearing.
4. Remove the drum from the spindle.
5. Thoroughly clean the old lubricant from the bearings and hub cavity. Inspect the bearing rollers for pitting or other signs of wear. Light discoloration is normal.
6. Repack the bearings with high temperature multi-purpose EP grease and add a small amount of new grease to the hub cavity. Be sure to force the lubricant between all rollers in the bearing.
7. Install the drum on the spindle after coating the polished spindle surfaces with wheel bearing lubricant.
8. Install the outer bearing cone, thrust washer and adjusting nut.

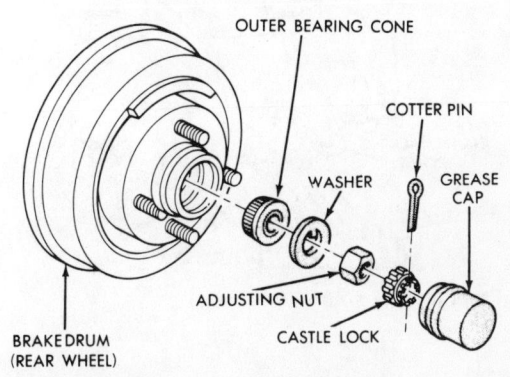

Exploded view of rear wheel bearing

GENERAL INFORMATION AND MAINTENANCE

9. Tighten the adjusting nut to 20–25 ft lbs while rotating the wheel.
10. Back off the adjusting nut to completely release the preload from the bearing.
11. Tighten the adjusting nut finger-tight.
12. Position the nut-lock with one pair of slots in line with the cotter pin hole. Install the cotter pin.
13. Clean and install the grease cap and wheel.
14. Lower the car.

PUSHING, TOWING, AND JUMP STARTING

If your car is equipped with a manual transaxle, it may be push started in an extreme emergency, but there is the possibility of damaging bumpers and/or fenders of both cars. Make sure that the bumpers of both cars are evenly matched. Depress the clutch pedal, select Second or Third gear, and switch the ignition On. When the car reaches a speed of approximately 10 or 15 mph, release the clutch to start the engine DO NOT ATTEMPT TO PUSH START AN AUTOMATIC OMNI OR HORIZON.

Manual transaxle models may be flat-towed short distances. Attach tow lines to the towing eye on the front suspension or the left or right bumper bracket at the rear. Flat-towing automatic transaxle models is not recommended more than 15 miles at more than 30 mph, and this only in an emergency. Cars equipped with the automatic should only be towed from the rear when the front wheels are on towing dollies.

If you plan on towing a trailer, don't exceed 1000 lbs (trailer without brakes). Towing a trailer with an automatic equipped car places an extra load on the transmission and a few items should be made note of here. Make doubly sure that the transmission fluid is at the correct level. Change the fluid more frequently if you're doing much trailer hauling. Start out in 1 or 2 and use the lower ranges when climbing hills. Aftermarket transmission coolers are available which greatly ease the load on your automatic and one should be considered if you often pull a trailer.

Jump starting is the favored method of starting a car with a dead battery. Make sure that the cables are properly connected, negative-to-negative and positive-to-positive, or you stand a chance of damaging the electrical systems of both cars. Keep the engine running in the donor car. If the car still fails to start, call a garage—continual grinding on the starter will overheat the unit and make repair or replacement necessary.

JACKING

Floor jacks can be used to raise the car at the locations shown. In addition a front jacking point is located at the center of the front crossmember. Four door models only can be jacked at the extreme rear provided a 2" x 4" x 25" (minimum dimensions) wood spacer is positioned as shown against the ledge of the rear bumper.

Jack receptacles are located at the front and rear of the body sill for use with jack supplied with a car. Do not use these lift points as bearing points for a floor jack.

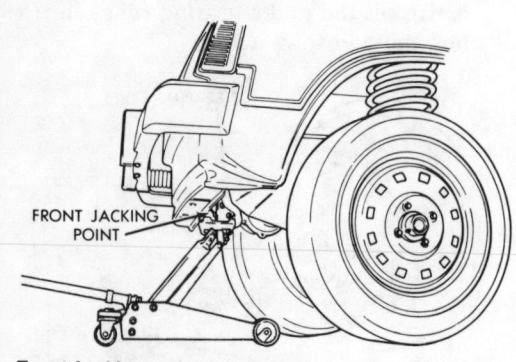

Front jacking point—floor jack

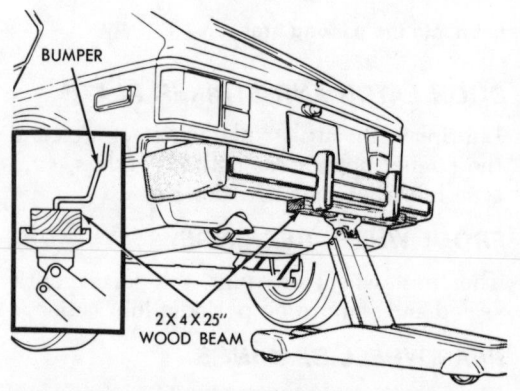

4-door model rear jacking point—floor jack

GENERAL INFORMATION AND MAINTENANCE 41

JUMP STARTING A DEAD BATTERY

The chemical reaction in a battery produces explosive hydrogen gas. This is the safe way to jump start a dead battery, reducing the chances of an accidental spark that could cause an explosion.

Jump Starting Precautions

1. Be sure both batteries are of the same voltage.
2. Be sure both batteries are of the same polarity (have the same grounded terminal).
3. Be sure the vehicles are not touching.
4. Be sure the vent cap holes are not obstructed.
5. Do not smoke or allow sparks around the battery.
6. In cold weather, check for frozen electrolyte in the battery.
7. Do not allow electrolyte on your skin or clothing.
8. Be sure the electrolyte is not frozen.

Jump Starting Procedure

1. Determine voltages of the two batteries; they must be the same.
2. Bring the starting vehicle close (they must not touch) so that the batteries can be reached easily.
3. Turn off all accessories and both engines. Put both cars in Neutral or Park and set the handbrake.
4. Cover the cell caps with a rag—do not cover terminals.
5. If the terminals on the run-down battery are heavily corroded, clean them.
6. Identify the positive and negative posts on both batteries and connect the cables in the order shown.
7. Start the engine of the starting vehicle and run it at fast idle. Try to start the car with the dead battery. Crank it for no more than 10 seconds at a time and let it cool off for 20 seconds in between tries.
8. If it doesn't start in 3 tries, there is something else wrong.
9. Disconnect the cables in the reverse order.
10. Replace the cell covers and dispose of the rags.

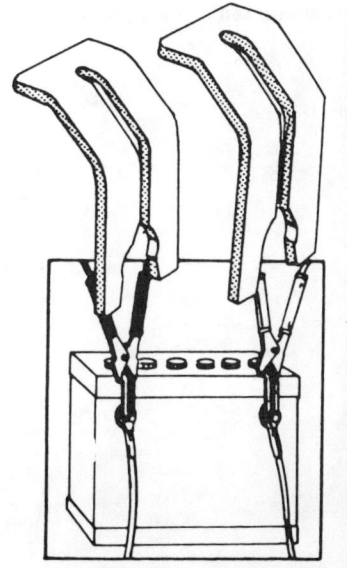

Side terminal batteries occasionally pose a problem when connecting jumper cables. There frequently isn't enough room to clamp the cables without touching sheet metal. Side terminal adaptors are available to alleviate this problem and should be removed after use.

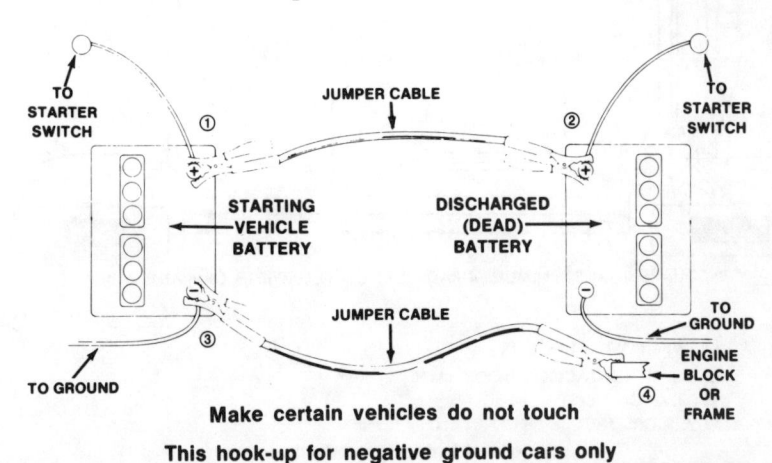

Make certain vehicles do not touch

This hook-up for negative ground cars only

42 GENERAL INFORMATION AND MAINTENANCE

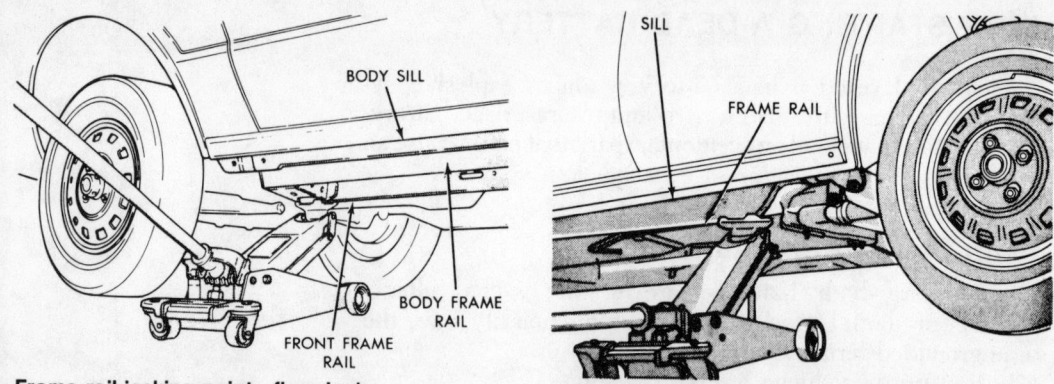

Frame rail jacking point—floor jack

Rear frame rail jacking point—floor jack

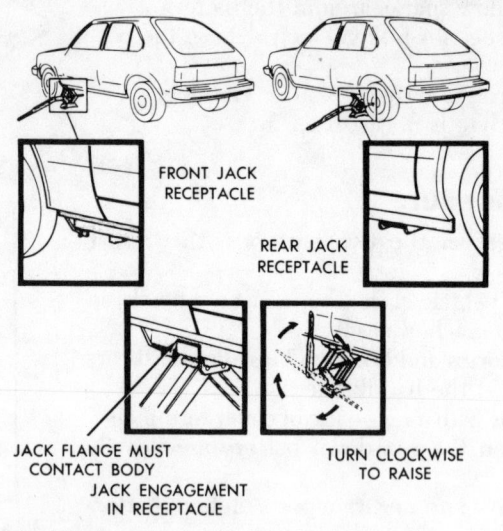

Jacking locations with tire changing jack

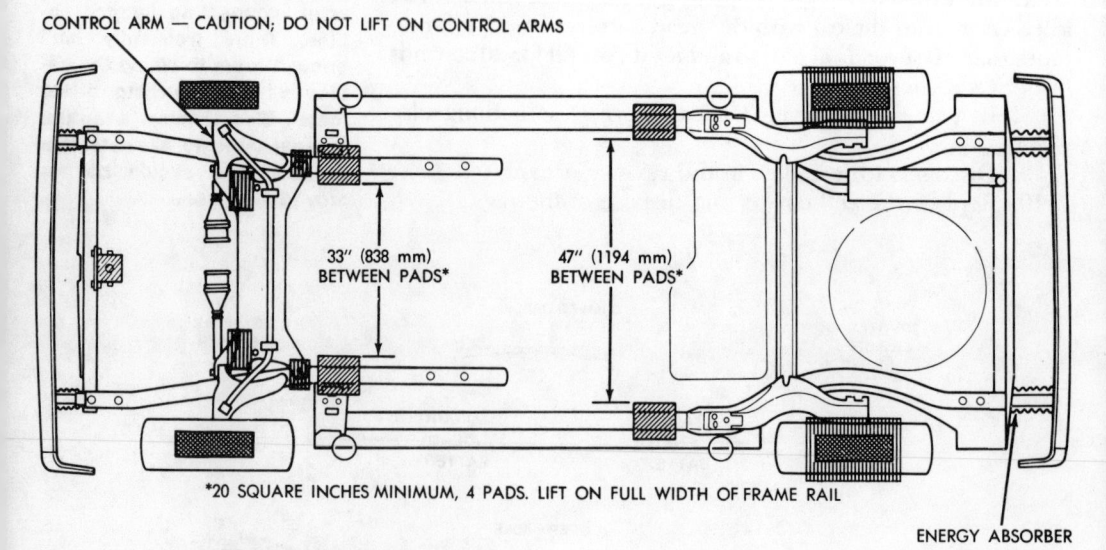

CONTROL ARM — CAUTION; DO NOT LIFT ON CONTROL ARMS

33" (838 mm) BETWEEN PADS*

47" (1194 mm) BETWEEN PADS*

*20 SQUARE INCHES MINIMUM, 4 PADS. LIFT ON FULL WIDTH OF FRAME RAIL

ENERGY ABSORBER

- ▥ TWIN POST LIFT POINTS
- ▨ FRAME CONTACT OR FLOOR JACK
- ▧ DRIVE ON HOIST
- O SCISSORS JACK (EMERGENCY) LOCATIONS

Jacking and hoisting contact locations

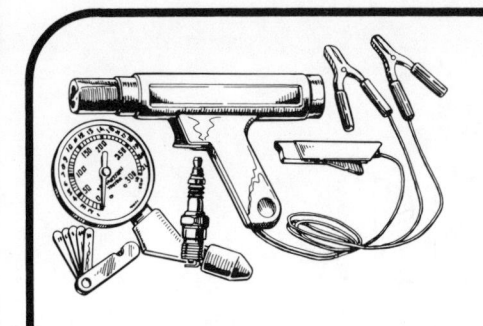

Tune-Up and Troubleshooting

TUNE-UP

The procedures listed here are intended as specific procedures. More general procedures are given in the "Tune-Up" section at the end of the chapter.

Neither tune-up nor troubleshooting can be considered independently, since each has a direct bearing on the other.

An engine tune-up is a service designed to restore the maximum capability of power, performance, economy and reliability in an engine, and, at the same time, assure the owner of a complete check and more lasting results in efficiency and trouble-free performance. Engine tune-up becomes increasingly important each year, to ensure that pollutant levels are in compliance with federal emissions standards.

It is advisable to follow a definite and thorough tune-up procedure. Tune-up consists of three separate steps: Analysis, the process of determining whether normal wear is responsible for performance loss, and whether parts require replacement or service; Parts Replacement or Service; and Adjustment, where engine adjustments are returned to the original factory specifications.

The extent of an engine tune-up is uaually determined by the length of time since the previous service, although the type of driving and the general mechanical condition of the engine must be considered. Specific maintenance should also be performed at regular intervals, depending on operating conditions.

Troubleshooting is a logical sequence of procedures designed to lead the owner or service man to the particular cause of trouble. The troubleshooting section of this manual is general in nature, yet specific enough to locate the problem. Service usually comprises two areas; diagnosis and repair. While the apparent cause of trouble, in many cases, is worn or damaged parts, performance problems are less obvious. The first job is to locate the problem and cause. Once the problem has been isolated, refer to the appropriate section for repair, removal or adjustment procedures.

It is advisable to read the entire chapter before beginning a tune-up, although those who are more familiar with tune-up procedures may wish to go directly to the instructions.

Spark Plugs

A typical spark plug consists of a metal shell surrounding a ceramic insulator. A metal electrode extends downward through the center of the insulator and protrudes a small distance. Located at the end of the plug and

TUNE-UP AND TROUBLESHOOTING

Tune-Up Specifications

Part numbers listed in this reference are not recommendations by Chilton for any product by brand name. They are references that can be used with interchange manuals and after market supplier catalogs to locate each brand supplier's discrete part number.

NOTE: When analyzing compression test results, look for uniformity among cylinders rather than specific pressures. The lowest reading cylinder should be within 20% of the highest.

Year	No. Cyl Displ Cu In.	hp	Spark Plugs Orig Type	Gap (in.)	Ignition Timing (deg) ▲ Man Trans	Ignition Timing (deg) ▲ Auto Trans	Intake Valve Opens (deg) ■	Fuel Pump Pressure (psi)	Idle Speed (rpm) ▲ Man Trans	Idle Speed (rpm) ▲ Auto Trans	Valve Lash (in.) ▲ Intake	Valve Lash (in.) ▲ Exhaust
'78	4—104.7	75	RN-12Y	.035	15B	15B	23	4.5–6	900	900	.008–.012H	.016–.020H
'79	4—104.7	75	RN-12Y	.035	15B	15B	14	4.4–5.8	900	900	.008–.012H	.016–.020H
'80	4—104.7	75	RN-12Y	.035	15B	15B	14	4.4–5.8	900	900	.008–.012H	.016–.020H

NOTE: The underhood specifications sticker often reflects tune-up specification changes made in production. Sticker figures must be used if they disagree with those in this chart.
▲ See text for procedure
■ Before Top Dead Center

TUNE-UP AND TROUBLESHOOTING

attached to the side of the outer metal shell is the side electrode. The side electrode bends in at a 90° angle so that its tip is even with, and parallel to, the tip of the center electrode. The distance between these two electrodes (measured in thousandths of an inch) is called the spark plug gap. The spark plug in no way produces a spark but merely provides a gap across which the current can arc. The coil produces anywhere from 20,000 to 40,000 volts which travels to the distributor where it is distributed through the spark plug wires to the spark plugs. The current passes along the center electrode and jumps the gap to the side electrode, and, in so doing, ignited the air/fuel mixture in the combustion chamber.

SPARK PLUG HEAT RANGE

Spark plug heat range is the ability of the plug to dissipate heat. The longer the insulator (or the farther it extends into the engine), the hotter the plug will operate; the shorter the insulator the cooler it will operate. A plug that absorbs little heat and remains too cool will quickly accumulate deposits of oil and carbon since it is not hot enough to burn them off. This leads to plug fouling and consequently to misfiring. A plug that absorbs too much heat will have no deposits, but, due to the excessive heat, the electrodes will burn away quickly and in some instances, preignition may result. Preignition takes place when plug tips get so hot that they glow sufficiently to ignite the fuel/air mixture before the actual spark occurs. This early ignition will usually cause a pinging during low speeds and heavy loads.

The general rule of thumb for choosing the correct heat range when picking a spark plug is: if most of your driving is long distance, high speed travel, use a colder plug; if most of your driving is stop and go, use a hotter plug. Original equipment plugs are compromise plugs, but most people never have occasion to change their plugs from the factory-recommended heat range.

REPLACING SPARK PLUGS

A set of spark plugs usually requires replacement after about 10,000 miles on cars with conventional ignition systems and after about 20,000 to 30,000 miles on cars with electronic ignition, depending on your style of driving. In normal operation, plug gap increases about 0.001 in. for every 1,000–2,500 miles. As the gap increases, the plug's voltage requirement also increases. It requires a greater voltage to jump the wider gap and about two to three times as much voltage to fire a plug at high speeds than at idle.

When you're removing spark plugs, you should work on one at a time. Don't start by removing the plug wires all at once, because unless you number them, they may become mixed up. Take a minute before you begin and number the wires with tape. The best location for numbering is near where the wires come out of the cap.

1. Twist the spark plug boot and remove the boot and wire from the plug. Do not pull on the wire itself as this will ruin the wire.
2. If possible, use a brush or rag to clean the area around the spark plug. Make sure that all the dirt is removed so that none will enter the cylinder after the plug is removed.
3. Remove the spark plug using the proper size socket. Turn the socket counterclockwise to remove the plug. Be sure to hold the socket straight on the plug to avoid breaking the plug, or rounding off the hex on the plug.
4. Once the plug is out, check it against

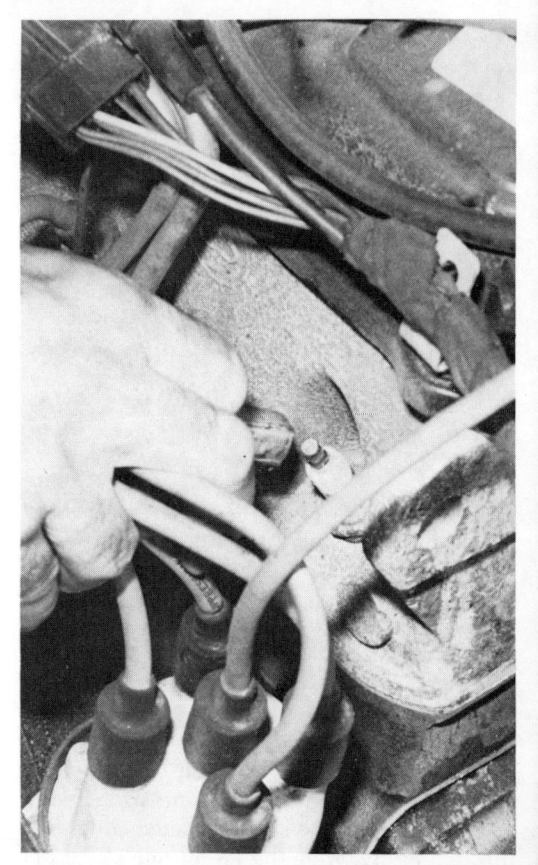

Remove the plug wires by pulling on the boot

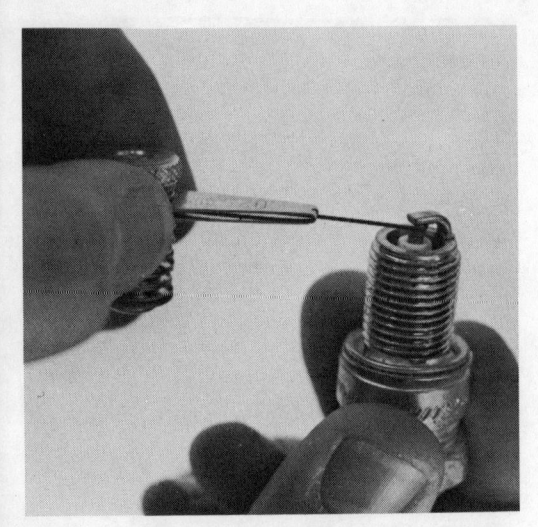

46 TUNE-UP AND TROUBLESHOOTING

Check the spark plug gap with a round feeler gauge

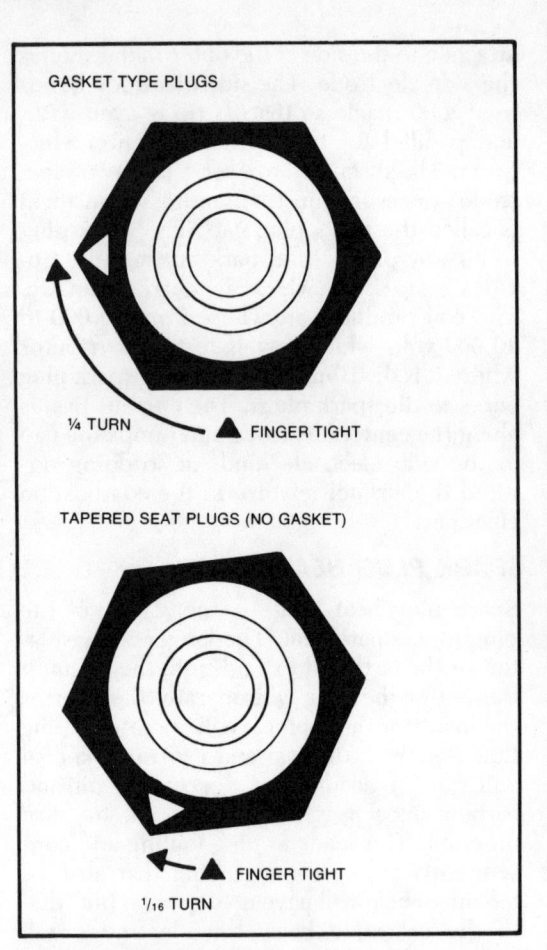

Tighten the plugs as shown in the absence of a specified torque

the plugs shown in this section to determine engine condition. This is crucial since plug readings are vital signs of engine condition.

5. Use a round wire feeler gauge to check the plug gap. The correct size gauge should pass through the electrode gap with a slight drag. If you're in doubt, try one size smaller and one larger. The smaller gauge should go through easily while the larger one shouldn't go through at all. If the gap is incorrect, use the electrode bending tool on the end of the gauge to adjust the gap. When adjusting the gap, always bend the side electrode. The center electrode is non-adjustable.

6. Squirt a drop of penetrating oil on the threads of the new plug and install it. Don't oil the threads too heavily. Turn the plug in clockwise by hand until it is snug.

7. When the plug is finger tight, tighten it with a wrench. If you don't have a torque wrench, tighten the plug as shown.

8. Install the plug boot firmly over the plug. Proceed to the next plug.

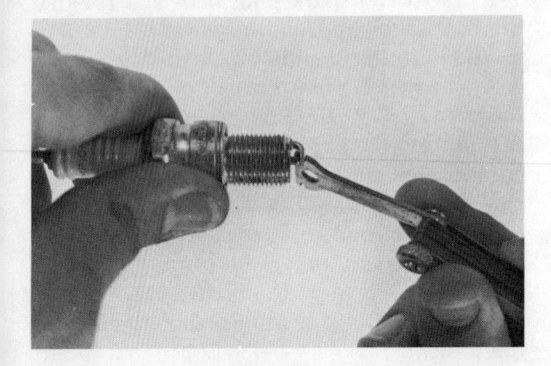

Bend the outer electrode to adjust the plug gap

CHECKING AND REPLACING SPARK PLUG CABLES

Visually inspect the spark plug cables for burns, cuts, or breaks in the insulation. Check the spark plug boots and the nipples on the distributor cap and coil. Replace any damaged wiring. If no physical damage is obvious, the wires can be checked with an ohmmeter for excessive resistance. (See the tune-up and troubleshooting section).

When installing a new set of spark plug cables, replace the cables one at a time so there will be no mixup. Start by replacing the longest cable first. Install the boot firmly over the spark plug. Route the wire exactly the same as the original. Insert the nipple firmly into the tower on the distributor cap. Repeat the process for each cable.

Breaker Points and Condenser

The Omni and Horizon models use a fully electronic hall effect ignition system that has

TUNE-UP AND TROUBLESHOOTING

no breaker points or condenser. No periodic maintenance or parts replacement is necessary.

DWELL ANGLE

The electronic ignition system has no dwell angle in the sense of a conventional point-type ignition system. No measurement of the dwell angle is necessary or possible.

Ignition Timing Adjustment

The engine is timed on No. 1 cylinder, which is the left-hand side of the car, facing the car.

1. Connect a timing light according to the manufacturer's instructions.
2. Run the engine to normal operating temperature.
3. Make sure the idle speed is correct.
4. Loosen the distributor holddown screw just enough so that the distributor can be rotated.
5. Ground the carburetor switch.
6. Remove the timing hole access cover and aim the timing light at the hole in the clutch housing. Carefully rotate the distributor until the mark is aligned with the pointer on the flywheel housing.
7. Tighten the distributor and recheck the timing.
8. Check, and if necessary adjust, the idle speed.

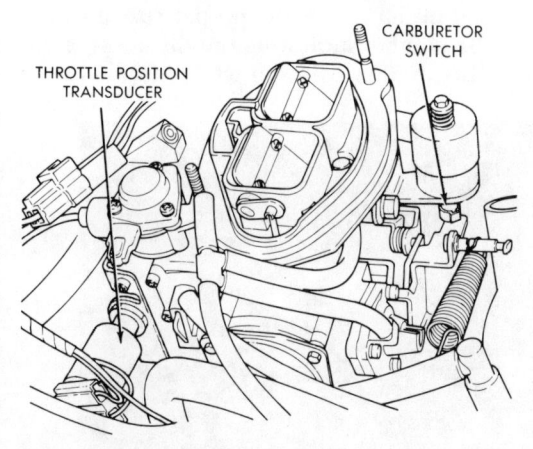

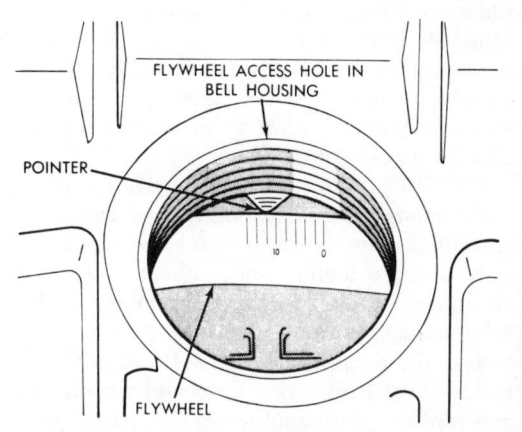

Carburetor switch location

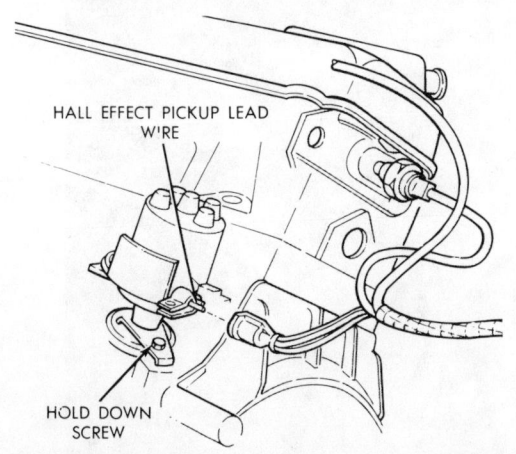

Timing marks—manual transaxle

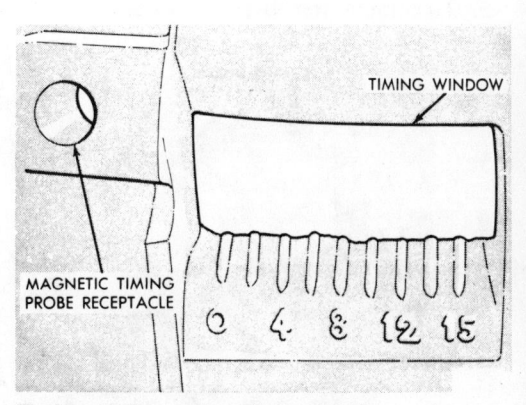

Timing marks—automatic transaxle

Loosen the distributor hold-down bolt to adjust the timing

Valve Adjustment

Valve adjustment is not required as a matter of routine maintenance. It is, however, necessary to check the valve clearance periodically. Adjusting clearance is a matter of substituting discs located in the top of the cam follower. The discs are available in .05mm increments from 3.00mm to 4.25mm. One disc is located in each follower. A special tool is required for disc removal and installation. Cold clearance should be .15–.25mm (.006–.010in.) intake and .35–.45mm (.014–.018in.) exhaust; warm clearance is .20–.30mm (.008–.012in.) intake and .40–.50mm (.016–.020in.) exhaust.

48 TUNE-UP AND TROUBLESHOOTING

CHECKING/ADJUSTING VALVE CLEARANCE

The valve should be checked with the engine warm and be checked in the firing order 1-3-4-2.

1. Run the engine to normal operating temperature.
2. Remove the valve cover.
3. Use a socket wrench on the crankshaft pulley or bump the engine around until the camshaft lobes of No. 1 cylinder are positioned as shown. Due to the design of the camshaft lobes, it is not necessary that the lobes be pointing directly away (perpendicular) to the adjusting disc.

CAUTION: *Do not turn the engine using the camshaft pulley, and only turn the engine in the direction of normal rotation.*

4. Using a feeler gauge, check the valve clearance between the camshaft lobe and the valve adjusting disc.
5. If the measure clearance is not as specified, the valve adjusting disc can be removed and replaced with another of the proper size to give the correct valve clearance.
6. To remove the disc:

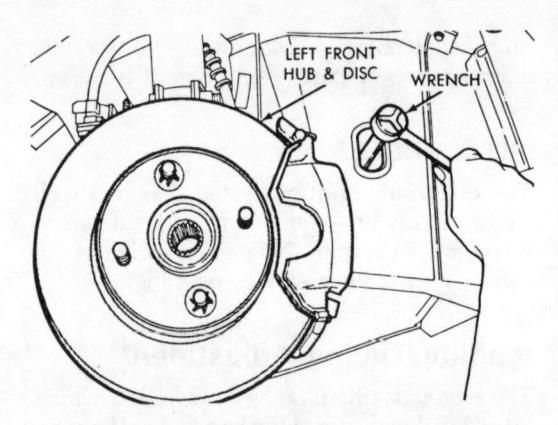

Rotate the engine by inserting a wrench through the access hole

a. Depress the cam follower with Tool L-4417. This tool is necessary to remove the disc without damaging the camshaft or cylinder head.

b. Remove the valve adjusting disc with a magnet.

c. Calculate the thickness of a new disc and install one of the proper size. Be sure the number indicating the thickness of the disc (mm) faces down when installed.

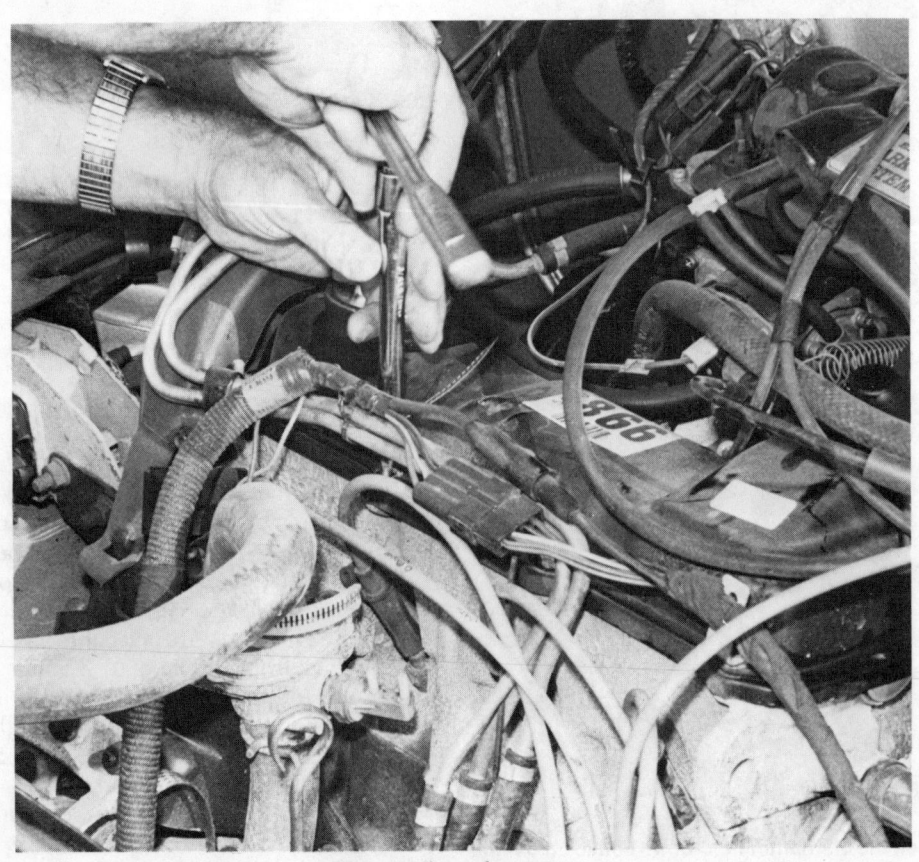

Remove the valve cover

TUNE-UP AND TROUBLESHOOTING 49

The valves of cylinters 1, 3, 4 can be adjusted when No. 1 is positioned as shown

Check valve clearance with a feeler gauge

Depress the cam followers with the special tool shown

TUNE-UP AND TROUBLESHOOTING

Remove the adjusting disc with a magnet

You may need an assortment of discs. The size is etched on the bottom side and faces down when installed

Valve Adjusting Discs

Thickness (mm)	Part Number	Thickness (mm)	Part Number
3.00	5240946	3.65	5240580
3.05	5240945	3.70	5240581
3.10	5240944	3.75	5240582
3.15	5240943	3.80	5240583
3.20	5240942	3.85	5240584
3.25	5240941	3.90	5240585
3.30	5240573	3.95	5240586
3.35	5240574	4.00	5240587
3.40	5240575	4.05	5240588
3.45	5240576	4.10	5240589
3.50	5240577	4.15	5240590
3.55	5240578	4.20	5240591
3.60	5240579	4.25	5240592

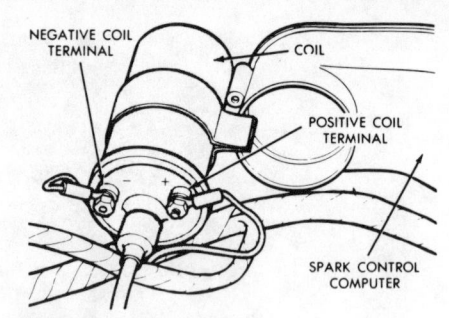

Tachometer connections

d. Recheck the valve clearance.

7. Recheck or adjust all other valves in the same manner.

NOTE: *When the camshaft is in position to check the valves of No. 1 cylinder, cylinders No. 3 and 4 can also be checked or adjusted. It is only necessary to turn the engine one time to position the camshaft to check No. 2 cylinder.*

8. Reinstall the camshaft cover.

Idle Speed

TACHOMETER HOOKUP

1. Connect the red lead of the test tachometer to the negative primary terminal of the coil and the black lead to a good ground.

2. Turn the selector switch to the appropriate cylinder position and read the idle on the 1000 rpm scale, if so equipped.

3. With the engine at normal operating temperature momentarily open the throttle to check for binding in the linkage. Make sure that the idle screw is against its stop.

4. Adjust the idle speed to specifications. If the engine is equipped with an idle solenoid, the solenoid must be energized and the adjusting screw must be resting on the solenoid plunger.

IDLE SPEED AND MIXTURE ADJUSTMENT

Chrysler recommends the use of a propane enrichment procedure to adjust the mixture. The equipment needed for this procedure is not readily available to the general public. An alternate method recommended by Chrysler is with the use of an exhaust gas analyzer. If this equipment is not available, and a mixture adjustment must be performed, follow this procedure:

TUNE-UP AND TROUBLESHOOTING 51

1. Run engine to normal operating temperature.
2. Place the transmission in Neutral (MT) or Drive (AT), turn off the lights and air conditioning and make certain that the electric cooling fan is operating.
3. Disconnect the EGR vacuum line, disconnect the distributor electrical advance connector, and ground the carburetor idle stop switch (if equipped) with a jumper wire.

4. Connect tachometer according to the manufacturer's specifications. (See previous procedure).
5. Adjust the idle screw to achieve the curb idle figure listed on the underhood sticker.
6. Back out the mixture screw to achieve the fastest possible idle.
7. Adjust the idle screw to the specified curb idle speed.

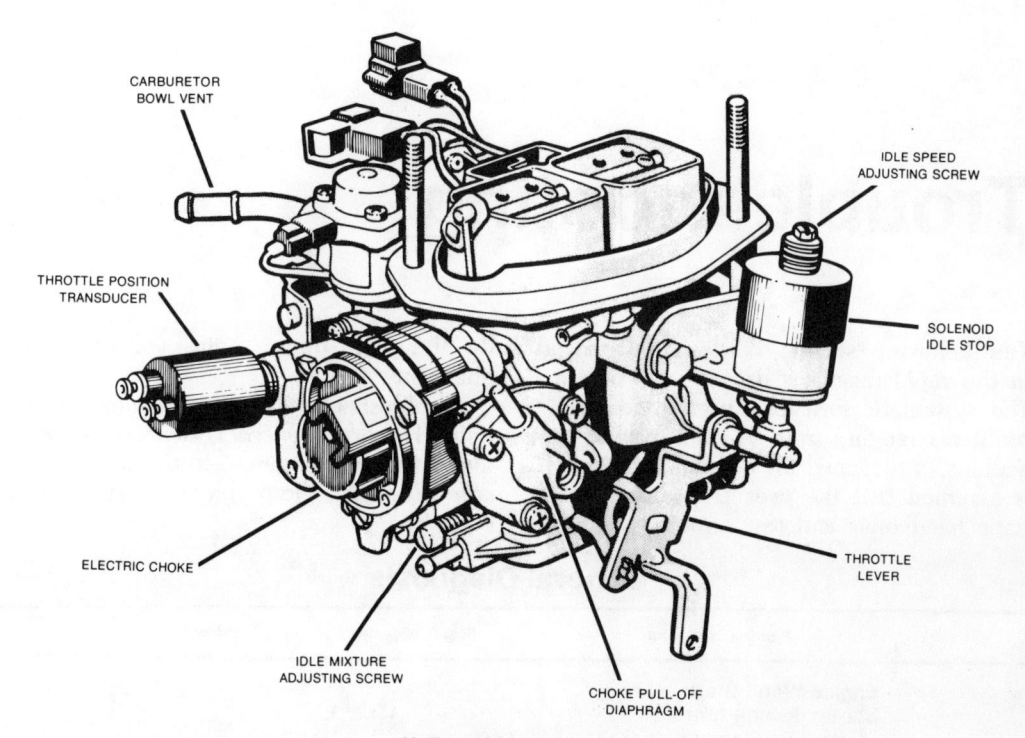

Holley 5220 carburetor

Troubleshooting

The following section is designed to aid in the rapid diagnosis of engine problems. The systematic format is used to diagnose problems ranging from engine starting difficulties to the need for engine overhaul. It is assumed that the user is equipped with basic hand tools and test equipment (tach- dwell meter, timing light, voltmeter, and ohmmeter).

Troubleshooting is divided into two sections. The first, *General Diagnosis*, is used to locate the problem area. In the second, *Specific Diagnosis*, the problem is systematically evaluated.

General Diagnosis

Problem: Symptom	Begin at Specific Diagnosis, Number _____
Engine Won't Start:	
Starter doesn't turn	1.1, 2.1
Starter turns, engine doesn't	2.1
Starter turns engine very slowly	1.1, 2.4
Starter turns engine normally	3.1, 4.1
Starter turns engine very quickly	6.1
Engine fires intermittently	4.1
Engine fires consistently	5.1, 6.1
Engine Runs Poorly:	
Hard starting	3.1, 4.1, 5.1, 8.1
Rough idle	4.1, 5.1, 8.1
Stalling	3.1, 4.1, 5.1, 8.1
Engine dies at high speeds	4.1, 5.1
Hesitation (on acceleration from standing stop)	5.1, 8.1
Poor pickup	4.1, 5.1, 8.1
Lack of power	3.1, 4.1, 5.1, 8.1
Backfire through the carburetor	4.1, 8.1, 9.1
Backfire through the exhaust	4.1, 8.1, 9.1
Blue exhaust gases	6.1, 7.1
Black exhaust gases	5.1
Running on (after the ignition is shut off)	3.1, 8.1
Susceptible to moisture	4.1
Engine misfires under load	4.1, 7.1, 8.4, 9.1
Engine misfires at speed	4.1, 8.4
Engine misfires at idle	3.1, 4.1, 5.1, 7.1, 8.4

TUNE-UP AND TROUBLESHOOTING

Engine Noise Diagnosis

Problem: Symptom	Probable Cause
Engine Noises:①	
Metallic grind while starting	Starter drive not engaging completely
Constant grind or rumble	*Starter drive not releasing, worn main bearings
Constant knock	Worn connecting rod bearings
Knock under load	Fuel octane too low, worn connecting rod bearings
Double knock	Loose piston pin
Metallic tap	*Collapsed or sticky valve lifter, excessive valve clearance, excessive end play in a rotating shaft
Scrape	*Fan belt contacting a stationary surface
Tick while starting	S.U. electric fuel pump (normal), starter brushes
Constant tick	*Generator brushes, shreaded fan belt
Squeal	*Improperly tensioned fan belt
Hiss or roar	*Steam escaping through a leak in the cooling system or the radiator overflow vent
Whistle	*Vacuum leak
Wheeze	Loose or cracked spark plug

①—It is extremely difficult to evaluate vehicle noises. While the above are general definitions of engine noises, those starred (*) should be considered as possibly originating elsewhere in the car. To aid diagnosis, the following list considers other potential sources of these sounds.

Metallic grind:
Throwout bearing; transmission gears, bearings, or synchronizers; differential bearings, gears; something metallic in contact with brake drum or disc.

Metallic tap:
U-joints; fan-to-radiator (or shroud) contact.

Scrape:
Brake shoe or pad dragging; tire to body contact; suspension contacting undercarriage or exhaust; something non-metallic contacting brake shoe or drum.

Tick:
Transmission gears; differential gears; lack of radio suppression; resonant vibration of body panels; windshield wiper motor or transmission; heater motor and blower.

Squeal:
Brake shoe or pad not fully releasing; tires (excessive wear, uneven wear, improper inflation); front or rear wheel alignment (most commonly due to improper toe-in).

Hiss or whistle:
Wind leaks (body or window); heater motor and blower fan.

Roar:
Wheel bearings; wind leaks (body and window).

Index

Topic		Group
Battery	*	1
Cranking system	*	2
Primary electrical system	*	3
Secondary electrical system	*	4
Fuel system	*	5
Engine compression	*	6
Engine vaccuum	**	7
Secondary electrical system	**	8
Valve train	**	9
Exhaust system	**	10
Cooling system	**	11
Engine lubrication	**	12

* The engine need not be running
**The engine must be running

54 TUNE-UP AND TROUBLESHOOTING

Sample Section

Test and Procedure	Results and Indications	Proceed to
4.1—Check for spark: Hold each spark plug wire approximately ¼" from ground with gloves or a heavy, dry rag. Crank the engine and observe the spark. **NOTE:** *Do not run the engine any longer than necessary with the spark plug wire disconnected.*	If no spark is evident:	4.2
	If spark is good in some cases:	4.3
	If spark is good in all cases:	4.6

Specific Diagnosis

This section is arranged so that following each test, instructions are given to proceed to another, until a problem is diagnosed.

1.1—Inspect the battery visually for case condition (corrosion, cracks) and water level. *Inspect the battery case*	If case is cracked, replace battery:	1.4
	If the case is intact, remove corrosion with a solution of baking soda and water (**CAUTION:** *do not get the solution into the battery*), and fill with water:	1.2
1.2—Check the battery cable connections: Insert a screwdriver between the battery post and the cable clamp. Turn the headlights on high beam, and observe them as the screwdriver is gently twisted to ensure good metal to metal contact. *Testing battery cable connections using a screwdriver*	If the lights brighten, remove and clean the clamp and post; coat the post with petroleum jelly, install and tighten the clamp:	1.4
	If no improvement is noted:	1.3
1.3—Test the state of charge of the battery using an individual cell tester or hydrometer. Spec. Grav. Reading — Charged Condition 1.260–1.280 — Fully Charged 1.230–1.250 — Three Quarter Charged 1.200–1.220 — One Half Charged 1.170–1.190 — One Quarter Charged 1.140–1.160 — Just About Flat 1.110–1.130 — All The Way Down **State of battery charge** *The effect of temperature on the specific gravity of battery electrolyte*	If indicated, charge the battery. **NOTE:** *If no obvious reason exists for the low state of charge (i.e., battery age, prolonged storage), the charging system should be tested:*	1.4
1.4—Visually inspect battery cables for cracking, bad connection to ground, or bad connection to starter.	If necessary, tighten connections or replace the cables:	2.1

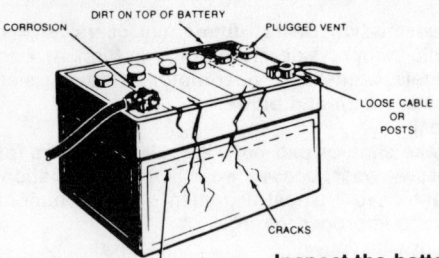

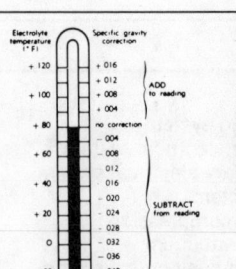

TUNE-UP AND TROUBLESHOOTING

Test and Procedure	Results and Indications	Proceed to
Tests in Group 2 are performed with coil high tension lead disconnected to prevent accidental starting.		
2.1—Test the starter motor and solenoid: Connect a jumper from the battery post of the solenoid (or relay) to the starter post of the solenoid (or relay).	If starter turns the engine normally:	2.2
	If the starter buzzes, or turns the engine very slowly:	2.4
	If no response, replace the solenoid (or relay):	3.1
	If the starter turns, but the engine doesn't, ensure that the flywheel ring gear is intact. If the gear is undamaged, replace the starter drive:	3.1
2.2—Determine whether ignition override switches are functioning properly (clutch start switch, neutral safety switch), by connecting a jumper across the switch(es), and turning the ignition switch to "start".	If starter operates, adjust or replace switch:	3.1
	If the starter doesn't operate:	2.3
2.3—Check the ignition switch "start" position: Connect a 12V test lamp between the starter post of the solenoid (or relay) and ground. Turn the ignition switch to the "start" position, and jiggle the key.	If the lamp doesn't light when the switch is turned, check the ignition switch for loose connections, cracked insulation, or broken wires. Repair or replace as necessary:	3.1
	If the lamp flickers when the key is jiggled, replace the ignition switch:	3.3

Checking the ignition switch "start" position

2.4—Remove and bench test the starter, according to specifications in the car section.	If the starter does not meet specifications, repair or replace as needed:	3.1
	If the starter is operating properly:	2.5
2.5—Determine whether the engine can turn freely: Remove the spark plugs, and check for water in the cylinders. Check for water on the dipstick, or oil in the radiator. Attempt to turn the engine using an 18″ flex drive and socket on the crankshaft pulley nut or bolt.	If the engine will turn freely only with the spark plugs out, and hydrostatic lock (water in the cylinders) is ruled out, check valve timing:	9.2
	If engine will not turn freely, and it is known that the clutch and transmission are free, the engine must be disassembled for further evaluation:	**Next Chapter**
3.1—Check the ignition switch "on" position: Connect a jumper wire between the distributor side of the coil and ground, and a 12V test lamp between the switch side of the coil and ground. Remove the	If the lamp lights:	3.2
	If the lamp flickers when the key is jiggled, replace the ignition switch:	3.3
	If the lamp doesn't light, check for loose or open connections. If none are found, remove	

56 TUNE-UP AND TROUBLESHOOTING

Test and Procedure	Results and Indications	Proceed to
high tension lead from the coil. Turn the ignition switch on and jiggle the key.	the ignition switch and check for continuity. If the switch is faulty, replace it:	3.3

Checking the ignition switch "on" position

3.2—Check the ballast resistor with an ohmmeter (low scale). The reading should be 0.5 to 0.6 ohms.	If readings differ from these, replace the ballast resistor.	

Ignition coil and ballast resistor

3.3—Test the coil primary resistance. Connect an ohmmeter between the battery(+) terminal and the negative(−) terminal of the coil. Resistance should be 1.6–1.79 ohms (Prestolite coil) 1.41–1.62 ohms (Essex coil).	If readings differ from these, check the coil secondary resistance before replacing the coil, or perform a coil substitution test.	4.1

Testing the coil primary resistance

4.1—Check for spark: Hold each spark plug wire approximately ¼" from ground with gloves or a heavy, dry rag. Crank the engine, and observe the spark.	If no spark is evident:	4.2
	If spark is good in some cylinders:	4.3
	If spark is good in all cylinders:	4.6

Check for spark at the plugs

TUNE-UP AND TROUBLESHOOTING

Test and Procedure	Results and Indications	Proceed to
4.2—Check for spark at the coil high tension lead: Remove the coil high tension lead from the distributor and position it approximately ¼" from ground. Crank the engine and observe spark. **CAUTION:** *This test should not be performed on cars equipped with transistorized ignition.*	If the spark is good and consistent:	4.3
	If the spark is good but intermittent, test the primary electrical system starting at 3.3:	3.3
	If the spark is weak or non-existent, replace the coil high tension lead, clean and tighten all connections and retest. If no improvement is noted:	4.4
4.3—Visually inspect the distributor cap and rotor for burned or corroded contacts, cracks, carbon tracks, or moisture. Also check the fit of the rotor on the distributor shaft (where applicable).	If moisture is present, dry thoroughly, and retest per 4.1:	4.1
	If burned or excessively corroded contacts, cracks, or carbon tracks are noted, replace the defective part(s) and retest per 4.1:	4.1
	If the rotor and cap appear intact, or are only slightly corroded, clean the contacts thoroughly (including the cap towers and spark plug wire ends) and retest per 4.1: If the spark is good in all cases:	4.6
	If the spark is poor in all cases:	4.5
4.4—Check the coil secondary resistance: Connect an ohmmeter between the coil battery (+) terminal and the coil tower. Resistance should be between 9400–11,700 ohms (Prestolite coil) 8000–11,200 ohms (Essex coil).	If readings differ from these, perform a coil substitution test, and retest per 4.1.	

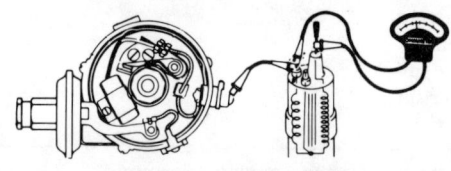

Testing the coil secondary resistance

4.5—Visually inspect the spark plug wires for cracking or brittleness. Ensure that no two wires are positioned so as to cause induction firing (adjacent and parallel). Remove each wire, one by one, and check resistance with an ohmmeter.	Replace any cracked or brittle wires. If any of the wires are defective, replace the entire set. Replace any wires with excessive resistance (over 8000Ω per foot for suppression wire), and separate any wires that might cause induction firing.	4.6

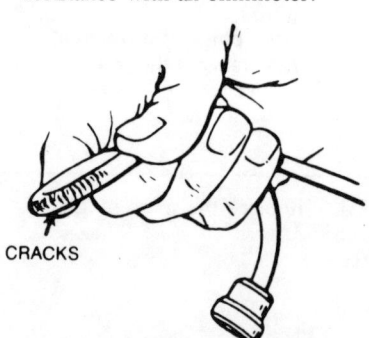

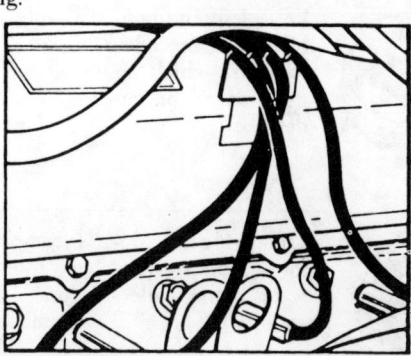

CRACKS

Check the spark plug wires for cracks

Be sure plug wires do not run adjacent or parallel to another

58 TUNE-UP AND TROUBLESHOOTING

Test and Procedure	Results and Indications	Proceed to
4.6—Remove the spark plugs, noting the cylinders from which they were removed, and evaluate according to the chart below.	See following.	See following.

Condition	Cause	Remedy	Proceed to
Electrodes eroded, light brown deposits.	Normal wear. Normal wear is indicated by approximately .001" wear per 1000 miles.	Clean and regap the spark plug if wear is not excessive: Replace the spark plug if excessively worn:	4.7
Carbon fouling (black, dry, fluffy deposits).	If present on one or two plugs: Faulty high tension lead(s).	Test the high tension leads:	4.5
	Burnt or sticking valve(s).	Check the valve train: (Clean and regap the plugs in either case.)	9.1
	If present on most or all plugs: Overly rich fuel mixture, due to restricted air filter, improper carburetor adjustment, improper choke or heat riser adjustment or operation.	Check the fuel system:	5.1
Oil fouling (wet black deposits).	Worn engine components. **NOTE:** *Oil fouling may occur in new or recently rebuilt engines until broken in.*	Check engine vacuum and compression: Replace with new spark plug.	6.1
Lead fouling (gray, black, tan, or yellow deposits, which appear glazed or cinder-like).	Combustion by-products.	Clean and regap the plugs: (Use plugs of a different heat range if the problem recurs.)	4.7
Gap bridging (deposits lodged between the electrodes).	Incomplete combustion, or transfer of deposits from the combustion chamber.	Replace the spark plugs:	4.7

TUNE-UP AND TROUBLESHOOTING

	Condition	Cause	Remedy	Proceed to
	Overheating (burnt electrodes, and extremely white insulator with small black spots).	Ignition timing advanced too far.	Adjust timing to specifications:	8.2
		Overly lean fuel mixture.	Check the fuel system:	5.1
		Spark plugs not seated properly.	Clean spark plug seat and install a new gasket washer: (Replace the spark plugs in all cases.)	4.7
	Fused spot deposits on the insulator.	Combustion chamber blow-by.	Clean and regap the spark plugs:	4.7
	Pre-ignition (melted or severely burned electrodes, blistered or cracked insulators, or metallic deposits on the insulator).	Incorrect spark plug heat range.	Replace with plugs of the proper heat range:	4.7
		Ignition timing advanced too far.	Adjust timing to specifications:	8.2
		Spark plugs not being cooled efficiently.	Clean the spark plug seat, and check the cooling system:	11.1
		Fuel mixture too lean.	Check the fuel system:	5.1
		Poor compression.	Check compression:	6.1
		Fuel grade too low.	Use higher octane fuel:	4.7

Test and Procedure	Results and Indications	Proceed to
4.7—Determine the static ignition timing. Using the flywheel or crankshaft pulley timing marks as a guide, locate top dead center on the *compression* stroke of the No. 1 cylinder. Remove the distributor cap.	Adjust the distributor so that the rotor points toward the No. 1 tower in the distributor cap, and the points are just opening:	4.8
4.8—Check coil polarity: Connect a voltmeter negative lead to the coil high tension lead, and the positive lead to ground (**NOTE:** *reverse the hook-up for positive ground cars*). Crank the engine momentarily. Checking coil polarity	If the voltmeter reads up-scale, the polarity is correct:	5.1
	If the voltmeter reads down-scale, reverse the coil polarity (switch the primary leads):	5.1
5.1—Determine that the air filter is functioning efficiently: Hold paper elements up to a strong light, and attempt to see light through the filter.	Clean permanent air filters in gasoline (or manufacturer's recommendation), and allow to dry. Replace paper elements through which light cannot be seen:	5.2

TUNE-UP AND TROUBLESHOOTING

Test and Procedure	Results and Indications	Proceed to
5.2—Determine whether a flooding condition exists: Flooding is identified by a strong gasoline odor, and excessive gasoline present in the throttle bore(s) of the carburetor.	If flooding is not evident:	5.3
	If flooding is evident, permit the gasoline to dry for a few moments and restart. If flooding doesn't recur:	5.6
	If flooding is persistent:	5.5
5.3—Check that fuel is reaching the carburetor: Detach the fuel line at the carburetor inlet. Hold the end of the line in a cup (not styrofoam), and crank the engine.	If fuel flows smoothly:	5.6
	If fuel doesn't flow (**NOTE:** *Make sure that there is fuel in the tank*), or flows erratically:	5.4

Check fuel pump output

5.4—Test the fuel pump: Disconnect all fuel lines from the fuel pump. Hold a finger over the input fitting, crank the engine (with electric pump, turn the ignition or pump on); and feel for suction.	If suction is evident, blow out the fuel line to the tank with low pressure compressed air until bubbling is heard from the fuel filler neck. Also blow out the carburetor fuel line (both ends disconnected):	5.6
	If no suction is evident, replace or repair the fuel pump: **NOTE:** *Repeated oil fouling of the spark plugs, or a no-start condition, could be the result of a ruptured vacuum booster pump diaphragm, through which oil or gasoline is being drawn into the intake manifold (where applicable).*	5.6
5.5—Check the needle and seat: Tap the carburetor in the area of the needle and seat.	If flooding stops, a gasoline additive (e.g., Gumout) will often cure the problem:	5.6
	If flooding continues, check the fuel pump for excessive pressure at the carburetor (according to specifications). If the pressure is normal, the needle and seat must be removed and checked, and/or the float level adjusted:	5.6
5.6—Test the accelerator pump by looking into the throttle bores while operating the throttle.	If the accelerator pump appears to be operating normally:	5.7
	If the accelerator pump is not operating, the pump must be reconditioned. Where possible, service the pump with the carburetor(s) installed on the engine. If necessary, remove the carburetor. Prior to removal:	5.7

Check for fuel at the carburetor throat

TUNE-UP AND TROUBLESHOOTING

Test and Procedure	Results and Indications	Proceed to
5.7—Determine whether the carburetor main fuel system is functioning: Spray a commercial starting fluid into the carburetor while attempting to start the engine.	If the engine starts, runs for a few seconds, and dies:	5.8
	If the engine doesn't start:	6.1
5.8—Uncommon fuel system malfunctions: See below:	If the problem is solved:	6.1
	If the problem remains, remove and recondition the carburetor.	

Condition	Indication	Test	Usual Weather Conditions	Remedy
Vapor lock	Car will not restart shortly after running.	Cool the components of the fuel system until the engine starts.	Hot to very hot.	Ensure that the exhaust manifold heat control valve is operating. Check with the vehicle manufacturer for the recommended solution to vapor lock on the model in question.
Carburetor icing	Car will not idle, stalls at low speeds.	Visually inspect the throttle plate area of the throttle bores for frost.	High humidity, 32–40°F.	Ensure that the exhaust manifold heat control valve is operating, and that the intake manifold heat riser is not blocked.
Water in the fuel	Engine sputters and stalls; may not start.	Pump a small amount of fuel into a glass jar. Allow to stand, and inspect for droplets or a layer of water.	High humidity, extreme temperature changes.	For droplets, use one or two cans of commercial gas dryer. For a layer of water, the tank must be drained, and the fuel lines blown out with compressed air.

Vapor lock will disappear quickly if lines are cooled with a wet rag

Test and Procedure	Results and Indications	Proceed to
6.1—Test engine compression: Remove all spark plugs. Insert a compression gauge into a spark plug port, crank the engine to obtain the maximum reading, and record.	If compression is within limits on all cylinders:	7.1
	If gauge reading is extremely low on all cylinders:	6.2
	If gauge reading is low on one or two cylinders: (If gauge readings are identical and low on two or more adjacent cylinders, the head gasket must be replaced.)	6.2

TUNE-UP AND TROUBLESHOOTING

Test and Procedure	Results and Indications	Proceed to
Testing compression		
6.2—Test engine compression (wet): Squirt approximately 30 cc. of engine oil into each cylinder, and retest per 6.1.	If the readings improve, worn or cracked rings or broken pistons are indicated:	**Next Chapter**
	If the readings do not improve, burned or excessively carboned valves or a jumped timing chain are indicated: NOTE: *A jumped timing chain is often indicated by difficult cranking.*	7.1
7.1—Perform a vacuum check of the engine: Attach a vacuum gauge to the intake manifold beyond the throttle plate. Start the engine, and observe the action of the needle over the range of engine speeds.	See below.	See below

	Reading	Indications	Proceed to
	Steady, from 17–22 in. Hg.	Normal:	8.1
	Low and steady.	Late ignition or valve timing, or low compression:	6.1
	Very low.	Vacuum leak:	7.2
	Needle fluctuates as engine speed increases.	Ignition miss, blown cylinder head gasket, leaking valve or weak valve spring:	6.1, 8.3
	Gradual drop in reading at idle.	Excessive back pressure in the exhaust system:	10.1

TUNE-UP AND TROUBLESHOOTING 63

Reading	Indications	Proceed to
Intermittent fluctuation at idle.	Ignition miss, sticking valve:	8.3, 9.1
Drifting needle.	Improper idle mixture adjustment, carburetors not synchronized (where applicable), or minor intake leak. Synchronize the carburetors, adjust the idle, and retest. If the condition persists:	7.2
High and steady.	Early ignition timing:	8.2

Test and Procedure	Results and Indications	Proceed to
7.2—Attach a vacuum gauge per 7.1, and test for an intake manifold leak. Squirt a small amount of oil around the intake manifold gaskets, carburetor gaskets, plugs and fittings. Observe the action of the vacuum gauge.	If the reading improves, replace the indicated gasket, or seal the indicated fitting or plug: If the reading remains low:	8.1 7.3
7.3—Test all vacuum hoses and accessories for leaks as described in 7.2. Also check the carburetor body (dashpots, automatic choke mechanism, throttle shafts) for leaks in the same manner.	If the reading improves, service or replace the offending part(s): If the reading remains low:	8.1 6.1
8.1—Connect a timing light (per manufacturer's recommendation) and check the dynamic ignition timing. Disconnect and plug the vacuum hose(s) to the distributor if specified, start the engine, and observe the timing marks at the specified engine speed.	If the timing is not correct, adjust to specifications by rotating the distributor in the engine: (Advance timing by rotating distributor opposite normal direction of rotor rotation, retard timing by rotating distributor in same direction as rotor rotation.)	8.2
8.2—Check the operation of the distributor advance mechanism(s): To test the mechanical advance, disconnect all but the mechanical advance, and observe the timing marks with a timing light as the engine speed is increased from idle. If the mark moves smoothly, without hesitation, it may be assumed that the mechanical advance is functioning properly. To test vacuum advance and/or retard systems, alternately crimp and release the vacuum line, and observe the timing mark for movement. If movement is noted, the system is operating.	If the systems are functioning: If the systems are not functioning, remove the distributor, and test on a distributor tester:	8.3 8.3

64 TUNE-UP AND TROUBLESHOOTING

Test and Procedure	Results and Indications	Proceed to
8.3—Locate an ignition miss: With the engine running, remove and replace each spark plug wire, one by one, until one is found that doesn't cause the engine to roughen and slow down.	When the missing cylinder is identified:	4.1
9.1—Evaluate the valve train: Remove the valve cover, and ensure that the valves are adjusted to specifications. A mechanic's stethoscope may be used to aid in the diagnosis of the valve train. A timing light also may be used to diagnose valve problems. Connect the light according to manufacturer's recommendations, and start the engine. Vary the firing moment of the light by increasing the engine speed (and therefore the ignition advance), and moving the trigger from cylinder to cylinder. Observe the movement of each valve.	See below.	**See below**
9.2—Check the valve timing: Locate top dead center of the No. 1 piston, and install a degree wheel or tape on the crankshaft pulley or damper with zero corresponding to an index mark on the engine. Rotate the crankshaft in its direction of rotation, and observe the opening of the No. 1 cylinder intake valve. The opening should correspond with the correct mark on the degree wheel according to specifications.	If the timing is not correct, the timing cover must be removed for further investigation:	
10.1—Determine whether the exhaust manifold heat control valve is operating: Operate the valve by hand to determine whether it is free to move. If the valve is free, run the engine to operating temperature and observe the action of the valve, to ensure that it is opening.	If the valve sticks, spray it with a suitable solvent, open and close the valve to free it, and retest. If the valve functions properly: If the valve does not free, or does not operate, replace the valve:	10.2 10.2
10.2—Ensure that there are no exhaust restrictions: Visually inspect the exhaust system for kinks, dents, or crushing. Also note that gasses are flowing freely from the tailpipe at all engine speeds, indicating no restriction in the muffler or resonator.	Replace any damaged portion of the system:	11.1
11.1—Visually inspect the fan belt for glazing, cracks, and fraying, and replace if necessary. Tighten the	Replace or tighten the fan belt as necessary:	11.2

TUNE-UP AND TROUBLESHOOTING 65

Test and Procedure	Results and Indications	Proceed to
belt so that the longest span has approximately ½" play at its midpoint under thumb pressure. **Checking belt tension**		
11.2—Check the fluid level of the cooling system.	If full or slightly low, fill as necessary: If extremely low:	11.5 11.3
11.3—Visually inspect the external portions of the cooling system (radiator, radiator hoses, thermostat elbow, water pump seals, heater hoses, etc.) for leaks. If none are found, pressurize the cooling system to 14–15 psi.	If cooling system holds the pressure: If cooling system loses pressure rapidly, reinspect external parts of the system for leaks under pressure. If none are found, check dipstick for coolant in crankcase. If no coolant is present, but pressure loss continues: If coolant is evident in crankcase, remove cylinder head(s), and check gasket(s). If gaskets are intact, block and cylinder head(s) should be checked for cracks or holes. If the gasket(s) is blown, replace, and purge the crankcase of coolant: NOTE: *Occasionally, due to atmospheric and driving conditions, condensation of water can occur in the crankcase. This causes the oil to appear milky white. To remedy, run the engine until hot, and change the oil and oil filter.*	11.5 11.4 12.6
11.4—Check for combustion leaks into the cooling system: Pressurize the cooling system as above. Start the **Radiator pressure tester**	Cylinders which reduce or eliminate the fluctuation, when the spark plug wire is removed, are leaking into the cooling system. Replace the head gasket on the affected cylinder bank(s).	

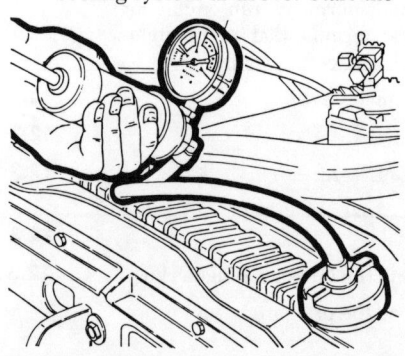

TUNE-UP AND TROUBLESHOOTING

Test and Procedure	Results and Indications	Proceed to
engine, and observe the pressure gauge. If the needle fluctuates, remove each spark plug wire, one by one, noting which cylinder(s) reduce or eliminate the fluctuation.		
11.5—Check the radiator pressure cap: Attach a radiator pressure tester to the radiator cap (wet the seal prior to installation). Quickly pump up the pressure, noting the point at which the cap releases.	If the cap releases within ± 1 psi of the specified rating, it is operating properly:	11.6
	If the cap releases at more than ± 1 psi of the specified rating, it should be replaced:	11.6

Testing radiator pressure cap

11.6—Test the thermostat: Start the engine cold, remove the radiator cap, and insert a thermometer into the radiator. Allow the engine to idle. After a short while, there will be a sudden, rapid increase in coolant temperature. The temperature at which this sharp rise stops is the thermostat opening temperature.	If the thermostat opens at or about the specified temperature:	11.7
	If the temperature doesn't increase: (If the temperature increases slowly and gradually, replace the thermostat.)	11.7
11.7—Check the water pump: Remove the thermostat elbow and the thermostat, disconnect the coil high tension lead (to prevent starting), and crank the engine momentarily.	If coolant flows, replace the thermostat and retest per 11.6:	11.6
	If coolant doesn't flow, reverse flush the cooling system to alleviate any blockage that might exist. If system is not blocked, and coolant will not flow, recondition the water pump.	—
12.1—Check the oil pressure gauge or warning light: If the gauge shows low pressure, or the light is on, for no obvious reason, remove the oil pressure sender. Install an accurate oil pressure gauge and run the engine momentarily.	If oil pressure builds normally, run engine for a few moments to determine that it is functioning normally, and replace the sender.	—
	If the pressure remains low:	12.2
	If the pressure surges:	12.3
	If the oil pressure is zero:	12.3
12.2—Visually inspect the oil: If the oil is watery or very thin, milky, or foamy, replace the oil and oil filter.	If the oil is normal:	12.3
	If after replacing oil the pressure remains low:	12.3
	If after replacing oil the pressure becomes normal:	—

TUNE-UP AND TROUBLESHOOTING

Test and Procedure	Results and Indications	Proceed to
12.3—Check to ensure that the oil pump is not cavitating (sucking air instead of oil): See that the crankcase is neither over nor underfull, and that the pickup in the sump is in the proper position and free from sludge.	Fill or drain the crankcase to the proper capacity, and clean the pickup screen in solvent if necessary. If no improvement is noted:	12.4
12.4—Inspect the oil pump drive and the oil pump.	If the pump drive or the oil pump appear to be defective, service as necessary and retest per 12.1:	12.1
	If the pump drive and pump appear to be operating normally, the engine should be disassembled to determine where blockage exists:	Next Chapter
12.5—Drain the engine of ethylene glycol coolant: Completely drain the crankcase and the oil filter. Obtain a commercial butyl cellosolve base solvent, designated for this purpose, and follow the instructions precisely. Following this, install a new oil filter and refill the crankcase with the proper weight oil. The next oil and filter change should follow shortly thereafter (1000 miles).		

3

Engine and Engine Rebuilding

ENGINE ELECTRICAL

Chrysler Corporation Electronic Spark Control Ignition

The Electronic Spark Control System is the heart of the Lean Burn emission control system used by Chrysler. Omni and Horizon models use what is known as a Hall Effect ignition system which is controlled by signals from the Lean Burn system. To understand how one system works, you must also understand the other.

OPERATION

Hall Effect Electronic Ignition

The Omni/Horizon Hall Effect electronic ignition is used in conjunction with the Chrysler Lean Burn System. It consists of a sealed Spark Control Computer, five engine sensors (vacuum transducer, coolant switch, Hall Effect pickup assembly, throttle position transducer, and carburetor switch), coil, spark plugs, ballast resistor, and the various wires needed to connect the components.

The distributor contains the Hall Effect pickup assembly which replaces the breaker points assembly in conventional systems. The pickup assembly supplies the computer with information on engine speed and crankshaft position, and is only one of five signals which the computer uses as input to determine ignition timing. The Hall Effect is a shift in magnetic field, caused, in this installation, when one of the rotor blades passes between the two arms of the sensor.

There are essentially two modes of operation of the Spark Control computer: the start mode and the run mode. The start mode is only used during engine cranking. During cranking only the Hall Effect pickup signals the computer. These signals are interpreted to provide a fixed number of degrees of spark advance. The computer shuts off coil primary current in accordance with the pickup signals. As in conventional ignition systems, primary current shutdown causes secondary field collapse, and the high voltage is sent from the coil to the distributor, which then sends it to the spark plug.

After the engine starts, and during normal engine operation, the computer functions in the run mode. In this mode the Hall Effect pickup serves as only one of the five signals to the computer. It is a reference signal of maximum possible spark advance. The computer then determines, from information provided by the other four sensors, how much of this advance is necessary, and shuts down the

ENGINE AND ENGINE REBUILDING

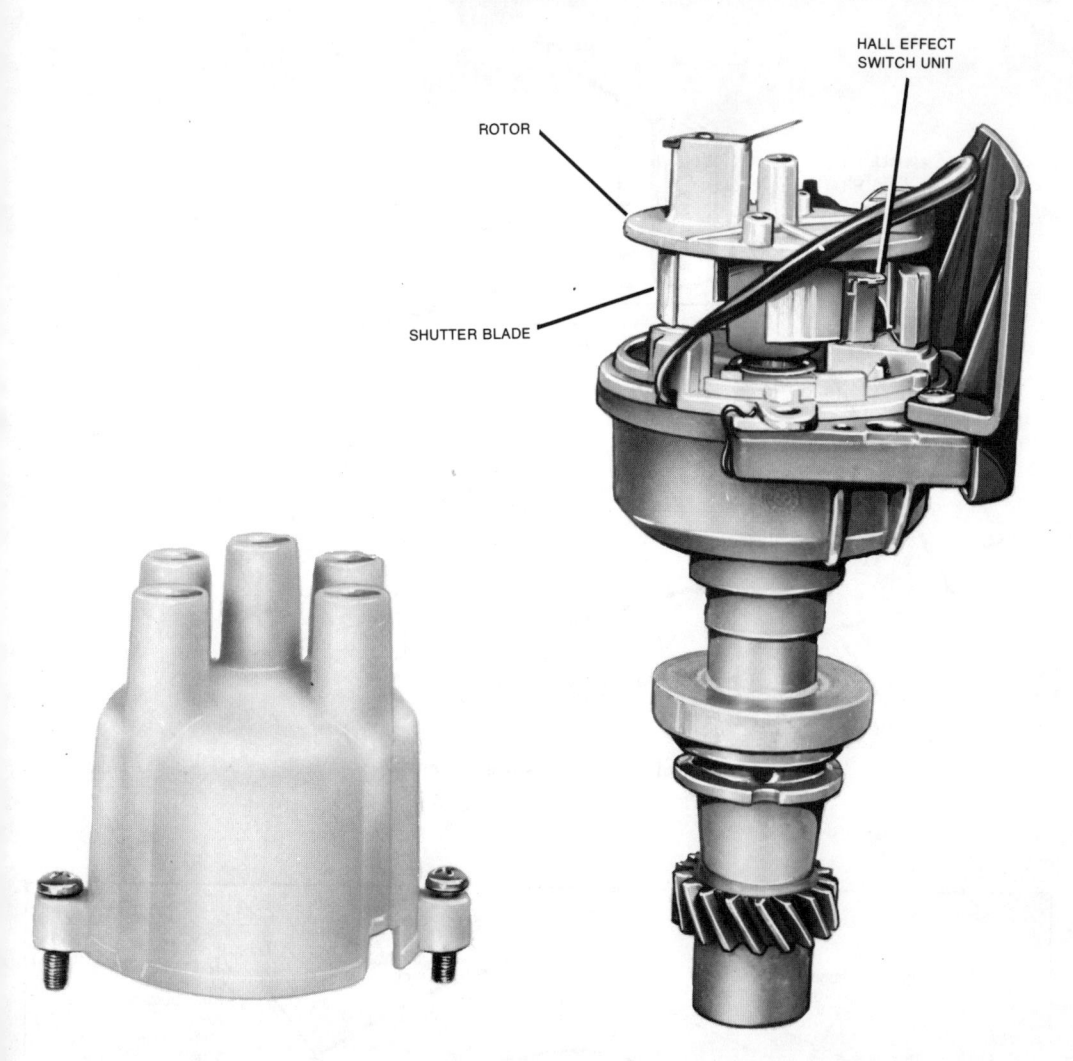

Hall effect distributor

primary current accordingly to fire the spark plug at the exact moment when this advance (crankshaft position) is reached.

There is a third mode of operation which only becomes functional when the computer fails. This is the limp-in mode. This mode functions on signals from the pickup only, and results in very poor engine performance. However, it does allow the car to be driven to a repair shop. If a failure occurs in the pickup assembly or the start mode of the computer, the engine will neither start nor run.

Lean Burn System

The Lean Burn system is based on the principle that lower NO_x emissions will occur if the air/fuel ratio in the cylinder is raised from the conventional 15.5:1 to approximately 18:1. This is a much leaner mixture (more air) and to make the engine workable, a solution to the problems of carburetion and timing had to be developed, since an engine running on leaner mixtures is not the most efficient in terms of driveability. Chrysler was able to adapt a conventional carburetor to handle the added air, but the real advance of the system is the Spark Control Computer. Since a lean burning engine demands precise ignition timing, additional spark control was needed for the distributor. The computer supplies this control by providing an infinitely variable advance curve. Input data is fed instantaneously to the computer by a series of sensors located in the engine compartment which monitor timing, water temperature, air temperature, throttle position, idle/off-idle operation, and intake manifold vacuum. The program schedule module of the Spark Control Computer receives the information

70 ENGINE AND ENGINE REBUILDING

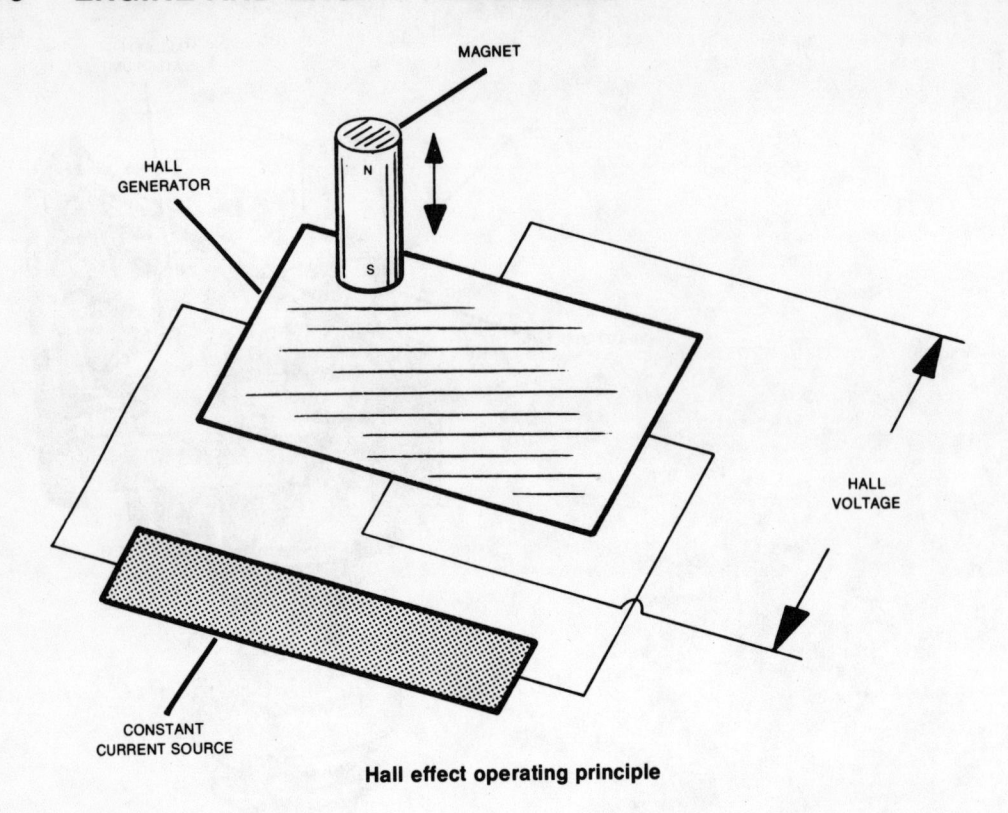

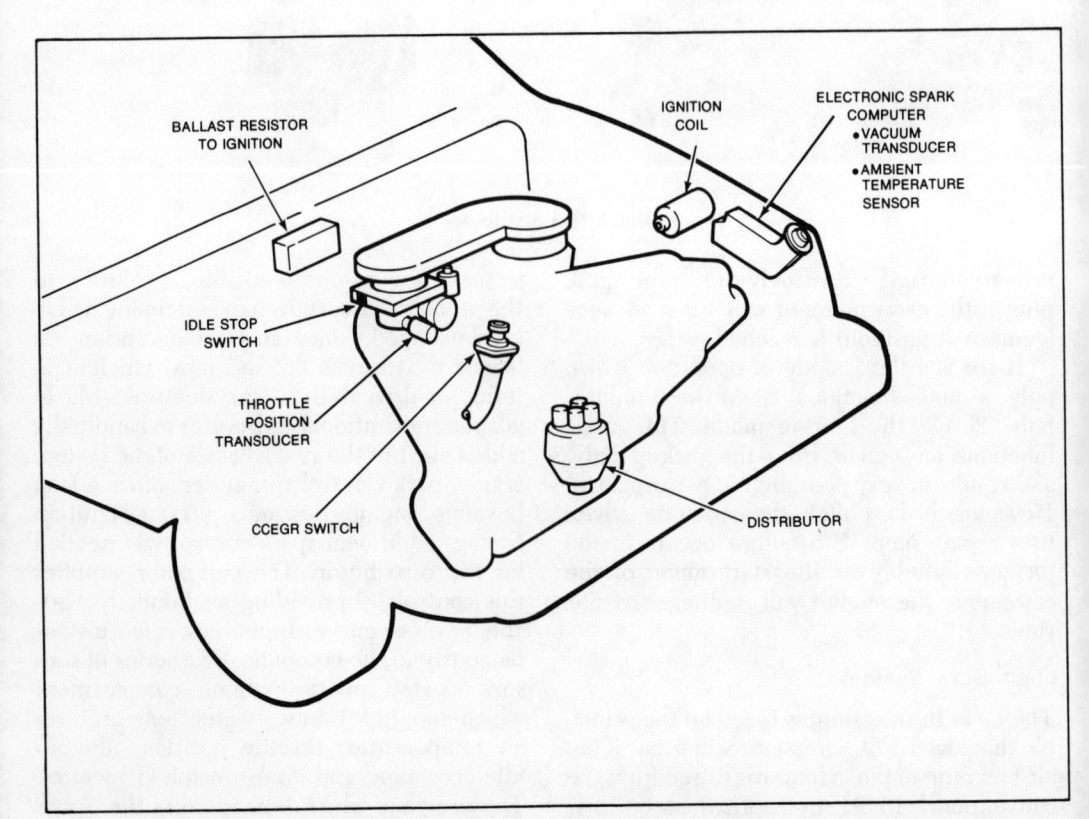

Hall effect operating principle

Electronic Lean Burn System Components

ENGINE AND ENGINE REBUILDING 71

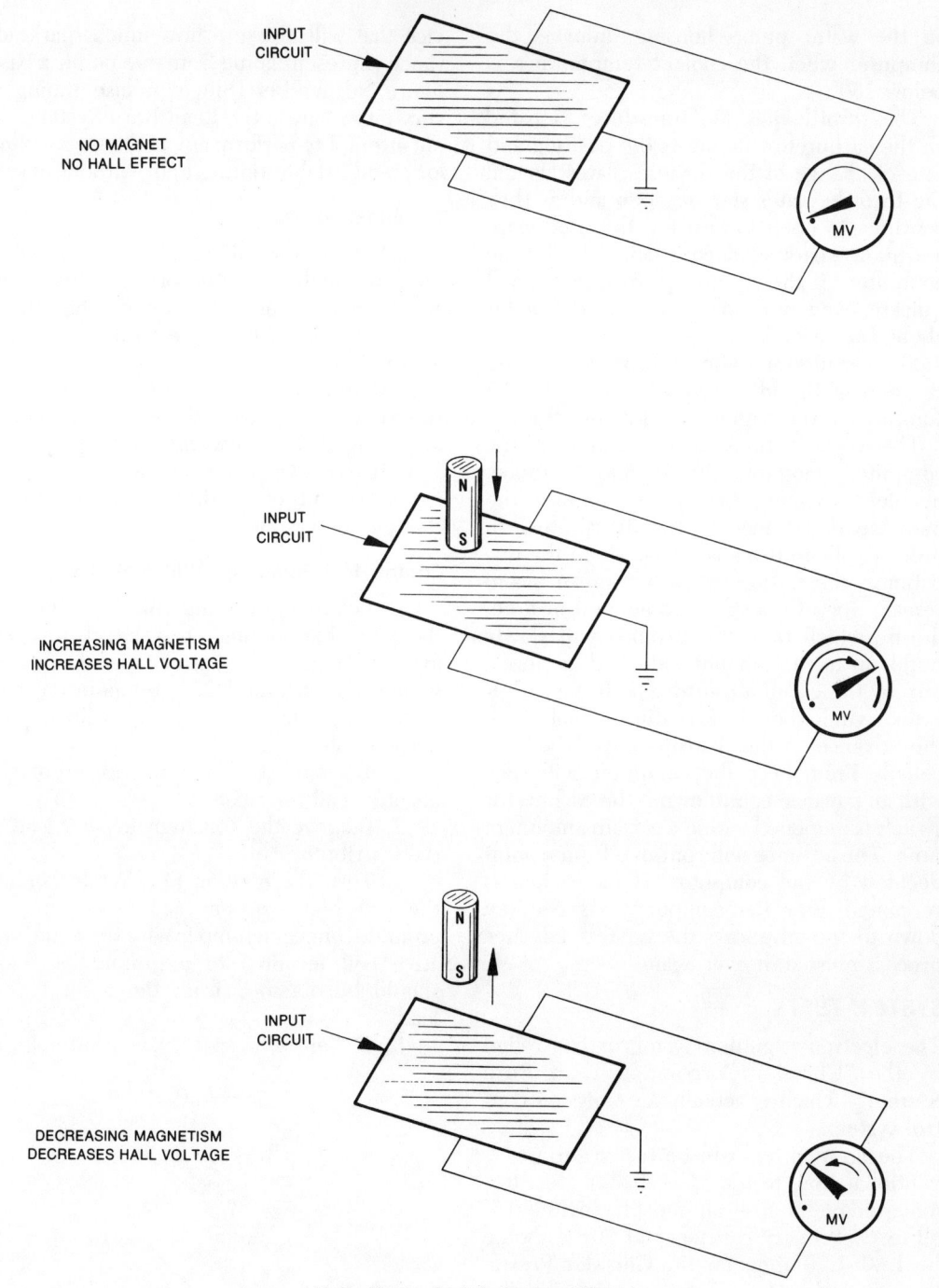

**NO MAGNET
NO HALL EFFECT**

INPUT CIRCUIT

**INCREASING MAGNETISM
INCREASES HALL VOLTAGE**

INPUT CIRCUIT

**DECREASING MAGNETISM
DECREASES HALL VOLTAGE**

INPUT CIRCUIT

Hall effect principle in operation

from the sensors, processes it, and then directs the ignition control module to advance or retard the timing as necessary. This whole process is going on continuously as the engine is running, taking only a thousandth of a second to complete a circuit from sensor to distributor. The components of the system are as follows: Modified carburetor; Spark Control Computer, consisting of two interacting modules, the Program Schedule Module which is responsible for translating input data, and the Ignition Control Module which transmits data to the distributor to advance or retard the timing.

The start pick-up sensor, located inside the distributor, supplies a signal to the computer providing a fixed timing point.

The coolant temperature sensor, located

ENGINE AND ENGINE REBUILDING

on the water pump housing, informs the computer when the coolant temperature is below 150°.

The throttle position transducer, located on the carburetor, monitors the position and rate of change of the throttle plates. When the throttle plates start to open and as they continue to open toward full throttle, more and more spark advance is called for by the computer. If the throttle plates are opened quickly, even more spark advance is given for about one second.

The carburetor switch sensor, located on the end of the idle stop solenoid, tells the computer if the engine is at idle or off-idle.

The vacuum transducer, located on the computer, monitors the amount of intake manifold vacuum; the more vacuum, the more spark advance to the distributor. In order to obtain this spark advance in the distributor, the carburetor switch sensor has to remain open for a specified amount of time, during which time the advance will slowly build up to the amount indicated as necessary by the vacuum transducer. If the carburetor switch should close during that time, the advance to the distributor will be cancelled. From here the computer will start with an advance countdown if the carburetor switch is reopened within a certain amount of time. The advance will continue from a point decided by the computer. If the switch is reopened after the computer has counted down to "no advance," the vacuum advance process must start over again.

SYSTEM TESTS

The electronic ignition system is controlled by the "Chrysler Corporation Lean Burn System", which is actually an emission control system.

The ignition coil can be tested on a conventional coil tester. The ballast resistor, mounted on the firewall, must be included in all tests. Primary resistance at 70° F should be 1.60–1.79 ohms for the Chrysler Prestolite coil, and 1.41–1.62 ohms for the Chrysler Essex coil. Secondary resistance should be 9400–11,700 ohms for the Prestolite, 8000–11,200 ohms for the Essex. The ballast resistor should measure 0.50–0.60 ohms resistance at 70° F.

Equipment

Some of the procedures in this section refer to an adjustable timing light. This is also known as a spark advance tester, i.e., a device that will measure how much spark advance is present going from one point, a base figure, to another. Since precise timing is very important to the Lean Burn System, do not attempt to perform any of the tests calling for an adjustable timing light without one.

Troubleshooting

1. Remove the coil wire from the distributor cap and hold it cautiously about ¼ in. away from an engine ground, then have someone crank the engine while you check for spark.
2. If you have a good spark, slowly move the coil wire away from the engine and check for arcing at the coil while cranking.
3. If you have good spark and it is not arcing at the coil, check the rest of the parts of the ignition system.

Engine Not Running—Will Not Start

1. Before performing this test, be sure the "Troubleshooting" test has been performed. Measure the battery specific gravity: it must be at least 1.220, temperature corrected. Measure the battery voltage and make a note of it.
2. Disconnect the thin wire from the negative coil terminal.
3. Remove the coil high tension lead at the distributor cap.
4. Turn the ignition On. While holding the coil high tension lead ¼ in. from a ground, connect a jumper wire from the negative coil terminal to a ground. A spark should be obtained from the high tension lead.
5. If there is no spark, use a voltmeter to

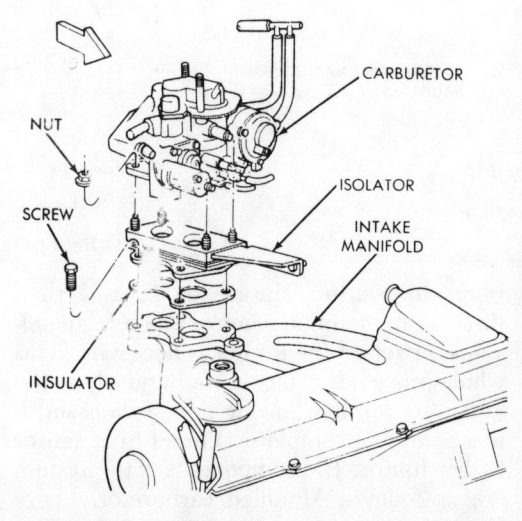

Testing the ignition coil

ENGINE AND ENGINE REBUILDING 73

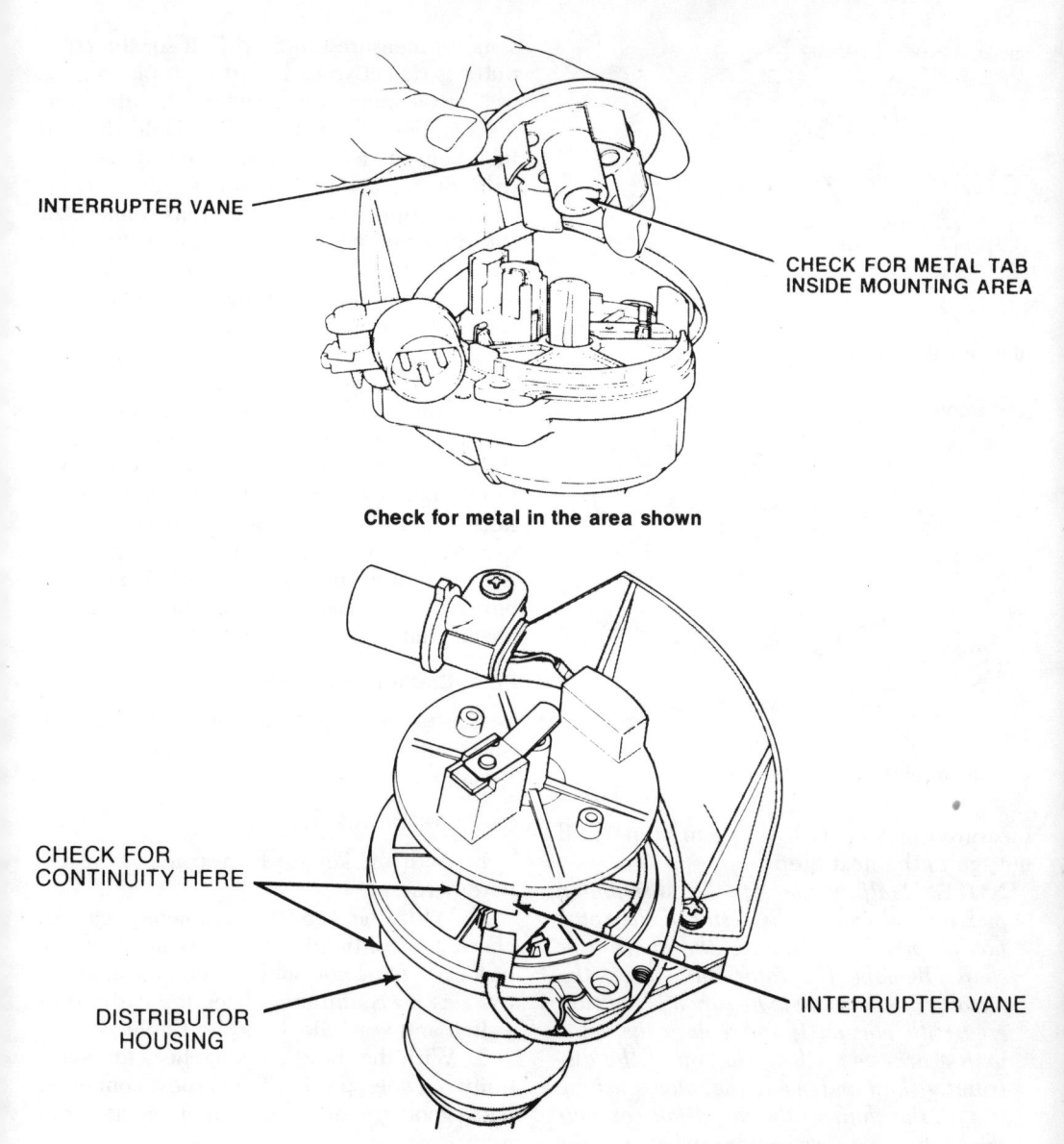

Check for metal in the area shown

Check for continuity between the interrupter vane and distributor housing

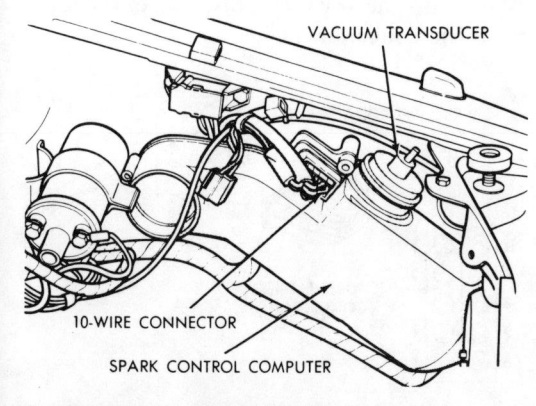

Spark control computer location

test for at least 9 volts at the positive coil terminal (ignition On). If so, the coil must be replaced. If less than 9 volts is obtained, check the ballast resistor, wiring, and connections. If the car still won't start, proceed to Step 6.

6. If there was a spark in Step 4, turn the ignition Off, reconnect the wire to the negative coil terminal, and disconnect the distributor pick-up coil connector.

7. Turn the ignition On, and measure voltage between pin B of the pick-up coil connector on the spark control computer side, and a good engine ground. Voltage should be the same as the battery voltage

74 ENGINE AND ENGINE REBUILDING

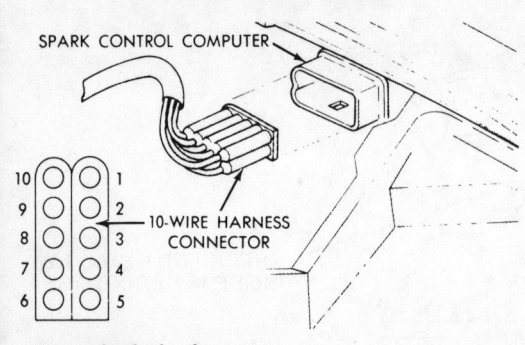

10-terminal wire harness

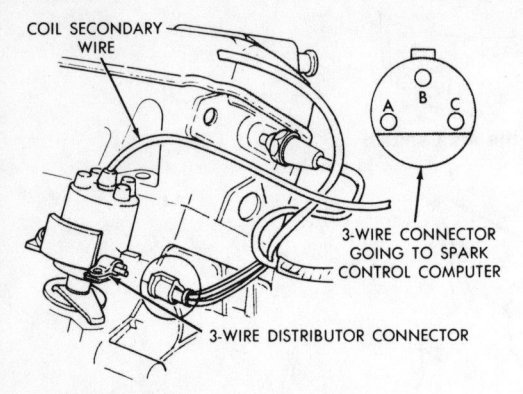

Distributor pick-up coil connector

measured in Step 1. If so, go to Step 11. If not, go to the next Step.

NOTE: *Malfunction of the distributor pick-up coil can be the result of the rotor not properly grounded to the distributor shaft. Remove the rotor and check the metal grounding tab to be sure it is not covered with plastic. If so, replace the rotor with a new one. Clean the top of the distributor shaft and install the rotor, pushing it onto the shaft so the metal tab contacts the shaft. Check for continuity between the interrupter vane and distributor housing. Do not try to start the engine with no continuity.*

8. Turn the ignition Off and disconnect the 10 terminal connector at the spark control computer.

NOTE: *Do not remove grease from the 10-wire harness connector.*

9. Check for continuity between pin B of the pick-up coil connector on the computer side, and terminal 3 of the computer connector. If there is no continuity, the wire must be replaced. If continuity exists, go to the next step.

10. With the ignition On, connect a voltmeter between terminals 2 and 10 of the computer connector. Voltage should be the same as measured in Step 1. If so, the computer is defective and must be replaced.

11. Reconnect the 10 wire computer connector. Turn the ignition On. Hold the coil high tension lead (disconnected at the distributor cap) about ¼ in. from a ground. Connect a jumper wire between pins A and C of the distributor pick-up coil connector. If a spark is obtained, the distributor pick-up is defective and must be replaced. If not, go to the next step.

12. Turn the ignition Off. Disconnect the 10 wire computer connector.

13. Check for continuity between pin C of the distributor connector and terminal 9 of the computer connector. Also check for continuity between pin A of the distributor connector and terminal 5 of the computer connector. If continuity exists, the computer is defective and must be replaced. If not, the wires are damaged. Repair them and recheck, starting at Step 11.

Poor Engine Performance

Before proceeding with these tests, be sure the ignition timing and idle speed are as specified.

CARBURETOR SWITCH TEST

1. With the key OFF, disconnect the 10-wire harness.
2. With the throttle completely closed, check for continuity between pin 7 of the harness connector and a good ground. If there is no continuity, check the carburetor switch and wire. Recheck the timing.
3. With the throttle open, check for continuity between pin 7 of the harness connector and a good ground. There should be no continuity.

COOLANT SWITCH TEST

1. With the key OFF, disconnect the wire from the coolant switch.

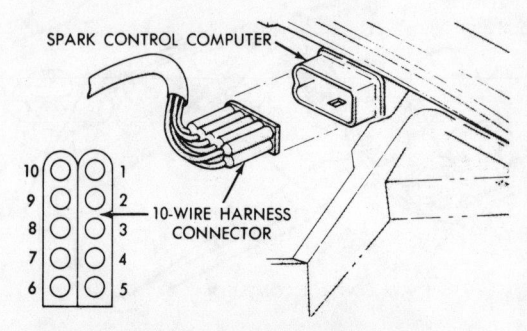

Carburetor switch continuity check

ENGINE AND ENGINE REBUILDING

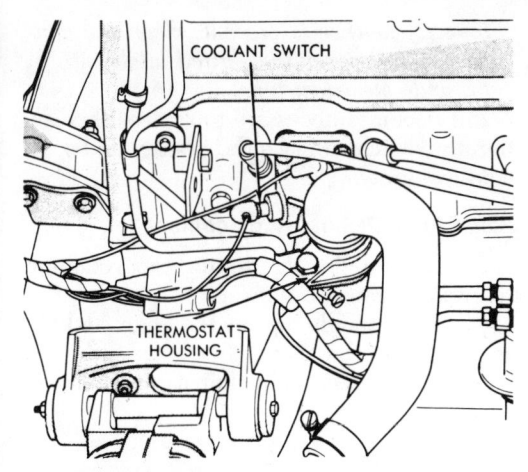

Location of coolant switch

2. Connect one lead of an ohmmeter to a good ground, on the engine.

3. Connect the other lead to the terminal of the coolant switch. On a cold engine, (below 150° F.) continuity should be present at the coolant switch. If not, replace the switch. On a warm engine (above 150° F.) or on an engine at operating temperature (thermostat open), the ohmmeter should show no continuity. If it does, replace the coolant switch.

START-UP ADVANCE TEST

1. Connect an adjustable timing light.
2. Connect a jumper wire from the carburetor switch to a ground.
3. Start the engine and immediately adjust the timing light so that the basic timing light is seen on the timing plate of the engine. The meter (on the timing light) should show an 8° advance. Continue to observe the mark for 90 seconds, adjusting the light as necessary. The additional advance will slowly decrease to the basic timing signal

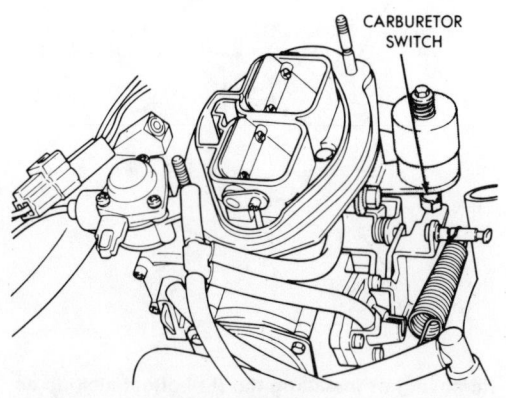

Location of carburetor switch

over a period of about one minute. If not, replace the Spark Control Computer and recheck. If it is ok, go on to the next test. Do not remove the timing light or jumper wire. They will be used for the next test.

SPEED ADVANCE TEST

1. Start and run the engine for 2 minutes.
2. Adjust the timing light so that the basic timing is shown at the timing indicator. Additional advance shown on the timing light meter should be:
   0–3° @ 1100 rpm
   8–12° @ 2000 rpm.

If not, replace the spark control computer and repeat the test. If as specified, go to the next test.

VACUUM ADVANCE TEST

The program for each computer is different. Specifications for individual computer numbers are:
   18–22° @ 2000 rpm (all part numbers)
   23–27° @ 3000 rpm (numbers 5206721, 5206784 and 5206793)
   28–32° @ 3000 rpm (numbers 5206785 and 5206790)

While performing these tests, use a metal exhaust tube. Use of rubber tube may cause a fire due to extremely high temperatures and a long test period.

If the spark control computer fails to meet these tests, it should be replaced.

1. Connect an adjustable timing light and tachometer.
2. Start the engine and warm it to normal operating temperature. Wait at least 1 minute for start up advance to return to basic timing. Place the transmission in Neutral and apply the parking brake. 3. Check, and, if necessary, adjust the basic timing.
3. Check, and, if necessary, adjust the basic timing.
4. Remove the vacuum line from the vacuum transducer and plug the line.
5. Ground the carburetor switch.
6. Increase the engine speed to 1100 rpm.
7. Check the speed advance timing.
8. Increase speed to 2000 rpm. Remove the carburetor switch ground and connect the vacuum line to the vacuum transducer.
9. Check the Zero Time Offset. Timing should be:
   6–10°—computer number 5206721
   2–6°—computer number 5206784
   3–7°—computer number 5206785

76 ENGINE AND ENGINE REBUILDING

0–3°—computer number 5206790, 5206793

10. Allow the accumulator in the computer to "clock-up" for 8 minutes.

11. With the accumulator "clocked-up" and the speed at 1100 rpm, check the vacuum advance. It should be 0–3° at 1100 rpm.

12. Disconnect and plug the vacuum line from the transducer and increase the engine speed to 3000 rpm. Note the speed advance timing.

13. Reconnect the vacuum line to the transducer and recheck the vacuum advance.

14. Return the engine to curb idle. Connect the wire to the carburetor switch if applicable.

REMOVAL AND OVERHAUL

None of the components of the Lean Burn System (except the carburetor) may be taken apart and repaired. When a part is known to be bad, it should be replaced.

The Spark Control Computer is held on by mounting screws. First remove the battery, then disconnect the 10 terminal connectors and the air duct from the computer. Next remove the vacuum line from the transducer. Remove the three screws securing the computer to the left front fender, and remove the computer.

To remove the vacuum transducer, replace the spark control computer.

NOTE: *When disconnecting the Spark Control Computer, check the following:*

1. *Discard any foam gasket found inside the connector cavity.*

2. *Be sure there is at least ¼ in. silicone grease in the cavity connector.*

3. *Computers built after 1/78 have a molded shroud around the connector. Cars built prior to 1/78 have a piece of Butyl tape. If neither is present, clean the connector and cover the slotted latch with ¾ in. wide electrical tape.*

If it becomes necessary to replace the carburetor switch, replace the bracket and solenoid assembly.

Hall Effect Pickup Replacement

1. Loosen the distributor cap retaining screws and remove the cap.

2. Pull straight up on the rotor and remove it from the shaft.

3. Disconnect the pickup assembly lead.

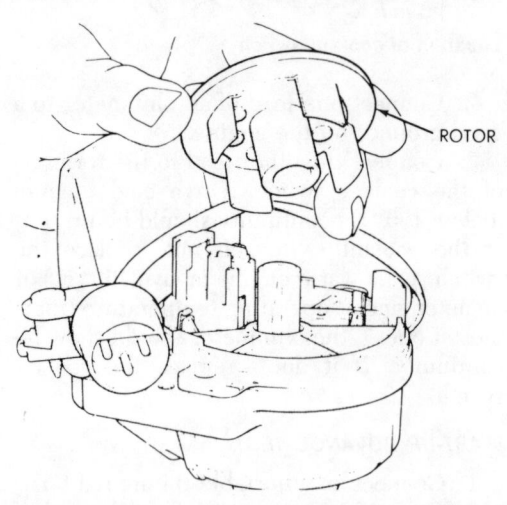

Removing or installing the Hall-effect distributor rotor

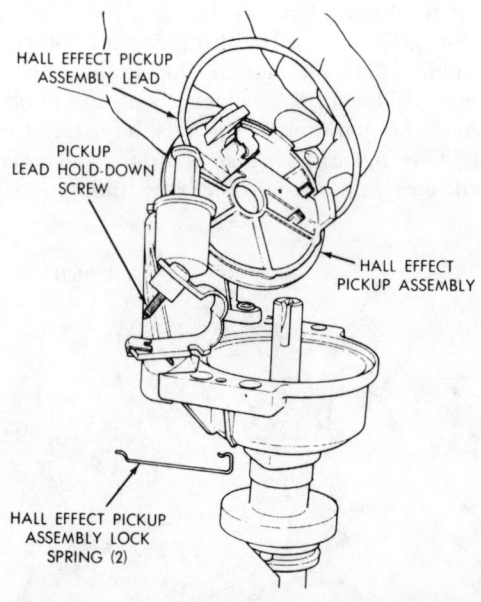

Removing or installing the Hall-effect pick-up assembly

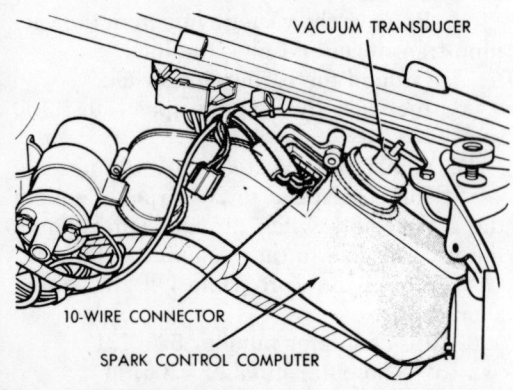

Spark control computer removal and installation

ENGINE AND ENGINE REBUILDING

4. Remove the pickup lead hold down screw.
5. Remove the pickup assembly lock springs and lift off the pickup.
6. Install the new pickup assembly onto the distributor housing and fasten it into place with the lock springs.
7. Fasten the pickup lead to the housing with the hold down screw.
8. Reconnect the lead to the harness.
9. Press the rotor back into place on the shaft. Do not wipe off the silicone grease on the metal portion of the rotor.
10. Replace the distributor cap and tighten the retaining screws.

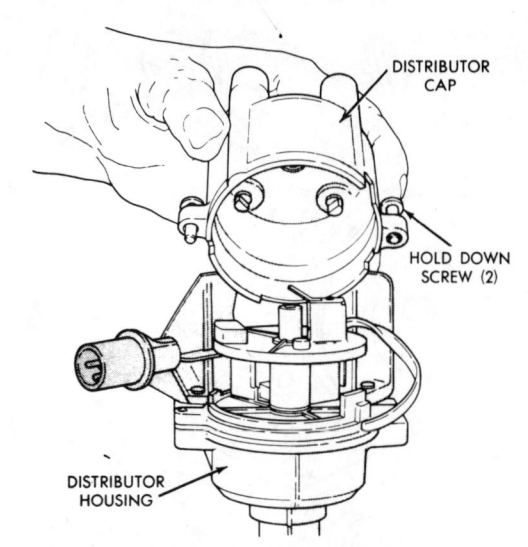

Distributor

REMOVAL AND INSTALLATION

1. Disconnect the distributor pickup lead wire at the harness connector.
2. Remove the distributor cap.
3. Rotate the engine crankshaft until the rotor is pointing toward the cylinder block. Make a mark on the block at this point for installation reference.
4. Remove the distributor holddown screw.
5. Carefully lift the distributor from the engine. The shaft will rotate slightly as the distributor is removed.

To install the distributor:
1. If the engine has been cranked over while the distributor was removed, rotate the crankshaft until the number one piston is at TDC on the compression stroke. This will be indicated by the O mark on the flywheel aligning with the pointer on the clutch housing. Position the rotor just ahead of the #1 terminal of the cap and lower the distributor into the engine. With the distributor fully seated, the rotor should be directly under the #1 terminal.
2. If the engine was not disturbed while the distributor was out, lower the distributor into the engine, engaging the gears and making sure that the gasket is properly seated in the block. The rotor should line up with the mark made before removal.
3. Tighten the holddown screw and connect the wires.
4. Check and adjust the ignition timing.

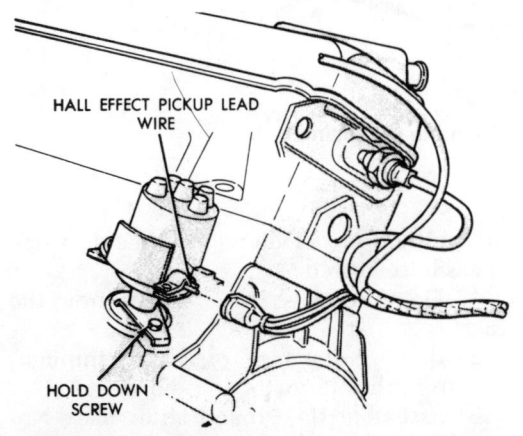

Removing or installing the distributor cap

Distributor hold-down bolt

Firing Order

NOTE: *To avoid confusion, replace spark plug wires or spark plugs one at a time.*

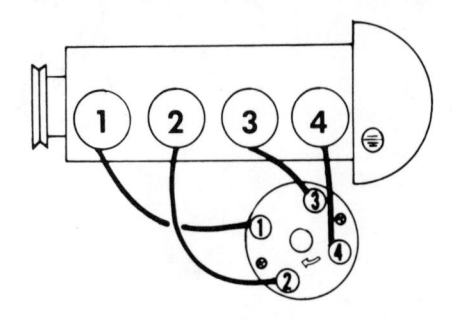

Alternator

A conventional alternator is used. It has six built-in rectifiers which convert AC current to DC current. Current at the output terminal is DC. The main components of the alternator are: the rotor, stator, rectifiers, end shields and the drive pulley.

The electronic voltage regulator is a device

78 ENGINE AND ENGINE REBUILDING

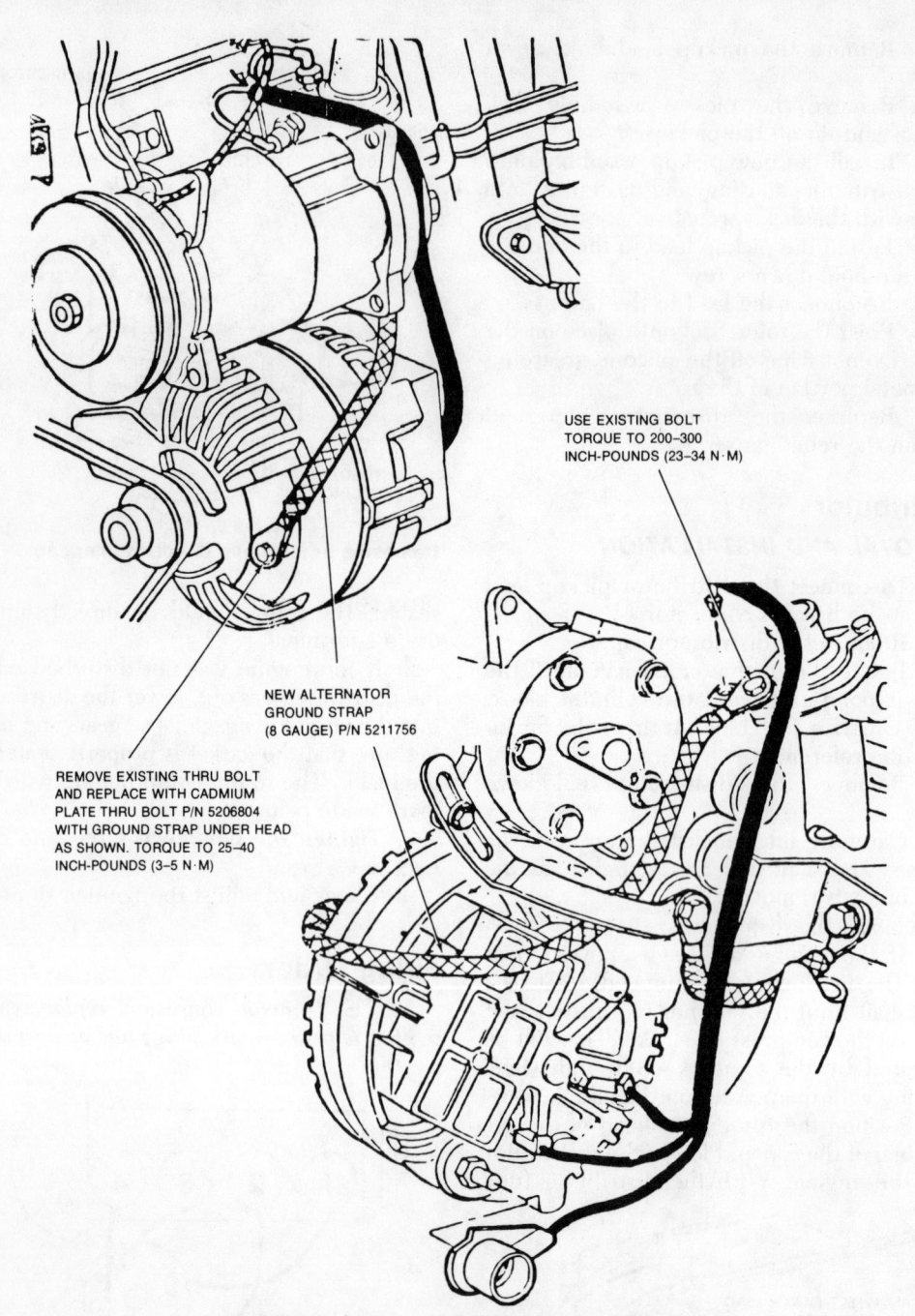

USE EXISTING BOLT
TORQUE TO 200–300
INCH-POUNDS (23–34 N·M)

NEW ALTERNATOR
GROUND STRAP
(8 GAUGE) P/N 5211756

REMOVE EXISTING THRU BOLT
AND REPLACE WITH CADMIUM
PLATE THRU BOLT P/N 5206804
WITH GROUND STRAP UNDER HEAD
AS SHOWN. TORQUE TO 25–40
INCH-POUNDS (3–5 N·M)

Modifications to improve alternator grounding

which regulates the vehicle electrical system voltage by limiting the output voltage that is generated by the alternator. This is accomplished by controlling the amount of current that is allowed to pass through the alternator field windings. The regulator has no moving parts and requires no adjustment.

Ammeter fluctuation may be caused by an intermittent loss of alternator ground, which is easily corrected.

1. Do not remove the alternator from the car.
2. Remove the forward (black) through-bolt from the alternator and discard.
3. Assemble the ground strap (Part No. 5211756) under the head of the cadmium

ENGINE AND ENGINE REBUILDING

plated (silver) replacement through-bolt (Part No. 5206804).

4. Route the ground strap as shown.

5. Remove the bolt from the thermostat housing and assemble the other end of the ground strap under the bolt.

6. Tighten the bolt.

ALTERNATOR PRECAUTIONS

To prevent damage to the alternator and regulator, the following precautions should be taken when working with the electrical system.

1. Never reverse the battery connections.

2. Booster batteries for starting must be connected properly—positive-to-positive and negative-to-negative.

3. Disconnect the battery cables before using a fast charger; the charger has a tendency to force current through the diodes in the opposite direction for which they were designed. This burns out the diodes.

4. Never use a fast charger as a booster for staring the vehicle.

5. Never disconnect the voltage regulator while the engine is running.

6. Avoid long soldering times when replacing diodes or transistors. Prolonged heat is damaging to AC generators.

7. Do not use test lamps of more than 12 volts (V) for checking diode continuity.

8. Do not short across or ground any of the terminals on the AC generator.

9. The polarity of the battery, generator, and regulator must be matched and consid-

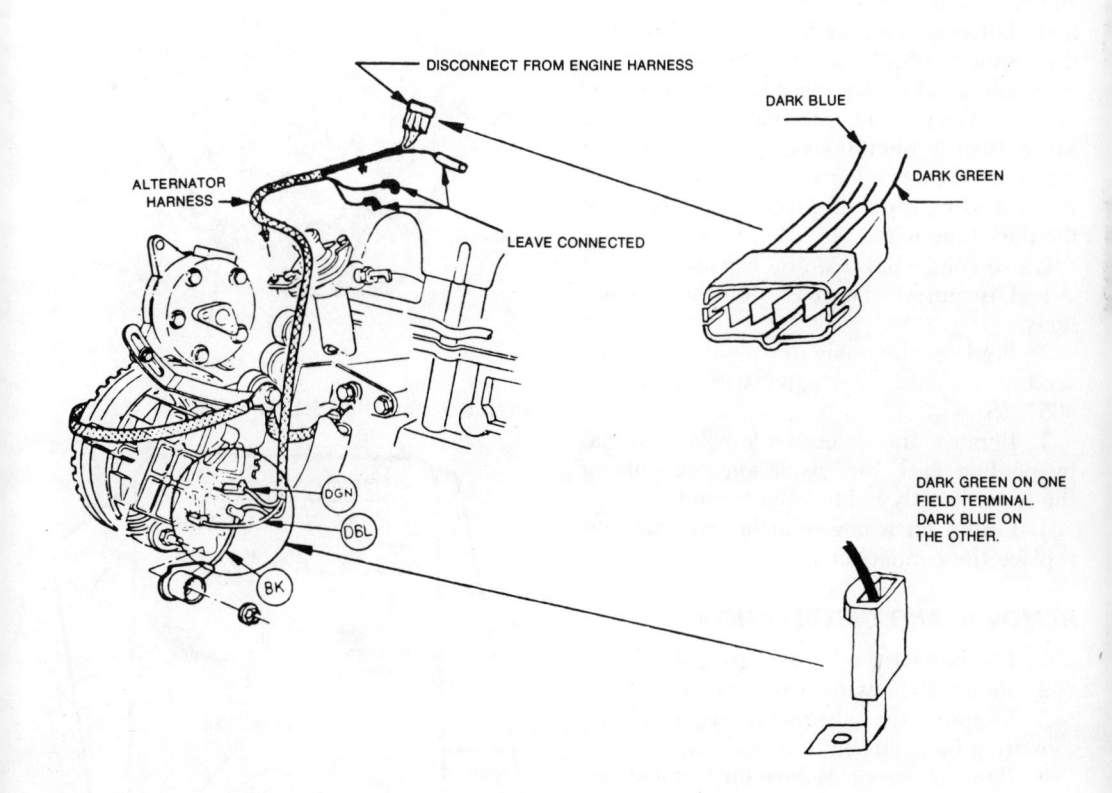

Modifications to alternator terminals

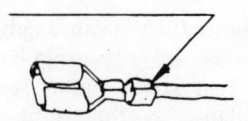

80 ENGINE AND ENGINE REBUILDING

ered before making any electrical connections within the system.

10. Never operate the alternator on an open circuit. Make sure that all connections within the circuit are clean and tight.

11. Disconnect the battery terminals when performing any service on the electrical system. This will eliminate the possibility of accidental reversal of polarity.

12. Disconnect the battery ground cable if arc welding is to be done on any part of the car.

Some 1978–79 Omni and Horizons may exhibit a tendency to inadequately charge the battery. This condition is probably due to a loose connection at the field terminals on the alternator.

A loose connection can be tested by disconnecting the 4-way connector between the alternator and engine harness. Test for continuity between the dark blue wire terminal in the connector and the male terminal brush assembly to which the dark blue wire is connected. Wiggle the alternator connecton. More than 1 ohm resistance or an erratic reading indicates a loose connection. Repeat the test using the dark green wire instead of the dark blue wire.

Loose connections can be repaired.

1. Disconnect the loose female connections.
2. Replace the male terminal brush assembly on the alternator with part no. 4057928.
3. Remove the defective female terminal by peeling back the insulation and cutting the wire directly behind the terminal.
4. Crimp on a new female terminal and replace the connections.

REMOVAL AND INSTALLATION

1. Disconnect the battery ground cable.
2. Remove the wires from the alternator.
3. Support the alternator, remove the mounting bolts and lift out the unit.
4. Reverse the procedure for installation.

Regulator

REMOVAL AND INSTALLATION

1. Disconnect the battery ground cable.
2. Remove the wires from the regulator.
3. Remove the two sheet metal screws securing the regulator to the right side fender skirt.
4. Installation is the reverse of removal.

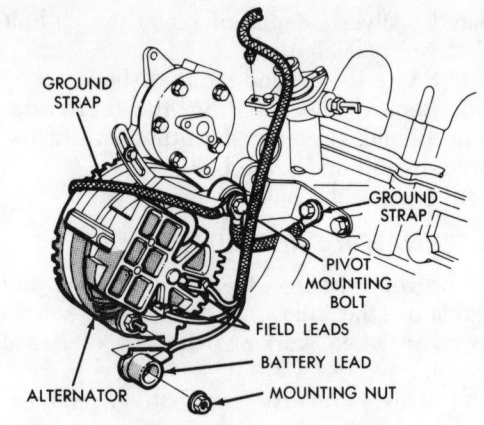

Alternator connections

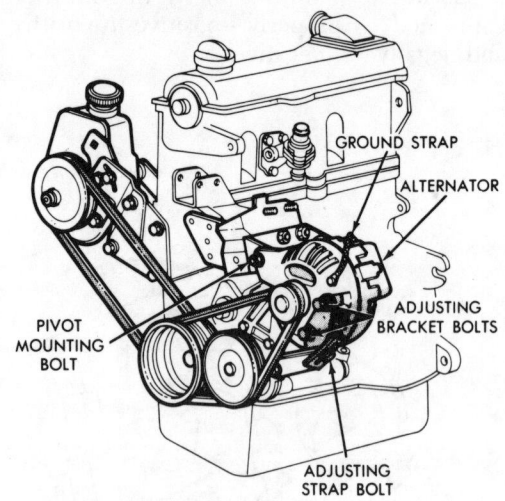

Alternator mounting details

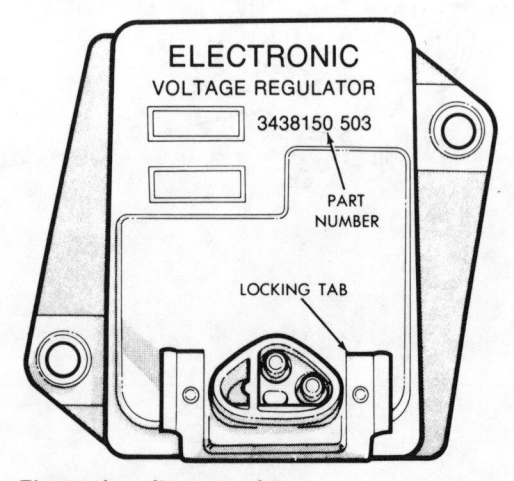

Electronic voltage regulator

Starter

The starter is an overrunning clutch drive type with a solenoid mounted on the starter

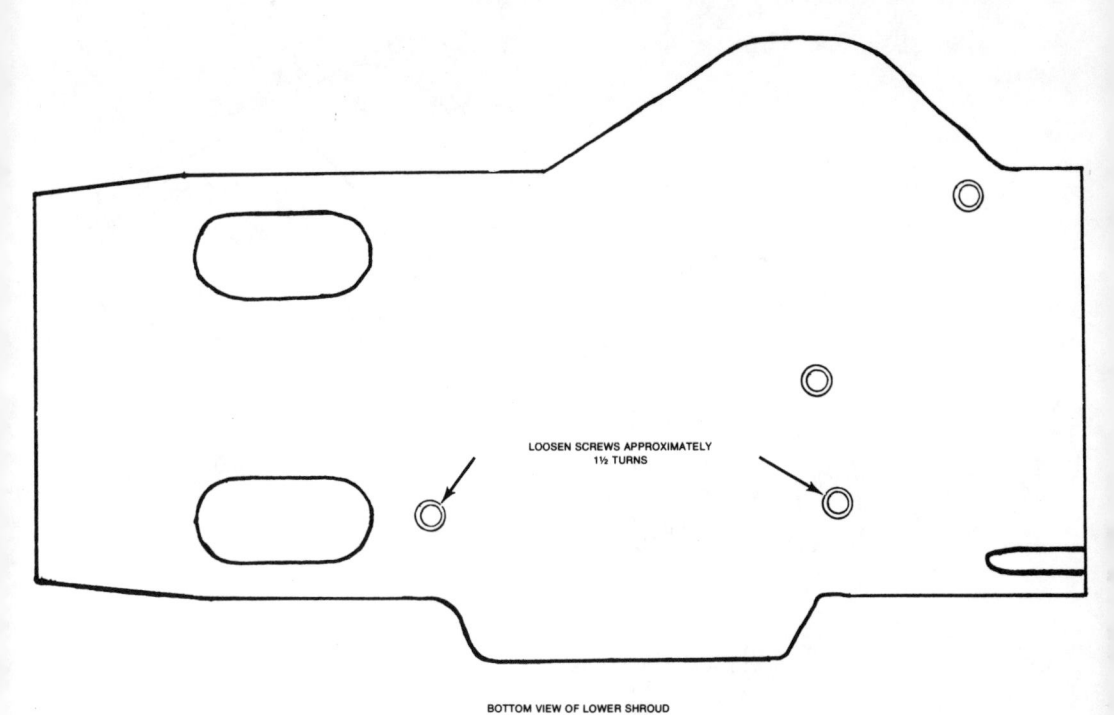

ENGINE AND ENGINE REBUILDING

Bottom view of lower shroud—loosen screws shown

motor. Four different starters are used on Omni/Horizon models. Two each are built by Nippondenso and Bosch for manual and automatic transmission applications. Removal and installation procedures are the same for all units.

Some early production models may experience starter motor damage due to improper fit of the upper and lower steering column shrouds. Irregularities in the mating surface of the key cylinder area may cause the ignition key to bind, causing the starter to be continuously engaged. The condition can be corrected by loosening the shroud cover screws about 1½ turns.

If loosening the screws does not solve the problem, the covers will have to be replaced with new parts, which are available only in black and must be painted to match interior trim.

REMOVAL AND INSTALLATION

1. Disconnect the battery ground cable.
2. Remove the wires from the starter and solenoid.
3. Support the starter, remove the bolts and lift the unit out from the flywheel housing.
4. Installation is the reverse of removal.

OVERHAUL

Service procedures are the same for the Bosch or Nippondenso starters. The starter drive is an over-running clutch type with a solenoid mounted externally on the motor.

Disassembly

1. Disconnect the field coil wire from the solenoid terminal.
2. Remove the solenoid mounting screws and work the solenoid off the shift fork.
3. On Nippondenso units, remove the bearing cover, armature shaft lock, washer, spring, and seal.
4. On Bosch units, remove the bearing cover, armature shaft lock, and shim.
5. Remove the two through-bolts and the commutator end frame cover.
6. Remove the two brushes and the brush holder.
7. Slide the field frame off over the armature.
8. Take out the shift lever pivot bolt.
9. Take off the rubber gasket and metal plate.
10. Remove the armature assembly and shift lever from the drive end housing.
11. Press the stop collar off the snap ring.

82 ENGINE AND ENGINE REBUILDING

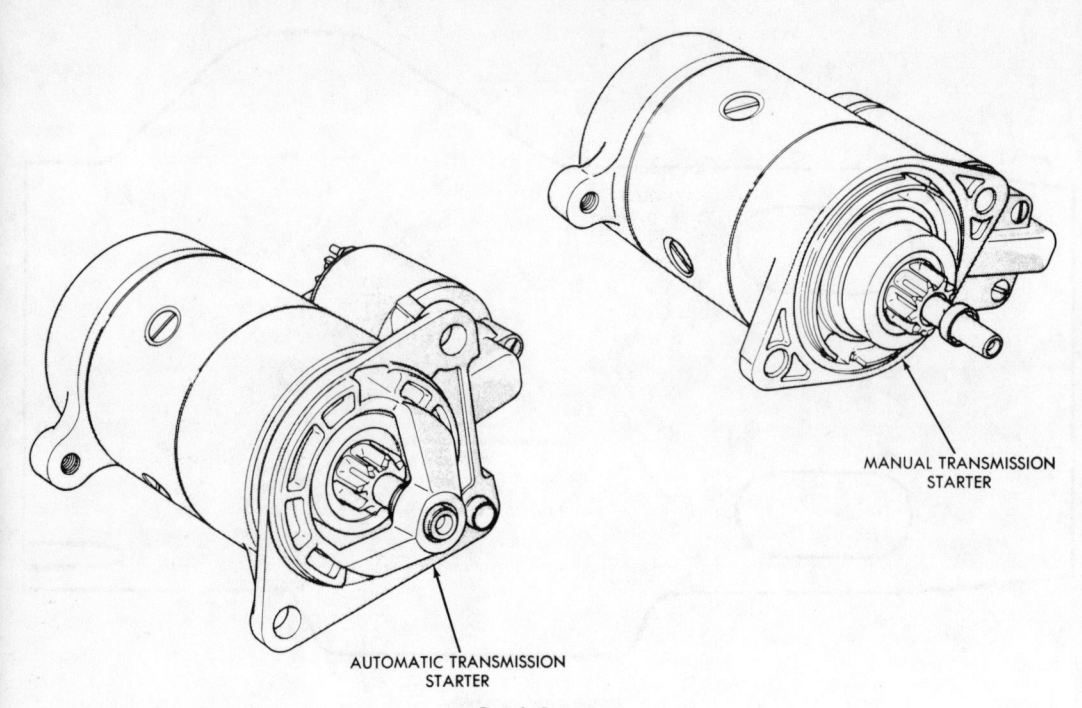

Bosch Starters

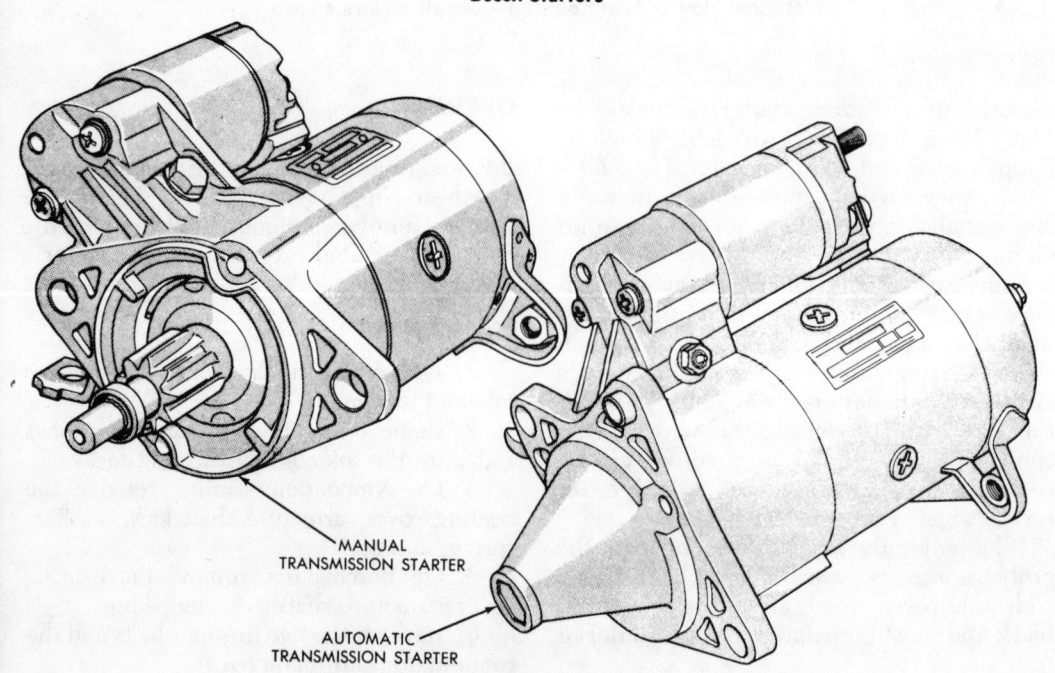

AUTOMATIC TRANSMISSION STARTER

MANUAL TRANSMISSION STARTER

Nippondenso Starters

MANUAL TRANSMISSION STARTER

AUTOMATIC TRANSMISSION STARTER

Starter identification

Remove the snap-ring, stop collar, and clutch.

Inspection

1. Brushes that are worn more than one-half the length of new brushes, or are oil-soaked, should be replaced.

2. Do not immerse the starter clutch unit in cleaning solvent. Solvent will wash the lubricant from the clutch.

3. Place the drive unit on the armature shaft and, while holding the armature, rotate the pinion. The drive pinion should rotate smoothly in one direction only. The pinion

ENGINE AND ENGINE REBUILDING

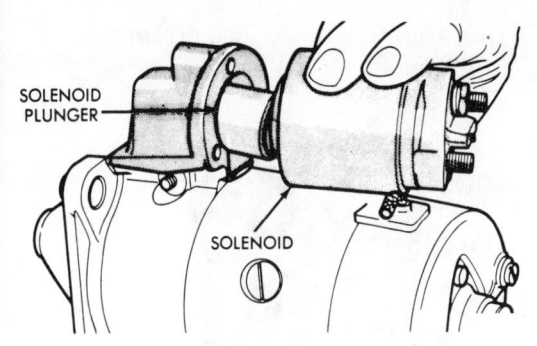

Solenoid removal (automatic transaxle shown)

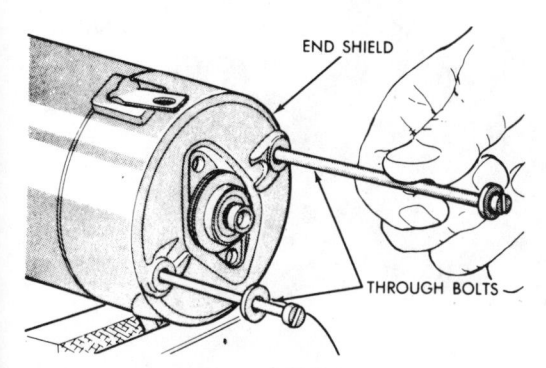

Removing starter through bolts

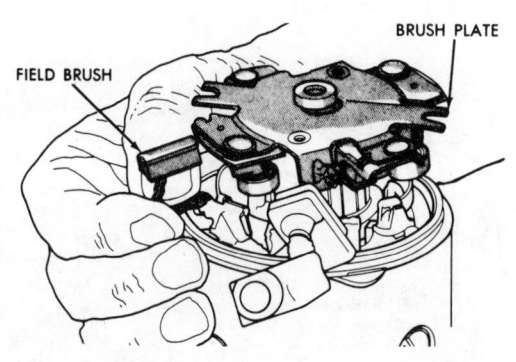

Brush assembly

may not rotate easily. If the clutch unit does not function properly, or if the pinion is worn, chipped, or burred, replace the unit.

Assembly

1. Lubricate the armature shaft and splines with SAE 10-W or 30 oil.
2. Install the clutch, stop collar, and lock ring on the armature.
3. Place the armature assembly and shift fork in the drive end housing. Install the shift lever pivot bolt.
4. Install the rubber gasket and metal plate.
5. Slide the field frame into position. Install the brush holder and brushes.

6. Position the commutator end frame cover and install the through bolts.
7. On Nippondenso units, install the seal, spring, washer, armature shaft lock, and bearing cover.
8. On Bosch units, install the shim and armature shaft lock. Check that end play is 0.05–0.3 mm (0.002–0.012 in.). Install the bearing cover.
9. Assemble the solenoid to the shift fork and install the mounting screws.
10. Connect the field coil wire to the solenoid.

Battery

The battery is located conventionally, under the hood. It can be easily removed by disconnecting the battery cables and removing the hold-down bolts from the battery tray. Coat the terminals with a small amount of petroleum jelly after installation.

ENGINE MECHANICAL

A 104.7 cu. in. (1.7L) displacement, four cylinder, overhead camshaft engine is used. The block is cast iron and the head is aluminum. A five main bearing forged steel crankshaft using no vibration damper is employed, rotated by cast aluminum pistons. A sintered iron timing belt sprocket is mounted on the end of the crankshaft. The intake manifold and oil filter base are aluminum.

A steel reinforced belt drives the intermediate shaft and camshaft. The intermediate shaft drives the oil pump, distributor, and fuel pump.

The cylinder head is lightweight aluminum alloy. The intake and exhaust manifolds are mounted on the same side of the cylinder head. The valves are opened and closed by the camshaft lobes operating on cupped cam followers which fit over the valves and springs. This design results in lighter valve train weight and fewer moving parts. The Omni/Horizon engine combines low maintenance and high power output along with low emissions and excellent fuel mileage.

ENGINE REMOVAL AND INSTALLATION
Manual Transmission

NOTE: *The engine and transmission must be removed together, or the transmission should be completely removed from the car*

84 ENGINE AND ENGINE REBUILDING

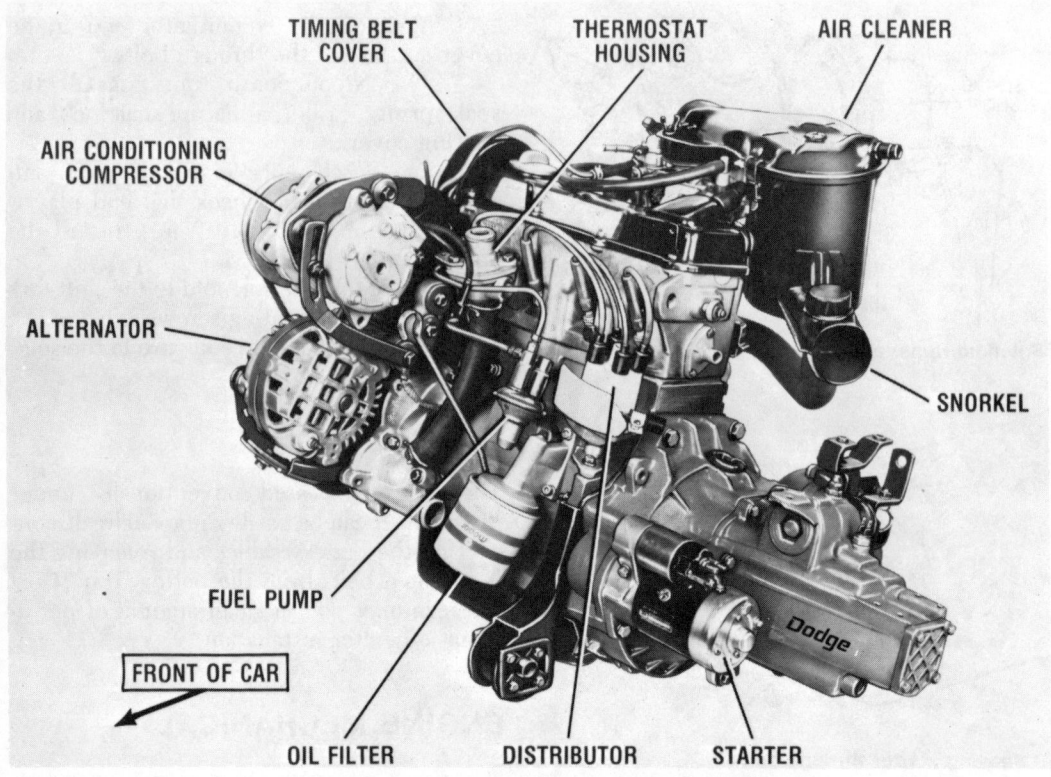

1.7 liter engine (shown with manual transaxle)

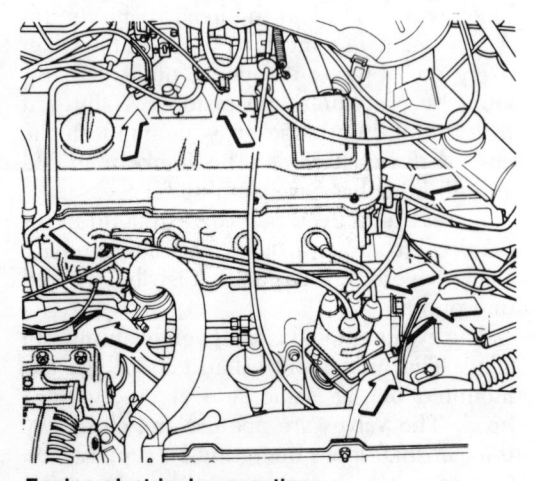

Labels: TIMING BELT COVER, THERMOSTAT HOUSING, AIR CLEANER, AIR CONDITIONING COMPRESSOR, ALTERNATOR, SNORKEL, FUEL PUMP, FRONT OF CAR, OIL FILTER, DISTRIBUTOR, STARTER

Engine electrical connections

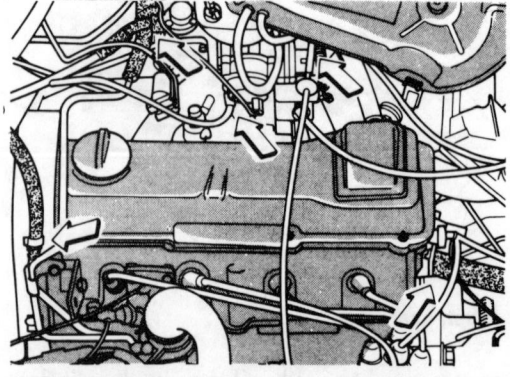

Fuel, heater and accelerator connections

first. The following is for engine/transmission assembly removal.

1. Disconnect the battery.
2. Mark the hood hinge outline and remove the hood.
3. Drain the cooling system.
4. Remove the radiator hoses and remove the radiator and shroud assembly.
5. Remove the air cleaner and hoses.
6. The air conditioning compressor does not have to be disconnected. Remove it from its bracket and position it out of the way. Securing it with wire is the best method.

NOTE: *On A/C cars do not disconnect any hoses from the A/C system. Disconnect compressor with hoses attached.*

7. Disconnect all wiring from the engine, alternator and carburetor.
8. Disconnect the fuel line, heater hoses and accelerator linkage.
9. Disconnect the air pump lines.
10. Remove the alternator.
11. Disconnect the clutch and speedometer cables.

ENGINE AND ENGINE REBUILDING 85

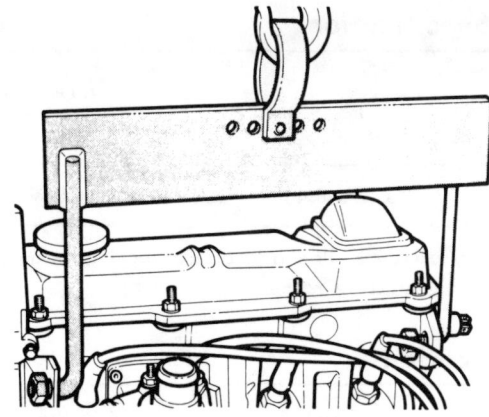

Attach a lifting sling to the engine

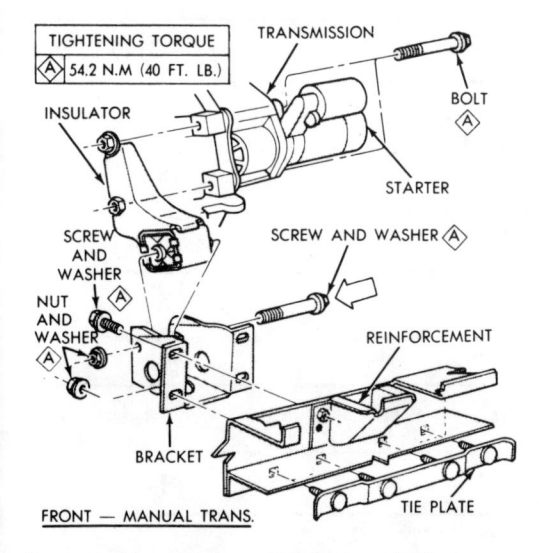

Front engine mount—manual transmission

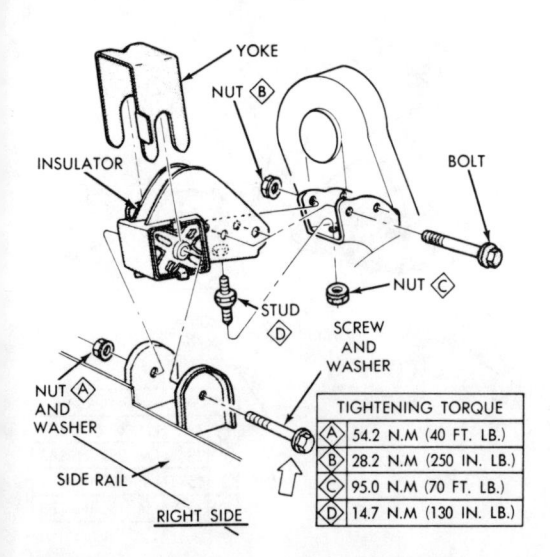

Right engine mount—manual transmission

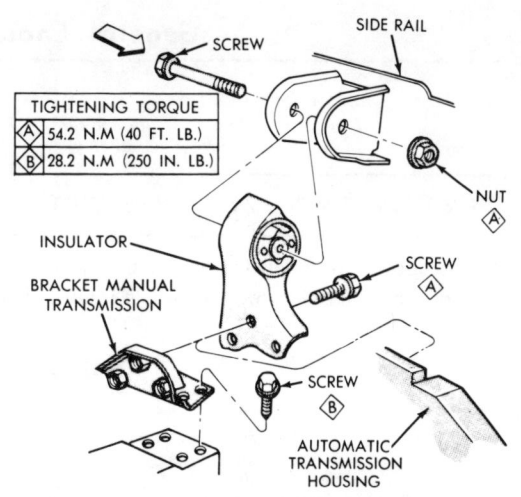

Left engine mount—manual and automatic transmission

12. Raise the vehicle and support it on jackstands.
13. Disconnect the driveshafts from the transmission and support them with wires.
14. Disconnect the exhaust pipe.
15. Remove the air pump.
16. Disconnect the transmission linkage.
17. Lower the vehicle.
18. Attach a lifting fixture and a shop crane to the engine. Raise the engine slightly to take up the weight and disconnect the engine mounts in this order: front, right, left. Lift the engine from the car.
19. Lower the engine into place and loosely install all mounting bolts. When all mounts have been hand tightened, torque each to 40 ft lbs.
20. Remove the lifting fixture and raise the vehicle, supporting it on jackstands.
21. Connect the driveshafts. Torque the bolts to 35 ft lbs.
22. Connect the transmission linkage, install the air pump, connect the exhaust pipe and lower the vehicle.
23. Connect the clutch and speedometer cables.
24. Install the alternator.
25. Install the air pump lines.
26. Connect the fuel line, heater hoses and accelerator linkage.
27. Connect all wiring.
28. Mount the air conditioning compressor.
29. Install the air cleaner.
30. Install the radiator and hoses.
31. Fill the cooling system.

ENGINE AND ENGINE REBUILDING

General Engine Specifications

Year	Engine No. Cyl Displ Cu In.	Carb Type	Horsepower at RPM ■	Torque (ft lb) at RPM ■	Bore X Stroke (In.)	Compression Ratio	Oil Pressure (psi) at 2000 rpm
'78–'80	4—104.7	2 bbl	75 @ 5600	90 @ 3200	3.13 x 3.40	8.2 : 1	60–90

■ Horsepower and torque are SAE net, with all accessories installed and operating. Figure may vary from model-to-model and is intended to be representative rather than exact.

Valve Specifications

Year	Engine	Seat Angle (deg)	Face Angle (deg)	Spring Test Pressure (lb in.)	Spring Installed Height (in.)	Stem-to-Guide Clearance (in.) Intake	Exhaust	Stem Diameter (in.) Intake	Exhaust
'78–80	4—104.7	45	①	②	③	.039 max	.051 max	.3140	.3140

① Intake: 45°33'
Exhaust: 43°33'
② outer: 101 @ .878
inner: 49 @ .720
③ outer: 1.28
inner: 1.13

Torque Specifications
(ft lbs)

Year	Engine	Cylinder Head Bolts	Connecting Rod Bearing Bolts	Main Bearing Bolts	Crankshaft Bolt	Flywheel to Crankshaft Bolts	Camshaft Cap Bolts
'78	4—104.7	60①	33	47	58	55②	14
'79–'80	4—104.7	60①	35	47	58	55②	14

① plus ¼ turn more
② 50 with auto trans

32. Install the hood.
33. Connect the battery.
34. Start the engine and run it to normal operating temperature.
35. Check the timing and adjust if necessary. Adjust the carburetor idle speed and mixture, and the transmission linkage.

Automatic Transmission

The engine is removed without the transmission.
1. Disconnect the battery.
2. Scribe the outline of the hood hinges and remove the hood.
3. Drain the cooling system.
4. Disconnect the hoses from the radiator and engine.
5. Remove the air cleaner and hoses.

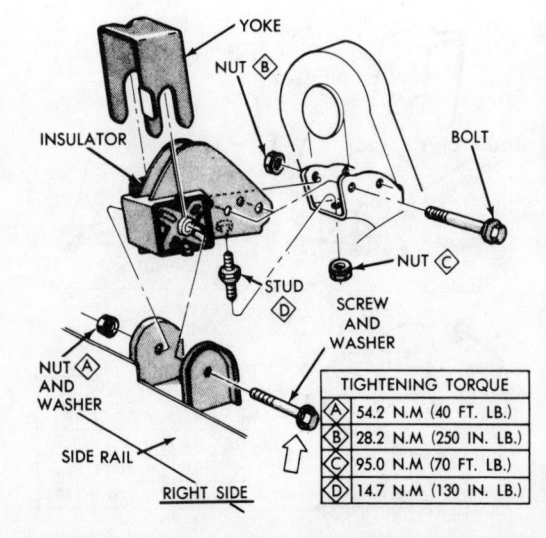

Right engine mount—automatic transmission

Crankshaft and Connecting Rod Specifications
(all specifications in inches)

Year	Engine	Main Brg Journal Dia	Main Brg Oil Clearance	Crankshaft End Play	Thrust on No.	Connecting Rod Journal Dia	Rod Bearing Oil Clearance	Rod Bearing Side Clearance
'78–'80	4—104.7	2.124–2.128	0.0008–0.003	.003–.007	3	1.809–1.813	.0011–.0034	.015

Piston, Ring and Pin Specifications
(all specifications in inches)

Year	Engine	Piston Clearance	Ring Gap Top Compression	Ring Gap Bottom Compression	Oil Control	Ring Side Clearance Top Compression	Ring Side Clearance Bottom Compression	Oil Control
'78–'79	4—104.7	.0011–.027	.012–.018	.012–.018	.010–.016	.0008–.0020	.0008–.0020	.0008–.0020
'80	4—104.7	.0004–.0015	.012–.018	.012–.018	.016–.045	.0016–.0028	.0008–.0020	.0008–.0020

ENGINE AND ENGINE REBUILDING

6. Disconnect the air conditioning compressor and set it aside, with refrigerant lines attached.

CAUTION: *Do not disconnect any of the refrigerant lines.*

7. Disconnect and tag all electrical connections from the engine.
8. Disconnect the fuel line, accelerator cable and heater hoses. Plug the lines to prevent leakage.
9. Remove the diverter valve and lines from the air pump.
10. Remove the alternator.
11. Remove the upper bell housing bolts.
12. Raise and support the vehicle.
13. Remove the wheels and right and left splash shields.
14. Remove the power steering pump and set it aside. Do not disconnect the lines.
15. Remove the water pump and crankshaft pulleys.
16. Remove the front engine mounting bolt.
17. Remove the inspection cover from the transmission and remove the bolts from the flex plate.
18. Remove the starter.
19. Remove the remaining lower bell housing bolts.
20. Lower the vehicle and support the transmission with a jack.
21. Remove the oil filter and drain the oil.
22. Attach a lifting fixture to the engine and remove the engine.
23. Installation is the reverse of removal. Be sure to connect all lines, hoses and wires. Fill the engine with oil and coolant and test for leaks.

Cylinder Head

REMOVAL AND INSTALLATION

The engine should be cold before the cylinder head is removed. The head is retained by 10 socket head bolts.

1. Disconnect the battery.
2. Drain the cooling system.
3. Remove the air cleaner assembly.
4. Disconnect all lines, hoses and wires from the head manifold and carburetor.
5. Disconnect the accelerator linkage.
6. Remove the distributor cap.
7. Disconnect the exhaust pipe.
8. Remove the carburetor.
9. Remove the intake and exhaust manifolds.

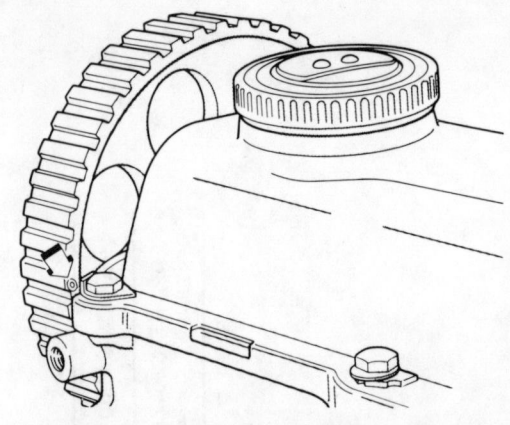

Align the camshaft timing dot with the edge of the cylinder head

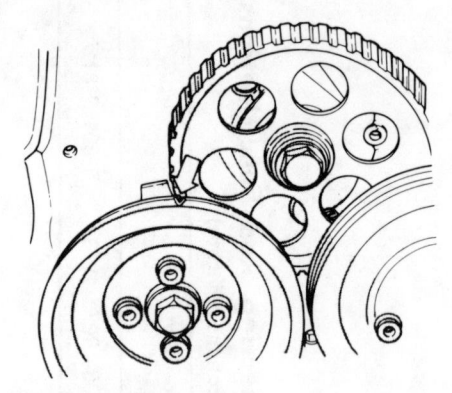

Align the timing marks on crankshaft and intermediate shaft

10. Remove the upper portion of the front cover.
11. Turn the engine by hand until all gear timing marks are aligned.
12. Loosen the drive belt tensioner and slip the belt off the camshaft gear.

NOTE: *The camshaft timing mark is on the back of the gear and is properly positioned when it is in line with the left corner of the camshaft cover at the head.*

13. If equipped with air conditioning, remove the compressor from the mounting brackets and support it out of the way with wires. Remove the mounting brackets from the head.
14. Remove the valve cover, gaskets and seals.
15. Remove head bolts in reverse order of the tightening sequence.
16. Lift off the head and discard the gasket.
17. Installation is the reverse of removal. Make certain all gasket surfaces are thoroughly cleaned and are free of deep nicks

ENGINE AND ENGINE REBUILDING

Work the belt off the gear

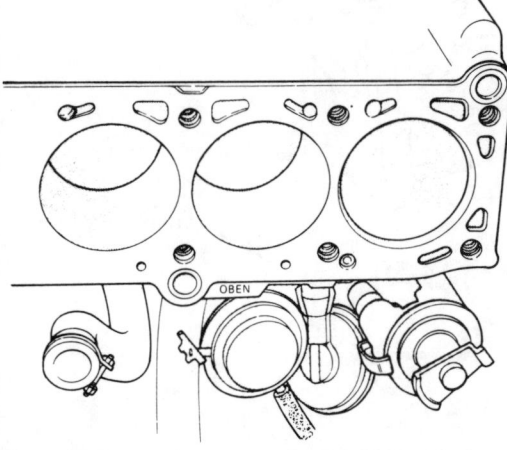

The cylinder head gasket is installed with the word "OBEN" facing up

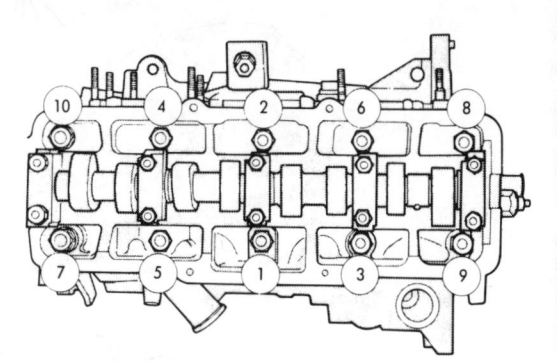

Cylinder head torque sequence

or scratches. Always use new gaskets and seals. The word "OBEN" (Top) faces up. Never reuse a gasket or seal, even if it looks good. When positioning the head on the block, insert bolts 8 and 10 (see illustration) to align the head. Tighten bolts in the order shown in the illustration. Bolts should be tightened to 30 ft lbs in rotation, then tightened to 60 ft lbs. When all bolts are at 60 ft lbs, tighten each ¼ turn more in sequence. Make sure all timing marks are aligned before installing the drive belt. The drive belt is correctly tensioned when it can be twisted 90° with the thumb and index finger midway between the camshaft and intermediate shaft.

OVERHAUL

Procedures for overhauling the cylinder head are given as part of the engine rebuilding section in this chapter.

VALVE GUIDES

Valve guides are replaceable, but they should not be replaced in a cylinder head in which the valve seats cannot be refaced.

Worn guides should be pressed out from the combustion chamber side and new guides pressed in as far as they will go.

> NOTE: *Service valve guides have a shoulder. Once the guide is seated, do not use more than 1 ton pressure or the guide shoulder could break.*

VALVE SEATS

Valve seats can be refaced if they are worn or burned, but the correction angle and seat width must be maintained. If not, the cylinder head must be replaced.

Intake valve seats should be ground to a 45° angle and the valve margin should not be less than 0.02 in. Check the valve stem diameter.

Exhaust valves are sodium filled and should not be ground by machine. Use lapping compound and lap by hand. Valve margin should be at least 0.02 in. Check the

90 ENGINE AND ENGINE REBUILDING

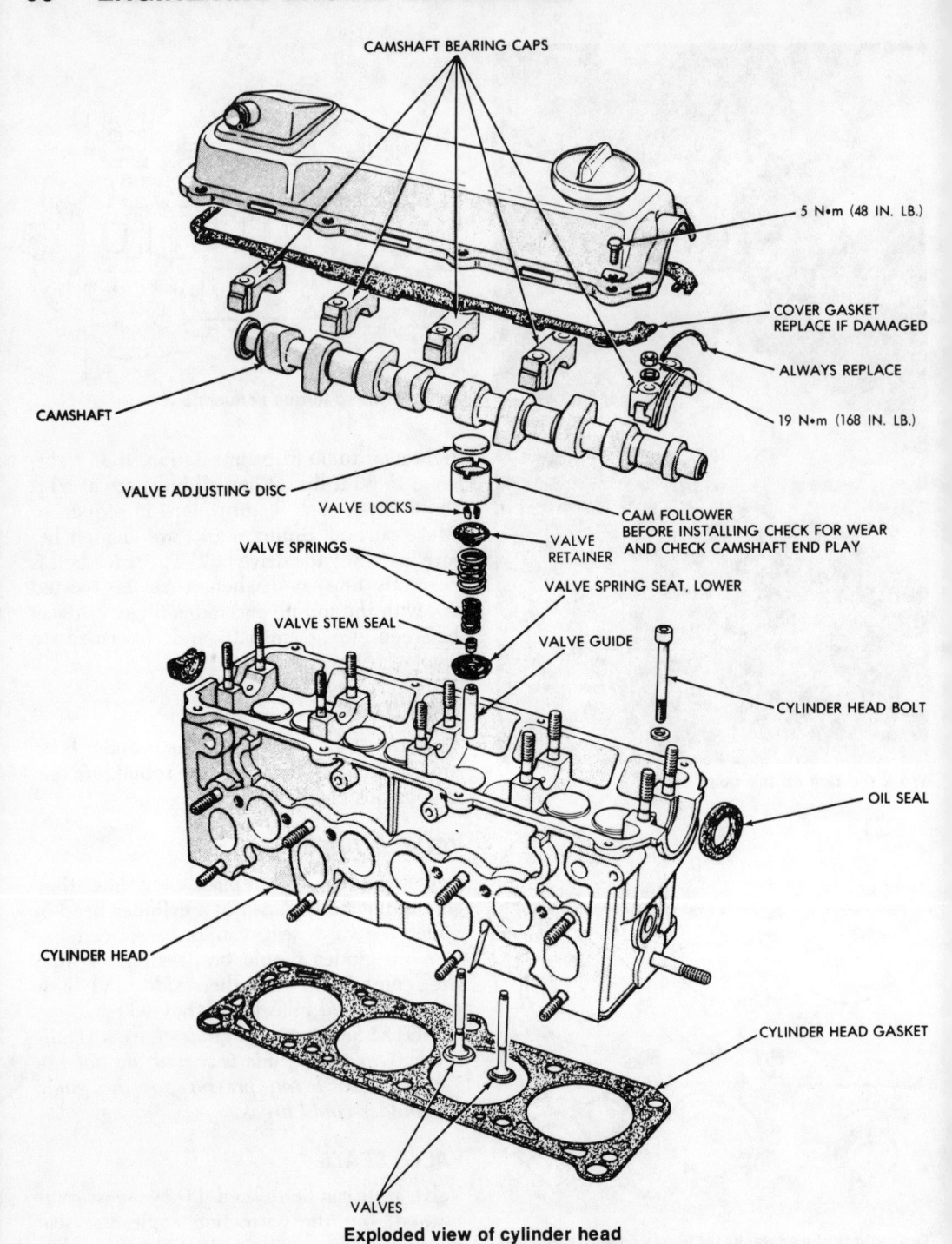

Exploded view of cylinder head

stem diameter. The exhaust valve seat should be ground to a 45° angle.

Intake and exhaust valves are available with stems 0.020 in. shorter than production valves. If the seats are cut too much during repairs, these shorter valves should be installed to allow the use of proper sized valve adjusting discs.

Intake Manifold

REMOVAL AND INSTALLATION

1. Remove the air cleaner and hoses.
2. Remove all wiring and any hoses connected to the carburetor and manifold.
3. Disconnect the accelerator linkage.

ENGINE AND ENGINE REBUILDING 91

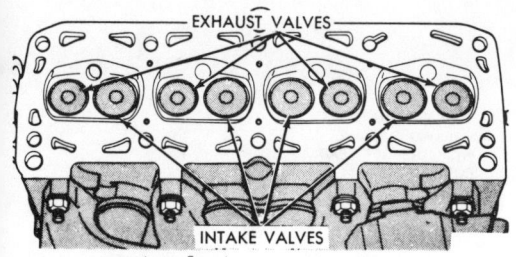

Valve identification

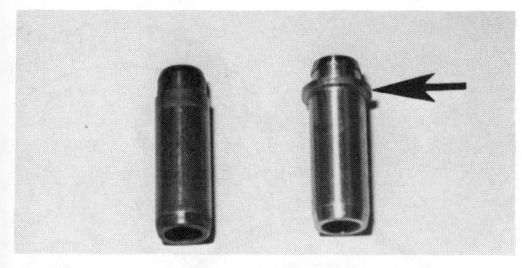

Service valve guides (right) have a shoulder

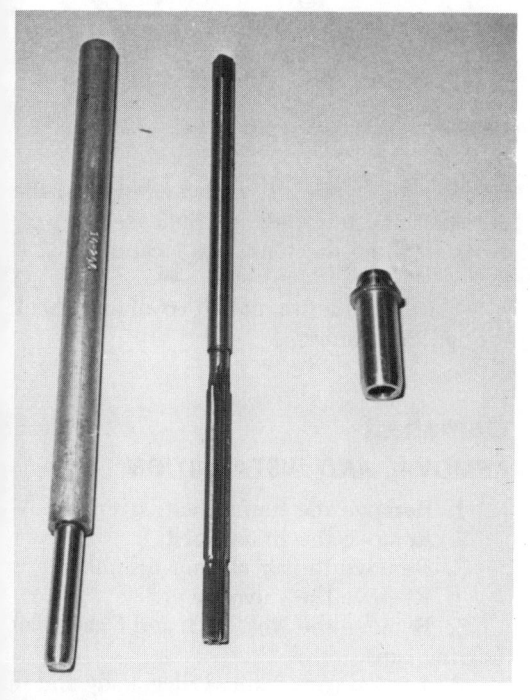

Valve guide tools

4. Remove the intake-to-exhaust manifold bolts.
5. Remove the manifold-to-head bolts and lift out the intake manifold.
6. Clean all gasket surfaces and, using new gaskets, install the manifold.
7. Connect all hoses and wires, and install the air cleaner.
8. Connect the accelerator linkage.

Exhaust Manifold
REMOVAL AND INSTALLATION

1. Follow the intake manifold removal procedures above.
2. Disconnect the exhaust pipe.
3. Unbolt and remove the exhaust manifold.
4. Clean the gasket surfaces, and using a new gasket, install the manifold.

Timing Cover
REMOVAL AND INSTALLATION

1. Loosen the alternator mounting bolts, pivot the alternator and remove the drive belt.
2. Do the same thing with the air conditioning compressor.
3. Remove the cover retaining nuts, washers and spacers.
4. Remove the cover.
5. Installation is the reverse of removal.

Timing Belt
REMOVAL AND INSTALLATION

The timing belt is designed to last a long time without requiring tension adjustments. If the belt is removed or replaced, basic valve timing must be checked and the belt retensioned.

1. Remove the timing belt cover.
2. While holding the large hex on the tension pulley, loosen the pulley nut.
3. Remove the belt from the tensioner.
4. Slide the belt off the three toothed pulleys.
5. Using the larger bolt on the crankshaft pulley, turn the engine until the #1 cylinder is at TDC of the compression stroke. At this point the valves for the #1 cylinder will be closed and the timing mark will be aligned with the pointer on the flywheel housing. Make sure that the timing mark on the rear face of the camshaft pulley is aligned with the lower left corner of the valve cover.
6. Check that the V-notch in the crankshaft pulley aligns with the dot mark on the intermediate shaft.

CAUTION: *If the timing marks are not perfectly aligned, poor engine performance and probable engine damage will result!*

7. Install the belt on the pulleys.
8. Adjust the tension by turning the large tensioner hex to the right. Tension is correct when the belt can be twisted 90° with the

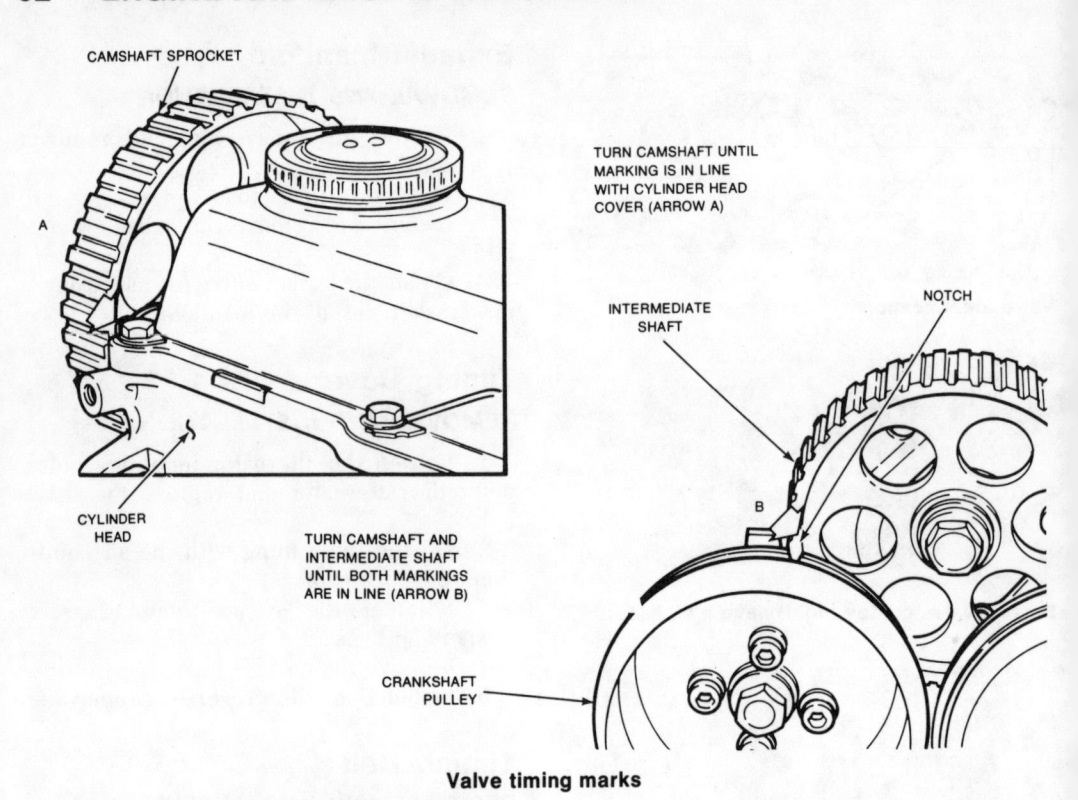

92 ENGINE AND ENGINE REBUILDING

Valve timing marks

Belt tension is correct when the belt can be twisted 90°

thumb and forefinger, midway between the camshaft and intermediate pulleys.

9. Tighten the tensioner locknut to 32 ft lb.

10. Install the timing belt cover and check the ignition timing.

Camshaft

REMOVAL AND INSTALLATION

1. Remove the timing belt cover.
2. Remove the timing belt.
3. Remove the air cleaner assembly.
4. Remove the valve cover.
5. Remove the Nos. 1, 3, and 5 camshaft bearing caps.
6. Loosen caps 2 and 4 diagonally and in increments.
7. Lift the camshaft out.
8. Lubricate the camshaft journals and lobes with engine assembly lubricant and position it in the head.
9. Install a new oil seal.
10. Install the Nos. 1, 3, 5 bearing caps and torque the nuts to 14 ft lbs.

NOTE: *All bearing caps are slightly offset. They should be installed so that the numbers on the cap read right side up from the driver's seat.*

ENGINE AND ENGINE REBUILDING

Timing Belt Wear

DESCRIPTION	FLAW CONDITIONS
1. Hardened back surface rubber	Back surface glossy. Non-elastic and so hard that even if a finger nail is forced into it, no mark is produced.
2. Cracked back surface rubber	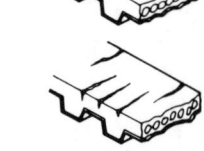
3. Cracked or exfoliated canvas	
4. Badly worn teeth (initial stage)	Canvas on load side tooth flank worn (Fluffy canvas fibers, rubber gone and color changed to white, and unclear canvas texture)
5. Badly worn teeth (last stage)	Canvas on load side tooth flank worn down and rubber exposed (tooth width reduced)
6. Cracked tooth bottom	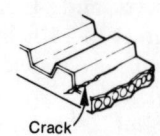
7. Missing tooth	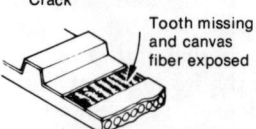
8. Side of belt badly worn	
9. Side of belt cracked	NOTE: *Normal belt should have clear-cut sides as if cut by a sharp knife.*

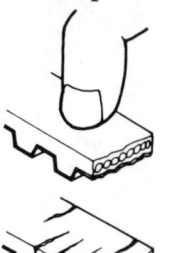

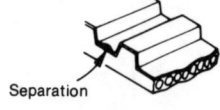

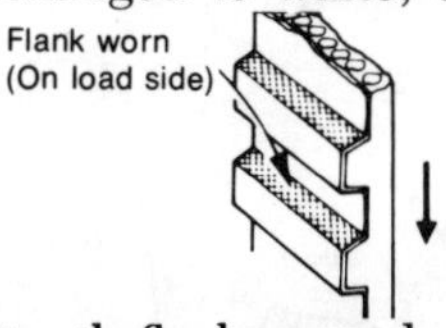

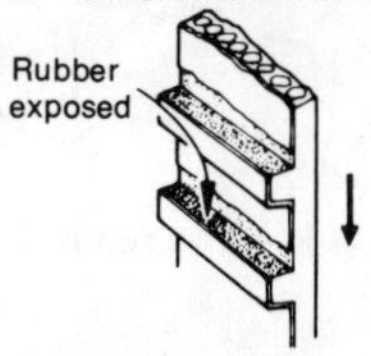

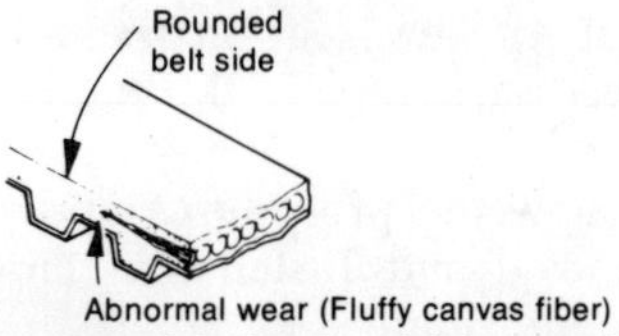

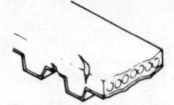

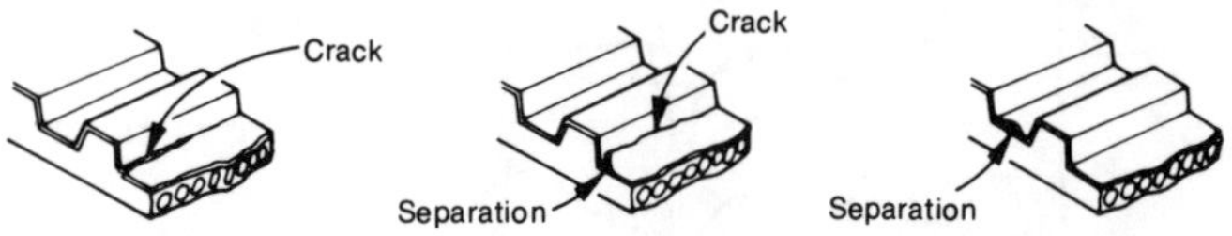

ENGINE AND ENGINE REBUILDING

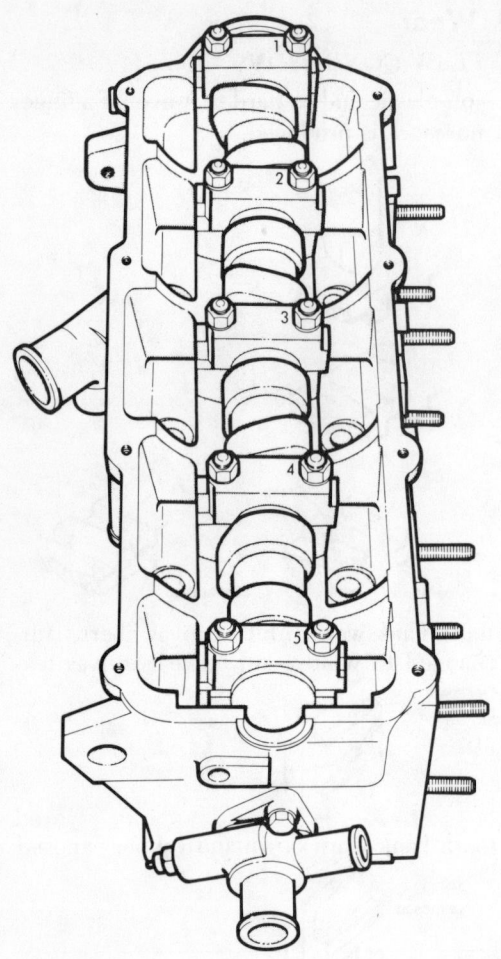

Bearing caps should be installed with the numbers as shown

11. Install the Nos. 2 and 4 caps and diagonally torque the nuts to 14 ft lbs.
NOTE: *All bearing caps are slightly offset. They should be installed so that the numbers on the cap read right side up from the driver's seat.*
12. Position a dial indicator so that the feeler touches the front end of the camshaft. Check for end play. Play should not exceed .006 in.
13. Place a new seal on the #1 bearing cap. If necessary, replace the end plug in the head.
14. Follow the procedures under Timing Belt Removal and Installation for belt installation and timing.
15. Check the valve clearance and ignition timing.

Timing Gears
REMOVAL AND INSTALLATION

The camshaft, intermediate shaft, and crankshaft pulleys are located by keys on their respective shafts and each is retained by a bolt. To remove any or all of the pulleys, first remove the timing belt cover and belt and then use the following procedure.

NOTE: *When removing the crankshaft pulley, don't remove the four socket head bolts which retain the outer belt pulley to the timing belt pulley.*

1. Remove the center bolt.
2. Gently pry the pulley off the shaft.
3. If the pulley is stubborn in coming off, use a gear puller. Don't hammer on the pulley.
4. Remove the pulley and key.
5. Install the pulley in the reverse order of removal.
6. Tighten the center bolt to 58 ft lbs.
7. Install the timing belt, check valve timing, tension belt, and install the cover.

Pistons and Connecting Rods
REMOVAL AND INSTALLATION

NOTE: *A complete step-by-step engine rebuilding section is included at the end of this chapter.*

1. Follow the instructions under "Cylinder Head" removal and "Timing Belt" removal.
2. Remove the oil pan as described later in this chapter.
3. This procedure is much easier performed with the engine out of the car.
4. Pistons should be removed in the order: 1-3-4-2. Turn the crankshaft until the piston to be removed is at the bottom of its stroke.
5. Place a cloth on the head of the piston to be removed and, using a ridge reamer, remove the deposits from the upper end of the cylinder bore.

NOTE: *Never remove more than $1/32$ in. from the ring travel area when removing the ridges.*

6. Mark all connecting rod bearing caps so that they may be returned to their original locations in the engine. The connecting rod caps are marked with rectangular forge marks which must be mated during assembly and be installed on the intermediate shaft side of the engine. Mark all pistons so they can be returned to their original cylinders.

CAUTION: *Don't score the cylinder walls or the crankshaft journal.*

7. Using an internal micrometer, measure the bores across the thrust faces of the cylinder and parallel to the axis of the crankshaft at a minimum of four equally spaced

ENGINE AND ENGINE REBUILDING 95

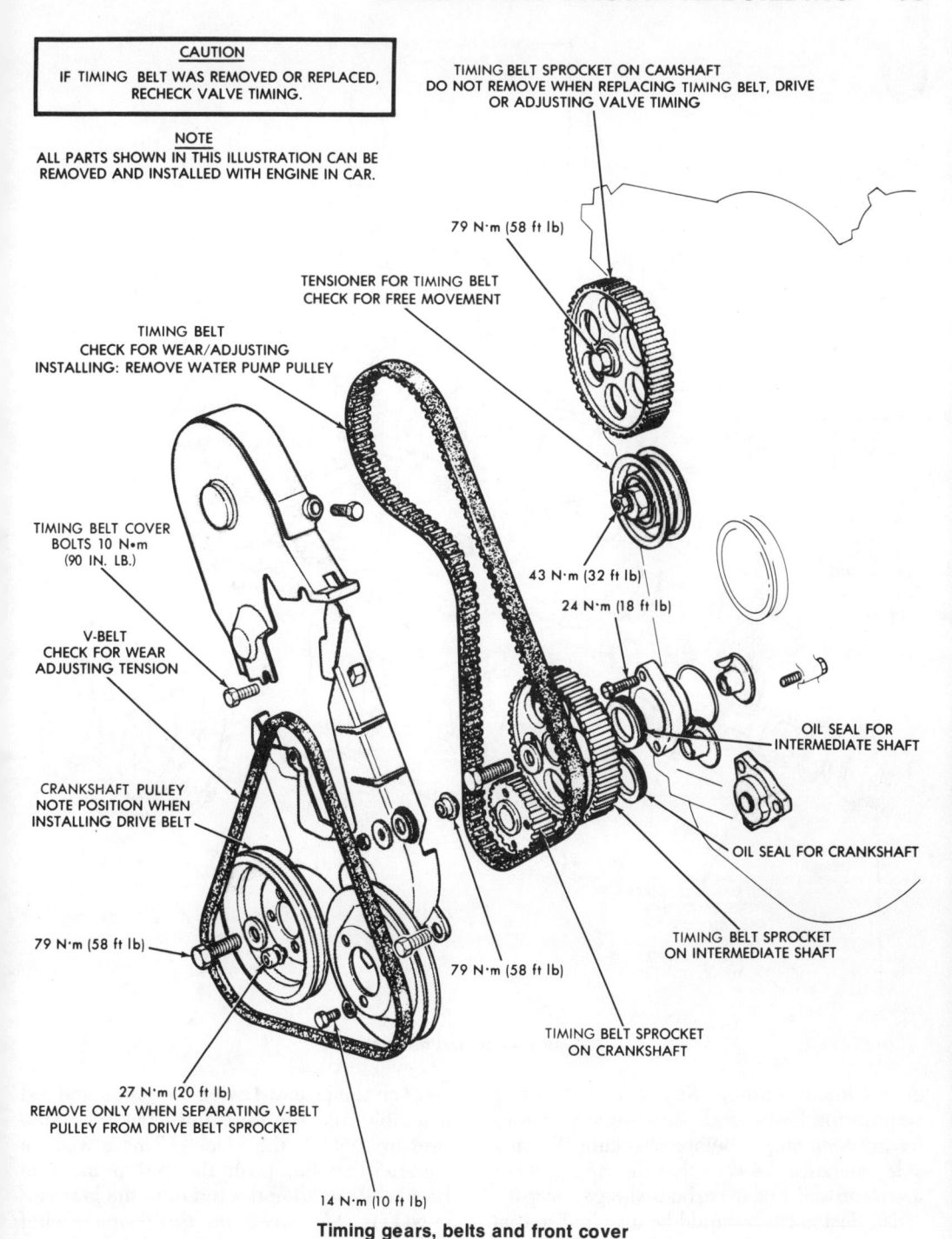

Timing gears, belts and front cover

locations. The bore must not be out-of-round by more than 0.005 in. and it must not taper more than 0.010 in. Taper is the difference in wear between two bore measurements in any cylinder. See the "Engine Rebuilding" section for complete details.

8. If the cylinder bore is in satisfactory condition, place each ring in the bore in turn and square it in the bore with the head of the piston. Measure the ring gap. If the ring gap is greater than the limit, get a new ring. If the ring gap is less than the limit, file the end of the ring to obtain the correct gap.

9. Check the ring side clearance by installing rings on the piston, and inserting a feeler gauge of the correct dimension between the ring and the lower land. The gauge should slide freely around the ring circumfer-

96 ENGINE AND ENGINE REBUILDING

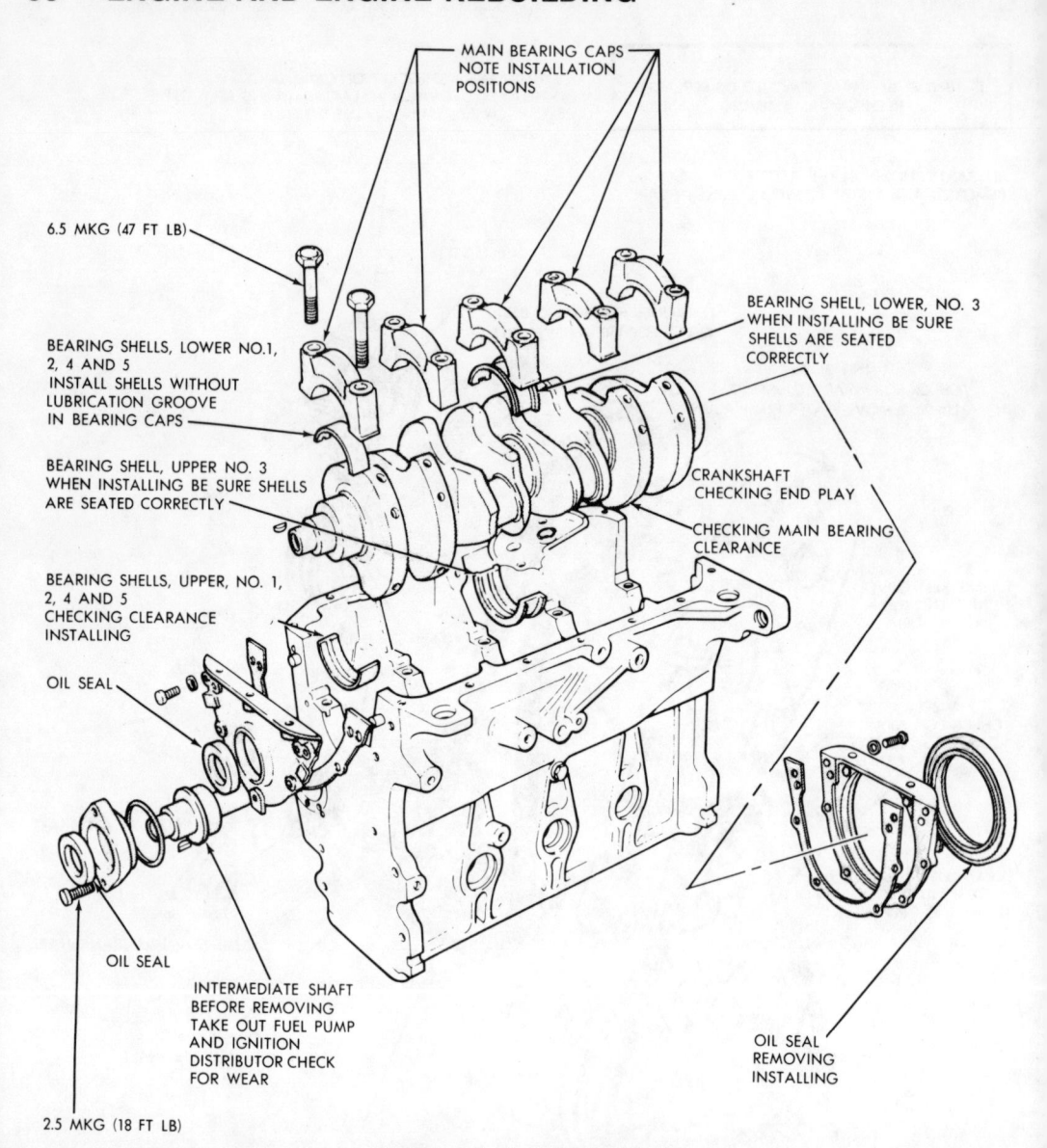

Cylinder block and crankshaft

ence without binding. Any wear will form a step on the lower land. Remove any pistons having high steps. Before checking the ring side clearance, be sure that the ring grooves are clean and free of carbon, sludge, or grit.

10. Piston rings should be installed so that their ends are at three equal spacings. Avoid installing the rings with their ends in line with the piston pin bosses and the thrust direction.

11. Install the pistons in their original bores, if you are reusing the same pistons. Install short lengths of rubber hose over the connecting rod bolts to prevent damage to the cylinder walls or rod journal.

12. Install a ring compressor over the rings on the piston. Lower the piston and rod assembly into the bore until the ring compressor contacts the block. Using a wooden hammer handle, push the piston into the bore while guiding the rod onto the journal.

NOTE: *The arrow on the piston should face toward the front (drive belt) of the engine.*

Engine Rebuilding Notes

Use the "Engine Rebuilding" section at the end of the chapter for cylinder head, block, and crankshaft refinishing. The main bearing shells with the lubricating grooves always go in the block, not the caps, for proper oiling.

ENGINE AND ENGINE REBUILDING 97

Piston and rings

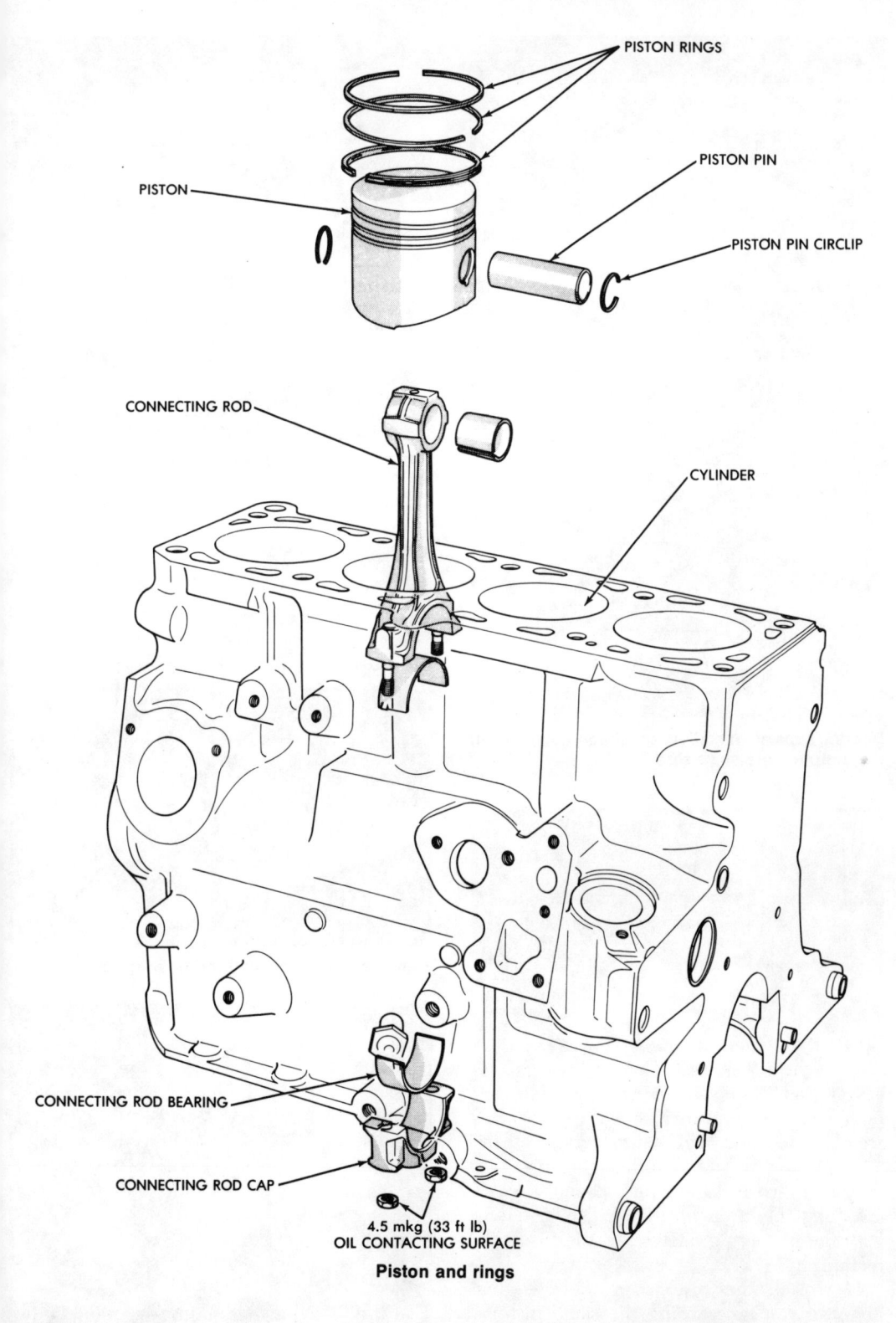

There is a piston size code stamped on the cylinder block above the water pump. Bring this number to the dealer when ordering a replacement piston(s).

ENGINE LUBRICATION

Lubrication is conventional with a gear type pump driven off the intermediate shaft. A

98 ENGINE AND ENGINE REBUILDING

Bearing caps are installed with the forge marks on the intermediate shaft side

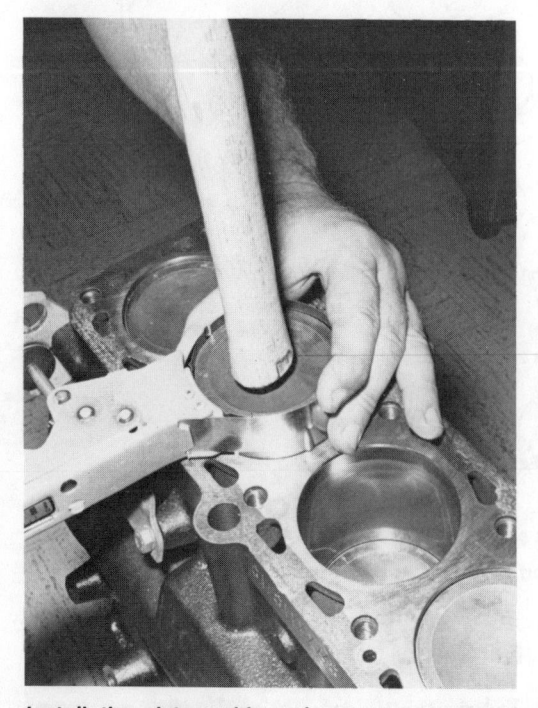

Tap the connecting rod bolts with a plastic mallet to loosen them

Remove the connecting rod bearing caps

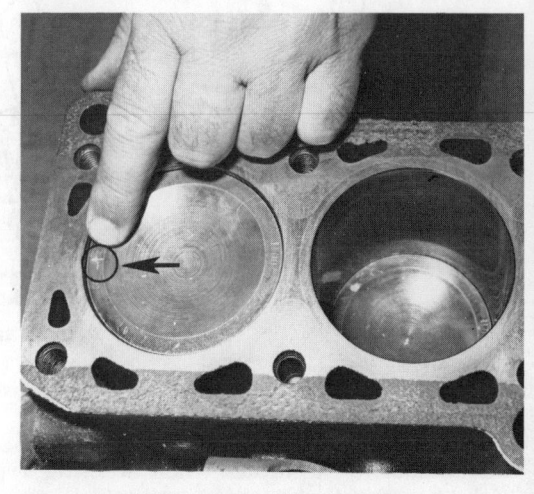

Install the piston with a ring compressor and wooden hammer handle

The arrow on the piston faces front

ENGINE AND ENGINE REBUILDING 99

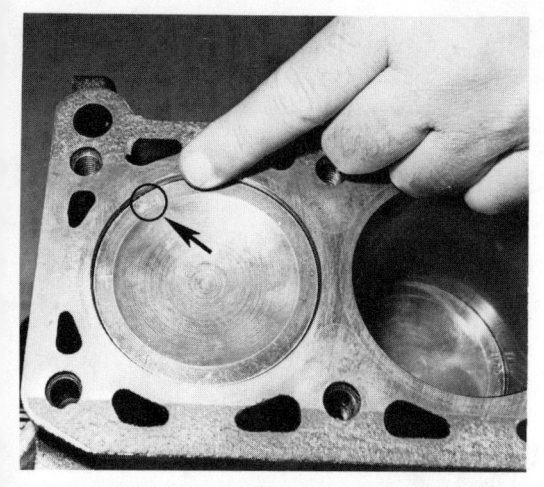

All pistons are stamped with a weight class

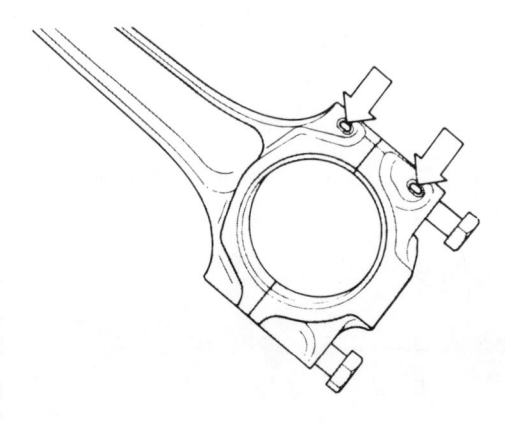

Connecting rod match marks

pressure relief valve prevents extreme pressure from building up in the system.

Oil Pan
REMOVAL AND INSTALLATION
1. Drain the oil pan.
2. Support the pan and remove the attaching bolts.
3. Lower the pan and discard the gaskets.
4. Clean all gasket surfaces thoroughly and install the pan using gasket sealer and a new gasket.
5. Torque the pan bolts to 7 ft lbs.
6. Refill the pan, start the engine, and check for leaks.

Oil Pump
REMOVAL AND INSTALLATION
1. Remove the oil pan.
2. Remove the two pump mounting bolts.
3. Pull the oil pump down and out of the engine.
4. Installation is the reverse of removal. Torque pump mounting bolts to 14 ft lbs.

Rear Main Seal
REMOVAL AND INSTALLATION

The rear main seal is located in a housing on the rear of the block. To replace the seal it is necessary to remove the engine.
1. Remove the transmission and flywheel.
CAUTION: *Before removing the transmission, align the dimple on the flywheel with the pointer on the flywheel housing. The transmission will not mate with the engine during installation unless this alignment is observed.*
2. Very carefully, pry the old seal out of the support ring with a screwdriver.
3. Coat the new seal with clean engine oil and press it into place with a flat piece of metal. Take great care not to scratch the seal or crankshaft.
4. Install the flywheel and transmission.

ENGINE COOLING

The cooling system consists of a radiator, overflow tank, water pump, thermostat, coolant temperature switch, electric fan and radiator fan switch. The use of an electric fan is necessitated by the transversely mounted engine. A radiator bypass system is used for faster warmup.

Radiator
REMOVAL AND INSTALLATION
1. Move the temperature selector to full on.
2. Open the radiator drain cock.
3. When the coolant reserve tank is empty, remove the radiator cap.
4. Remove the hoses.
5. Remove the upper and lower mounting brackets.
6. Remove the shroud.
7. Remove the fan motor attaching bolts.
8. Remove the top radiator attaching bolts.
9. Remove the bottom radiator attaching bolts.
10. Lift radiator from engine compartment.
11. Installation is the reverse of removal.

100 ENGINE AND ENGINE REBUILDING

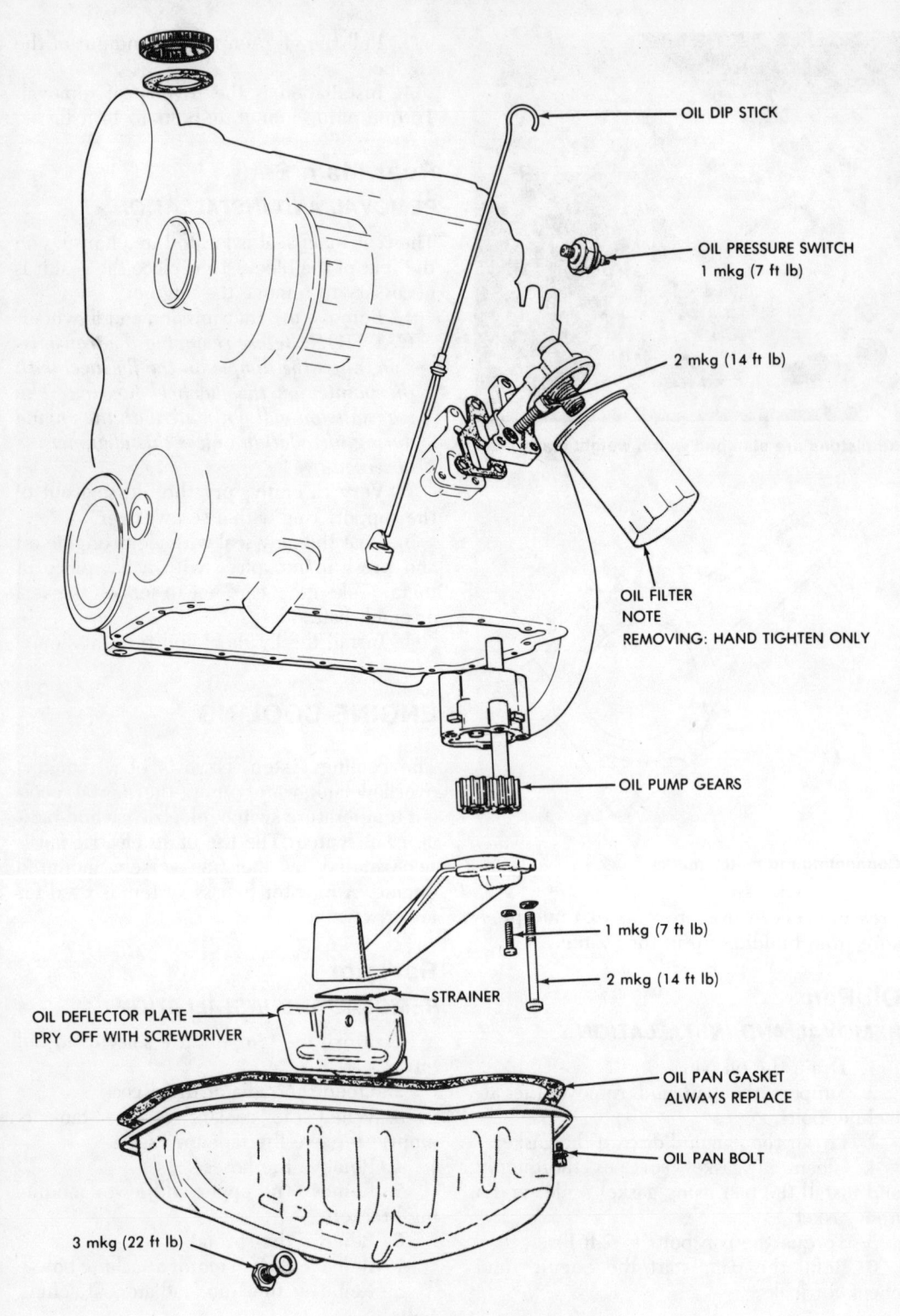

Engine lubrication components

- OIL DIP STICK
- OIL PRESSURE SWITCH — 1 mkg (7 ft lb)
- 2 mkg (14 ft lb)
- OIL FILTER NOTE REMOVING: HAND TIGHTEN ONLY
- OIL PUMP GEARS
- 1 mkg (7 ft lb)
- 2 mkg (14 ft lb)
- STRAINER
- OIL DEFLECTOR PLATE PRY OFF WITH SCREWDRIVER
- OIL PAN GASKET ALWAYS REPLACE
- OIL PAN BOLT
- 3 mkg (22 ft lb)

ENGINE AND ENGINE REBUILDING 101

Water Pump

REMOVAL AND INSTALLATION

1. Drain the cooling system.
2. Remove the drive belts.
3. Remove the water pump pulley.

Pry the rear main seal housing off as shown

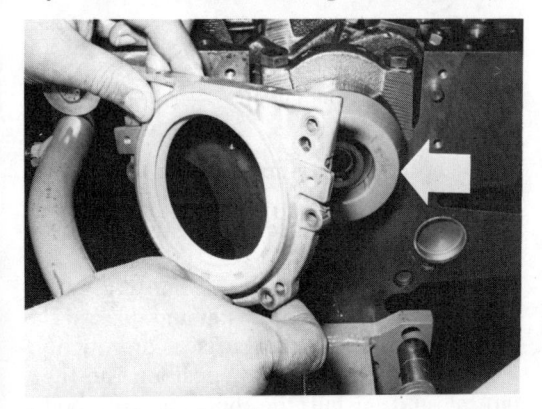

A rear main seal protector is necessary when installing the new seal

Check the rubber O-ring before installing the water pump

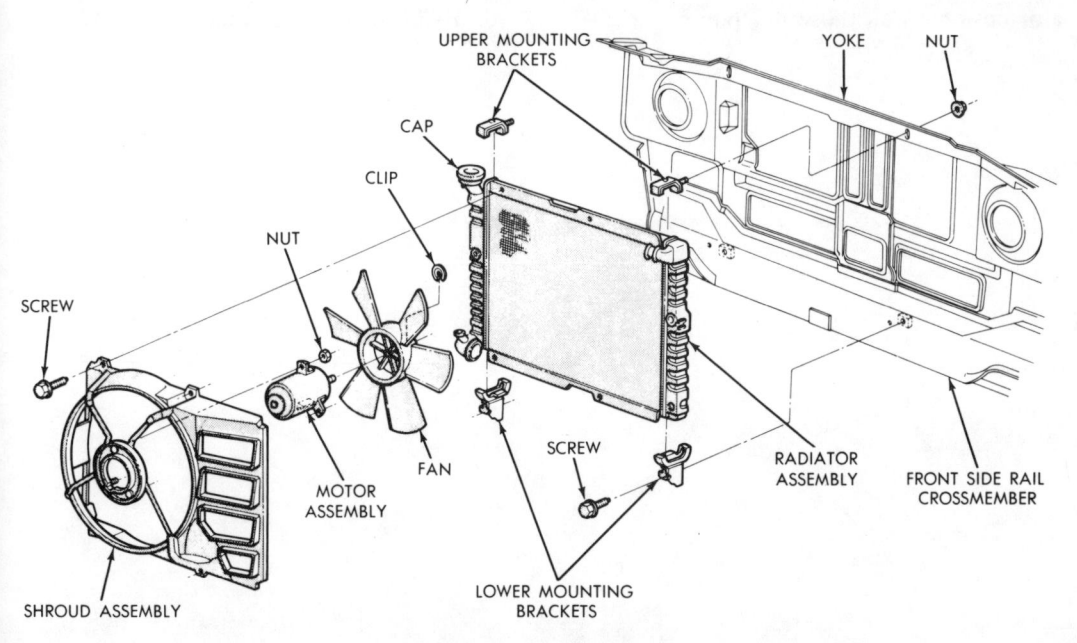

Radiator, fan and shroud

ENGINE AND ENGINE REBUILDING

The long bolt goes in the location shown

4. Unbolt the compressor and/or air pump brackets from the water pump and secure them out of the way.
5. Position the bypass hose lower clamp in the center of the hose and disconnect the heater hose.
6. Unbolt and remove the water pump. Discard the gasket and clean the gasket surfaces.
7. Installation is the reverse of removal. Torque the water pump bolts to 25 ft lbs, the alternator adjusting bolt to 30–50 ft lbs; the pulley bolts to 85–125 in. lbs.

Thermostat

REMOVAL AND INSTALLATION

The thermostat is located in the bottom radiator hose neck on the water pump.

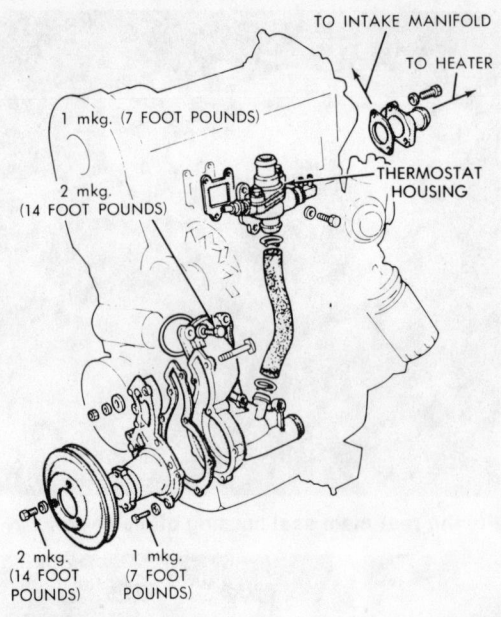

Engine cooling components

1. Drain the cooling system to a level below the thermostat.
2. Remove the hoses from the thermostat housing.
3. Remove the thermostat housing.
4. Remove the thermostat and discard the gasket. Clean the gasket surfaces thoroughly.
5. Using a new gasket, position the thermostat and install the housing and bolts. Make sure that the thermostat is seated properly.
6. Refill the cooling system.

Engine Rebuilding

This section describes, in detail, the procedures involved in rebuilding a typical engine. The procedures specifically refer to an inline engine, however, they are basically identical to those used in rebuilding engines of nearly all design and configurations. Procedures for servicing atypical engines (i.e., horizontally opposed) are described in the appropriate section, although in most cases, cylinder head reconditioning procedures described in this chapter will apply.

The section is divided into two sections. The first, Cylinder Head Reconditioning, assumes that the cylinder head is removed from the engine, all manifolds are removed, and the cylinder head is on a workbench. The camshaft should be removed from overhead cam cylinder heads. The second section, Cyl-

Torque (ft. lbs.)*

U.S./Bolt Grade (SAE)

Bolt Diameter (inches)	1 and 2	5	6	8	Wrench Size (inches) Bolt	Nut
1/4	5	7	10	10.5	3/8	7/16
5/16	9	14	19	22	1/2	9/16
3/8	15	25	34	37	9/16	5/8
7/16	24	40	55	60	5/8	3/4
1/2	37	60	85	92	3/4	13/16
9/16	53	88	120	132	7/8	7/8
5/8	74	120	167	180	15/16	1
3/4	120	200	280	296	1 1/8	1 1/8
7/8	190	302	440	473	1 5/16	1 5/16
1	282	466	660	714	1 1/2	1 1/2

Metric/Bolt Grade

Bolt Diameter (mm)	5D	8G	10K	12K	Wrench Size (mm) Bolt and Nut
6	5	6	8	10	10
8	10	16	22	27	14
10	19	31	40	49	17
12	34	54	70	86	19
14	55	89	117	137	22
16	83	132	175	208	24
18	111	182	236	283	27
22	182	284	394	464	32
24	261	419	570	689	36

*—Torque values are for lightly oiled bolts. CAUTION: Bolts threaded into aluminum require much less torque.

ENGINE AND ENGINE REBUILDING

inder Block Reconditioning, covers the block, pistons, connecting rods and crankshaft. It is assumed that the engine is mounted on a work stand, and the cylinder head and all accessories are removed.

Procedures are identified as follows:

Unmarked—Basic procedures that must be performed in order to successfully complete the rebuilding process.

Starred (*)—Procedures that should be performed to ensure maximum performance and engine life.

Double starred (**)—Procedures that may be performed to increase engine performance and reliability. These procedures are usually reserved for extremely heavy-duty or competition usage.

In many cases, a choice of methods is also provided. Methods are identified in the same manner as procedures. The choice of method for a procedure is at the discretion of the user.

The tools required for the basic rebuilding procedure should, with minor exceptions, be those included in a mechanic's tool kit. An accurate torque wrench, and a dial indicator (reading in thousandths) mounted on a universal base should be available. Bolts and nuts with no torque specification should be tightened according to size (see chart). Special tools, where required, all are readily available from the major tool suppliers (i.e., Craftsman, Snap-On, K-D). The services of a competent automotive machine shop must also be readily available.

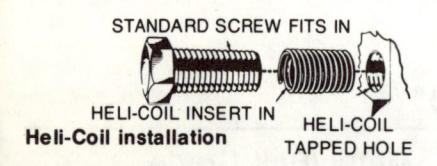

Heli-Coil installation

When assembling the engine, any parts that will be in frictional contact must be pre-lubricated, to provide protection on initial start-up. Vortex Pre-Lube, STP, or any product specifically formulated for this purpose may be used. NOTE: *Do not use engine oil*. Where semi-permanent (locked but removable) installation of bolts or nuts is desired, threads should be cleaned and coated with Loctite. Studs may be permanently installed using Loctite Stud and Bearing Mount.

Aluminum has become increasingly popular for use in engines, due to its low weight and excellent heat transfer characteristics. The following precautions must be observed when handling aluminum engine parts:

—Never hot-tank aluminum parts.

—Remove all aluminum parts (identification tags, etc.) from engine parts before hot-tanking (otherwise they will be removed during the process).

—Always coat threads lightly with engine oil or anti-seize compounds before installation, to prevent seizure.

—Never over-torque bolts or spark plugs in aluminum threads. Should stripping occur, threads can be restored according to the following procedure, using Heli-Coil thread inserts:

Tap drill the hole with the stripped threads to the specified size (see chart). Using the specified tap (NOTE: *Heli-Coil tap sizes refer to the size thread being replaced, rather than the actual tap size*), tap the hole for the Heli-Coil. place the insert on the proper installation tool (see chart). Apply pressure on the insert while winding it clockwise into the hole, until the top of the insert is one turn below the surface. Remove the installation tool, and break the installation tang from the bottom of the insert by moving it up and down. If the Heli-Coil must be removed, tap the removal tool firmly into the hole, so that it engages the top thread, and turn the tool counter-clockwise to extract that insert.

Snapped bolts or studs may be removed, using a stud extractor (unthreaded) or Vise-Grip pliers (threaded). Penetrating oil (e.g., Liquid Wrench) will often aid in breaking frozen threads. In cases where the stud or bolt is flush with, or below the surface, proceed as follows:

Drill a hole in the broken stud or bolt, approximately $1/2$ its diameter. Select a screw extractor (e.g., Easy-Out) of the proper size, and tap it into the stud or bolt. Turn the extractor counter-clockwise to remove the stud or bolt.

Magnaflux and Zyglo are inspection techniques used to locate material flaws, such as stress cracks. Magnafluxing coats the part with

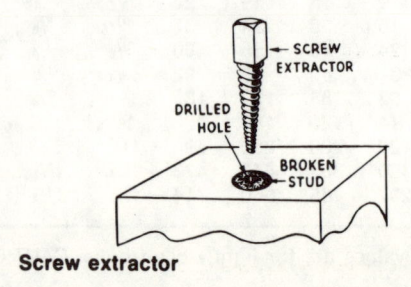

Screw extractor

ENGINE AND ENGINE REBUILDING

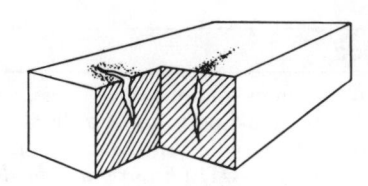

Magnaflux indication of cracks

fine magnetic particles, and subjects the part to a magnetic field. Cracks cause breaks in the magnetic field, which are outlined by the particles. Since Magnaflux is a magnetic process, it is applicable only to ferrous materials. The Zyglo process coats the material with a fluorescent dye penetrant, and then subjects it to blacklight inspection, under which cracks glow brightly. Parts made of any material may be tested using Zyglo. While Magnaflux and Zyglo are excellent for general inspection, and locating hidden defects, specific checks of suspected cracks may be made at lower cost and more readily using spot check dye. The dye is sprayed onto the suspected area, wiped off, and the area is then sprayed with a developer. Cracks then will show up brightly. Spot check dyes will only indicate surface cracks; therefore, structural cracks below the surface may escape detection. When questionable, the part should be tested using Magnaflux or Zyglo.

NOTE: *This engine rebuilding section is a guide to accepted engine rebuilding procedures. Every effort is made to illustrate the engine(s) used by this manufacturer; but, occasionally, typical examples of standard engine rebuilding practice are illustrated.*

Cylinder Head Reconditioning

Procedure	Method
Identify the valves:	Invert the cylinder head, and number the valve faces front to rear, using a permanent felt-tip marker.
Remove the valves and springs:	Using an appropriate valve spring compressor (depending on the configuration of the cylinder head), compress the valve springs. Lift out the keepers with needlenose pliers, release the compressor, and remove the valve, spring, and spring retainer.
Check the valve stem-to-guide clearance:	Clean the valve stem with lacquer thinner or a similar solvent to remove all gum and varnish. Clean the valve guides using solvent and an expanding wire-type valve guide cleaner. Mount a dial indicator so that the stem is at 90° to the valve stem, as close to the valve guide as possible. Move the valve off its seat, and measure the valve guide-to-stem clearance by moving the stem back and forth to actuate the dial indicator. Measure the valve stems using a micrometer, and compare to specifications, to determine whether stem or guide wear is responsible for excessive clearance.

Valve identification

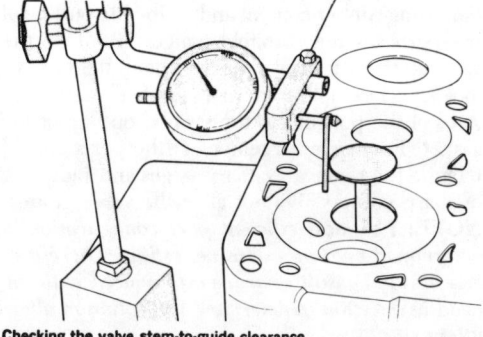

Checking the valve stem-to-guide clearance

106 ENGINE AND ENGINE REBUILDING

Procedure	Method
De-carbon the cylinder head and valves: 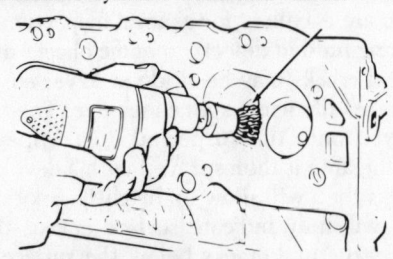 *Removing carbon from the cylinder head*	Chip carbon away from the valve heads, combustion chambers, and ports, using a chisel made of hardwood. Remove the remaining deposits with a stiff wire brush. **NOTE:** *Ensure that the deposits are actually removed, rather than burnished.*
Degrease the cylinder head: **CAUTION:** *Do not hot-tank the aluminum cylinder head.*	Have the cylinder head degreased to remove grease, corrosion, and scale from the water passages. **NOTE:** *In the case of overhead cam cylinder heads, consult the operator to determine whether the camshaft bearings will be damaged by the caustic solution.*
Check the cylinder head for warpage: 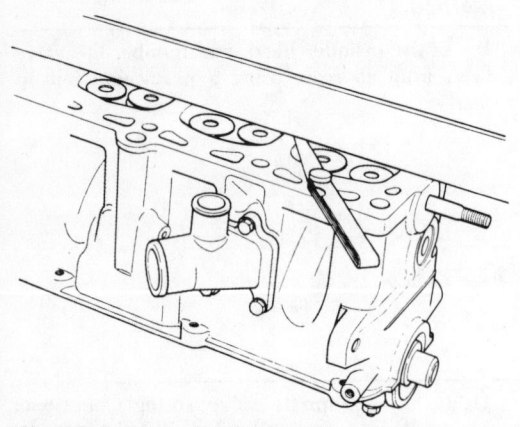 *Checking the cylinder head for warpage*	Place a straight-edge across the gasket surface of the cylinder head. Using feeler gauges, determine the clearance at the center of the straight-edge. Measure across both diagonals, along the longitudinal centerline, and across the cylinder head at several points. If warpage exceeds .003" in a 6" span, or .006" over the total length, the cylinder head must be resurfaced. **NOTE:** *If warpage exceeds the manufacturers maximum tolerance for material removal, the cylinder head must be replaced.* When milling the cylinder heads of V-type engines, the intake manifold mounting position is altered, and must be corrected by milling the manifold flange a proportionate amount.
Porting and gasket matching:	** Coat the manifold flanges of the cylinder head with Prussian blue dye. Glue intake and exhaust gaskets to the cylinder head in their installed position using rubber cement and scribe the outline of the ports on the manifold flanges. Remove the gaskets. Using a small cutter in a hand-held power tool (i.e., Dremel Moto-Tool), gradually taper the walls of the port out to the scribed outline of the gasket. Further enlargement of the ports should include the removal of sharp edges and radiusing of sharp corners. Do not alter the valve guides. **NOTE:** *The most efficient port configuration is determined only by extensive testing. Therefore, it is best to consult someone experienced with the head in question to determine the optimum alterations.*

ENGINE AND ENGINE REBUILDING 107

Procedure	Method
Polish the ports:	** Using a grinding stone with the above mentioned tool, polish the walls of the intake and exhaust ports, and combustion chamber. Use progressively finer stones until all surface imperfections are removed. **NOTE:** *Through testing, it has been determined that a smooth surface is more effective than a mirror polished surface in intake ports, and vice-versa in exhaust ports.*
* Knurling the valve guides: 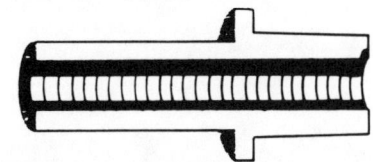 Cut-away view of a knurled valve guide	* Valve guides which are not excessively worn or distorted may, in some cases, be knurled rather than replaced. Knurling is a process in which metal is displaced and raised, thereby reducing clearance. Knurling also provides excellent oil control. The possibility of knurling rather than replacing valve guides should be discussed with a machinist.
Checking/replacing the valve guides: **NOTE:** *Valve guides should only be replaced if damaged or if an oversize valve stem is not available.* 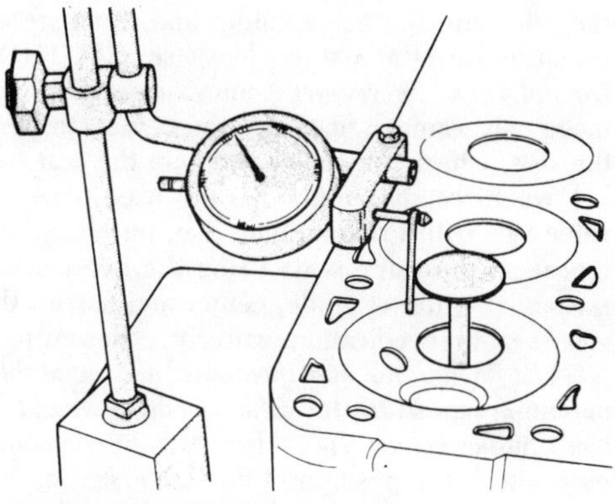 Checking valve guide for wear	** Check the valve guides by inserting a new valve in the guide and rocking it back and forth against a dial indicator. The dial indicator reading shows wear (max. 0.039 in. intake or 0.051 in. exhaust). Worn guides can be pressed out from the combustion chamber side. Coat new guides with oil and press them in from the camshaft side as far as they will go. Once the guide is seated, do not use more than 1 ton pressure.
Ream the valve guides: 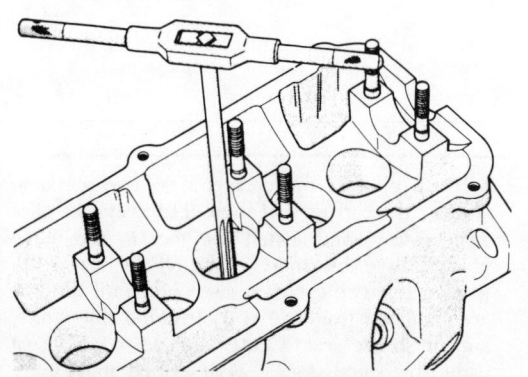 Reaming valve guides with a hand reamer	Using the proper cutting lubricant, ream the valve guides to the individual valves.

ENGINE AND ENGINE REBUILDING

Procedure	Method
Replacing valve seat inserts:	Replacement of valve seat inserts which are worn beyond resurfacing or broken, if feasible, must be done by a machine shop.
Resurfacing (grinding) the valve face:	Using a valve grinder, resurface the valves according to specifications. **CAUTION:** *Valve face angle is not always identical to valve seat angle.* A minimum margin of 1/32" should remain after grinding the valve. The valve stem tip should also be squared and resurfaced, by placing the stem in the V-block of the grinder, and turning it while pressing lightly against the grinding wheel.

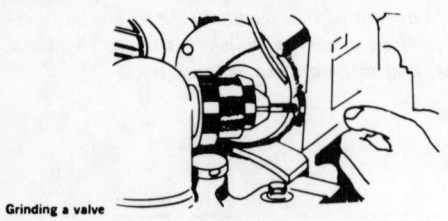

Grinding a valve

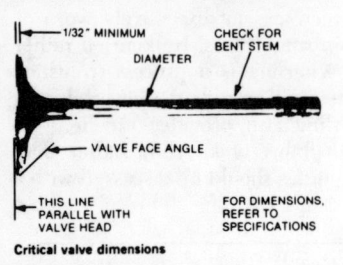

Critical valve dimensions

| Resurfacing the valve seats using reamers: | Select a reamer of the correct seat angle, slightly larger than the diameter of the valve seat, and assemble it with a pilot of the correct size. Install the pilot into the valve guide, and using steady pressure, turn the reamer clockwise. **CAUTION:** *Do not turn the reamer counter-clockwise.* Remove only as much material as necessary to clean the seat. Check the concentricity of the seat (see below). If the dye method is not used, coat the valve face with Prussian blue dye, install and rotate it on the valve seat. Using the dye marked area as a centering guide, center and narrow the valve seat to specifications with correction cutters. **NOTE:** *When no specifications are available, minimum seat width for exhaust valves should be 5/64", intake valves 1/16".* After making correction cuts, check the position of the valve seat on the valve face using Prussian blue dye. |

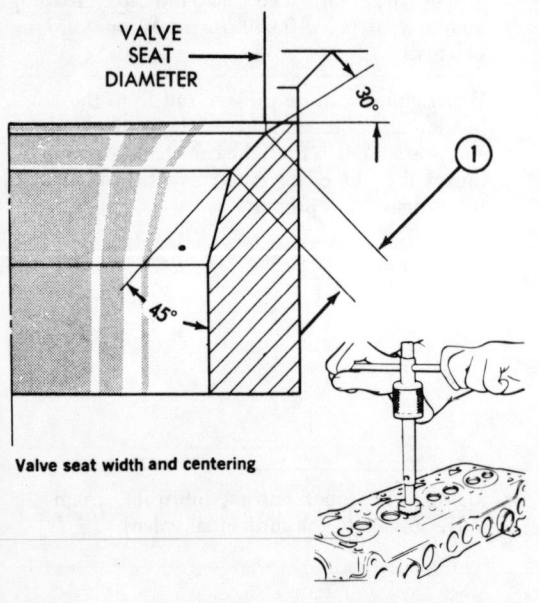

Valve seat width and centering

Reaming the valve seat

| * Resurfacing the valve seats using a grinder: | Select a pilot of the correct size, and a coarse stone of the correct seat angle. Lubricate the pilot if necessary, and install the tool in the valve guide. Move the stone on and off the seat at approximately two cycles per second, until all flaws are removed from the seat. Install a fine stone, and finish the seat. Center and narrow the seat using correction stones, as described above. |

ENGINE AND ENGINE REBUILDING 109

Procedure	Method
Checking the valve seat concentricity:	Coat the valve face with Prussian blue dye, install the valve, and rotate it on the valve seat. If the entire seat becomes coated, and the valve is known to be concentric, the seat is concentric.
	* Install the dial gauge pilot into the guide, and rest the arm on the valve seat. Zero the gauge, and rotate the arm around the seat. Run-out should not exceed .002".

Checking the valve seat concentricity using a dial gauge

* Lapping the valves: NOTE: *Valve lapping is done to ensure efficient sealing of resurfaced valves and seats. Valve lapping alone is not recommended for use as a resurfacing procedure.*	* Invert the cylinder head, lightly lubricate the valve stems, and install the valves in the head as numbered. Coat valve seats with fine grinding compound, and attach the lapping tool suction cup to a valve head (NOTE: *Moisten the suction cup*). Rotate the tool between the palms, changing position and lifting the tool often to prevent grooving. Lap the valve until a smooth, polished seat is evident. Remove the valve and tool, and rinse away all traces of grinding compound.
	** Fasten a suction cup to a piece of drill rod, and mount the rod in a hand drill. Proceed as above, using the hand drill as a lapping tool. CAUTION: *Due to the higher speeds involved when using the hand drill, care must be exercised to avoid grooving the seat.* Lift the tool and change direction of rotation often.

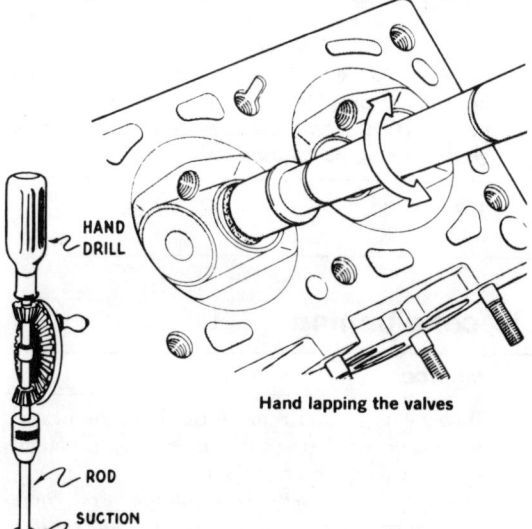

Hand lapping the valves

Home made mechanical valve lapping tool

Check the valve springs:	Place the spring on a flat surface next to a square. Measure the height of the spring, and rotate it against the edge of the square to measure distortion. If spring height varies (by comparison) by more than $1/16$" or if distortion exceeds $1/16$", replace the spring.
	** In addition to evaluating the spring as above, test the spring pressure at the installed and compressed (installed height minus valve lift) height using a valve spring tester. Springs used on small displacement engines (up to 3 liters) should be ± 1 lb of all other springs in either position. A tolerance of ± 5 lbs is permissible on larger engines.

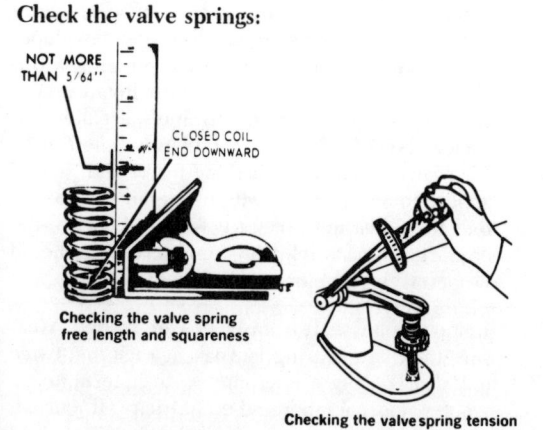

Checking the valve spring free length and squareness

Checking the valve spring tension

110 ENGINE AND ENGINE REBUILDING

Procedure	Method
* Install valve stem seals: *Installing valve stem seals*	* Due to the pressure differential that exists at the ends of the intake valve guides (atmospheric pressure above, manifold vacuum below), oil is drawn through the valve guides into the intake port. This has been alleviated somewhat since the addition of positive crankcase ventilation, which lowers the pressure above the guides. Several types of valve stem seals are available to reduce blow-by. Certain seals simply slip over the stem and guide boss, while others require that the boss be machined. Recently, Teflon guide seals have become popular. Consult a parts supplier or machinist concerning availability and suggested usages. **NOTE:** *When installing seals, ensure that a small amount of oil is able to pass the seal to lubricate the valve guides; otherwise, excessive wear may result.*
Install the valves:	Lubricate the valve stems, and install the valves in the cylinder head as numbered. Lubricate and position the seals (if used, see above) and the valve springs. Install the spring retainers, compress the springs, and insert the keys using needlenose pliers or a tool designed for this purpose. **NOTE:** *Retain the keys with wheel bearing grease during installation.*
Inspect the camshaft bushings and the camshaft (overhead cam engines):	See next section.

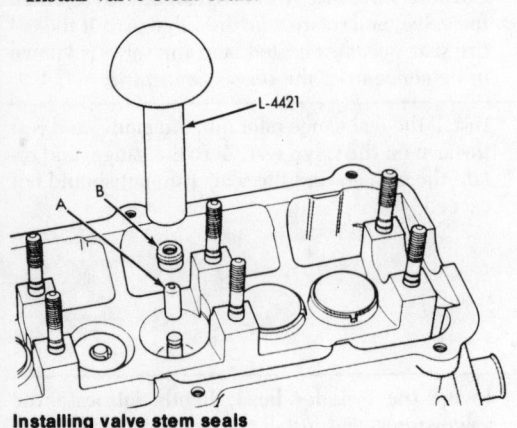

Cylinder Block Reconditioning

Procedure	Method
Checking the main bearing clearance: *Installing Plastigage on lower bearing shell* *Measuring Plastigage to determine bearing clearance*	Invert engine, and remove cap from the bearing to be checked. Using a clean, dry rag, thoroughly clean all oil from crankshaft journal and bearing insert. **NOTE:** *Plastigage is soluble in oil; therefore, oil on the journal or bearing could result in erroneous readings.* Place a piece of Plastigage along the full length of journal, reinstall cap, and torque to specifications. Remove bearing cap, and determine bearing clearance by comparing width of Plastigage to the scale on Plastigage envelope. Journal taper is determined by comparing width of the Plastigage strip near its ends. Rotate crankshaft 90° and retest, to determine journal eccentricity. **NOTE:** *Do not rotate crankshaft with Plastigage installed.* If bearing insert and journal appear intact, and are within tolerances, no further main bearing service is required. If bearing or journal appear defective, cause of failure should be determined before replacement. * Remove crankshaft from block (see below). Measure the main bearing journals at each end twice (90° apart) using a micrometer, to determine diameter, journal taper and eccentricity. If journals are within tolerances, reinstall bearing caps at

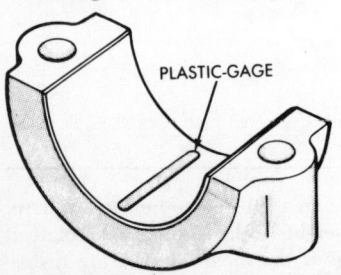

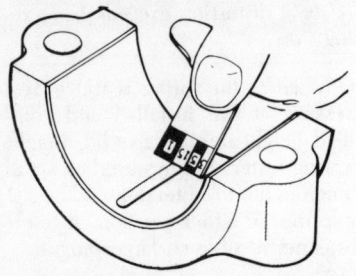

ENGINE AND ENGINE REBUILDING 111

Procedure	Method
	their specified torque. Using a telescope gauge and micrometer, measure bearing I.D. parallel to piston axis and at 30° on each side of piston axis. Subtract journal O.D. from bearing I.D. to determine oil clearance. If crankshaft journals appear defective, or do not meet tolerances, there is no need to measure bearings; for the crankshaft will require grinding and/or undersize bearings will be required. If bearing appears defective, cause for failure should be determined prior to replacement.
Checking the connecting rod bearing clearance:	Connecting rod bearing clearance is checked in the same manner as main bearing clearance, using Plastigage. Before removing the crankshaft, connecting rod side clearance also should be measured and recorded.
	* Checking connecting rod bearing clearance, using a micrometer, is identical to checking main bearing clearance. If no other service is required, the piston and rod assemblies need not be removed.
Removing the crankshaft: 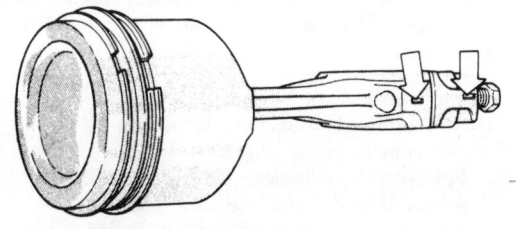 **Connecting rod matchmarks**	Using a punch, mark the corresponding main bearing caps and saddles according to position (i.e., one punch on the front main cap and saddle, two on the second, three on the third, etc.). Using number stamps, identify the corresponding connecting rods and caps, according to cylinder (if no numbers are present). Remove the main and connecting rod caps, and place sleeves of plastic tubing over the connecting rod bolts, to protect the journals as the crankshaft is removed. Lift the crankshaft out of the block.
Remove the ridge from the top of the cylinder: RIDGE CAUSED BY CYLINDER WEAR CYLINDER WALL TOP OF PISTON **Cylinder bore ridge**	In order to facilitate removal of the piston and connecting rod, the ridge at the top of the cylinder (unknown area; see illustration) must be removed. Place the piston at the bottom of the bore, and cover it with a rag. Cut the ridge away using a ridge reamer, exercising extreme care to avoid cutting too deeply. Remove the rag, and remove cuttings that remain on the piston. **CAUTION:** *If the ridge is not removed, and new rings are installed, damage to rings will result.*
Removing the piston and connecting rod: 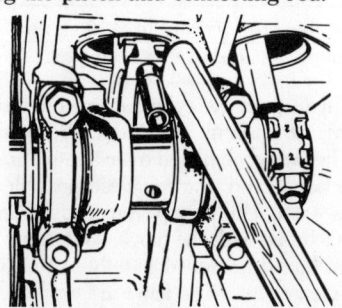 **Removing the piston**	Invert the engine, and push the pistons and connecting rods out of the cylinders. If necessary, tap the connecting rod boss with a wooden hammer handle, to force the piston out. **CAUTION:** *Do not attempt to force the piston past the cylinder ridge* (see above).

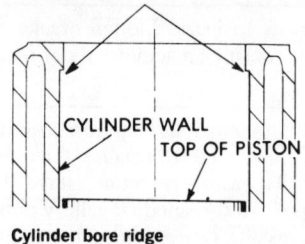

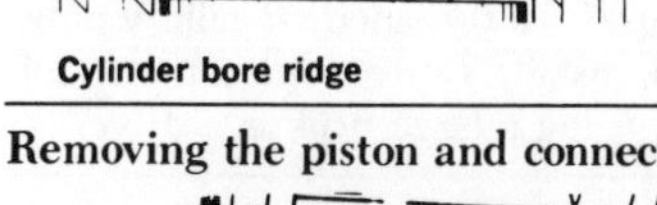

112 ENGINE AND ENGINE REBUILDING

Procedure	Method
Service the crankshaft:	Ensure that all oil holes and passages in the crankshaft are open and free of sludge. If necessary, have the crankshaft ground to the largest possible undersize.
	** Have the crankshaft Magnafluxed, to locate stress cracks. Consult a machinist concerning additional service procedures, such as surface hardening (e.g., nitriding, Tuftriding) to improve wear characteristics, cross drilling and chamfering the oil holes to improve lubrication, and balancing.
Removing freeze plugs:	Drill a small hole in the center of the freeze plugs, and remove them with a sheetmetal screw and slide hammer.
Remove the oil gallery plugs:	Threaded plugs should be removed using an appropriate (usually square) wrench. To remove soft, pressed in plugs, drill a hole in the plug, and thread in a sheet metal screw. Pull the plug out by the screw using a slide hammer.
Hot-tank the block:	Have the block hot-tanked to remove grease, corrosion, and scale from the water jackets. **NOTE:** *Consult the operator to determine whether the bearings will be damaged during the hot-tank process.*

Check the block for cracks:	Visually inspect the block for cracks or chips. The most common locations are as follows:
	     Adjacent to freeze plugs.
	     Between the cylinders and water jackets.
	     Adjacent to the main bearing saddles.
	     At the extreme bottom of the cylinders.
	 Check only suspected cracks using spot check dye (see introduction). If a crack is located, consult a machinist concerning possible repairs.

	** Magnaflux the block to locate hidden cracks. If cracks are located, consult a machinist about feasibility of repair.
Install the oil gallery plugs and freeze plugs:	Coat freeze plugs with sealer and tap into position using a piece of pipe, slightly smaller than the plug, as a driver. To ensure retention, stake the edges of the plugs. Coat threaded oil gallery plugs with sealer and install. Drive replacement soft plugs into block using a large drift as a driver.
	* Rather than reinstalling lead plugs, drill and tap the holes, and install threaded plugs.
Check the bore diameter and surface:	Visually inspect the cylinder bores for roughness, scoring, or scuffing. If evident, the cylinder bore must be bored or honed oversize to eliminate imperfections, and the smallest possible oversize piston used. The new pistons should be given to the machinist with the block, so that the cylinders can be bored or honed exactly to the piston size (plus clearance). If no flaws are evident, measure the bore diameter using a telescope gauge and mi-

ENGINE AND ENGINE REBUILDING   113

Procedure	Method

crometer, or dial gauge, parallel and perpendicular to the engine centerline, at the top (below the ridge) and bottom of the bore. Subtract the bottom measurements from the top to determine taper, and the parallel to the centerline measurements from the perpendicular measurements to determine eccentricity. If the measurements are not within specifications, the cylinder must be bored or honed, and an oversize piston installed. If the measurements are within specifications the cylinder may be used as is, with only finish honing (see below). **NOTE:** *Prior to submitting the block for boring, perform the following operation(s).*

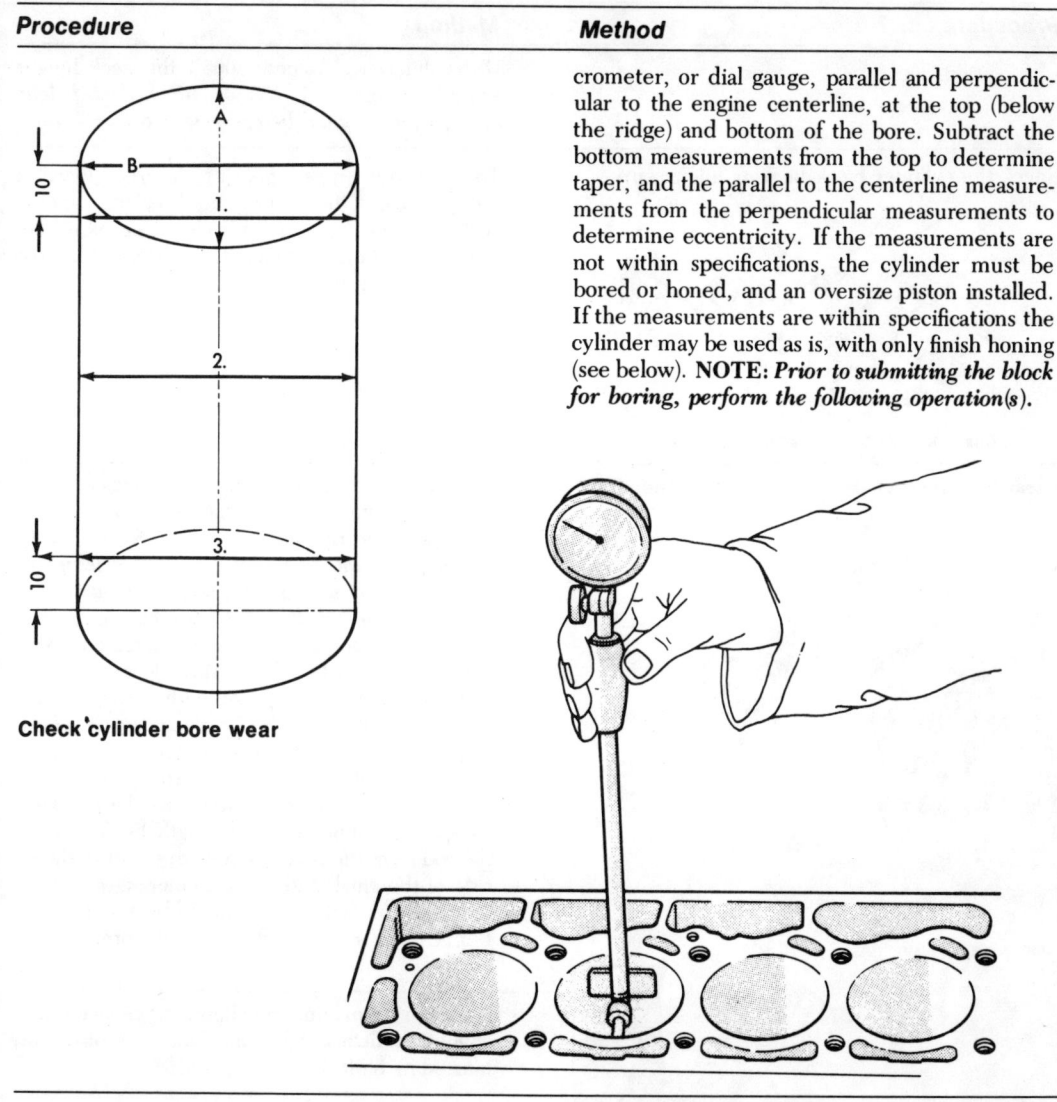

Check cylinder bore wear

Check the block deck for warpage:

Using a straightedge and feeler gauges, check the block deck for warpage in the same manner that the cylinder head is checked (see Cylinder Head Reconditioning). If warpage exceeds specifications, have the deck resurfaced. **NOTE:** *In certain cases a specification for total material removal (cylinder head and block deck) is provided. This specification must not be exceeded.*

* Check the deck height:

The deck height is the distance from the crankshaft centerline to the block deck. To measure, invert the engine, and install the crankshaft, retaining it with the center main cap. Measure the distance from the crankshaft journal to the block deck, parallel to the cylinder centerline. Measure the diameter of the end (front and rear) main journals, parallel to the centerline of the cylinders, divide the diameter in half, and subtract it from the previous measurement. The results of the front and rear measurements should be identical.

ENGINE AND ENGINE REBUILDING

Procedure	Method
	If the difference exceeds .005" the deck height should be corrected. **NOTE:** *Block deck height and warpage should be corrected concurrently.*
Check the cylinder block bearing alignment:  *Checking main bearing saddle alignment*	Remove the upper bearing inserts. Place a straightedge in the bearing saddles along the centerline of the crankshaft. If clearance exists between the straightedge and the center saddle, the block must be align-bored.
Clean and inspect the pistons and connecting rods: *Removing the piston rings* *Connecting rod length checking dimension*	Using a ring expander, remove the rings from the piston. Remove the retaining rings (if so equipped) and remove piston pin. **NOTE:** *If the piston pin must be pressed out, determine the proper method and use the proper tools; otherwise the piston will distort.* Clean the ring grooves using an appropriate tool, exercising care to avoid cutting too deeply. Thoroughly clean all carbon and varnish from the piston with solvent. **CAUTION:** *Do not use a wire brush or caustic solvent on pistons.* Inspect the pistons for scuffing, scoring, cracks, pitting, or excessive ring groove wear. If wear is evident, the piston must be replaced. Check the connecting rod length by measuring the rod from the inside of the large end to the inside of the small end using calipers (see illustration). All connecting rods should be equal length. Replace any rod that differs from the others in the engine. * Have the connecting rod alignment checked in an alignment fixture by a machinist. Replace any twisted or bent rods. * Magnaflux the connecting rods to locate stress cracks. If cracks are found, replace the connecting rod.
Fit the pistons to the cylinders: 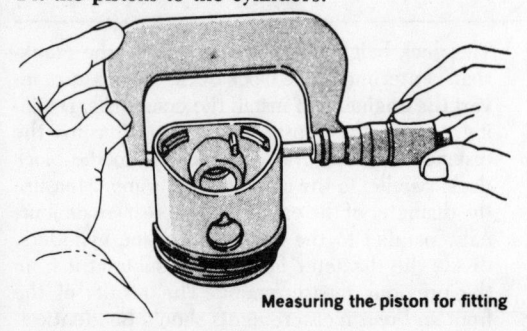 *Measuring the piston for fitting*	Using a telescope gauge and micrometer, or a dial gauge, measure the cylinder bore diameter perpendicular to the piston pin, 2½" below the deck. Measure the piston perpendicular to its pin on the skirt. The difference between the two measurements is the piston clearance. If the clearance is within specifications or slightly below (after boring or honing), finish honing is all that is required. If the clearance is excessive, try to obtain a slightly larger piston to bring clearance within specifications. Where this is not possible, obtain the first oversize piston, and hone (or if necessary, bore) the cylinder to size.

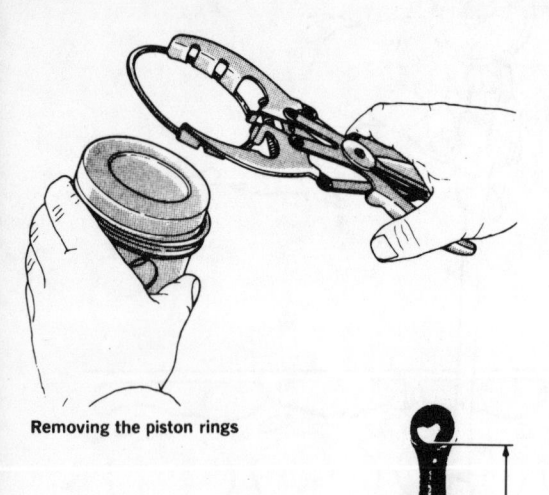

ENGINE AND ENGINE REBUILDING 115

Procedure	Method
Assemble the pistons and connecting rods: *Installing piston pin lock rings*	Inspect piston pin, connecting rod small end bushing, and piston bore for galling, scoring, or excessive wear. If evident, replace defective part(s). Measure the I.D. of the piston boss and connecting rod small end, and the O.D. of the piston pin. If within specifications, assemble piston pin and rod. **CAUTION:** *If piston pin must be pressed in, determine the proper method and use the proper tools; otherwise the piston will distort.* Install the lock rings; ensure that they seat properly. If the parts are not within specifications, determine the service method for the type of engine. In some cases, piston and pin are serviced as an assembly when either is defective. Others specify reaming the piston and connecting rods for an oversize pin. If the connecting rod bushing is worn, it may in many cases be replaced. Reaming the piston and replacing the rod bushing are machine shop operations.
Clean and inspect the camshaft: *Checking the camshaft for straightness* *Camshaft lobe measurement*	Degrease the camshaft, using solvent, and clean out all oil holes. Visually inspect cam lobes and bearing journals for excessive wear. If a lobe is questionable, check all lobes as indicated below. If a journal or lobe is worn, the camshaft must be reground or replaced. **NOTE:** *If a journal is worn, there is a good chance that the bushings are worn.* If lobes and journals appear intact, place the front and rear journals in V-blocks, and rest a dial indicator on the center journal. Rotate the camshaft to check straightness. If deviation exceeds .001″, replace the camshaft. * Check the camshaft lobes with a micrometer, by measuring the lobes from the nose to base and again at 90° (see illustration). The lift is determined by subtracting the second measurement from the first. If all exhaust lobes and all intake lobes are not identical, the camshaft must be reground or replaced.
Replace the camshaft bearings: *Note the off-center installation of the bearing caps*	If excessive wear is indicated, or if the engine is being completely rebuilt, camshaft bearings should be replaced. Lubricate the bearing shells, journals and the faces of the bearing caps. Install the caps in the proper order. Note the off-center bearing installation and that the numbers on the cap are not always on the same side.

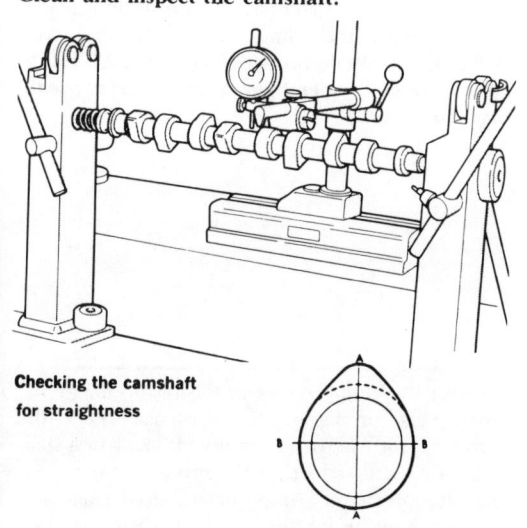

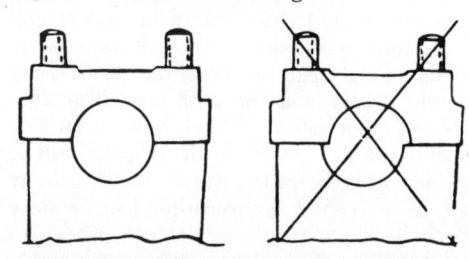

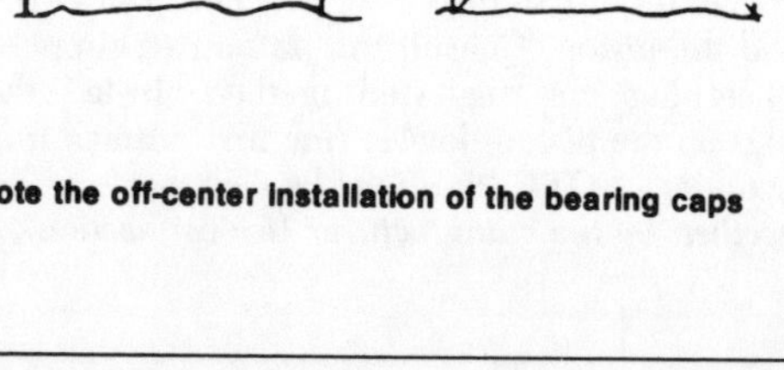

116 ENGINE AND ENGINE REBUILDING

Procedure	Method
Finish hone the cylinders: *Finish honed cylinder (CROSS-HATCH PATTERN, 50°–60°)*	Chuck a flexible drive hone into a power drill, and insert it into the cylinder. Start the hone, and move it up and down in the cylinder at a rate which will produce approximately a 60° cross-hatch pattern (see illustration). **NOTE:** *Do not extend the hone below the cylinder bore.* After developing the pattern, remove the hone and recheck piston fit. Wash the cylinders with a detergent and water solution to remove abrasive dust, dry, and wipe several times with a rag soaked in engine oil.
Check piston ring end-gap: *Checking ring end-gap*	Compress the piston rings to be used in a cylinder, one at a time, into that cylinder, and press them approximately 1″ below the deck with an inverted piston. Using feeler gauges, measure the ring end-gap, and compare to specifications. Pull the ring out of the cylinder and file the ends with a fine file to obtain proper clearance. **CAUTION:** *If inadequate ring end-gap is utilized, ring breakage will result.*
Install the piston rings: *Checking ring side clearance* *Piston groove depth: CORRECT, INCORRECT* *Correct ring spacer installation (SPACER)*	Inspect the ring grooves in the piston for excessive wear or taper. If necessary, recut the groove(s) for use with an overwidth ring or a standard ring and spacer. If the groove is worn uniformly, overwidth rings, or standard rings and spacers may be installed without recutting. Roll the outside of the ring around the groove to check for burrs or deposits. If any are found, remove with a fine file. Hold the ring in the groove, and measure side clearance. If necessary, correct as indicated above. **NOTE:** *Always install any additional spacers above the piston ring.* The ring groove must be deep enough to allow the ring to seat below the lands (see illustration). In many cases, a "go-no-go" depth gauge will be provided with the piston rings. Shallow grooves may be corrected by recutting, while deep grooves require some type of filler or expander behind the piston. Consult the piston ring supplier concerning the suggested method. Install the rings on the piston, lowest ring first, using a ring expander. **NOTE:** *Position the ring markings as specified by the manufacturer (see car section).*

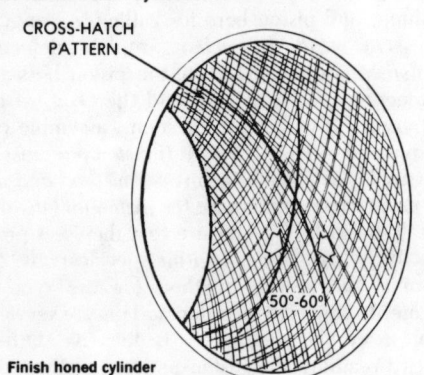

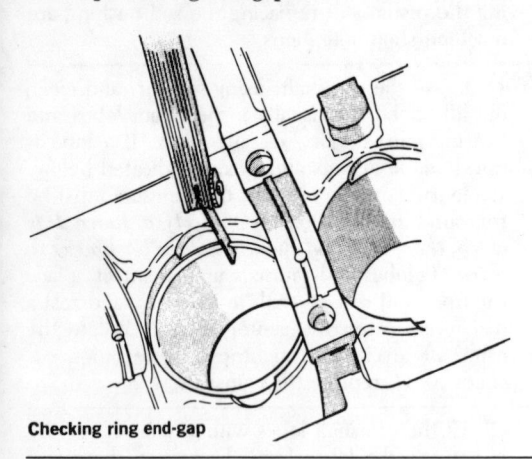

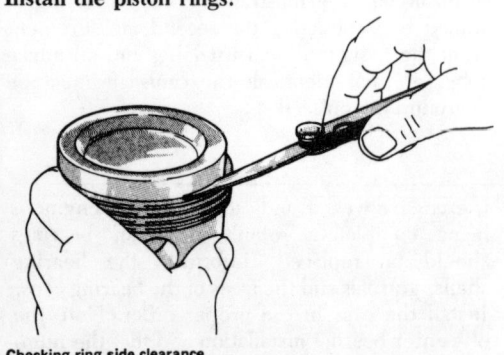

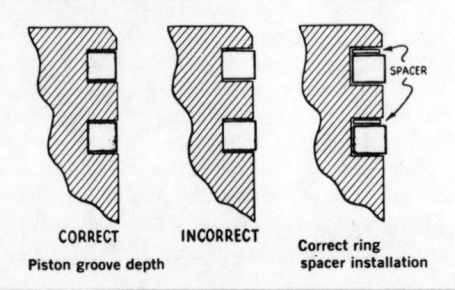

ENGINE AND ENGINE REBUILDING 117

Procedure	Method
Install the camshaft:	Liberally lubricate the camshaft lobes and journals, and slide the camshaft into the block. **CAUTION:** *Exercise extreme care to avoid damaging the bearings when inserting the camshaft.* Install and tighten the camshaft thrust plate retaining bolts.
Check camshaft end-play:	* Mount a dial indicator stand so that the stem of the dial indicator rests on the nose of the camshaft, parallel to the camshaft axis. Push the camshaft as far in as possible and zero the gauge. Move the camshaft outward to determine the amount of camshaft end-play. If the end-play is not within tolerance, install shims behind the thrust plate, or reposition the camshaft gear and retest.

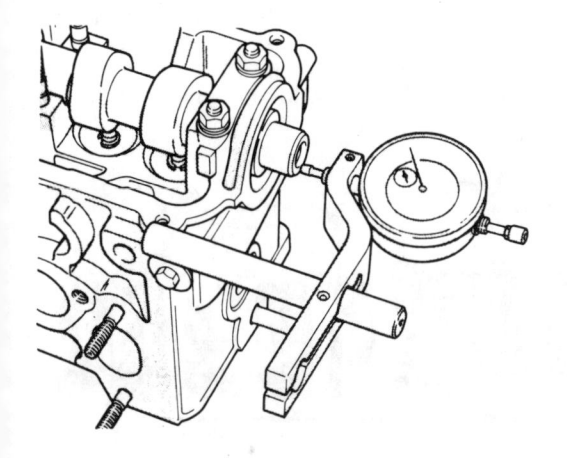

Checking camshaft end-play with a dial indicator

| Install the rear main seal (where applicable): | Position the block with the bearing saddles facing upward. Lay the rear main seal in its groove and press it lightly into its seat. Place a piece of pipe the same diameter as the crankshaft journal into the saddle, and firmly seat the seal. Hold the pipe in position, and trim the ends of the seal flush if required. |

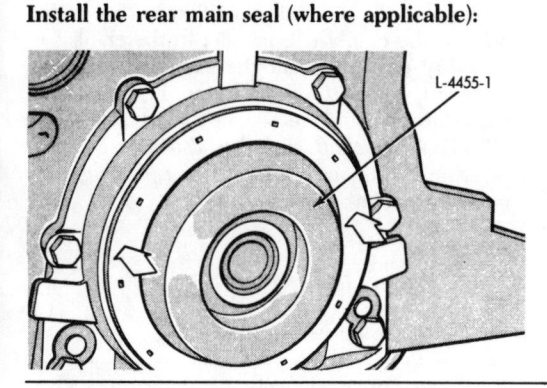

Seating the rear main seal

| Install the crankshaft: | Thoroughly clean the main bearing saddles and caps. Place the upper halves of the bearing inserts on the saddles and press into position. **NOTE:** *Ensure that the oil holes align.* Press the corresponding bearing inserts into the main bearing caps. Lubricate the upper main bearings, and lay the crankshaft in position. Place a strip of Plastigage on each of the crankshaft journals, install the main caps, and torque to specifications. Remove the main caps, and compare the Plastigage to the scale on the Plastigage envelope. If clearances are within tolerances, remove the Plastigage, turn the crankshaft 90°, wipe off all oil and retest. If all clearances are correct, remove all Plastigage, thoroughly lubricate the main caps and bearing journals, and install the main caps. If |

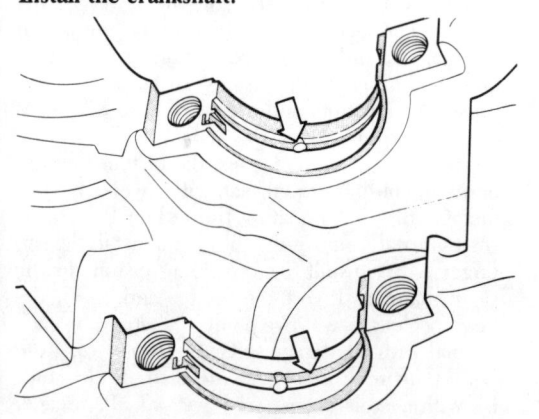

ENGINE AND ENGINE REBUILDING

Procedure	Method

clearances are not within tolerance, the upper bearing inserts may be removed, without removing the crankshaft, using a bearing roll out pin. Roll in a bearing that will provide proper clearance, and retest. Torque all main caps, excluding the thrust bearing cap, to specifications. Tighten the thrust bearing cap finger tight. To properly align the thrust bearing, pry the crankshaft the extent of its axial travel several times, the last movement held toward the front of the engine, and torque the thrust bearing cap to specifications. Determine the crankshaft end-play (see below), and bring within tolerance with thrust washers.

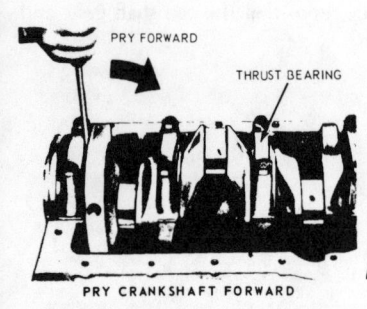

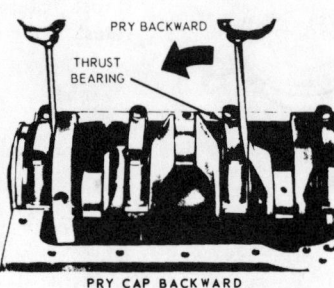

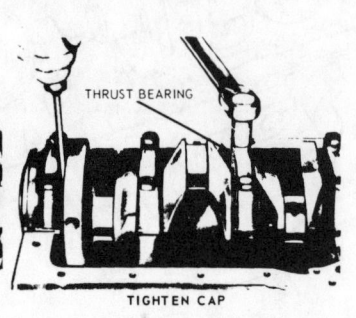

Aligning the thrust bearing

Measure crankshaft end-play:

Mount a dial indicator stand on the front of the block, with the dial indicator stem resting on the nose of the crankshaft, parallel to the crankshaft axis. Pry the crankshaft the extent of its travel rearward, and zero the indicator. Pry the crankshaft forward and record crankshaft end-play. **NOTE:** *Crankshaft end-play also may be measured at the thrust bearing, using feeler gauges (see illustration).*

Checking crankshaft end-play with a dial indicator

Install the pistons:

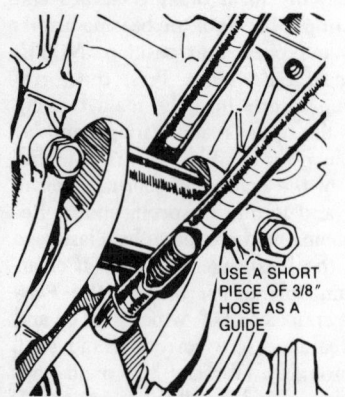

Press the upper connecting rod bearing halves into the connecting rods, and the lower halves into the connecting rod caps. Position the piston ring gaps according to specifications (see car section), and lubricate the pistons. Install a ring compresser on a piston, and press two long (8″) pieces of plastic tubing over the rod bolts. Using the plastic tubes as a guide, press the pistons into the bores and onto the crankshaft with a wooden hammer handle. After seating the rod on the crankshaft journal, remove the tubes and install the cap finger tight. Install the remaining pistons in the same manner. Invert the engine and check the bearing clearance at two points (90° apart) on each journal with Plastigage. **NOTE:** *Do not turn the crankshaft with Plastigage installed.* If clearance is within tolerances, remove *all* Plastigage,

Tubing used as guide when installing a piston

ENGINE AND ENGINE REBUILDING 119

Procedure	Method
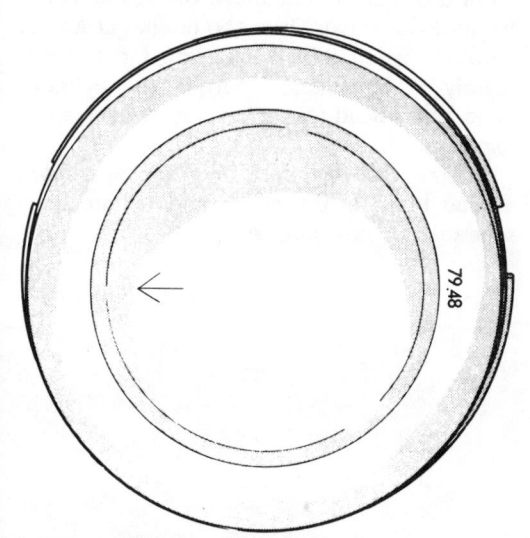 *Installing the piston*	thoroughly lubricate the journals, and torque the rod caps to specifications. If clearance is not within specifications, install different thickness bearing inserts and recheck. **CAUTION:** *Never shim or file the connecting rods or caps.* Always install plastic tube sleeves over the rod bolts when the caps are not installed, to protect the crankshaft journals.

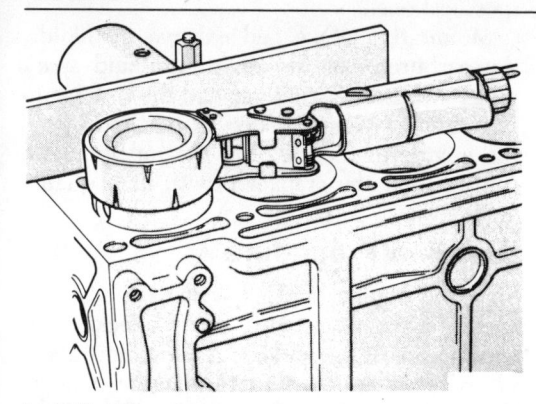

Arrow on piston faces forward

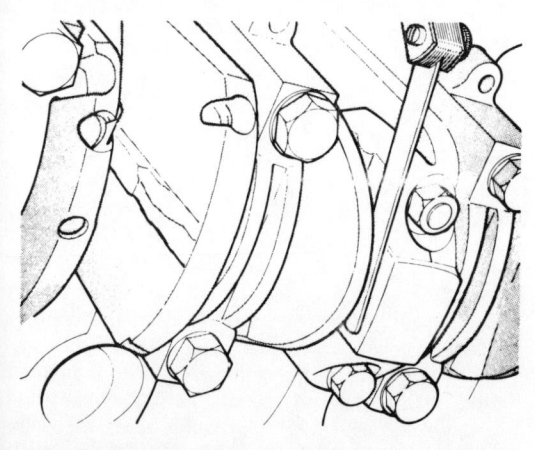 Check connecting rod side clearance:	Determine the clearance between the sides of the connecting rods and the crankshaft, using feeler gauges. If clearance is below the minimum tolerance, the rod may be machined to provide adequate clearance. If clearance is excessive, substitute an unworn rod, and recheck. If clearance is still outside specifications, the crankshaft must be welded and reground, or replaced.

Check the connecting rod side clearance with a feeler gauge

Completing the Rebuilding Process

Following the above procedures, complete the rebuilding process as follows:

Fill the oil pump with oil, to prevent cavitating (sucking air) on initial engine start up. Install the oil pump and the pickup tube on the engine. Coat the oil pan gasket as necessary, and install the gasket and the oil pan. Mount the flywheel and the crankshaft vibrational damper or pulley on the crankshaft. NOTE: *Always use new bolts when installing the flywheel*. Inspect the clutch shaft pilot bushing in the crankshaft. If the bushing is excessively worn, remove it with an expanding puller and a slide hammer, and tap a new bushing into place.

Position the engine, cylinder head side up. Lubricate the lifters, and install them into their bores. Install the cylinder head, and torque it as specified in the car section. Insert the pushrods (where applicable), and install the rocker shaft(s) (if so equipped) or position the rocker arms on the pushrods. If solid lifters are utilized, adjust the valves to the "cold" specifications.

Mount the intake and exhaust manifolds, the carburetor(s), the distributor and spark plugs. Adjust the point gap and the static ignition timing. Mount all accessories and install the engine in the car. Fill the radiator with coolant, and the crankcase with high quality engine oil.

Break-in Procedure

Start the engine, and allow it to run at low speed for a few minutes, while checking for leaks. Stop the engine, check the oil level, and fill as necessary. Restart the engine, and fill the cooling system to capacity. Check the point dwell angle and adjust the ignition timing and the valves. Run the engine at low to medium speed (800–2500 rpm) for approximately ½ hour, and retorque the cylinder head bolts. Road test the car, and check again for leaks.

Follow the manufacturer's recommended engine break-in procedure and maintenance schedule for new engines.

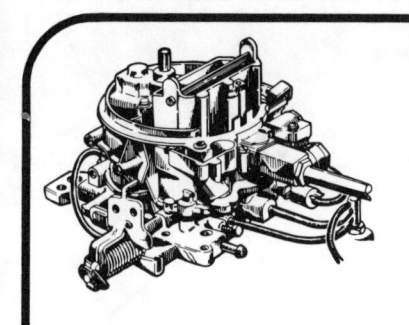

Fuel System and Emission Controls

EMISSION CONTROLS

Several different systems are used on each car. Most require no service and those which may require service also require sophisticated equipment for testing purposes. Following is a brief description of each system.

Catalytic Converter

Two catalysts are used in a small one located just after the exhaust manifold and a larger one located under the car body. Catalysts promote complete oxidation of exhaust gases through the effect of a platinum coated mass in the catalyst shell. Two things act to destroy

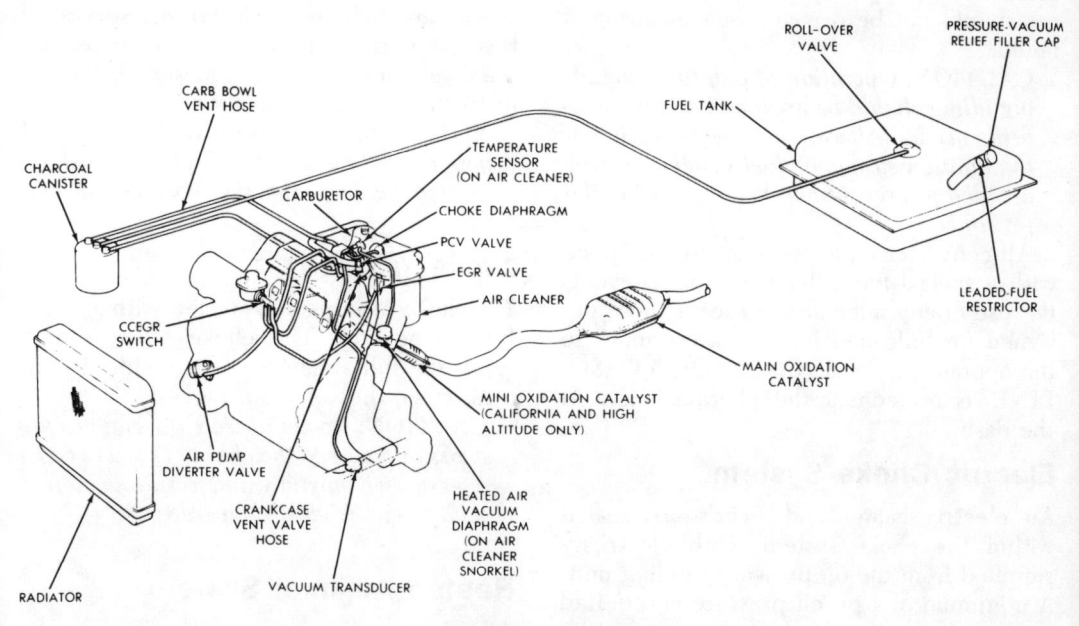

Emission control system

122 FUEL SYSTEM AND EMISSION CONTROLS

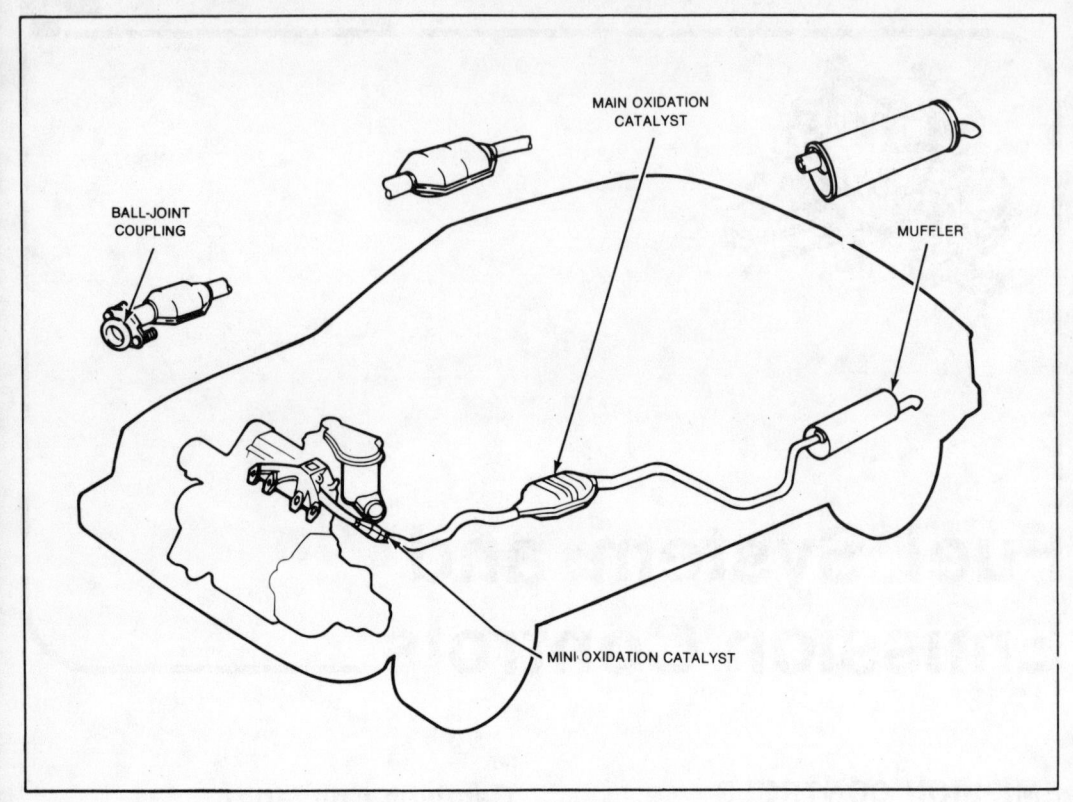

Exhaust system with catalytic converter

the catalyst, functionally: excessive heat and leaded gas. Excessive heat during misfiring and prolonged testing with the ignition system in any way altered is the most common occurrence. Test procedures should be accomplished as quickly as possible, and the car should not be driven when misfiring is noted.

> CAUTION: *Operation of any type including idling should be avoided if engine misfiring occurs. Alteration or deterioration of the ignition system or fuel system must be avoided to prevent overheating the catalytic converter.*

All converter equipped cars are equipped with a special fuel filler neck that prevents the use of any filler nozzle except those designed for unleaded fuel. As a reminder to the operator, a decal "UNLEADED GASOLINE" is located near the fuller neck, and on the dash.

Electric Choke System

An electric heater and switch are sealed within the choke system, with electricity supplied from the oil pressure sending unit. A minimum of 4 psi oil pressure is required to close the contacts and send current to the choke control switch.

The electric choke unit is located on the side of the carburetor. The initial setting is made by the manufacturer, but it is adjustable. The thermostat housing mark is positioned opposite a specified reference line on the black plastic adapter, after which, the 3 screws are tightened. No normal service of this system is required, but if, for any reason, the 3 retaining screws are loosened, the adjustment must be made again.

> NOTE: *If the choke is removed, be careful you don't lose the small plastic bushing located between the thermostat loop and pin.*

CHOKE HEATER TEST

The choke heater can be tested with a direct B+ connection. The choke valve should reach the fully open position within 5 minutes, when the vehicle is parked.

> CAUTION: *Do not operate the engine with a loss of power to the choke. This will cause a very rich mixture and result in abnormally high exhaust temperatures.*

Heated Air Inlet System

All engines are equipped with a vacuum device located in the carburetor air cleaner

FUEL SYSTEM AND EMISSION CONTROLS

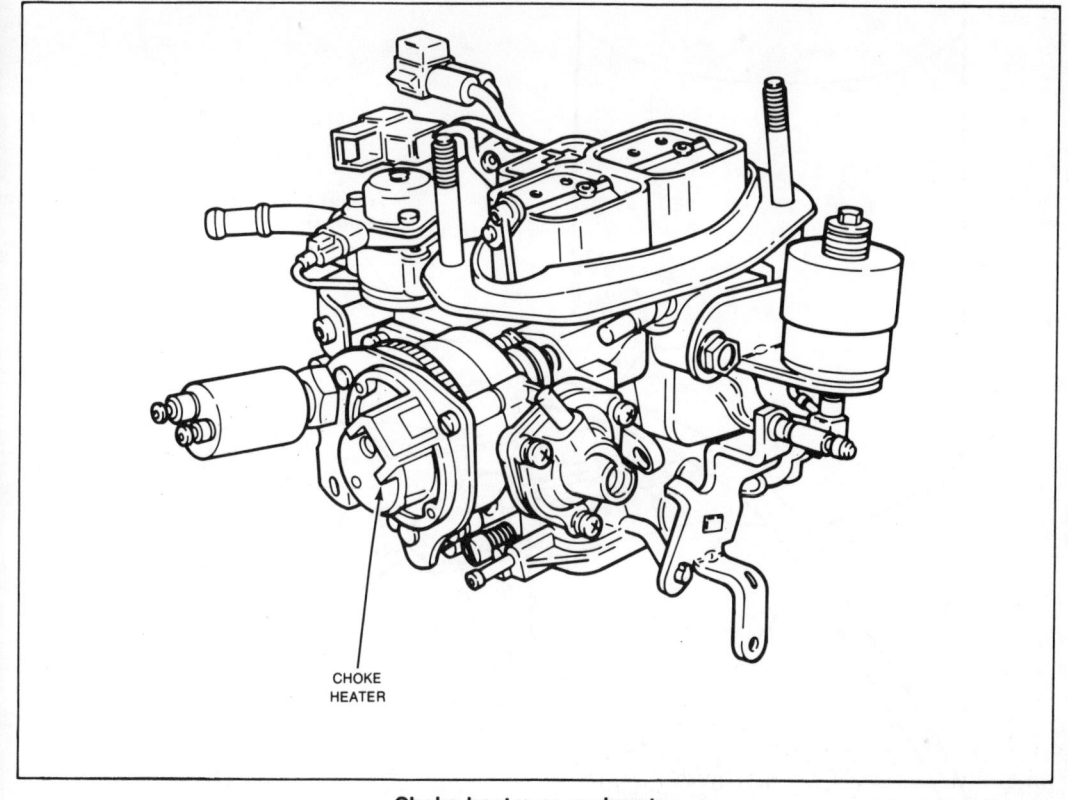

Choke heater on carburetor

intake. A small door is operated by a vacuum diaphragm and a thermostatic spring. When the air temperature outside is 40° F or lower, the door will block off air entering from outside and allow air channelled from the exhaust manifold area to enter the intake. This air is heated by the hot manifold. At 65° F or above, the door fully blocks off the heated air. At temperatures in between, the door is operated in intermediate positions. During acceleration the door is controlled by engine vacuum to allow the maximum amount of air to enter the carburetor.

TESTING THE SYSTEM

To determine if the system is functioning properly, use the following procedures.

1. Make sure all vacuum hoses and the flexible pipe from the heat stove are in good condition.
2. On a cold engine and the outside air temperature less than 50° F, the heat control door in the air cleaner snorkel should be up in the up or "Heat On" position.
3. With the engine warmed and running, the door in the snorkel should be in the down or "Heat Off" position.
4. Remove the air cleaner. Allow it to cool to 50° F, or less. Using a hand vacuum pump, apply 20 in./Hg to the sensor. The door in the air cleaner snorkel should be in the up or "Heat On" position. If not, check the vacuum diaphragm.

5. To test the diaphragm, use a hand vacuum pump to apply about 20 in./Hg to the diaphragm. It should not leak down more than 10 in./Hg in 3 minutes. The door should not lift from the snorkel at less than 2 in./Hg, and be in the full up position with no more than 4 in./Hg.

6. If these conditions in Step 6 are not met, replace the diaphragm and repeat the checks in Steps 2 and 3. If the vacuum diaphragm performs properly, but proper temperature is not maintained, replace the sensor and repeat the checks in Steps 2 and 3.

VACUUM DIAPHRAGM

Removal and Installation

1. Remove the air cleaner housing.
2. Disconnect the vacuum hose from the diaphragm.
3. Drill through the metal (welded) tab and tip the diaphragm slightly forward to disengage the lock. Rotate the diaphragm counterclockwise.
4. When the diaphragm is free, slide the

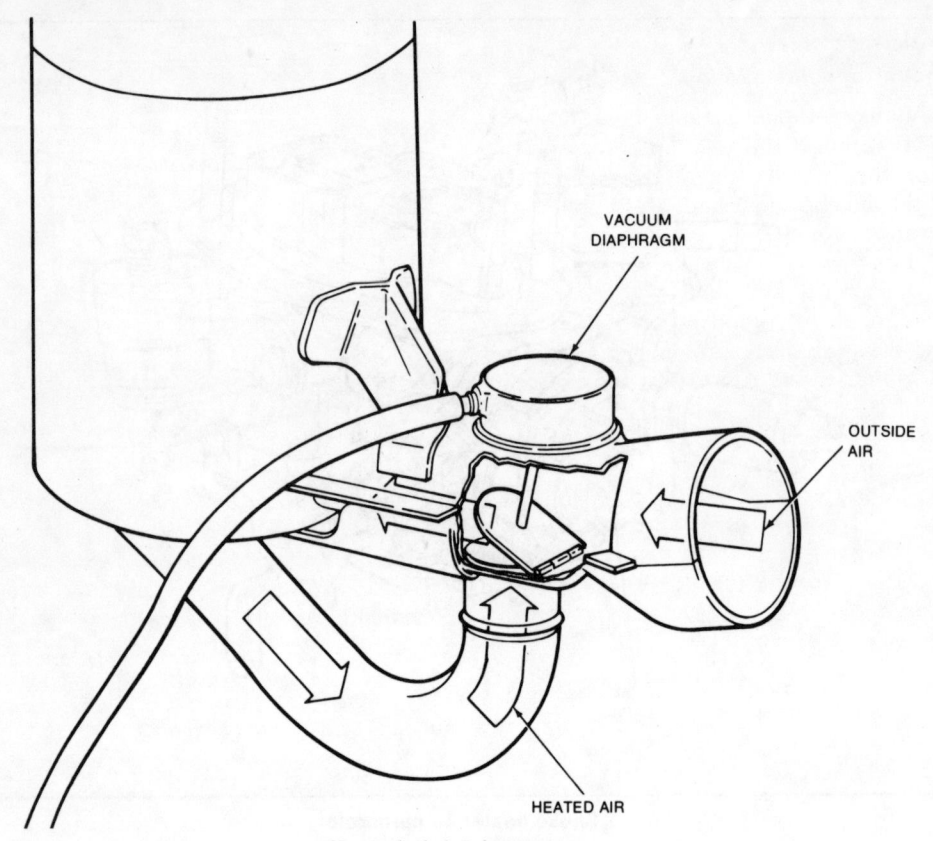

FUEL SYSTEM AND EMISSION CONTROLS

Heated air intake system

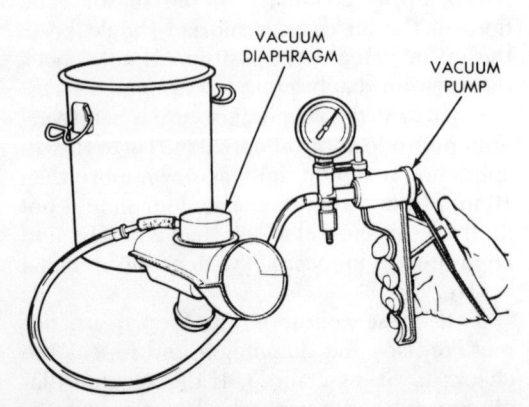

Testing vacuum diaphragm with hand vacuum pump

7. Apply 9 in. of vacuum to the diaphragm hose nipple and check to be sure the heat control door operates freely.

CAUTION: *Manually operating the heat control door could cock the operating rod and restrict proper operation of the system.*

8. Assemble the air cleaner and install it on the car. Test the operation.

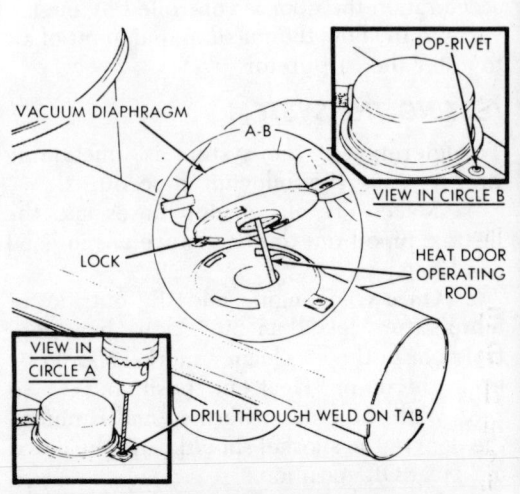

complete assembly to one side and remove the operating rod from the heat control door.

5. With the diaphragm removed, check the door for freedom of operation. When the door is raised, it should fall freely when released. If not, check the snorkel walls for interference, or check the hinge pin.

6. Insert the operating rod into the heat control door. Position the diaphragm tangs in the openings in the snorkel and turn clockwise until the lock is engaged.

Removing or installing the vacuum diaphragm

FUEL SYSTEM AND EMISSION CONTROLS

SENSOR

Removal and Installation

1. Remove the air cleaner housing.
2. Disconnect the vacuum hoses from the sensor and remove the retainer clips. Discard the old clips; new ones are supplied with a new sensor.
3. Remove the sensor and gasket.
4. Install a new gasket and sensor. Hold the sensor in place and install new retainer clips. Be sure the gasket forms a tight air seal. Do not attempt to adjust the sensor.

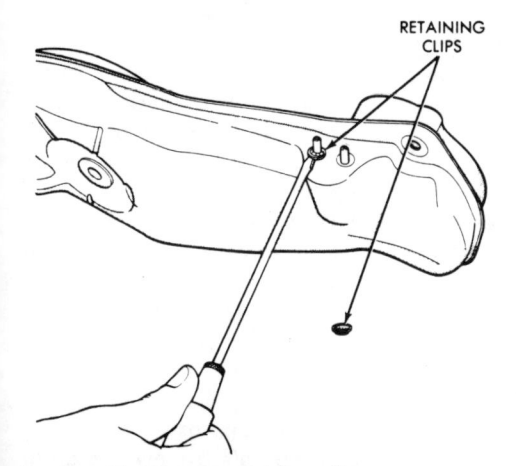

Remove the sensor retaining clip

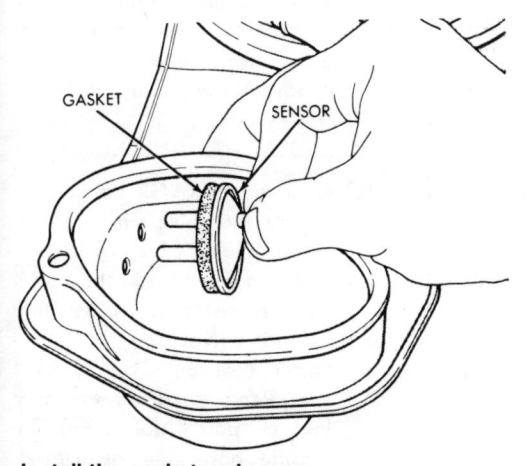

Install the gasket and sensor

Exhaust Gas Recirculation System

This system reduces the amount of oxides of nitrogen in the exhaust by allowing a predetermined amount of hot exhaust gases to recirculate and dilute the incoming fuel/air mixture. The principal components of the

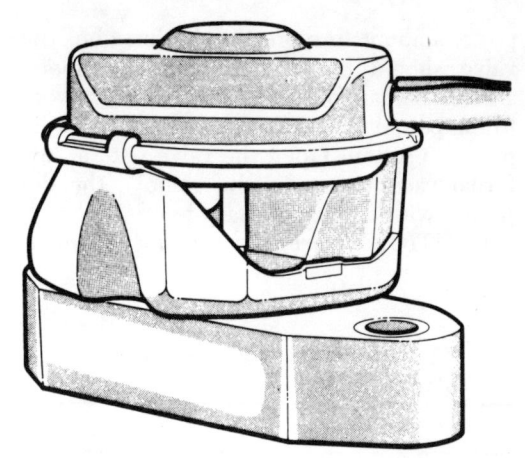

EGR valve

system are the EGR valve and the Coolant Control Exhaust Gas Recirculation Valve (CCEGR). The former is located in the intake manifold and directly regulates the flow of exhaust gases into the intake. The latter is located in the thermostat housing and overrides the EGR valve when coolant temperature is below 125° F.

Ported vacuum uses a slot in the carburetor throttle body which is exposed to an increasing percentage of manifold vacuum as the throttle opens. The throttle bore port is connected to the EGR valve. The flow rate of recirculation is dependent on manifold vacuum, throttle position and exhaust gas back pressure. Recycling at wide open throttle is eliminated, by calibrating the valve opening point above the manifold vacuum available at wide open throttle, which provides maximum performance.

TESTING THE SYSTEM

EGR Valve

1. Inspect all hose connections between the carburetor, intake manifold and EGR valve.
2. Check the valve with the engine warmed and running.
3. Allow the engine to idle in Neutral for 70 seconds, with the throttle closed. Abruptly accelerate the engine to about 2000 rpm, but not more than 3000 rpm.
4. Visible movement of the EGR valve stem should occur during this operation. Movement can be seen by the position of the groove on the EGR valve stem. You may have to repeat the operation several times to definitely ascertain movement.

Inspect the EGR valve for deposits, particularly around the poppet and seat area. If deposits amount to more than a thin film, the valve should be cleaned. Apply a liberal amount of manifold heat control valve solvent to the poppet and seat area and allow the deposits to soften. Open the valve with an external vacuum source and remove the deposits, with a suitable sharp tool.

CAUTION: *During the cleaning operation, do not spill solvent on the valve diaphragm or it will cause failure of the diaphragm. Do not push on the diaphragm to operate the valve; use an external vacuum source.*

An alternate procedure to this messy operation is to simply replace the valve if it is extremely clogged.

EGR Diagnosis

NOTE: *All tests must be made with fully warm engine running continuously for at least two minutes*

Condition	Possible Cause	Correction
EGR valve stem does not move on system test.	(a) Cracked, leaking, disconnected or plugged hoses.	(a) Verify correct hose connections and leak check and confirm that all hoses are open. If defective hoses are found, replace hose harness.
	(b) Defective EGR valve.	(b) Disconnect hose harness from EGR valve. Connect external vacuum source, 10 in./Hg or greater, to valve diaphragm while checking valve movement. If no valve movement occurs, replace valve. If valve opens, approx. $\frac{1}{8}$" travel, clamp off supply hose to check for diaphragm leakage. Valve should remain open 30 seconds or longer. If leakage occurs, replace valve. If valve is satisfactory, evaluate control system.
EGR valve stem does not move on system test, operates normally on external vacuum source.	(a) Defectvie thermal control valve.	(a) Disconnect CCEGR valve and bypass the valve with a short length of $\frac{3}{16}$" tubing. If normal movement of the EGR valve is restored, replace the thermal valve.
	(b) Defective control system—Plugged passages.	(b) Ported Vacuum Control System: Remove carburetor and inspect port (slot type) in throttle bore and associated vacuum passages in carburetor throttle body including limiting orifice at hose end of passages. Use suitable solvent to remove deposits and check for flow with light air pressure. Normal operation should be restored to ported vacuum control EGR system.

FUEL SYSTEM AND EMISSION CONTROLS

EGR Diagnosis (cont.)

NOTE: *All tests must be made with fully warm engine running continuously for at least two minutes*

Condition	Possible Cause	Correction
Engine will not idle, dies out on return to idle or idle is very rough or slow. EGR valve open at idle.	(a) Control system defective.	(a) Disconnect hose from EGR valve and plug hose. If idle is unsatisfactory, replace EGR valve. If idle is still unsatisfactory, install a vacuum gauge on ported signal tap and observe gauge for vacuum reading. If vacuum signal is greater than 1 inch/Hg, check idle set (refer to Carburetor, Engine Idle Check and Set Procedure). If vacuum is ok, remove carburetor, Group 14, Fuel System, and check linkage and throttle blades for binding.
Engine will not idle, dies out on return to idle or idle is rough or slow. EGR valve closed at idle.	(a) High EGR valve leakage in closed position.	(a) If removal of vacuum hose from EGR valve does not correct rough idle, remove EGR valve and inspect to insure that poppet is seated. Clean deposits if necessary or replace EGR valve if found defective.

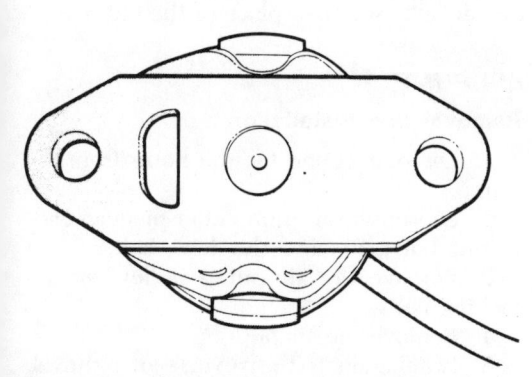

Bottom view (poppet seat area) of EGR valve

NOTE: *A new EGR valve was used on models built after February 20, 1978. Vehicles built prior to the change can increase fuel economy slightly by using the new EGR valve (part no. 4131219) and gasket (part no. 3671425).*

CCEGR Valve

This valve is mounted in the thermostat housing and is color coded yellow for its calibrated temperature of 120–130° F. During warm-up, when engine coolant temperature exceeds 125° F., the valve opens, allowing vacuum to reach the EGR valve, causing recirculation of exhaust gasses.

1. Remove the valve from the housing.
2. Place it an ice bath below 40° F. so that the threaded portion of the valve is covered.
3. Connect a hand vacuum pump to the

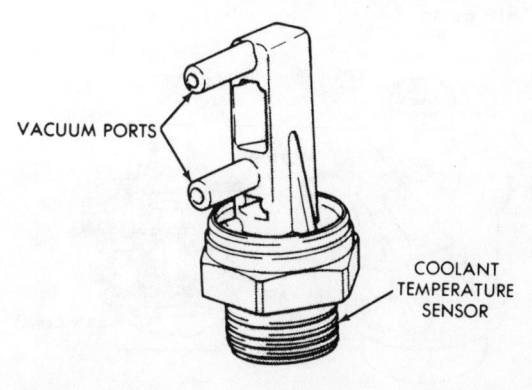

VACUUM PORTS

COOLANT TEMPERATURE SENSOR

CCEGR valve

FUEL SYSTEM AND EMISSION CONTROLS

valve nipple corresponding to the yellow stripe hose. Apply 10 in. vacuum. There should be no more than 1 in. drop in vacuum in one (1) minute. If the vacuum reading falls off, the valve should be replaced.

Air Injection System

This system is used on all California and Canada cars and all other cars built through January 10, 1978. Its job is to reduce carbon monoxide and hydrocarbons to required levels. The system adds a controlled amount of air to exhaust gases, via an air pump and induction tubes, causing oxidation of the gases. The California and other American cars, introduces air through the head at the exhaust port. The system is composed of an air pump, a combination diverter/pressure-relief valve, hoses, a check valve to protect the hoses from exhaust gas, and an injection tube.

NOTE: *The system is not noiseless. A certain squeal is present in pump operation.*

SERVICING THE SYSTEM

For proper operation of the system, the drive belt should be in good condition and properly tensioned. The air pump is not a serviceable item; if necessary, it should be replaced.

NOTE: *Do not attempt to disassemble the pump or clamp it in a vise.*

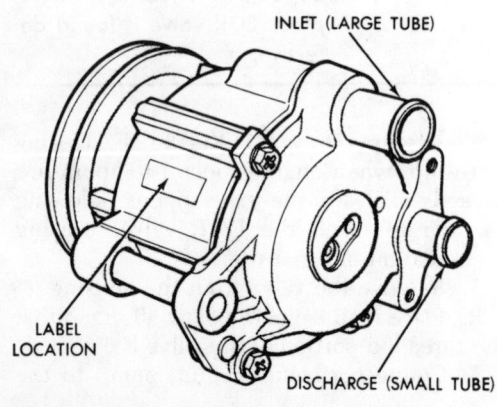

Complaints of road load surge at about 40-60 mph on 1978 Federal models equipped with manual transmission and AIR pump can be corrected, in most cases, by installing a kit (Part No. 4131207).

The kit consists of a vacuum bleed, an idle air bleed, a carburetor ID tag, main metering jet, air horn gasket and hose routing label.

1. Remove the carburetor air horn.
2. Replace the primary main metering jet with the one supplied in the kit.
3. Install the new carburetor air horn gasket.
4. Install the air horn.
5. Install the idel air bleed in the opening next to the primary choke housing. It should be installed flush with the surface. Use a driver (brass drift) larger than the diameter of the bleed fitting.
6. Install the vacuum bleed between the EGR ported vacuum nipple of the carburetor and install the CCEGR valve hose in place of the existing plastic reducer. The large end of the vacuum bleed should be toward the carburetor.
7. Install the new hose routing label over the old one.
8. Install the new carburetor ID tag under the air horn screw in place of the old one.

AIR PUMP

Removal and Installation

1. Disconnect and tag the hoses from the pump.
2. Loosen the air pump idler pivot and adjusting bolts. Remove the drive belt.
3. Remove the air pump pulley and attaching bolts.
4. Remove the air pump.
5. Installation is the reverse of removal. Tension the drive belt (see Chapter 1).

DIVERTER VALVE

Removal and Installation

Servicing the diverter valve is limited to replacement. If the valve fails it will become extremely noisy. If air escapes from the silencer at idle speed, either the diverter valve or the relief valve has failed and the entire valve assembly should be replaced.

1. Remove the air and vacuum hoses.

AIR pump

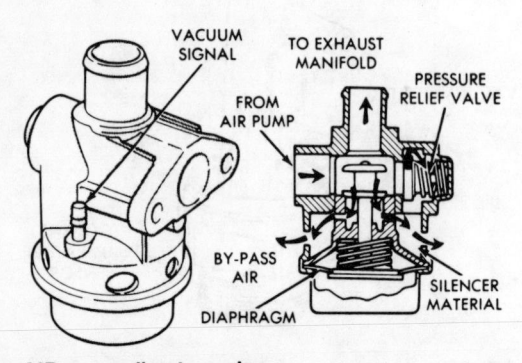

AIR pump diverter valve

FUEL SYSTEM AND EMISSION CONTROLS

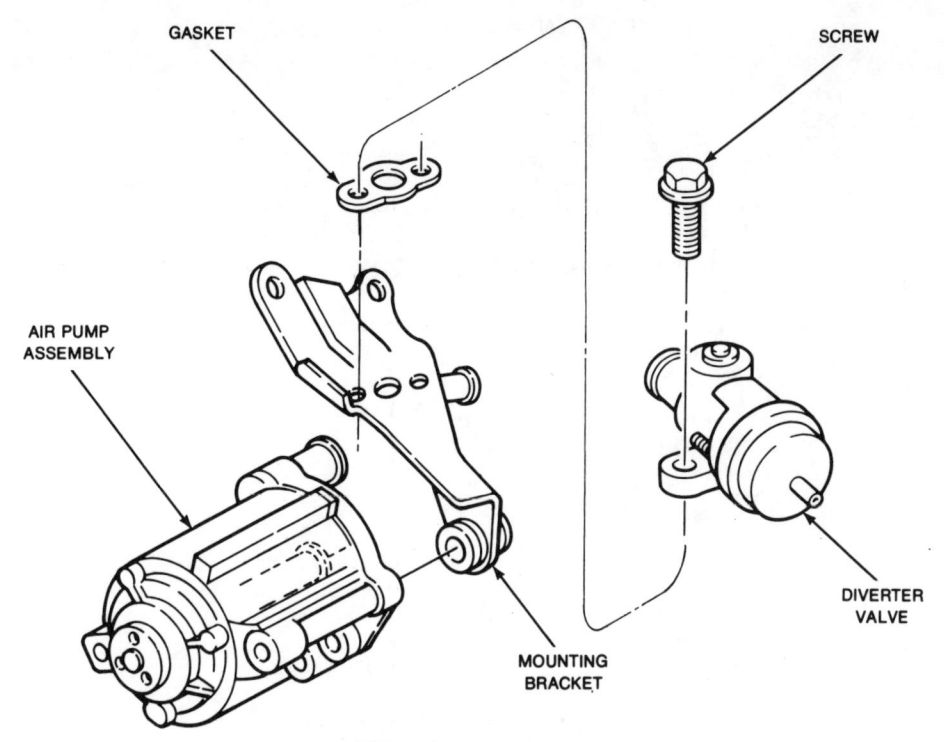

AIR system components

2. Remove the 2 screws holding the diverter valve to the mounting flange and remove the valve.
3. Remove the old gasket.
4. Installation is the reverse of removal. Use a new gasket and connect the hoses properly.

CHECK VALVE

The check valve is not repairable; if necessary to service it, replace it with a new one. The valve can be tested by removing the hose from the valve inlet tube. If exhaust gasses escape from the inlet tube the valve has failed. On California cars, if the tube nut joint is leaking, retorque the nut to 25–35 ft lbs. If the adapter to the exhaust manifold joint is leaking, retorque the connection to a maximum of 40 ft lbs. On Canadian cars, if the air injection tube to the head joint is leaking, retorque the hollow bolts to 20 ft lbs.

Removal and Installation—California Cars

1. Release the clamp and disconnect the air hose from the check valve.
2. Remove the tube nut holding the injection tube to the exhaust manifold.
3. Remove the injection tube from the engine.
4. Installation is the reverse of removal.

Removal and Installation—Canadian Cars

1. Release the clamp and remove the air hose from the check valve inlet.
2. On A/C cars, remove the air conditioning compressor from the mount.
CAUTION: *Do not disconnect any A/C system hoses.*
Remove the 4 isolated rubber compressor mounting bracket bolts and the compressor-to-cylinder head bolt. Set the compressor aside and keep it upright.
3. Drain the cooling system to a level below the thermostat housing.
4. Remove the housing from the bypass hose.
5. Remove the 4 hollow bolts holding the injection tube assembly to the cylinder head.
6. Install the injection tube assembly on the cylinder head. The 4 copper washers must be used between the tube assembly and the cylinder head.
7. Install the 4 hollow bolts with copper washers between each bolt and the injection tube assembly. The washers must be used. Torque the bolts to 20 ft lbs.
8. Install the thermostat housing and connect the bypass hose.
9. On engines with A/C, reinstall the compressor. Adjust the drive belt (see Chapter 1).

130 FUEL SYSTEM AND EMISSION CONTROLS

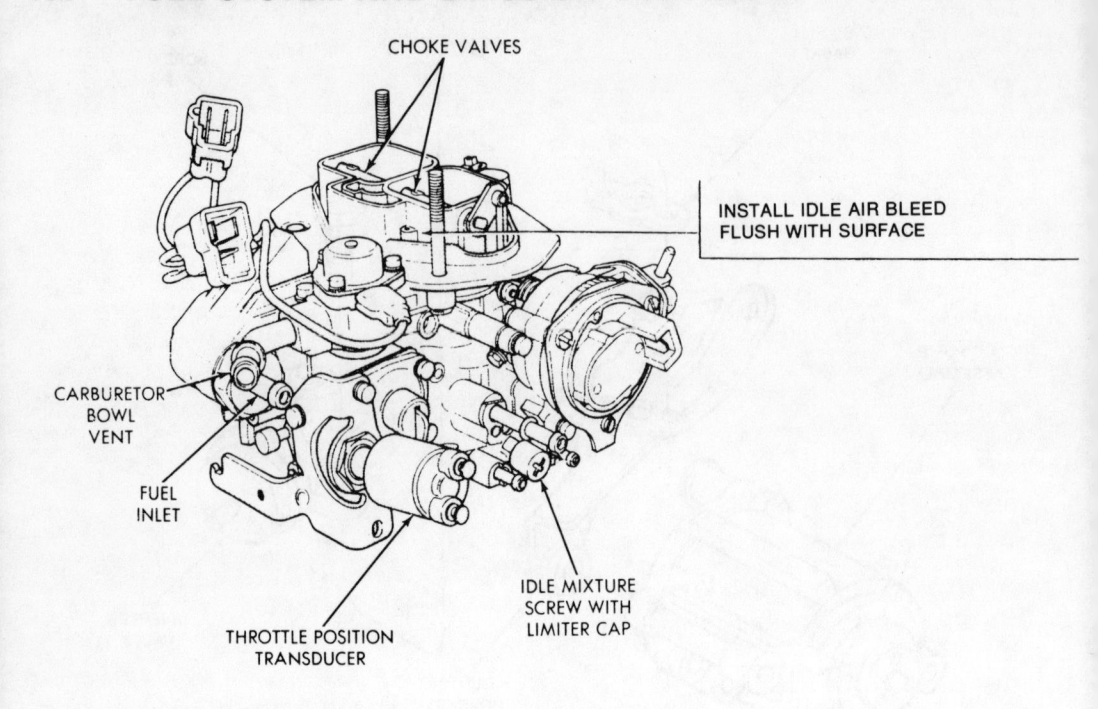

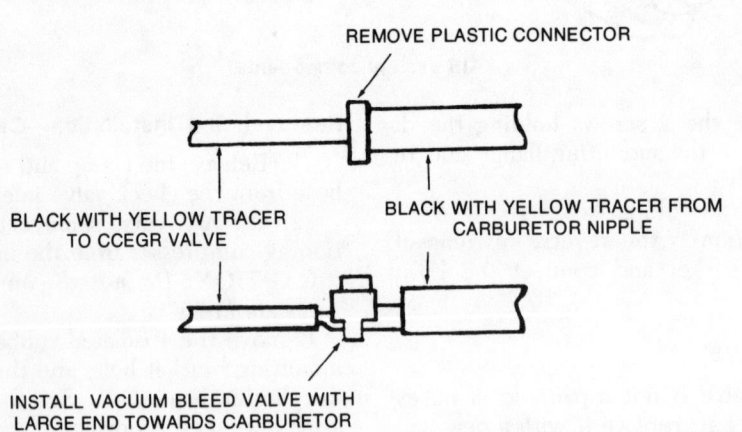

Carburetor modification

10. Reconnect the air hose to the check valve inlet.
11. Refill the cooling system (see Chapter 1).

Air Aspirator System

All models built after January 10, 1978, except California cars, will have an aspirator valve. This valve utilizes exhaust pressure pulsation to draw clean air from the inside of the air cleaner into the exhaust system. The function is to reduce HC (hydrocarbon) emissions. It is located in a tube between the exhaust manifold and the air cleaner.

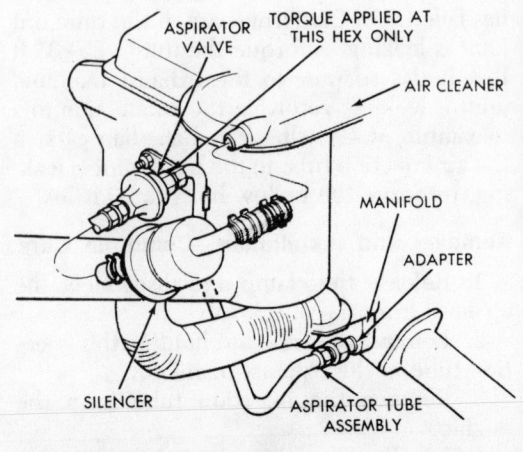

AIR aspirator system

FUEL SYSTEM AND EMISSION CONTROLS

TESTING THE SYSTEM

To determine if the air aspirator valve has failed, disconnect the hose from the aspirator inlet. With the engine idling in Neutral, vacuum exhaust pulses can be felt at the aspirator inlet. If hot exhaust gas is escaping from the aspirator inlet, the valve has failed and should be replaced.

ASPIRATOR VALVE

Removal and Installation

1. Disconnect the air hose from the aspirator valve inlet and unscrew the valve from the aspirator tube assembly.
2. Installation is the reverse of removal. Replace the hose if it has hardened.

ASPIRATOR TUBE ASSEMBLY

Removal and Installation

1. Disconnect the air hose from the aspirator valve inlet.
2. Remove the nut securing the aspirator tube assembly to the engine.
3. Remove the aspirator tube.
4. Installation is the reverse of removal. Tighten the tube nut to 25–35 ft lbs.

Evaporation Control System

This system prevents the release of gasoline vapors from the fuel tank and the carburetor into the atmosphere. The system is vacuum operated and draws the fumes into a charcoal canister where they are temporarily held until they are drawn into the intake manifold for burning. For proper operation of the system and to prevent gas tank failure, the lines should never be plugged, and no other cap other than the one specified should be used on the fuel tank filler neck.

The Evaporation Control System should not require service other than replacement of the charcoal canister filter. All hoses should be inspected and replaced if cracked or leaking. Any loss of fuel or vapor from the filler cap would indicate one of the following conditions:

1. Poor seal between cap and filler neck,
2. Malfunction of fuel cap release valve,
3. Plugged vent line roll-over valve in the fuel tank, or
4. Plugged vapor vent lines between fuel tank and charcoal canister.

FUEL TANK ROLL-OVER VALVE AND LIQUID VAPOR SEPARATOR VALVE

Removal and Installation

1. Remove the fuel tank.
2. Wedge the blade of a suitable pry bar between the rubber grommet and the support rib on the fuel tank.

NOTE: *Chrysler recommends the use of 2 screwdrivers for this operation. Before performing this operation with screwdrivers, read the Safety Notice on the acknowledgements page of this book and read the section in Chapter 1 concerning Safety.*

3. Use a second screwdriver as a support and pry the valve and grommet from the tank.

CAUTION: *Do not pry between the valve and grommet.*

4. To remove the grommet from the valve, place the valve upright on a flat surface and push down on the grommet.
5. Install the rubber grommet in the fuel tank and work it around the curled lip.

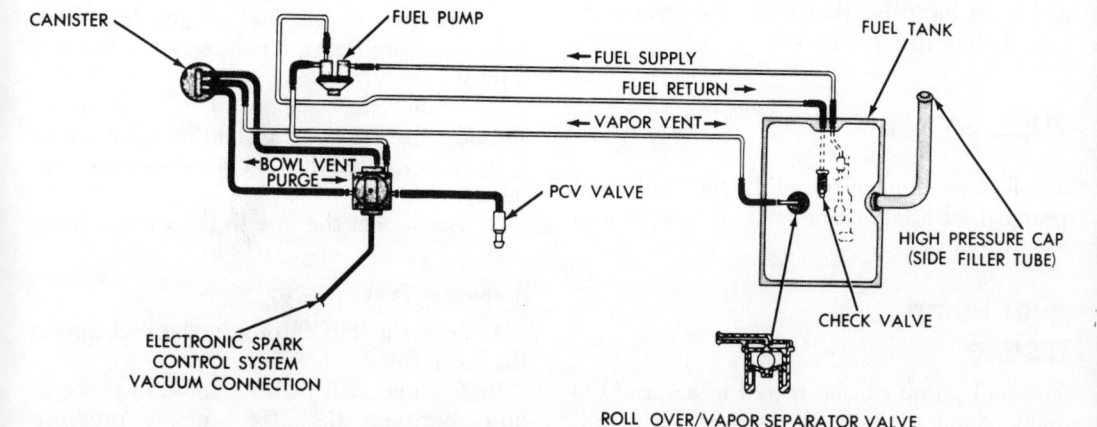

Fuel evaporation control system schematic

132 FUEL SYSTEM AND EMISSION CONTROLS

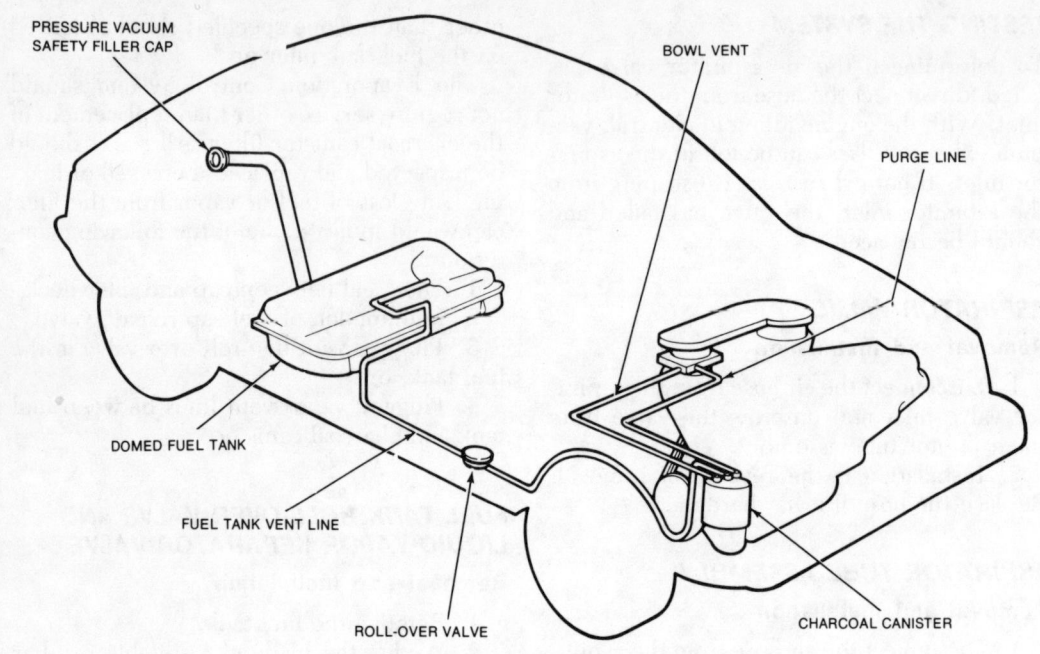

Components of Fuel Evaporation system

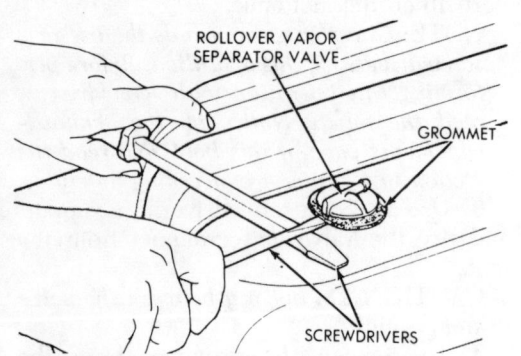

Removing rollover/vapor separation valve from fuel tank

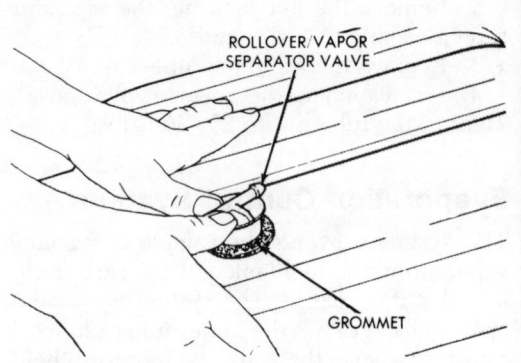

Installing the rollover/vapor separator valve

6. Lubricate the grommet with engine oil and twist the valve down into the grommet.
7. Install the fuel tank.

FUEL SYSTEM

The fuel system consists of the fuel tank, fuel pump, fuel filter, carburetor, fuel lines and vacuum lines.

Fuel Pump
TESTING

The fuel pump can be tested in a variety of ways, depending on the equipment available.

Volume Test

1. Disconnect the fuel supply line from the carburetor (leave it connected to the fuel pump).
2. Crank the engine. The fuel pump should supply 1 quart of fuel in 1 minute or less. Do not catch the fuel in a styrofoam container.
3. Reconnect the line to the carburetor.

Pressure Test

1. Insert a "tee" fitting in the fuel line at the carburetor.
2. Connect a 6 inch (maximum) piece of hose between the "tee" and a pressure gauge.

FUEL SYSTEM AND EMISSION CONTROLS 133

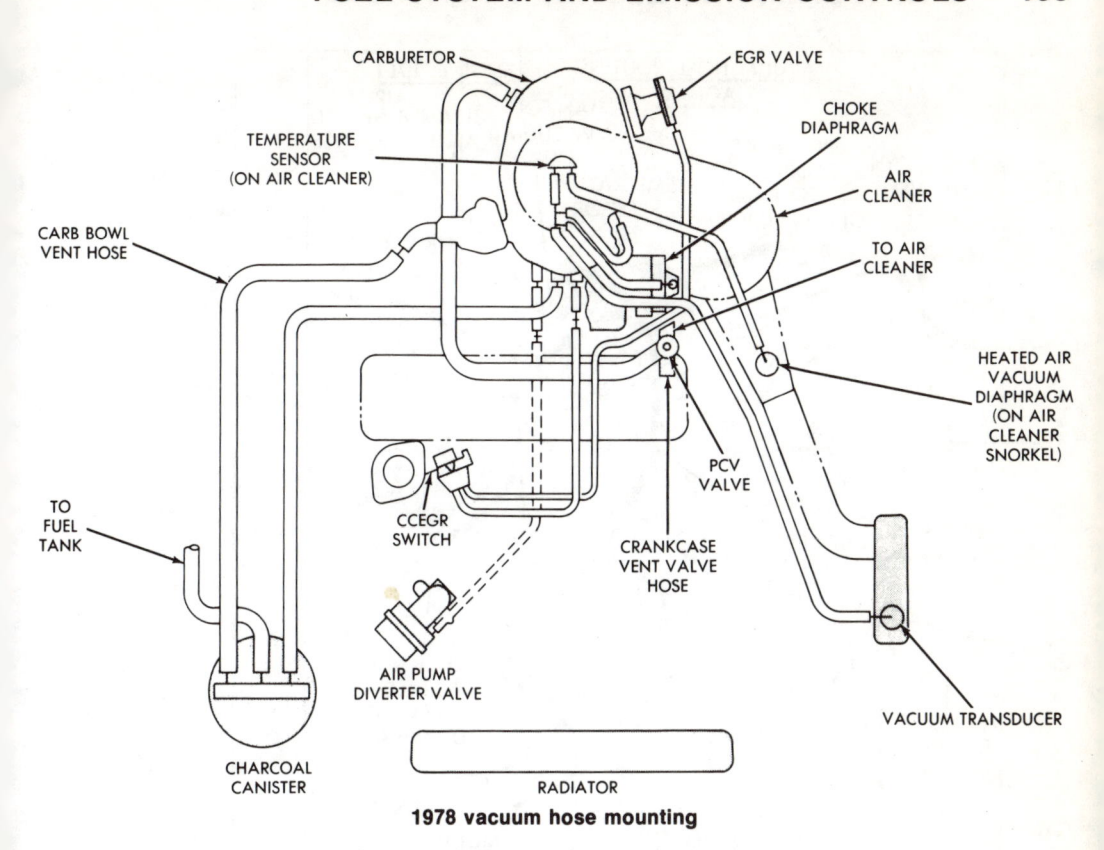

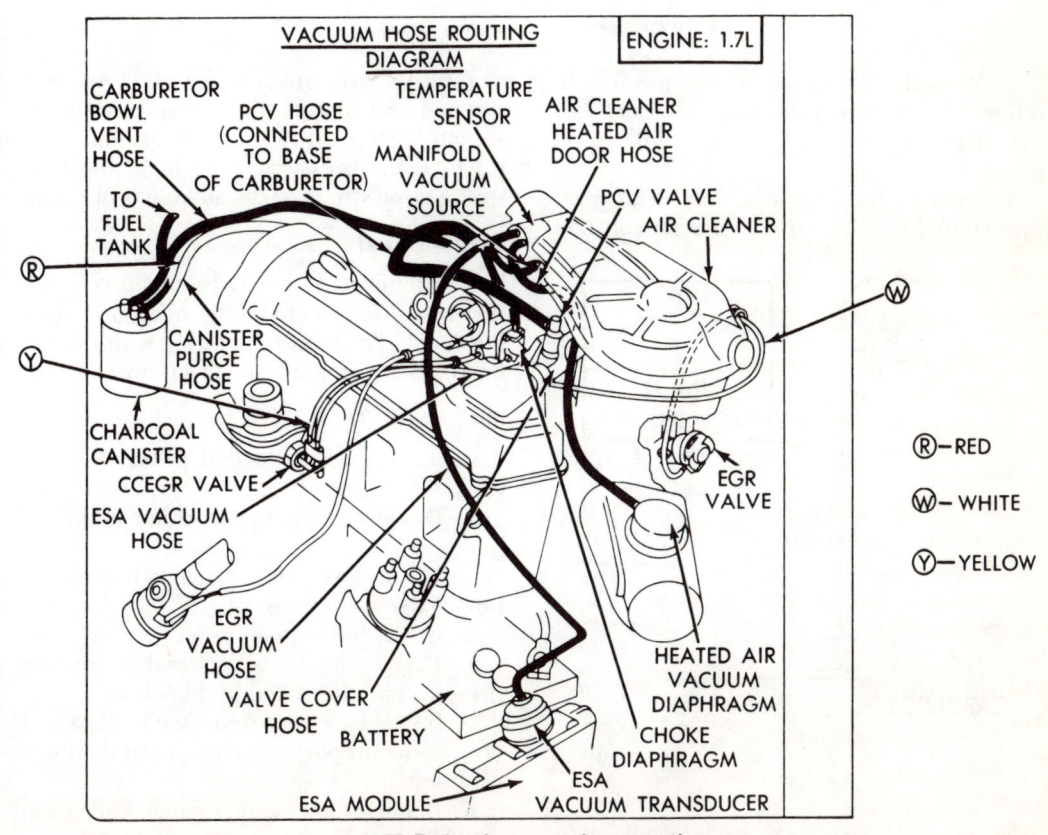

1978 vacuum hose mounting

1979 Federal vacuum hose routing

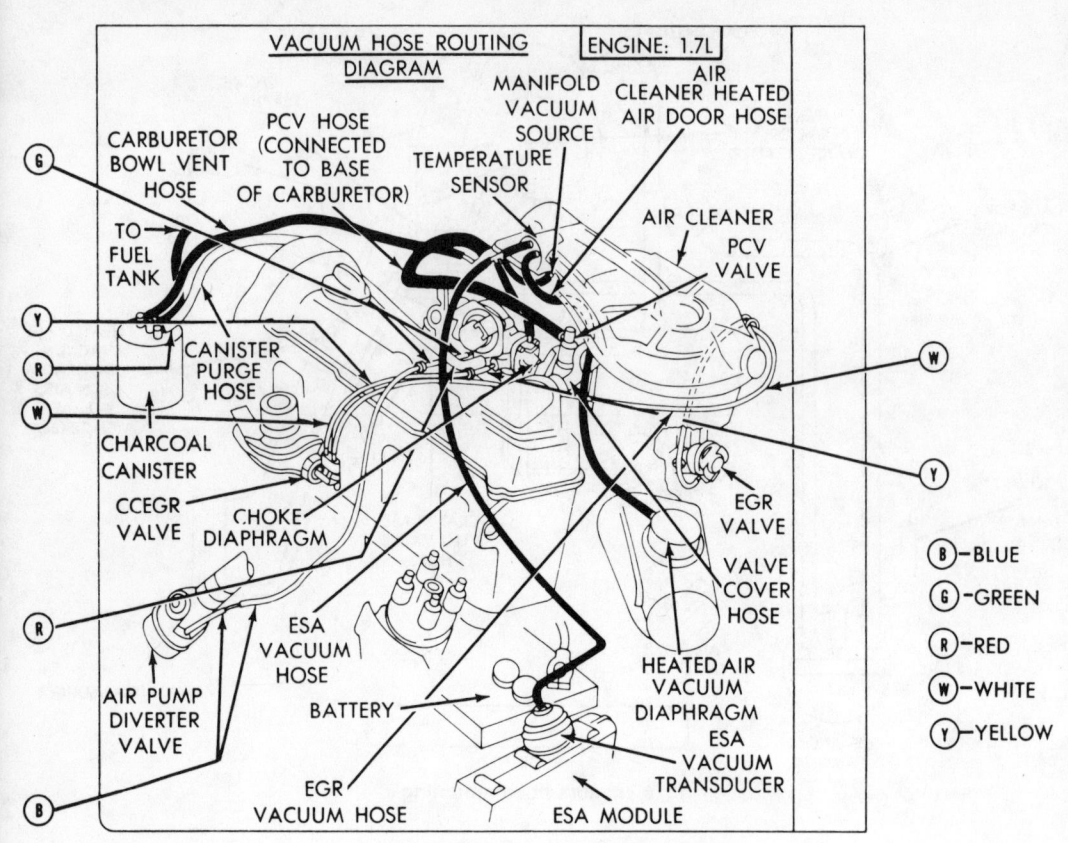

134 FUEL SYSTEM AND EMISSION CONTROLS

1979 California vacuum hose routing

3. Vent the pump for a few seconds to relieve air trapped in the fuel chamber. This will allow the pump to operate at full capacity.

4. Operate the engine at idle. The pressure should be 4–6 psi and remain constant or return slowly to zero when the engine is stopped. An instant drop to zero when the engine is stopped indicates a leaking outlet valve. If the pressure is too high, the main spring is too strong or the air vent is plugged.

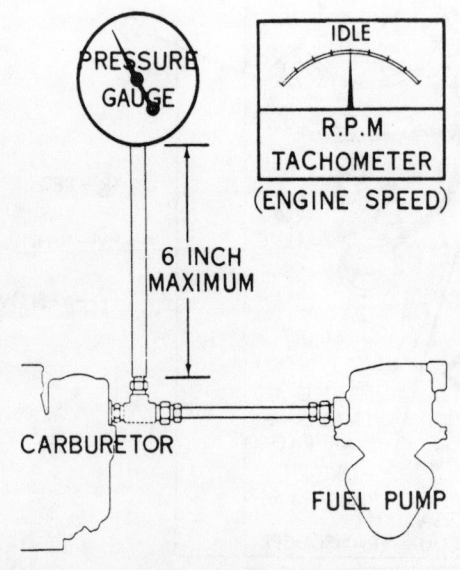

Vacuum Test

The vacuum test should be made with the fuel line disconnected. The minimum reading should be at least 10 in./Hg with the fuel line disconnected at the carburetor.

Inlet Valve Test

A vacuum gauge is needed to test the inlet valve.

1. Disconnect the fuel inlet line at the fuel pump.
2. Connect a vacuum gauge to the inlet fitting of the fuel pump.
3. Crank the engine.
4. There should a noticeable vacuum present, not alternated by blowback.
5. If blowback is present, the inlet valve is not seating properly and the pump should be replaced.
6. Remove the vacuum gauge and reconnect the fuel line.

Testing fuel pump pressure

FUEL SYSTEM AND EMISSION CONTROLS 135

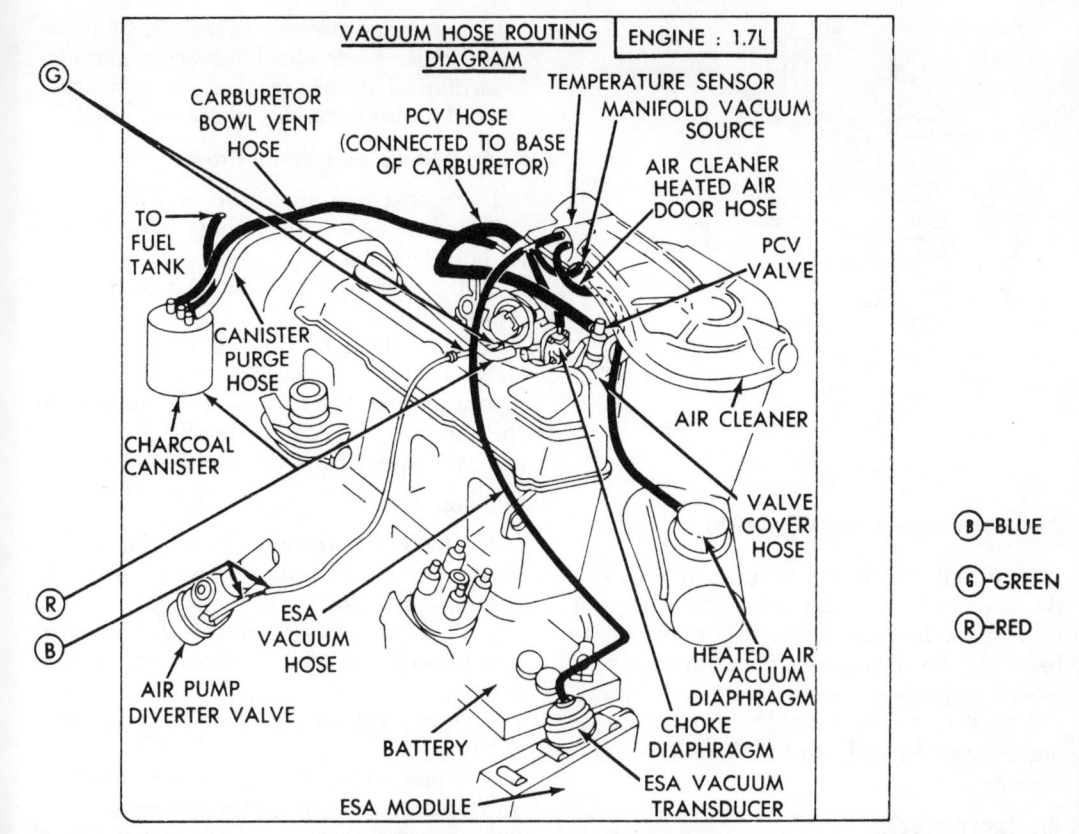

1979 Canada vacuum hose routing

REMOVAL AND INSTALLATION

A mechanical fuel pump is located on the left side of the engine. To remove the pump, disconnect the fuel and vapor lines and remove the attaching bolts. Installation is the reverse of removal. Always use a new gasket when installing the pump and make certain the gasket surfaces are clean.

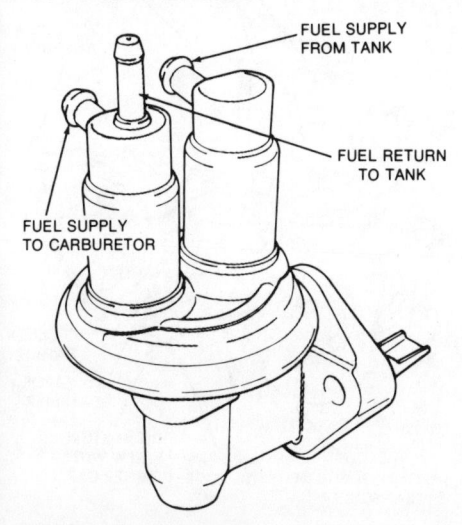

Fuel pump connections

Carburetor

A Holley model 5220 is used. This unit is a staged 2-barrel unit.

REMOVAL AND INSTALLATION

Do not attempt to remove the carburetor from a hot engine that has just been run. Allow the engine to cool sufficiently. When removing the carburetor, it should not be necessary to disturb the intake manifold isolator mounting screws, unless you have determined that a leak exists in the isolator.

1. Disconnect the negative battery cable.
2. Remove the air cleaner.
3. Remove the fuel filler cap to relieve pressure.
4. Disconnect the fuel inlet fitting and catch any excess fuel that may flow out.
5. Disconnect all electrical connections. Tag these for installation.
6. Disconnect the throttle linkage.
7. Disconnect and tag all hoses.
8. Remove the carburetor mounting nuts and remove the carburetor. Hold the carburetor level to avoid spilling fuel on a hot engine.

136 FUEL SYSTEM AND EMISSION CONTROLS

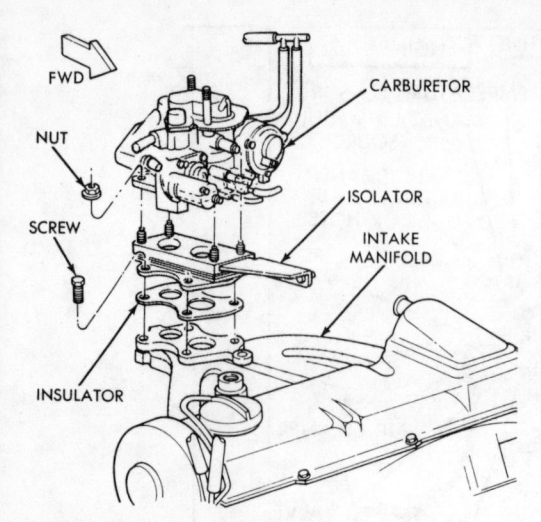

Carburetor removal and installation

9. Installation is the reverse of removal. Be careful when installing the mounting nut nearest the fast idle lever. It is very easy to bend the lever. Tighten the mounting nuts evenly to prevent vacuum leaks.

Check to be sure the choke plate opens and closes fully and that full throttle travel is obtained.

ADJUSTMENTS

NOTE: *Before attempting any adjustments, complaints of fuel loading on a cold engine on all 1978 models (except those with Federal emission package and aspirator and manual transmission) can be cured by removing the secondary choke blade and choke blade attaching screws and discarding. This change has been incorporated in production as of May 15, 1978.*

Float Setting and Float Drop

1. Remove and invert the air horn.
2. Insert a .480 inch gauge between the air horn and float.
3. If necessary, bend the tang on the float arm to adjust.
4. Turn the air horn right side up and allow the float to hang freely. Measure the float drop from the bottom of the air horn to the bottom of the float. It should be exactly ⅞ inches. Correct by bending the float tang.

Vacuum Kick

1. Open the throttle, close the choke, then close the throttle to trap the fast idle system at the closed choke position.
2. Disconnect the vacuum hose to the carburetor and connect it to an auxiliary vacuum source.
3. Apply at least 15 inches Hg. vacuum to the unit.
4. Apply sufficient force to close the choke valve without distorting the linkage.
5. Insert a gauge (see Specification Chart) between the top of the choke plate and the air horn wall.
6. Adjust by rotating the Allen screw in the center diaphragm housing.
7. Replace the vacuum hose.

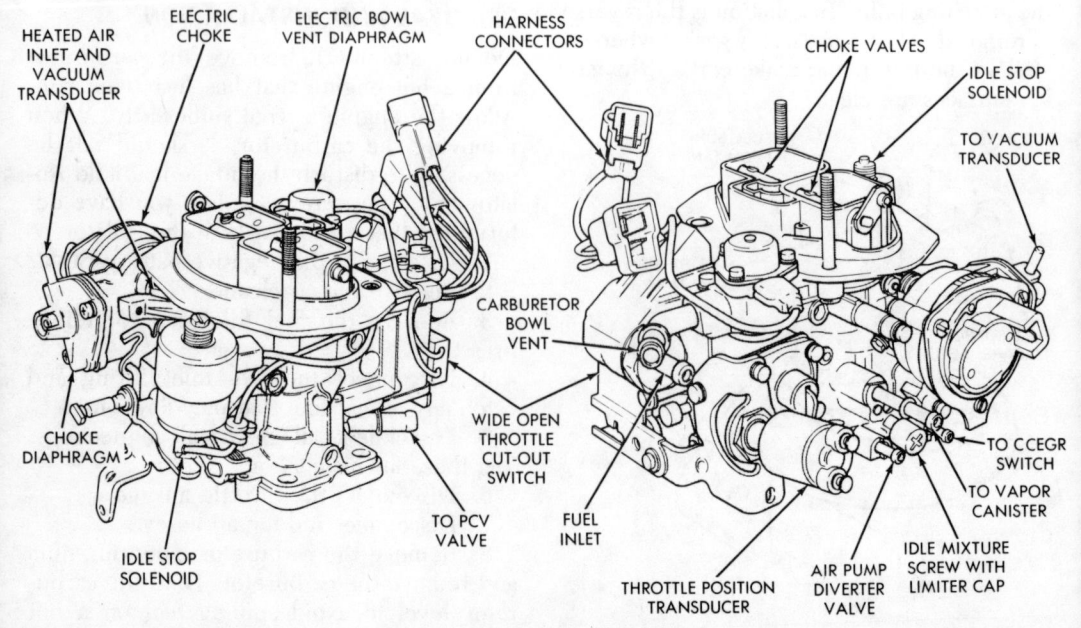

1978 Carburetor (with A/C)

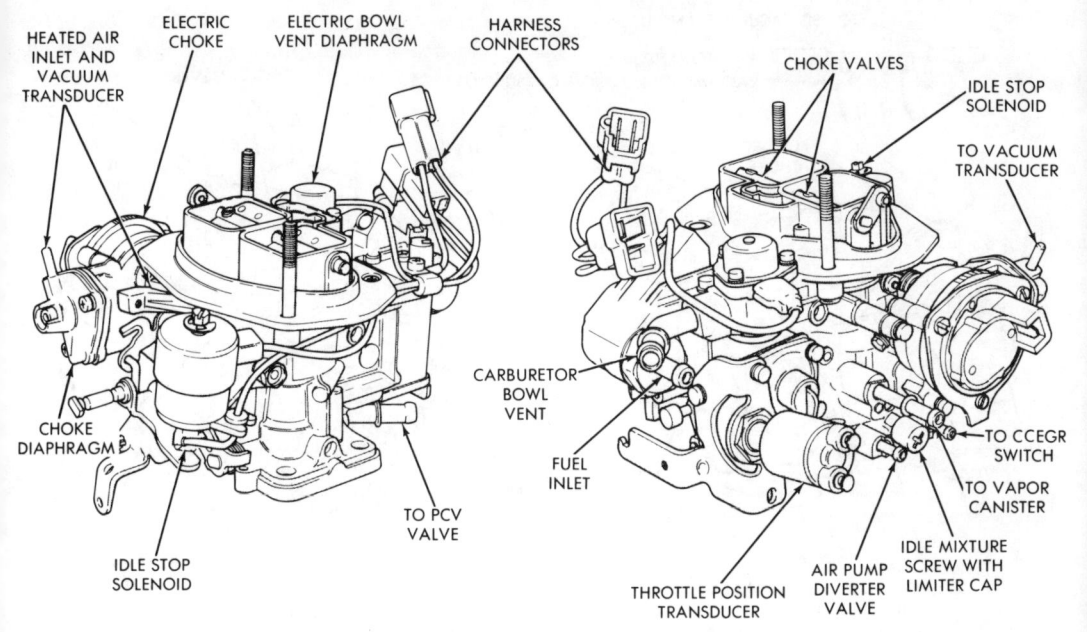

FUEL SYSTEM AND EMISSION CONTROLS 137

1978 Carburetor (w/o A/C)

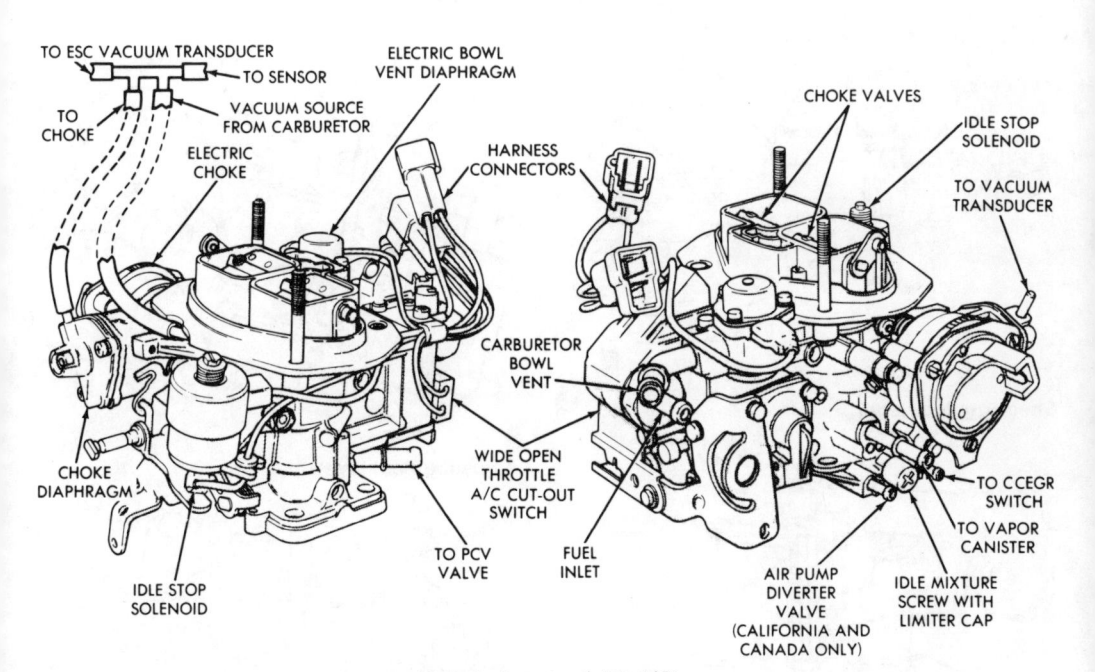

1979 Carburetor (with A/C)

Throttle Position Transducer

1978 ONLY

1. Disconnect the wire from the transducer.
2. Loosen the locknut.
3. Place an 11/16 inch gauge between the outer portion of the transducer and the mounting bracket.
4. To adjust the gap, turn the transducer.
5. Tighten the locknut.

Fast Idle

1. Remove the top of the air cleaner.
2. Disconnect and plug the EGR vacuum line.
3. Plug any open vacuum lines, which were connected to the air cleaner.

138 FUEL SYSTEM AND EMISSION CONTROLS

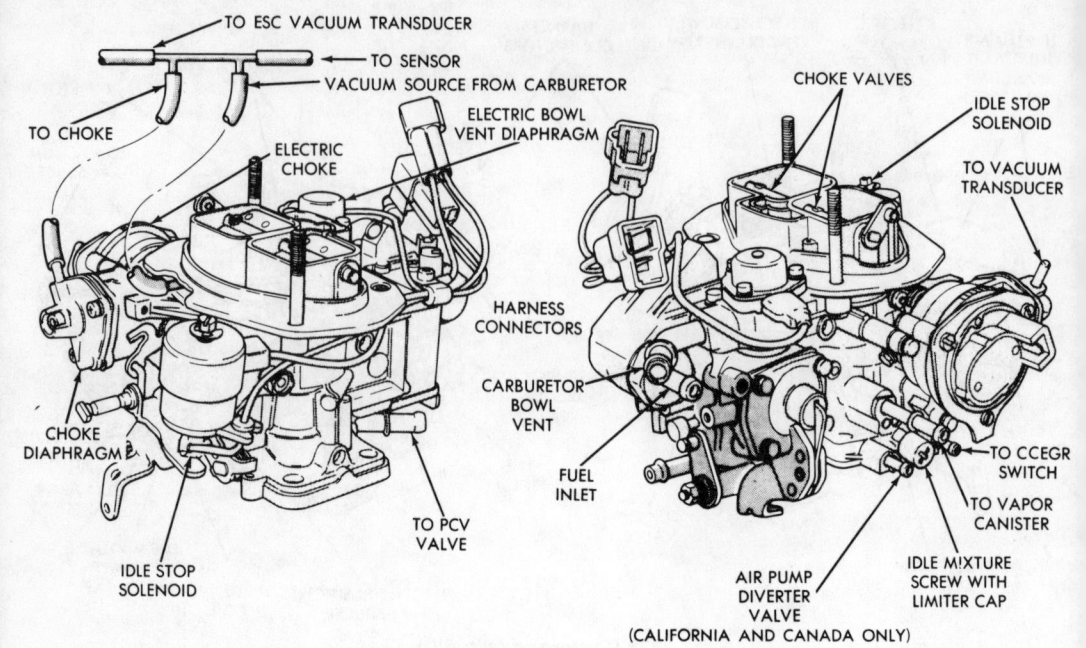

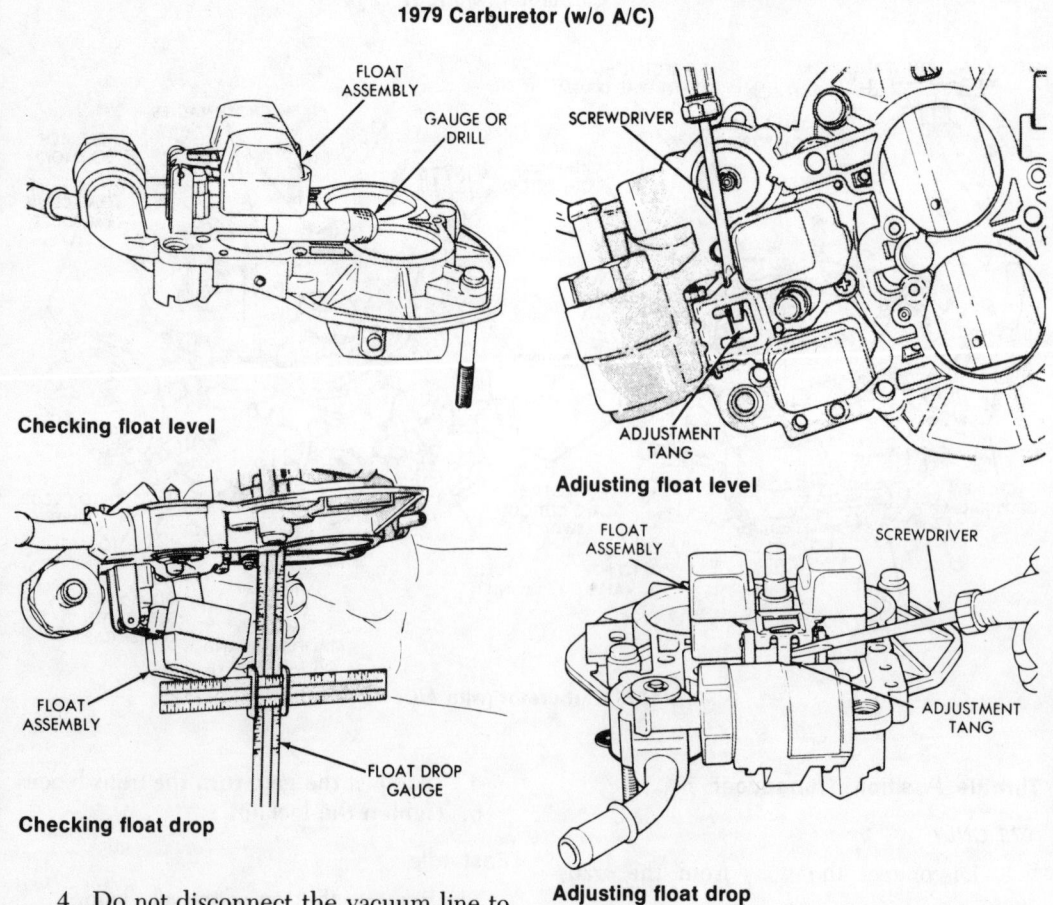

1979 Carburetor (w/o A/C)

Checking float level

Adjusting float level

Checking float drop

Adjusting float drop

4. Do not disconnect the vacuum line to the spark control computer. Instead, use a jumper wire to ground the idle stop switch. The air conditioning should be off.

5. Disconnect the engine cooling fan at the radiator and complete the circuit at the plug with a jumper wire to energize the fan.

6. Set the brake, place the transmission

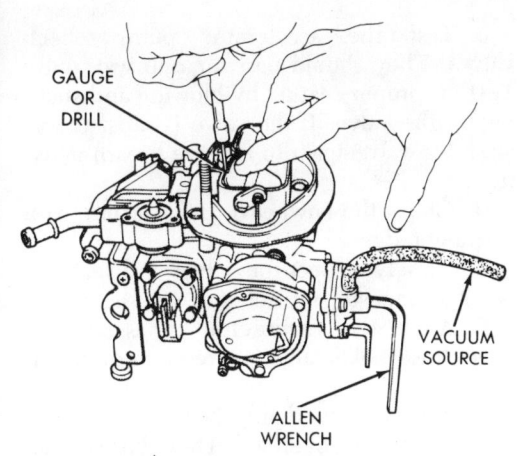

FUEL SYSTEM AND EMISSION CONTROLS   139

Adjusting choke vacuum kick

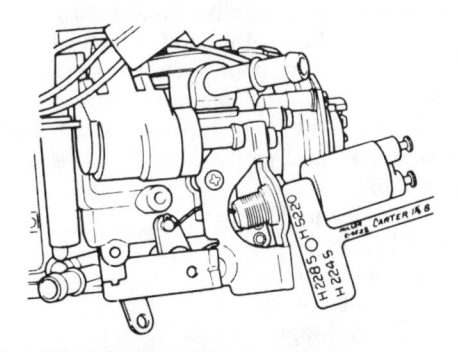

Adjusting throttle position transducer

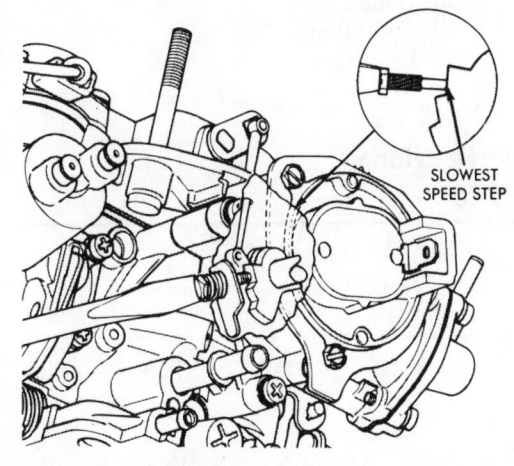

Adjusting fast idle speed

rpm. Do not adjust with the screw contacting the plastic cam.

10. Operate the throttle linkage a few times and return the screw to the first cam step to recheck rpm.

Throttle Stop Speed Adjustment (w/o Air Conditioning)

1. engine should be fully warmed.
2. Put the transmission in Neutral and set the parking brake.
3. Turn the headlights off.
4. Using a jumper wire, ground the idle stop carburetor switch.
5. Disconnect the idle stop solenoid wire at the connector.
6. Adjust the throttle stop speed screw to 700 5pm.
7. Reconnect the idle stop solenoid wire.
8. Disconnect the jumper wire from the carburetor switch.

OVERHAUL

Efficient carburetion depends greatly on careful cleaning and inspection during overhaul, since dirt, gum, varnish, water in or on the carburetor parts are mainly responsible for poor performance.

Carburetor overhaul should be performed in a clean, dust-free area. Carefully disassemble the carburetor, keeping look-alike parts segregated. Note all jet sizes.

Once the carburetor is disassembled, wash all parts (except diaphragms, electric choke units, pump plunger and any other plastic, leather or fiber parts) in clean carburetor solvent. Do not leave the parts in solvent any

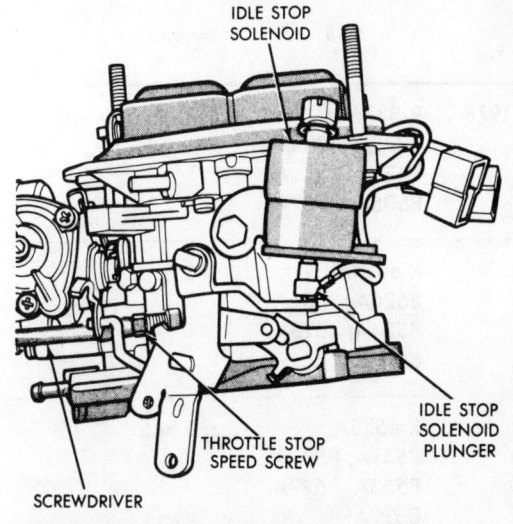

in Neutral and position the first step of the fast idle cam under the adjusting screw.

7. Connect a tachometer according to the manufacturer's specifications.
8. Start the engine and observe the idle speed. With the choke fully open, the speed should remain steady. If it gradually increases, the idle stop switch is not properly grounded.
9. Turn the adjusting screw to give 1100

Adjusting throttle stop speed (w/o A/C)

FUEL SYSTEM AND EMISSION CONTROLS

longer than necessary to sufficiently loosen the deposits. Excessive cleaning may remove the special finish from the float bowl and choke valve bodies, leaving them unfit for service. Rinse all parts in clean solvent and blow dry with compressed air. Wipe all plastic, leather or fiber parts with a clean, lint-free cloth.

Blow out all passages and jets with compressed air and be sure there are no restrictions or blockages. Never use wire to clean jets, fuel passages or air bleeds.

Check all parts for wear or damage. If wear or damage is found, replace the complete assembly. Especially check the following.

1. Check the float and needle seat for wear. If any is found, replace the assembly.
2. Check the float hinge pin for wear and the floats for distortion or dents. Replace the float if fuel has leaked into it.
3. Check the throttle and choke shaft bores for out-of-round. Damage or wear to the throttle arm, shaft or shaft bore will often require replacement of the throttle body. These parts require close tolerances and an air leak here can cause poor starting and idling.
4. Inspect the idle mixture adjusting needles for burrs or grooves. Burrs or grooves will usually require replacement of the needles since a satisfactory idle cannot be obtained.

5. Test the accelerator pump check valves. They should pass air one way only. Test for proper seating by blowing and sucking on the valve. If the valve is satisfactory, wash the valve again to remove breath moisture.
6. Check the bowl cover for warping with a straightedge.
7. Closely inspect the valves and seats for wear or damage, replacing as necessary.
8. After the carburetor is assembled, check the choke valve for freedom of operation.

Carburetor overhaul kits are recommended for each overhaul. These kits contain all gaskets and new parts to replace those that deteriorate most rapidly. Failure to replace all parts supplied with the kit (especially gaskets) can result in poor performance later.

Some carburetor manufacturers supply overhaul kits of three types—minor repair, major repair and gasket kits. They basically consist of:

Minor Repair Kits:
    All gaskets
    Float needle valve
    Volume control screw
    All diaphragms
    Pump diaphragm spring

Major Repair Kits:
    All jets and gaskets
    All diaphragms

Carburetor Specifications
Holley 5220

Year	Carb Part No.	Accelerator Pump	Dry Float Level (in.)	Vacuum Kick (in.)	Fast Idle RPM (w/fan)	Throttle Position Transducer (in.)	Throttle Stop Speed RPM	Choke
1978	R-8376A, 8378A, 8384A, 8439A, 8441A, 8505A, 8507A	#2 hole	.480	.070	1100	.547	700	2 Rich
1979	R-8524A, 8526A, 8532A, 8534A, 8528A, 8530A	#2 hole	.480	.040	1700	—	700	2 Rich
	R-8525A, 8541A, 8531A, 8533A, 8527A, 8529A	#2 hole	.480	.070	1400	—	700	2 Rich

FUEL SYSTEM AND EMISSION CONTROLS 141

Float needle valve
Volume control screw
Pump ball valve
Main jet carrier
Float
Complete intermediate rod
Intermediate pump lever
Complete injector tube
Assorted screws and washers

Gasket Kits:
All gaskets.

After cleaning and checking all components, reassemble the carburetor using new parts, using the exploded views in the car sections, if necessary. Make sure that all screws and jets are tight in their seats, but do not overtighten or the tips will be distorted. Do not tighten needle valves into their seats or uneven jetting will result. Always use new gaskets and adjust the float.

Fuel Tank

REMOVAL AND INSTALLATION

1. Raise and support the car.
2. Disconnect the negative battery cable.
3. Remove the fuel filler cap.
4. Disconnect the fuel supply line at the right front shock tower. Connect a drain or siphon line and empty the tank into another container.

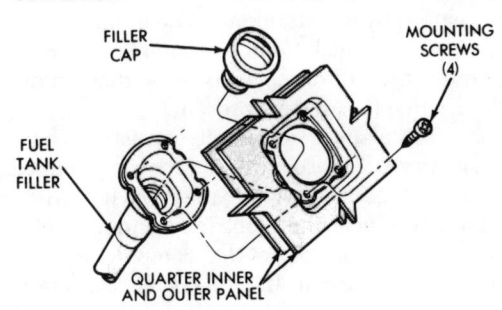

NOTE: *Do not begin the siphoning process by sucking on the line.*

5. Remove the screws holding the filler tube to the inner and outer quarter panel.
6. Disconnect and tag the wiring and lines from the tank.
7. Remove the exhaust pipe shield. Allow the shield to rest on the exhaust pipe.
8. Support the fuel tank and disconnect the fuel tank straps.
9. Lower the tank slightly and work the tank from the filler tube.
10. Lower the tank some more and disconnect the vapor separator roll-over valve hose.
11. Remove the fuel tank and insulating pad.
12. Installation is the reverse of removal. Be sure the vapor vent hose is clipped to the tank and not pinched between the tank and floorpan. Also be sure the fuel tank straps are not twisted when they are installed.

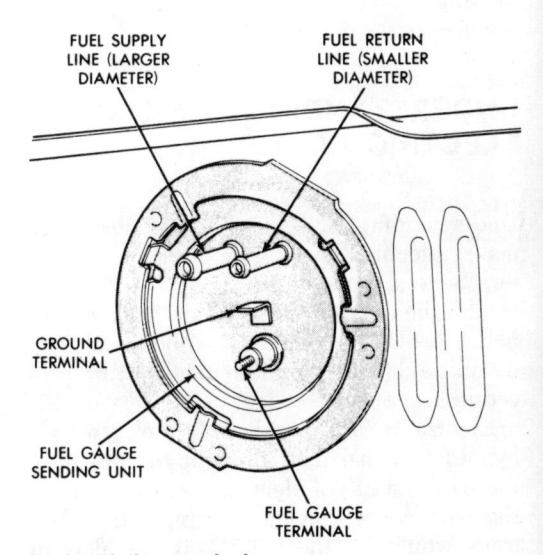

Fuel filler mounting

Fuel tank lines and wing

5

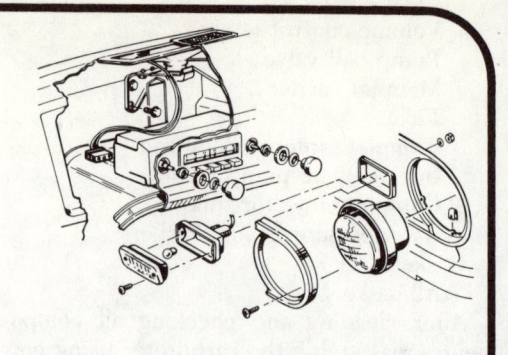

Chassis Electrical

UNDERSTANDING BASIC ELECTRICITY

Understanding the basic theory of electricity makes electrical troubleshooting much easier. Several gauges are used in electrical troubleshooting to see inside the circuit being tested. Without a basic understanding, it will be difficult to understand testing procedures.

Electricity is the flow of electrons—hypothetical particles thought to constitute the basic "stuff" of electricity. In a comparison with water flowing in a pipe, the electrons would be the water. As the flow of water can be measured, the flow of electricity can be measured. The unit of measurement is amperes, frequently abbreviated "amps." An ammeter will measure the actual amount of current flowing in the circuit.

Just as the water pressure is measured in units such as pounds per square inch, electrical pressure is measured in volts. When a voltmeter's two probes are placed on two "live" portions of an electrical circuit with different electrical pressures, current will flow through the voltmeter and produce a reading which indicates the difference in electrical pressure between the two parts of the circuit.

While increasing the voltage in a circuit will increase the flow of current, the actual flow depends not only on voltage, but on the resistance of the circuit. The standard unit for measuring circuit resistance is an ohm, measured by an ohmmeter. The ohmmeter is somewhat similar to an ammeter, but incorporates its own source of power so that a standard voltage is always present.

An actual electric circuit consists of four basic parts. These are: the power source, such as a generator or battery; a hot wire, which conducts the electricity under a relatively high voltage to the component supplied by the circuit; the load, such as a lamp, motor, resistor, or relay coil; and the ground wire, which carries the current back to the source under very low voltage. In such a circuit the bulk of the resistance exists between the point where the hot wire is connected to the load, and the point where the load is grounded. In an automobile, the vehicle's frame, which is made of steel, is used as a part of the ground circuit for many of the electrical devices.

Remember that, in electrical testing, the voltmeter is connected in parallel with the circuit being tested (without disconnecting any wires) and measures the difference in voltage between the locations of the two probes; that the ammeter is connected in series with the load (the circuit is separated at one point and the ammeter inserted so it becomes a part of the circuit); and the ohmmeter is self-powered, so that all the power in the circuit should be off and the portion of the circuit to be measured contacted at either end by one of the probes of the meter.

For any electrical system to operate, it must make a complete circuit. This simply means that the power flow from the battery must make a complete circle. When an electrical component is operating, power flows from the battery to the component, passes through the component causing it to perform its function (lighting a light bulb) and then returns to the battery through the ground of the circuit. This ground is usually (but not always) the metal part of the car on which the electrical component is mounted.

Perhaps the easiest way to visualize this is to think of connecting a light bulb with two wires attached to it to your car battery. The battery in your car has two posts (negative and positive). If one of the two wires attached to the light bulb was attached to the negative post of the battery and the other wire was attached to the positive post of the battery, you would have a complete circuit. Current from the battery would flow out one post, through the wire attached to it and then to the light bulb, where it would pass through causing it to light. It would then leave the light bulb, travel through the other wire, and return to the other post of the battery.

The normal automotive circuit differs from this simple example in two ways. First, instead of having a return wire from the bulb to the battery, the light bulb returns the current to the battery through the chassis of the vehicle. Since the negative battery cable is attached to the chassis and the chassis is made of electrically conductive metal, the chassis of the vehicle can serve as a ground wire to complete the circuit. Secondly, most automotive circuits contain switches to turn components on and off when it is turned off.

Some electrical components which require a large amount of current to operate also have a relay in their circuit. Since these circuits carry a large amount of current, the thickness of the wire in the circuit (gauge size) is also greater. If this large wire were connected from the component to the control switch on the instrument panel, and then back to the component, a voltage drop would occur in the circuit. To prevent this potential drop in voltage, an electromagnetic switch (relay) is used. The large wires in the circuit are connected from the car battery to one side of the relay, and from the opposite side of the relay to the component. The relay is normally open, preventing current from passing through the circuit. An additional, smaller, wire is connected from the relay to the control switch for the circuit. When the control switch is turned on, it grounds the smaller wire from the relay and completes the circuit. This closes the relay and allows current to flow from the battery to the component. The horn, headlight, and starter circuits are three which use relays.

Your alternator (which supplies the battery) puts out more current at speeds above idle. This is normal. However, it is possible for larger surges of current to pass through the electrical system of your car. If this surge of current were to reach an electrical component, it could burn it out. To prevent this from happening, fuses are connected into the current supply wires of the major electrical systems of your car. The fuse serves to head off the surge at the pass. When an electrical current of excessive power passes through the component's fuse, the fuse blows out and breaks the circuit, saving it from destruction.

The fuse also protects the component from damage if the power supply wire to the component is grounded before the current reaches the component.

Every complete circuit from a power source must include a component which is using the power from the power source. If you were to disconnect the light bulb (from the previous example of a light bulb being connected to the battery by two wires) from the wires and touch the two wires together (please take our word for this; don't try it), the result will be a shower of sparks. A similar thing happens (on a smaller scale) when the power supply wire to a component or the electrical component itself becomes grounded before the normal ground connection for the circuit. To prevent damage to the system, the fuse for the circuit blows to interrupt the circuit—protecting the components from damage. Because grounding a wire from a power source makes a complete circuit—less the required component to use the power—the phenomenon is called a short circuit. The most common causes of short circuits are: the rubber insulation on a wire breaking or rubbing through to expose the current carrying core of the wire to a metal part of the car, or a shorted switch.

CHASSIS ELECTRICAL

Some electrical systems on the car are protected by a circuit breaker which is, basically, a self-repairing fuse. When either of the above-described events takes place in a system which is protected by a circuit breaker, the circuit breaker opens the circuit the same way a fuse does. However, when either the short is removed from the circuit or the surge subsides, the circuit breaker resets itself and does not have to be replaced as a fuse does.

The final protective device in the chassis electrical system is a fuse link. A fuse link is a wire that acts as a fuse. It is connected between the starter relay and the main wiring harness for the car. This connection is under the hood, very near a similar fuse link which protects the engine electrical system. Since the fuse link protects all the chassis electrical components, it is the probable cause of trouble when none of the electrical components function, unless the battery is disconnected or dead.

Electrical problems generally fall into one of three areas:

1. The component that is not functioning is not receiving current.
2. The component itself is not functioning.
3. The component is not properly grounded.

Problems that fall into the first category are by far the most complicated. It is the current supply system to the component which contains all the switches, relays, fuses, etc.

The electrical system can be checked with a test light and a jumper wire. A test light is a device that looks like a pointed screwdriver with a wire attached to it. It has a light bulb in its handle. A jumper wire is a piece of insulated wire with an alligator clip attached to each end.

If a light bulb is not working, you must follow a systematic plan to determine which of the three causes is the villain.

1. Turn on the switch that controls the inoperable bulb.
2. Disconnect the power supply wire from the bulb.
3. Attach the ground wire on the test light to a good metal ground.
4. Touch the probe end of the test light to the end of the power supply wire that was disconnected from the bulb. If the bulb is receiving current, the test light will go on.

NOTE: *If the bulb is one which works only when the ignition key is turned on (turn signal), make sure the key is turned on.*

If the test light does not go on, then the problem is in the circuit between the battery and the bulb. As mentioned before, this includes all the switches, fuses, and relays in the system. Turn to the wiring diagram and find the bulb on the diagram. Follow the wire that runs back to the battery. The problem is an open circuit between the battery and the bulb. If the fuse is blown and, when replaced, immediately blows again, there is a short circuit in the system which must be located and repaired. If there is a switch in the system, bypass it with a jumper wire. This is done by connecting one end of the jumper wire to the power supply wire into the switch and the other end of the jumper wire to the wire coming out of the switch. If the test light lights with the jumper wire installed the switch or whatever was bypassed is defective.

NOTE: *Never substitute the jumper wire for the bulb, as the bulb is the component required to use the power from the power source.*

5. If the bulb in the test light goes on, then the current is getting to the bulb that is not working in the car. This eliminates the first of the three possible causes. Connect the power supply wire and connect a jumper wire from the bulb to a good metal ground. Do this with the switch which controls the bulb turned on, and also the ignition switch turned on if it is required for the light to work. If the bulb works with jumper wire installed, then it has a bad ground. This is usually caused by the metal area on which the bulb mounts to the car being coated with some type of foreign matter.

6. If neither test located the source of the trouble, then the light bulb itself is defective.

The above test procedure can be applied to any of the components of the chassis electrical system by substituting the component that is not working for the light bulb. Remember that for any electrical system to work, all connections must be clean and tight.

HEATER

Heater Assembly

REMOVAL AND INSTALLATION— WITHOUT AIR CONDITIONING

1. Disconnect the battery and drain the cooling system.

CHASSIS ELECTRICAL

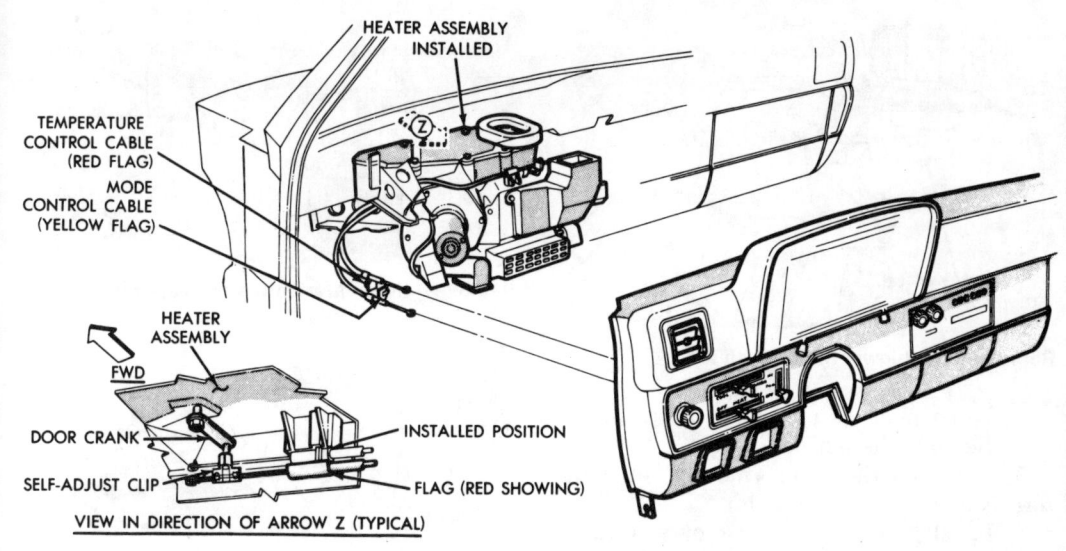

Heater control holders and attachment

2. Remove the center outside air floor vent housing.
3. Remove the ash tray.
4. Remove the two defroster duct adapter screws. The left one is reached through the ash tray opening.
5. Remove the defrost duct adapter and push the flexible hose up out of the way.
6. Disconnect the temperature control cable.
7. Disconnect the blower motor wiring connector.
8. Disconnect the hoses from the heater core and plug the core openings.
9. Remove the two nuts retaining the heater unit to the firewall.
10. Remove the glove compartment and door.
11. Remove the screw attaching the heater brace bracket to the instrument panel.
12. Remove the heater assembly support strap nut. Disconnect the strap from the plenum stud and lower the heater from the instrument panel.
13. Disconnect the control cable and remove the unit from the car.
14. Connect the control cable and raise the unit into position so that the core tubes and mounting studs fit through their holes in the firewall.
15. Install the support strap and hand tighten the nut.
16. Install and tighten the two heater-to-firewall nuts.
17. Unplug and connect the core tubes.
18. Install the defroster duct adaptor.
19. Install the ash tray.
20. Install the center outside air floor vent housing.
21. Install the glove compartment.
22. Refill the cooling system.

Blower Motor

REMOVAL AND INSTALLATION

Without Air Conditioning

The blower motor is located under the instrument panel on the left side of the heater assembly.

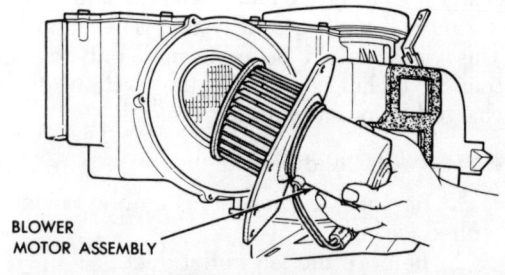

Removing or installing the heater

Removing or installing the blower motor

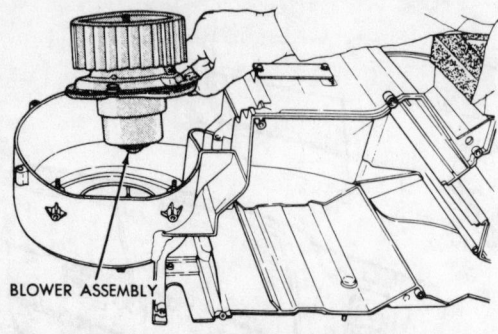

CHASSIS ELECTRICAL

Removing the blower motor (with A/C)

1. Disconnect the motor wiring.
2. Remove the left outlet duct.
3. Remove the four motor retaining screws and remove the motor.
4. Installation is the reverse of removal.

Air Conditioned Cars

1. Disconnect the battery ground.
2. Remove the three screws securing the glovebox to the instrument panel.
3. Disconnect the wiring from the blower and case.
4. Remove the blower vent tube from the case.
5. Loosen the recirculating door from its bracket and remove the actuator from the housing. Leave the vacuum lines attached.
6. Remove the seven screws attaching the recirculating housing to the A/C unit and remove the housing.
7. Remove the three mounting flange nuts and washers.
8. Remove the blower motor from the unit.
9. Installation is the reverse of removal. Replace any damaged sealer.

Heater Core
REMOVAL AND INSTALLATION
Air Conditioned Cars

Removal of the Heater-Evaporator Unit is required for core removal. Two people will be required to perform the operation. Discharge, evacuation and recharge and leak testing of the refrigerant system is necessary. This work should be performed only by a trained technician. Have the system discharged before attempting removal.

Without Air Conditioning

1. Remove the heater assembly as described earlier.
2. Remove the left outlet duct.

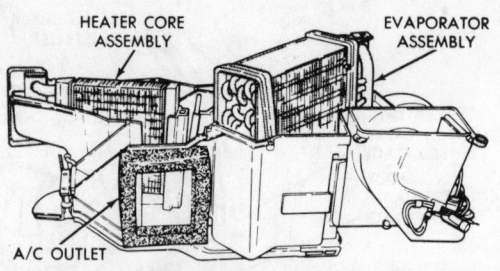

Removing the heater core and evaporator coil

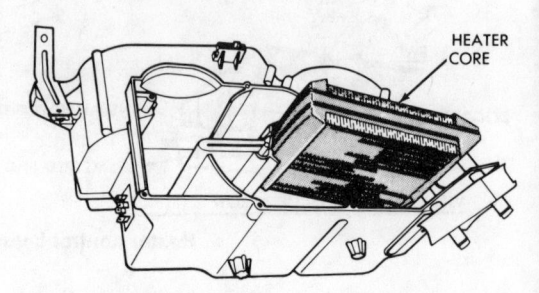

Removing the heater core

3. Remove the blower motor.
4. Remove the defroster duct adapter.
5. Remove the outside air and defroster door cover.
6. Remove the defroster door.
7. Remove the defroster door control rod.
8. Remove the core cover.
9. Lift the core from the unit.
10. Installation is the reverse of removal.

During installation, a small can of refrigerant oil will be necessary.

1. Disconnect the battery ground.
2. Drain the coolant.
3. Disconnect the temperature door cable from the heater-evaporator unit.
4. Disconnect the temperature door cable from the retaining clips.
5. Remove the glovebox.
6. Disconnect the vacuum harness from the control head.
7. Disconnect the blower motor lead and anti-diesel relay wire.
8. Remove the seven screws fastening the right trim bezel to the instrument panel. Starting at the right side, swing the bezel clear and remove it.
9. Remove the three screws on the bottom of the center distribution duct cover and slide the cover rearward and remove it.
10. Remove the center distribution duct.
11. Remove the defroster duct adaptor.
12. Remove the H-type expansion valve, located on the right side of the firewall:

CHASSIS ELECTRICAL 147

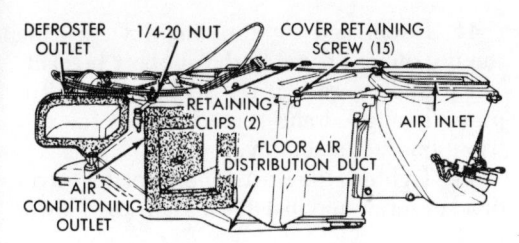

Heater/evaporator unit positioned for disassembly

a. remove the 5/16 in. bolt in the center of the plumbing sealing plate.

b. carefully pull the refrigerant lines toward the front of the car, taking care to avoid scratching the valve sealing surfaces.

c. remove the two ¼–20 Allenhead capscrews and remove the valve.

13. Cap the pipe openings at once. Wrap the valve in a plastic bag.
14. Disconnect the hoses from the core tubes.
15. Disconnect the vacuum lines at the intake manifold and water valve.
16. Remove the unit-to-firewall retaining nuts.
17. Remove the panel support bracket.
18. Remove the right cowl lower panel.
19. Remove the instrument panel pivot bracket screw from the right side.
20. Remove the screws securing the lower instrument panel at the steering column.
21. Pull back the carpet from under the unit as far as possible.
22. Remove the nut from the evaporator-heater unit-to-plenum mounting brace and blower motor ground cable. While supporting the unit, remove the brace from its stud.
23. Lift the unit, pulling it rearward to allow clearance. These operations may require two people.
24. Slowly lower the unit taking care to keep the studs from hanging-up on the insulation.
25. When the unit reaches the floor, slide it rearward until it is out from under the instrument panel.
26. Remove the unit from the car.
27. Place the unit on a workbench. On the inside-the-car-side, remove the ¼-20 nut from the mode door actuator on the top cover and the two retaining clips from the front edge of the cover. To remove the mode door actuator, remove the two screws securing it to the cover.
28. Remove the fifteen screws attaching the cover to the assembly and lift off the cover. Lift the mode door out of the unit.

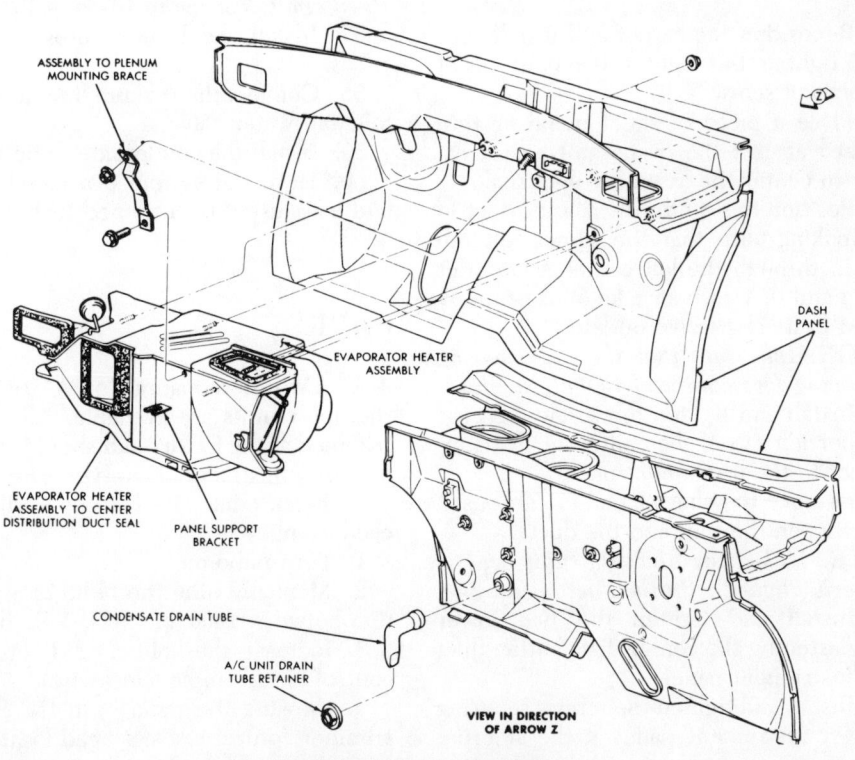

Heater/evaporator assembly

CHASSIS ELECTRICAL

29. Remove the screw from the core retaining bracket and lift out the core.

To install:

30. Place the core in the unit and install the bracket.

31. Install the actuator arm.

CAUTION: *When installing the unit in the car, care must be taken that the vacuum lines to the engine compartment do not hang-up on the accelerator or become trapped between the unit and the firewall. If this happens, kinked lines will result and the unit will have to be removed to free them. Proper routing of these lines will require two people. The portion of the vacuum harness which is routed through the steering column support MUST be positioned BEFORE the distribution housing is installed. The harness MUST be routed ABOVE the temperature control cable.*

32. Place the unit on the floor as far under the panel as possible.

33. Raise the unit carefully, at the same time pull the lower instrument panel rearward as far as possible.

34. Position the unit in place and attach the brace to the stud.

35. Install the lower ground cable and attach the nut.

36. Install and tighten the unit-to-firewall nuts.

37. Reposition the carpet and install, but do not tighten the right instrument panel pivot bracket screw.

38. Place a piece of sheet metal or thin cardboard against the evaporator-heater assembly to center the assembly duct seal.

39. Position the center distributor duct in place making sure that the upper left tab comes in through the left center A/C outlet opening and that each air take-off is properly inserted in its respective outlet.

NOTE: *Make sure that the radio wiring connector does not interfere with the duct.*

40. Install and tighten the screw securing the upper left tab of the center air distribution duct to the instrument panel.

41. Remove the sheet metal or cardboard from between the unit and the duct.

NOTE: *Make sure that the unit seal is properly aligned with the duct opening.*

42. Install and tighten the two lower screws fastening the center distribution duct to the instrument panel.

43. Install and tighten the screws securing the lower instrument panel at the steering column.

44. Install and tighten the nut securing the instrument panel to the support bracket.

45. Make sure that the seal on the unit is properly aligned and seated against the distribution duct assembly.

46. Tighten the instrument panel pivot bracket screw and install the right cowl lower trim.

47. Slide the distributor duct cover assembly onto the center distribution duct so that the notches lock into the tabs and the tabs slide over the rear and side ledges of the center duct assembly.

48. Install the three screws securing the ducting.

49. Install the right trim bezel.

50. Connect the vacuum harness to the control head.

51. Connect the blower lead and the anti-diesel wire.

52. Install the glovebox.

53. Connect the temperature door cable.

54. Install new O-rings on the evaporator plate and the plumbing plate. Coat the new O-rings with clean refrigerant oil.

55. Place the H-valve against the evaporator sealing plate surface and install the two ¼-20NC throughbolts. Torque to 6–10 ft lb.

56. Carefully hold the refrigerant line connector against the valve and install the $5/16$-18-NC bolt. *Torque to 14–20 ft lb.*

57. Install the heater hoses at the core tubes.

58. Connect the vacuum lines at the manifold and water valve.

59. Install the condensate drain tube.

60. Have the system evacuated, charged and leak tested by a trained technician.

RADIO

AM, AM/FM monaural, or AM/FM stereo multiplex units are available. All radios are trimmed at the factory and should require no further adjustment. However, after a repair or if the antenna trim is to be verified, proceed as follows:

1. Turn radio on.

2. Manually tune the radio to a weak station between 1400 and 1600 KHz on AM.

3. Increase the volume and set the tone control to full treble (clockwise).

4. Viewing the radio from the front, the trimmer control is a slot-head located at the rear of the right side. Adjust it carefully by

CHASSIS ELECTRICAL 149

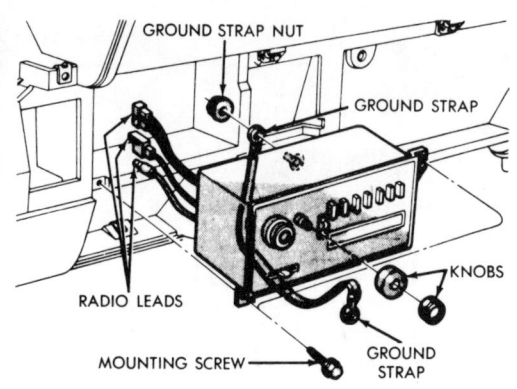

Radio removed or installation

turning it back and forth with a screwdriver until maximum loudness is achieved.

NOTE: *Some 1978 and early production 1979 cars exhibit an ignition noise interfering with radio reception. This can be corrected by installing the following items:*
1. *Ground Strap (Engine-mount-to-frame) (Chrysler Part No. 5211212)*
2. *Ground Strap (Engine-to-Cowl) (Chrysler Part No. 5211211).*
3. *Ground Strap (A/C Evaporator-to-Cowl) (Chrysler Part No. 5211210)*

Ground straps can also be obtained in kit form from local radio or CB shops.

REMOVAL AND INSTALLATION

1. Remove the seven bezel attaching screws and open the glove compartment.
2. Remove the bezel, guiding the right end around the glove compartment and away from the panel.
3. Disconnect the radio ground strap and remove the two radio mounting screws.
4. Pull the radio from the panel and disconnect the wiring and antenna lead.
5. Installation is the reverse of removal.

WINDSHIELD WIPERS

Front Wipers

WIPER REFILL

Removal and Installation

See Chapter 1 for wiper refill replacement.

WIPER BLADE REPLACEMENT

1. Lift the wiper arm away from the glass.
2. Depress the release lever on the bridge and remove the blade assembly from the arm.
3. Lift the tab and pinch the end bridge to release it from the center bridge.
4. Slide the end bridge from the blade element and the element from the opposite end bridge.
5. Assembly is the reverse of removal. Make sure that the element locking tabs are securely locked in position.

MOTOR

Removal and Installation

1. Disconnect the linkage from the motor crank arm.
2. Remove the wiper motor plastic cover.
3. Disconnect the wiring harness from the motor.
4. Remove the three mounting bolts from the motor bracket and remove the motor.
5. Installation is the reverse of removal.

Rear Wipers

BLADE AND ARM

Removal and Installation

1. Turn the wipers ON and position the blade at a convenient place on the glass by turning the ignition OFF.
2. Lift the wiper arm off the glass.
3. Depress the release lever on the center bridge and remove the center bridge.
4. Depress the release button on the end bridge to release it from the center bridge.
5. Remove the wiper element from the end bridge.
6. To remove the arm, pull out the latch knob and remove the arm from the pivot.
7. Installation is the reverse of removal. Be sure the element is engaged in all 4 bridge claws.

WIPER MOTOR

A new wiper motor was used beginning with mid-February 1978 production. The new motor is Part No. 5211024 with date code 0378 imprinted on red ink. Early motors have the date code in black ink (same part no.) If failure of the early motor occurs, replace it with the new motor.

Removal and Installation

1. Open the liftgate.
2. Remove the wiper motor plastic cover.
3. Remove the blade and arm assembly.
4. Remove the chrome nut from the pivot shaft and the chrome ring from the pivot shaft.

150 CHASSIS ELECTRICAL

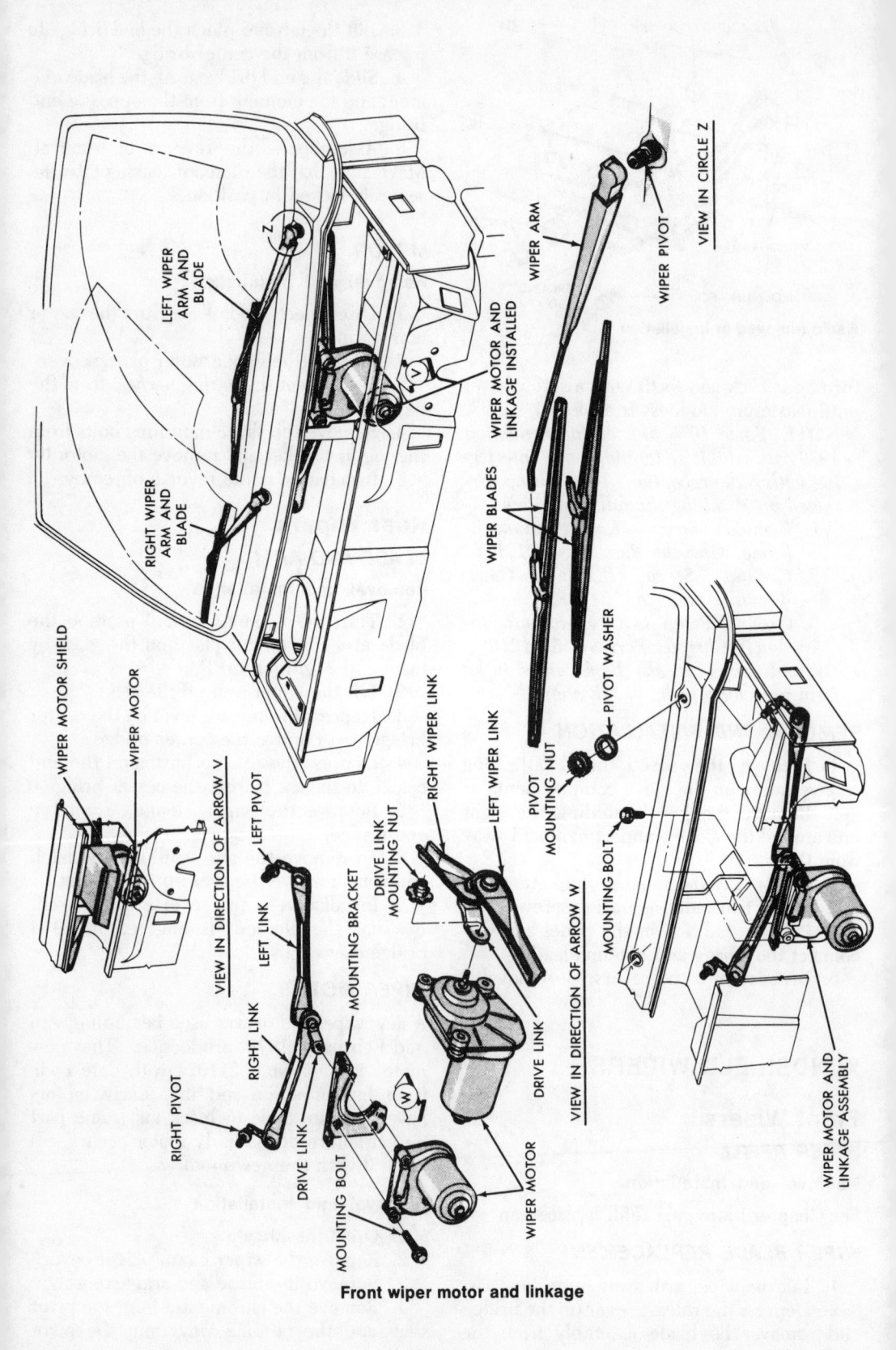

Front wiper motor and linkage

CHASSIS ELECTRICAL 151

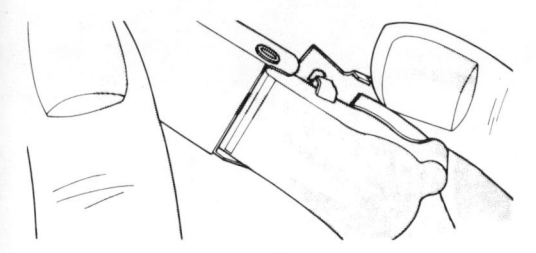

Removing front wiper arm

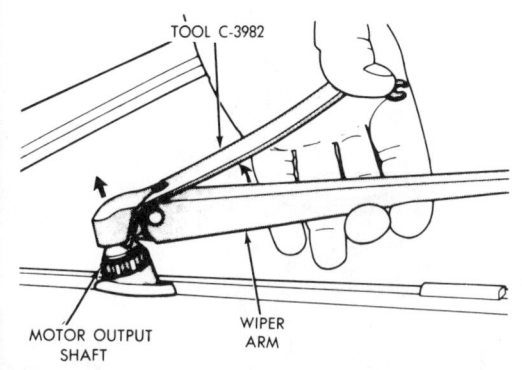

Removing liftgate wiper arm with tool available locally

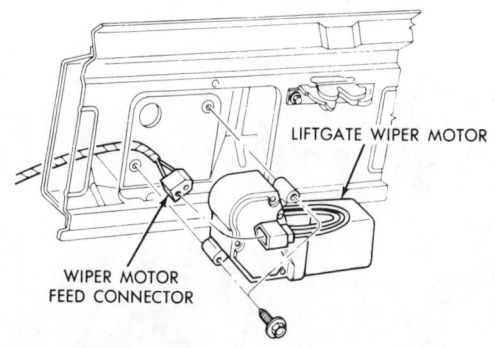

Liftgate wiper motor

5. From inside the tailgate, remove the motor mounting screws.
6. Disconnect the main liftgate wiring harness from the motor pigtail wire.
7. Remove the motor.
8. Installation is the reverse of removal.

Windshield Washer Reservoir and Pump

REMOVAL AND INSTALLATION
Front

1. Open the hood and disconnect the wiring harness from the pump.
2. Remove the sheet metal screws holding the reservoir to the inner fender shield.
3. Disconnect the washer hose and remove the reservoir. Keep your thumb over the liquid outlet to avoid spilling the washer solvent on painted surfaces.
4. Drain the reservoir to remove the pump. Insert a $19/32''$ socket and extension through the filler opening and remove the pump filter and nut.
5. Disconnect the outside portion of the pump and remove the inner and outer portions of the pump.
6. Installation is the reverse of removal. Be sure the rubber grommet is in place when installing the pump.

Rear

1. Open the liftgate.
2. Remove the plastic cap and mounting retainer from the reservoir filler on the right side of the liftgate. Reach through the side drain and remove the sheet metal screws.
3. Disconnect the wiring from the pump.
4. Remove the 2 side panel reservoir mounting screws.
5. Disconnect the washer hose from the reservoir.
6. Remove the reservoir and pump from the side panel through the aperture panel access hole. Try not to spill windshield washer solvent on the paint.
7. Drain the reservoir to remove the pump. Insert a $19/32''$ socket and extension through the filler opening and remove the pump filter and nut.
8. Disconnect the outside portion of the pump and remove the inner and outer parts of the pump.
9. Installation is the reverse of removal. Be sure the rubber grommet is in place when installing the pump.

INSTRUMENT PANEL

The fuel, temperature and oil pressure gauges work on the constant voltage principle through a common voltage limiter which pulses to provide intermittent current to the gauge system.

Cluster Assembly

REMOVAL AND INSTALLATION

1. Remove the two lens assembly lower attaching retaining springs by pulling rearward with a pliers.
2. Allow the lens assembly to drop as it is pulled rearward.

CHASSIS ELECTRICAL

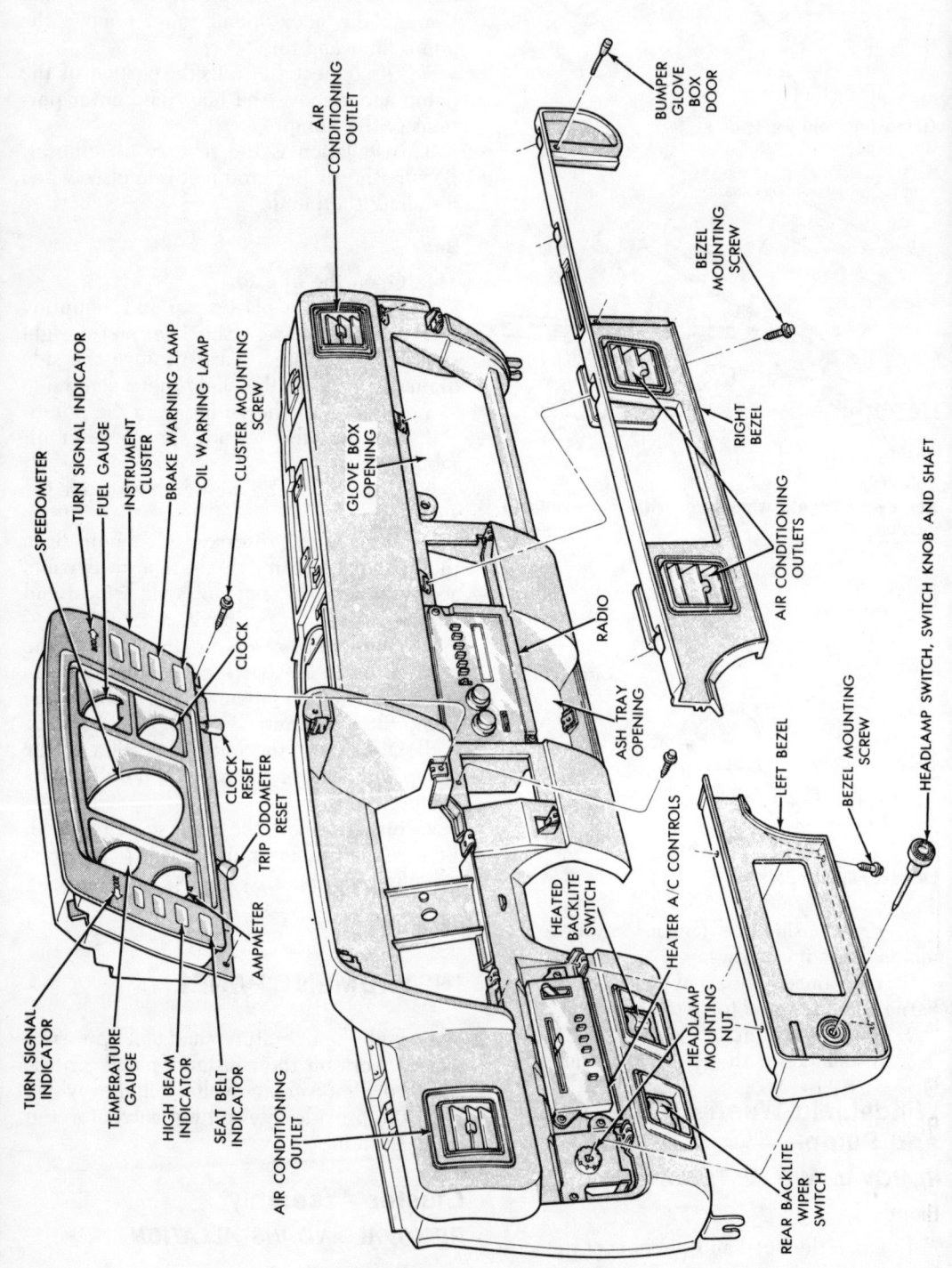

Exploded view of instrument panel

CHASSIS ELECTRICAL

3. Remove the speedometer assembly (two screws).
4. Remove the two wiring harness connectors.
5. Remove the two cluster attaching screws.
6. Pull the two upper spring retainers away from the panel.
7. If equipped with a clock, reach behind the panel and disconnect the wires.
8. Remove the cluster assembly.
9. Installation is the reverse of removal.

Rattles in a 1978 or 1979 instrument cluster may be caused by loose or missing upper cluster mounting clips. To correct rattles, a screw (Chrysler Part No. 9414172) in the screw holes provided in the upper part of the cluster.

Headlight Switch

REMOVAL AND INSTALLATION

1. Disconnect the battery ground.
2. Pull the headlight knob from the switch.
3. Unscrew the collar from the instrument panel side of the switch.
4. Push the switch through the panel and let it drop; disconnect the wires.
5. Installation is the reverse of removal.

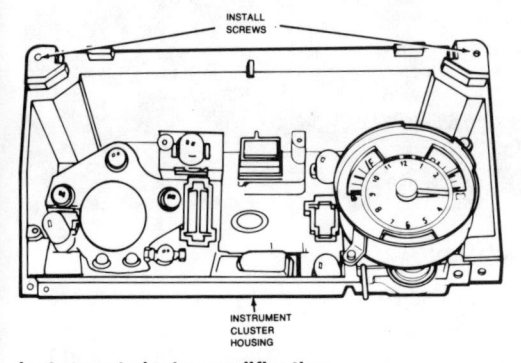

Instrument cluster modification

Speedometer Cable

REMOVAL AND INSTALLATION

1. Reach under the instrument panel and depress the spring clip retaining the cable to the speedometer head. Pull the cable back and away from the head.
2. If the core is broken, raise and support the vehicle and remove the cable retaining screw from the cable bracket. Carefully slide the cable out of the transaxle.
3. Coat the new core sparingly with speedometer cable lubricant and insert it in the cable. Install the cable at the transaxle, lower the car and install the cable at the speedometer head.

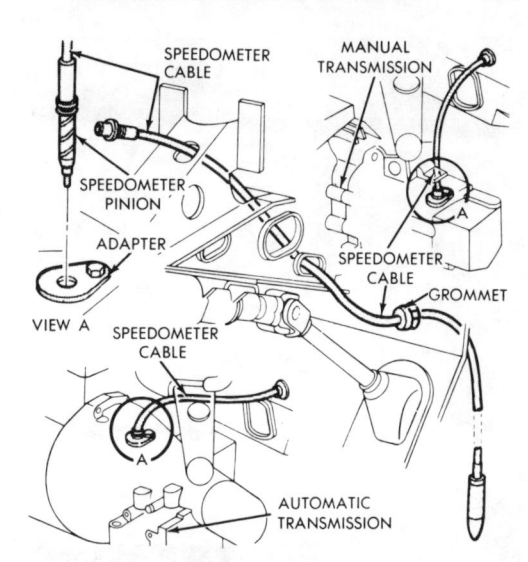

Speedometer cable mounting

Ignition Switch

REMOVAL AND INSTALLATION

See Chapter 7 for Ignition Switch replacement.

HEADLIGHTS

REMOVAL AND INSTALLATION

1. Be sure the light switch is OFF.
2. Remove the 4 screws that hold the headlight bezel in place.
3. Remove the headlight bezel. Pull the bezel away and disconnect the parking/turn signal light. Twist to remove the light and socket.
4. Set the bezel aside.
5. Remove the 4 screws securing the headlight retainer and remove the retainer.
6. Pull the headlight out and disconnect the socket.
7. Install a new headlight in the reverse order of removal. Check the operation of the lights before completing the assembly.

154 CHASSIS ELECTRICAL

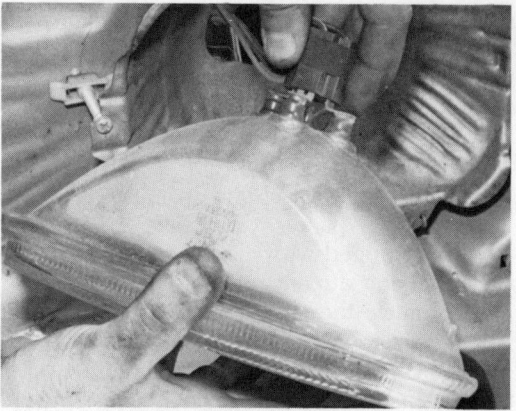

Interior Light Bulbs

Illumination	Bulb No. *

HEADLIGHT SWITCH RHEOSTAT DIMMING

Air Conditioning Controls	#158
Ash Tray	#161
Clock Conventional①	#168
Gear Shift Selector Console	#158
Heated Rear Window Control	#158
Heater Controls	#158
Instrument Cluster	#158
Radio AM	#158
Radio AM-FM	#158
Radio AM-FM Stereo	#363
Speedometer	#158
Switch Callouts	#161

NON-DIMMING

Brake Indicator	#158
Courtesy Lamp	#562
Dome Lamp	#211-2
Fasten Seat Belts	#158
Glove Compartment	#1891
Heated Rear Window Indicator	#161
High Beam Indicator	#158
Ignition Lamp	#1445
Map Lamp	#562
Oil Pressure Temperature Indicator	#158
Radio AM-FM Stereo Indicator	#73
Trunk Lamp, Underhood Lamp	#912
Turn Signal Indicator	#158

* All bulbs are glass or brass wedge base. Do not use aluminum bulbs.

① Included w/instrument cluster lighting.

CHASSIS ELECTRICAL

Exterior Light Bulbs

Illumination	Bulb No.
Back Up Lamps	1156
Fender Mounted Turn Signal Indicator	168
Headlamps	6052
License Plate Lamp	168
Park and Turn Signal Lamp	1157
Side Marker Lamps (Front)	①
Side Marker Lamps (Rear)	168
Tail and Stop Lamps	1157
Turn Signal Lamps (Rear)	1156

① Parking light serves as front side marker.

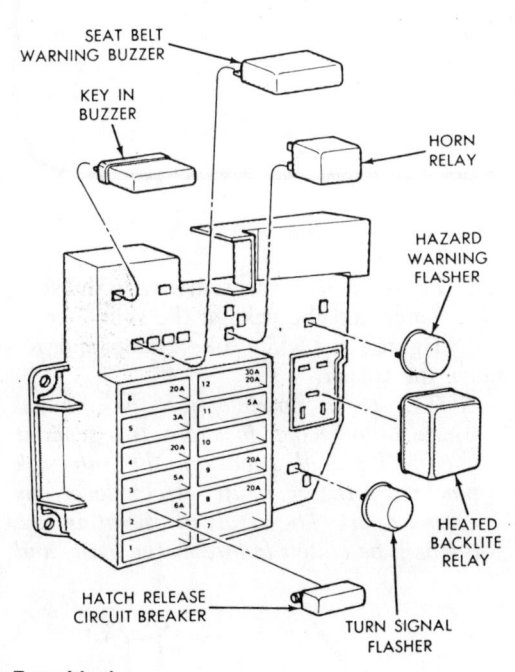

Fuse block

WIRING DIAGRAMS

NOTE: *Wiring diagrams have been left out of this book. As cars have become more complex and available with longer and longer option lists, wiring diagrams have grown in size and complexity also. It has become virtually impossible to provide a readable reproduction in a reasonable number of pages.*

Fuses and Circuit Breakers

Cavity	Fuse	Items Fused
1		
2	6 AMP C/BRKR	Rear Wash & Wipe Hatch Release (2-door)
3	5 AMP	Radio
4	20 AMP	A/C Clutch, Turn Signal & Back-Up Lamps & Tachometer
5	3 AMP	Cluster, Radio, A/C, HRT, Ash Rec, Gear Sel, Heated RR Wdo, Rear Wash/Wipe & Hatch Release Lamps
6	20 AMP	Hazard Flasher
7	—	—
8	20 AMP	Stop, Dome, Cargo, Glove box, Map & Ign Lamps; Time Delay Relay, Clock, Cigar Lighter & Key-In Buzzer
9	20 AMP	Horn & Horn Relay; Park, Tail, Side Marker (RR), License & Cluster Lamps
10	—	—
11	5 AMP	Seat Belt, Oil Pressure & Brake Warning Lamps; Seat Belt Buzzer, Voltage Limiter & Fuel & Temp Gauge
12	30 AMP 20 AMP	A/C & Heater Blower Motor Heater Blower Motor

6

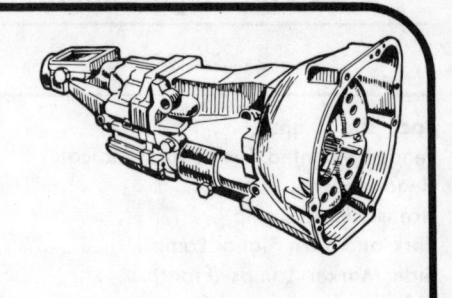

Clutch and Transmission

MANUAL TRANSAXLE

The Omni and Horizon use a Chrysler A-412 manual transaxle, so named, because the transmission and rear axle functions are contained in the same housing. A pad, located on top of the clutch housing contains the transaxle and VIN identification numbers. See Chapter 1 for further identification information.

SHIFT LINKAGE ADJUSTMENT

1. Place the transmission in neutral at the 3–4 position.
2. Loosen the shift tube clamp. Align the hole in the blocker bracket with the tab in the slider.
3. Place a ⅝ inch spacer between the shift tube flange and the yoke at the shift base.
4. Tighten the shift tube clamp and remove the spacer.

NOTE: *It is possible for the manual transaxle to become locked in two gears at once. This will occur if the interlock blocker on the gearshift selector lever has spread apart. The result of operating like this will be clutch failure at the least, and*

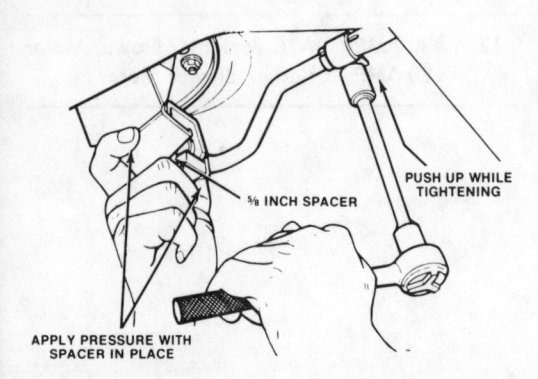

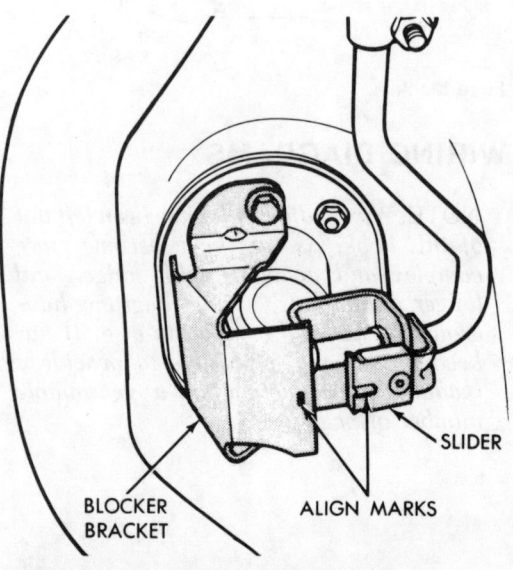

Adjusting shift linkage

Align the marks on blocker and slides

CLUTCH AND TRANSMISSION 157

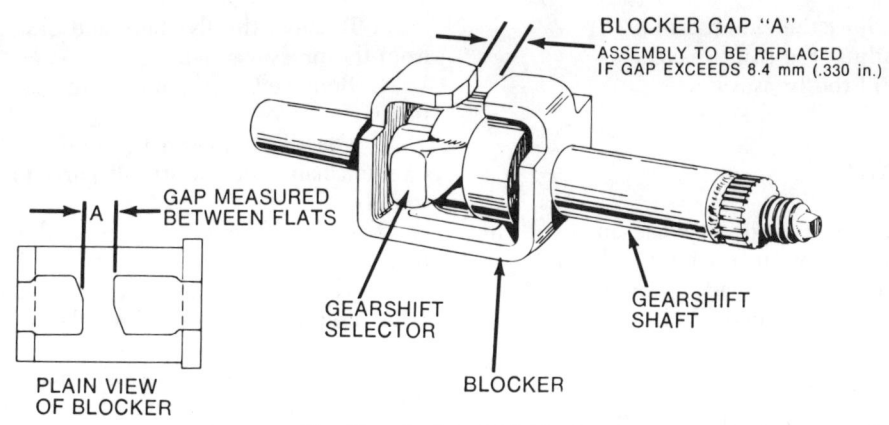

Checking the interlock blocker

driveline failure at the worst. To correctly diagnose the problem, the interlock should be checked using the following procedure:

1. Disconnect the shift linkage operating lever from the transaxle selector shaft.
2. Remove the transaxle detent spring assembly and selector shaft boot.
3. Remove the aluminum selector shaft plug.
4. Place the transaxle in neutral and pull the selector shaft assembly out of the case.
5. Measure the interlock blocker gap "A", in the accompanying picture. If gap "A" exceeds .330 in. replace the gearshift selector shaft assembly.
6. Apply a thick coating of chassis grease to the selector shaft shoulder at the threaded end and carefully insert the shaft through the selector shaft oil seal. Reverse steps 1–4 to install.
7. Adjust the shift linkage.

REMOVAL AND INSTALLATION

NOTE: *Anytime the differential cover is removed, a new gasket should be formed from RTV sealant. See Chapter 1.*

1. Remove the engine timing mark access plug.
2. Rotate the engine to align the drilled mark on the flywheel with the pointer on the engine.
3. Disconnect the battery ground.
4. Disconnect the shift linkage rods.
5. Disconnect the starter and ground wires.
6. Disconnect the backup light switch wire.
7. Remove the starter.
8. Disconnect the clutch cable.
9. Disconnect the speedometer cable.
10. Support the weight of the engine from

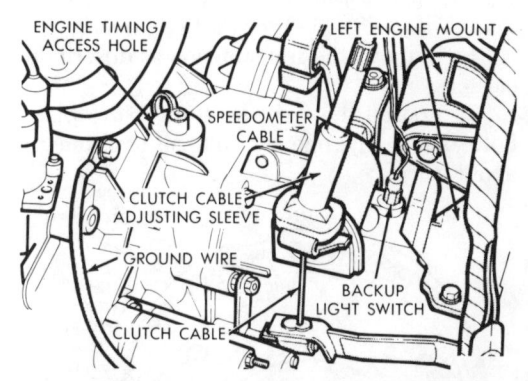

Transmission connections in the engine compartment

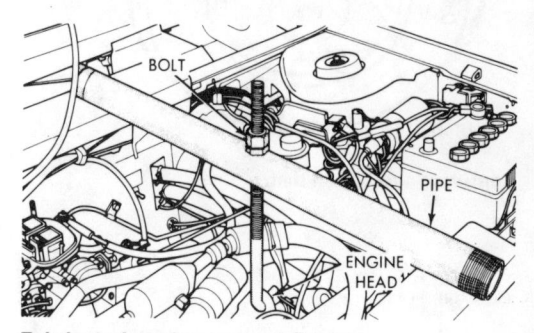

Fabricated engine support fixture

above, preferably with a shop hoist or the fabricated holding fixture.

11. Raise and support the vehicle.
12. Disconnect the drive shafts and support them out of the way.
13. Remove the left splash shield.
14. Drain the transaxle.
15. Unbolt the left engine mount.
16. Remove the transaxle-to-engine bolts.
17. Slide the transaxle to the left until the mainshaft clears, then, carefully lower it from the car.
18. Installation is the reverse of removal.

158 CLUTCH AND TRANSMISSION

19. Adjust the clutch cable.
20. Adjust the shift linkage.
21. Fill the transaxle.

CLUTCH

The clutch is a single dry disc unit, with no adjustment for wear provided in the clutch itself. Adjustment is made through an adjustable sleeve in the pedal linkage.

Clutch Disc

REMOVAL AND INSTALLATION

NOTE: *Chrysler recommends the use of special tool L-4533 for disc alignment.*

1. Remove the transmission as described earlier.
2. Loosen the flywheel-to-pressure plate bolts diagonally, one or two turns at a time to avoid warpage.

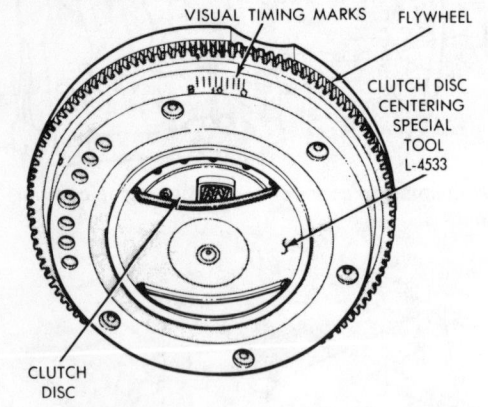

3. Remove the flywheel and clutch disc from the pressure plate.
4. Remove the retaining ring and release plate.
5. Diagonally loosen the pressure plate-to-crankshaft bolts. Mark all parts for reassembly.
6. Remove the bolts, spacer and pressure plate.
7. The flywheel and pressure plate surfaces should be cleaned thoroughly with fine sandpaper.
8. It is false economy to replace either the clutch disc or pressure plate separately, since this will only lead to premature failure of the other component. In order to reuse any of the components, the following conditions should be met:

   a. There should be no oil leakage through the rear main oil seal or transmission front oil seal.

   b. The friction surface of the pressure plate should have a uniform appearance over the entire surface contact area. The pressure plate may be improperly mounted or sprung if a heavy wear pattern occurs directly opposite a light wear pattern.

   c. The friction face of the flywheel should be free from discoloration, burned areas, cracks or grooves. Frequently the face of the flywheel must be machined smooth before installing a new clutch.

   d. The disc should be free of oil or grease. If it is worn to within less than 0.015 in. of the rivet heads, replace the disc.

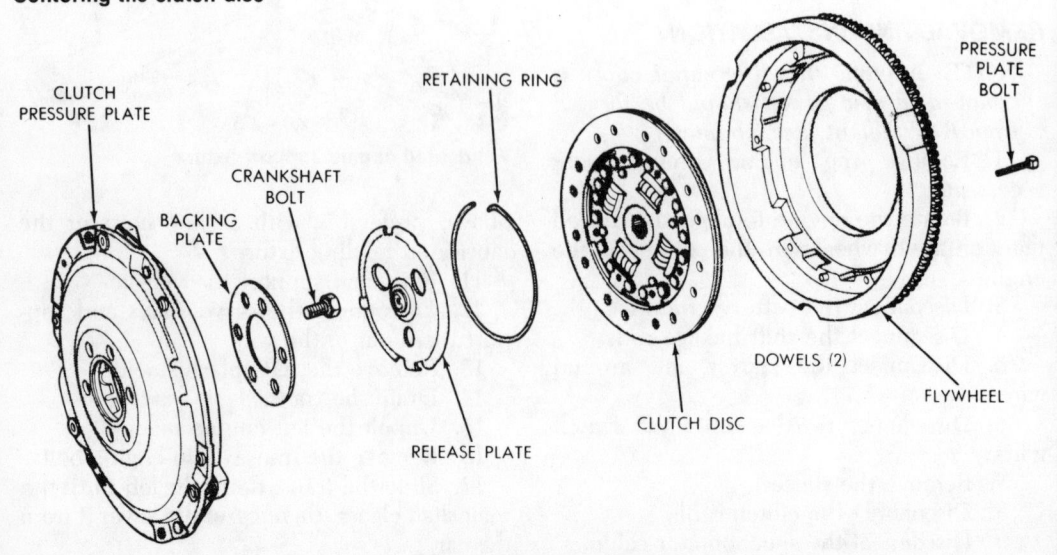

Centering the clutch disc

Exploded view of clutch

CLUTCH AND TRANSMISSION

e. Check the pressure plate for flatness. It should be flat within 0.020 in. across the friction area, and be free from cracks, burns, grooves or ridges.

f. Inspect the cover outer mounting flange for flatness, burrs, nicks or dents.

g. The 2 dowels in the flywheel should be tight and undamaged.

h. Inspect the center of the release plate for cracks or heavy wear. Wear up to 0.010 in. is acceptable.

If the clutch assembly does not meet these conditions, it should be replaced.

9. Align marks and install the pressure plate, spacer and bolts. Coat the bolts with thread compound and torque them to 55 ft lbs.

10. Install the release plate and retaining ring.

11. Using special tool L-4533 or its equivalent, install the clutch disc and flywheel on the pressure plate.

CAUTION: *Make certain that the drilled mark on the flywheel is at the top, so that the two dowels on the flywheel align with the proper holes in the pressure plate.*

12. Install the six flywheel bolts and tighten them to 14.5 ft lbs.

13. Remove the aligning tool.

14. Install the transmission.

15. Adjust the freeplay.

CLUTCH FREEPLAY ADJUSTMENT

1. Pull up on the clutch plate.
2. While holding the cable up, rotate the adjusting sleeve downward until a snug contact is made against the grommet.
3. Rotate the sleeve slightly to allow the end of the sleeve to seat in the rectangular hole in the grommet.

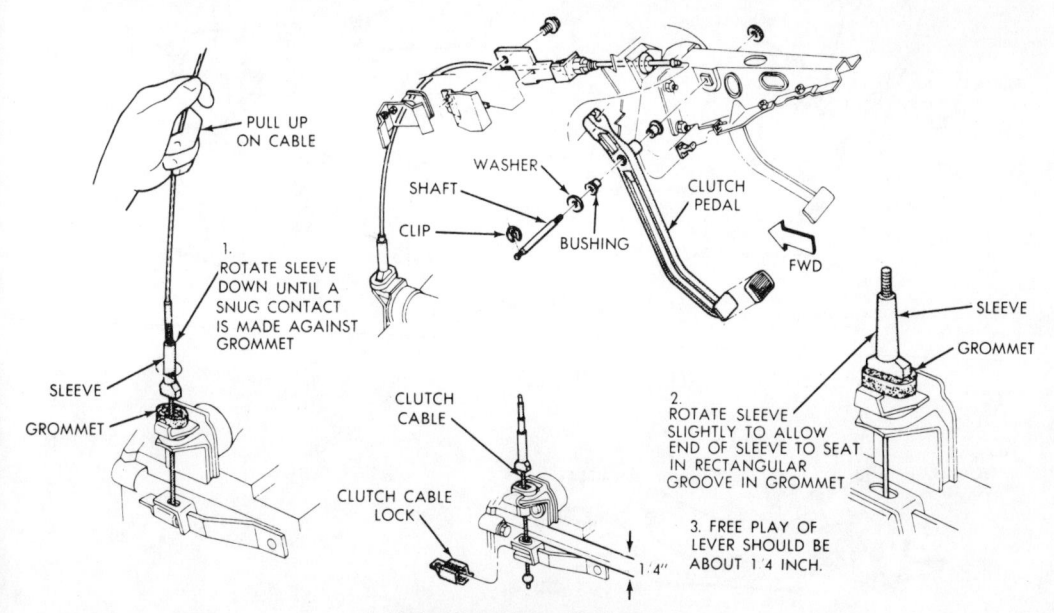

Hole for dowel pin

Dowel pin in the clutch cover

Clutch free-play adjustment

CLUTCH AND TRANSMISSION

AUTOMATIC TRANSAXLE

The automatic transaxle combines a torque converter, fully automatic 3-speed transmission, final drive gearing and differential into a compact front wheel drive system. Officially, it is designated the A-404 Torqueflite Automatic Transaxle.

SHIFT LINKAGE ADJUSTMENT

NOTE: *When it is necessary to disconnect the linkage cable from the lever, which uses plastic grommets as retainers, the grommets should be replaced.*
1. Make sure that the adjustable swivel block is free to slide on the shift cable.
2. Place the shift lever in Park.
3. With the linkage assembled, and the swivel lock bolt loose, move the shift on the transaxle all the way to the rear detent.
4. Tighten the adjuster swivel lock bolt to 8 ft lb.
5. Check the linkage action.

NOTE: *The automatic transmission gear selector release button may pop up in the knob when shifting from PARK to DRIVE. This is caused by inadequate retention of the selector release knob retaining tab. The release button will always work but the loose button can be annoying. A sleeve (Chrysler Part No. 5211984) and washers (Chrysler Part No. 6500380) are available to cure this condition. If these are unavailable, do the following:*
1. Remove the release button.
2. Cut and fold a standard paper match stem as shown.
3. Using tweezers, insert the folded match as far as possible into the clearance slot as shown. The match should be below the knob surface.
4. Insert the button, taking care not to break the button stem.

THROTTLE CABLE ADJUSTMENT

1. Adjust the idle speed as previously described.
2. Run the engine to normal operating temperature.
3. Loosen the adjustment bracket lock screw.
4. Make sure the adjustment bracket is free to slide in its slot.
5. Hold the transmission lever firmly rearward against its internal stop and tighten the adjustment bracket lock screw to 9 ft lb.
6. Test the cable operation.

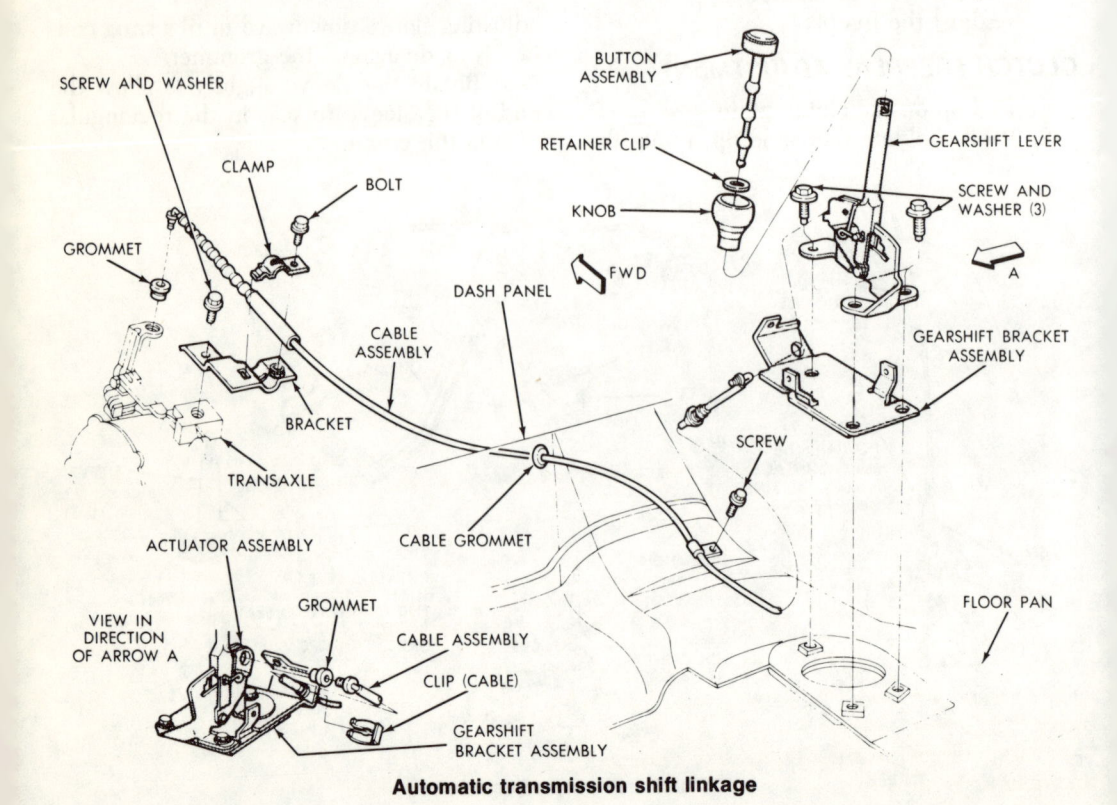

Automatic transmission shift linkage

CLUTCH AND TRANSMISSION   161

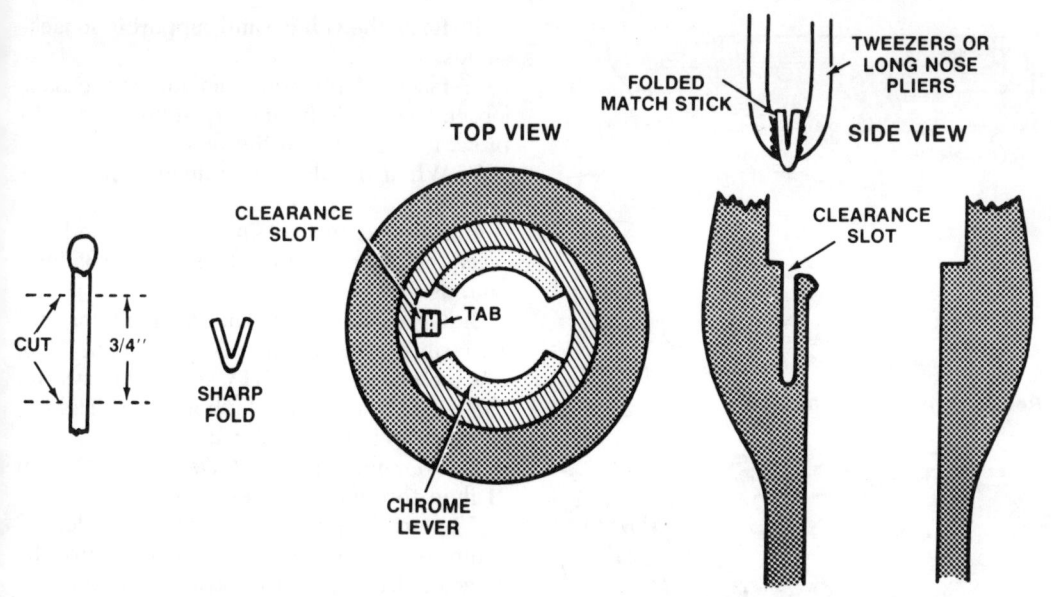

Automatic transmission shifter modification

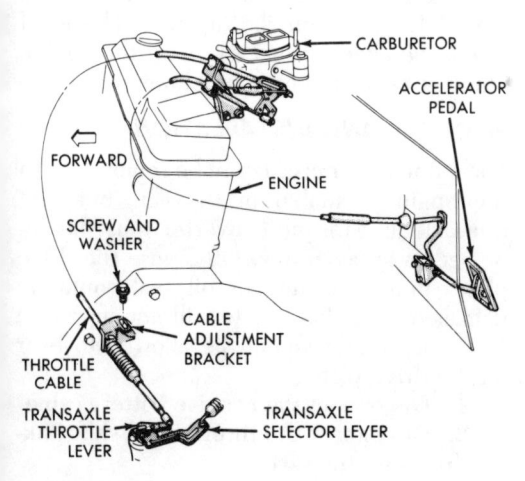

Throttle cable

BAND ADJUSTMENTS

Front (Kickdown) Band

Chrysler recommends that the band be adjusted at each fluid change. The adjusting screw is located on the left side of the case.

1. Loosen the lock nut and back off the nut about five full turns.
2. Tighten the band adjusting screw to 72 inch pounds.
3. Back off the adjusting screw exactly 2.5 turns.
4. Hold the adjusting screw and tighten the locknut to 35 ft lb.

NEUTRAL START SWITCH ADJUSTMENT

The neutral start circuit is the center contact of the three-terminal switch located in the transmission case.

1. Remove the wiring connector and test for continuity between the center pin and the case. Continuity should exist only in Park and Neutral.
2. Remove the switch and check that the operating lever fingers are centered in the switch opening.
3. Install the switch and a new seal and tighten to 24 ft lb. Retest with a lamp.
4. Replace the lost transmission fluid.
5. If shift linkage adjustment is correct and the switch still malfunctions, replace the switch.

PAN REMOVAL AND INSTALLATION, FLUID AND FILTER CHANGE

NOTE: *RTV silicone sealer is used in place of a pan gasket.*

Chrysler recommends no fluid or filter changes during the normal service life of the

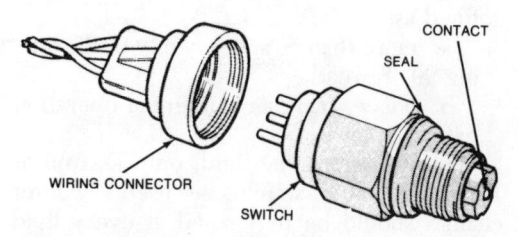

Neutral safety switch

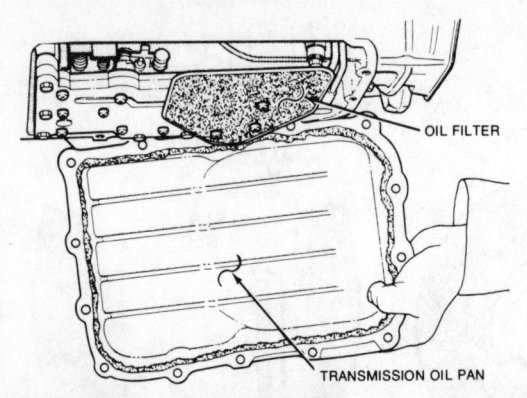

CLUTCH AND TRANSMISSION

Removing transmission oil pan

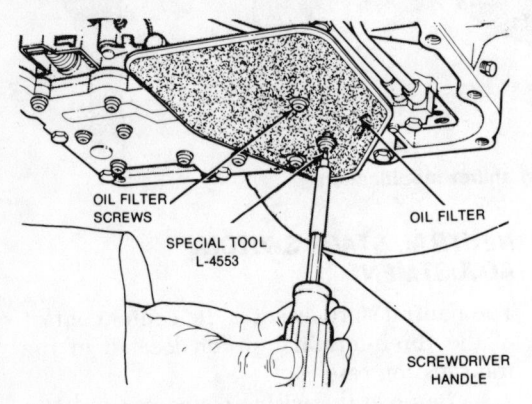

Automatic transmission oil filter attaching screws

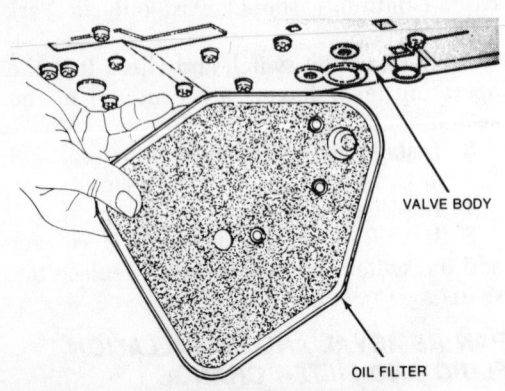

Removing automatic transmission filter

1. Raise the vehicle and support it on jackstands.
2. Place a large container under the pan, loosen the pan bolts and tap at one corner to break it loose. Drain the fluid.
3. When the fluid is drained remove the pan bolts.
4. Remove the retaining screws and replace the filter. Tighten the screws to 35 inch pounds.
5. Clean the fluid pan, peel off the old RTV silicone sealer and install the pan, using a ⅛ inch bead of new RTV sealer. Always run the sealer bead inside the bolt holes. Tighten the pan bolts to 10–12 ft lb.
6. Pour four quarts of Dexron or Dexron II fluid through the filler tube.
7. Start the engine and idle it for at least 2 minutes. Set the parking brake and move the selector through each position, ending in Park.
8. Add sufficient fluid to bring the level to the FULL mark on the dipstick. The level should be checked in Park, with the engine idling at normal operating temperature.

REMOVAL AND INSTALLATION

The automatic transaxle can be removed with the engine installed in the car, but, the transaxle and torque converter must be removed as an assembly. Otherwise the drive plate, pump bushing or oil seal could be damaged. The drive plate will not support a load—no weight should be allowed to bear on the drive plate.

1. Disconnect the positive battery cable.
2. Disconnect the throttle and shift linkage from the transaxle.

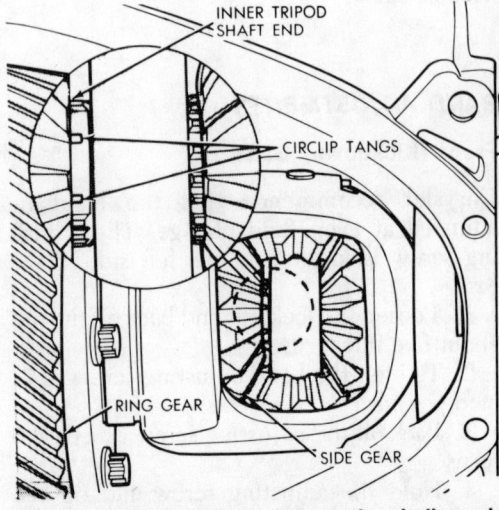

car. Severe usage requires a fluid and filter change every 15,000 miles. Severe usage is defined as:
 a. more than 50% heavy city traffic during 90° F weather.
 b. police, taxi or commercial operation or trailer towing.

When changing the fluid, only Dexron or Dexron II fluid should be used. A filter change should be performed at every fluid change.

Rotate the driveshafts to expose the circlip ends

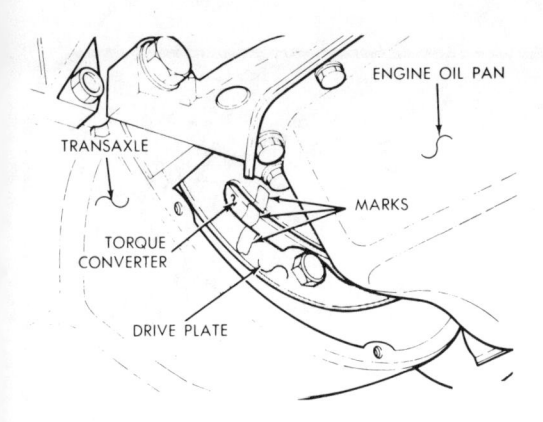

CLUTCH AND TRANSMISSION 163

Matchmark the torque converter and drive plate

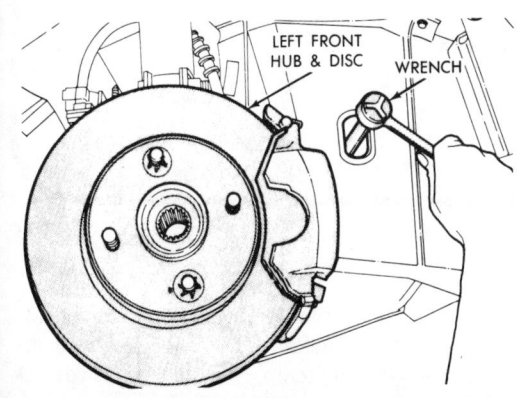

Access plug (in right splash shield) to rotate engine by hand

3. Raise and support the car. Remove the front wheels. Refer to the following chapter to remove or install the driveshafts.
4. Remove the upper oil cooler tube.
5. Remove the left splash shield. Drain the differential and remove the cover.
6. Remove the speedometer adaptor, cable and gear.
7. Remove the sway bar.
8. Remove both lower ball joint-to-steering knuckle bolts.
9. Pry the lower ball joint from the steering knuckle.
10. Remove the driveshaft from the hub.
11. Rotate both driveshafts to expose the circlip ends. Note the flat surface on the inner ends of both axle tripod shafts. Pry the circlip out.
12. Remove both driveshafts.
13. Matchmark the torque converter and drive plate. Remove the torque converter mounting bolts. Remove the access plug in the right splash shield to rotate the engine.
14. Remove the lower cooler tube and the wire to the neutral safety switch.
15. Install some means of supporting the engine.
16. Remove the upper bell-housing bolts.
17. Remove the engine mount bracket from the front crossmember.
18. Support the transmission.
19. Remove the front mount insulator through-bolts and the bell housing mount.
21. Remove the long through-bolt from the left-hand engine mount.
22. Raise the transaxle and pry it away from the engine.
23. Installation is the reverse of removal. Fill the differential with DEXRON automatic transmission fluid before lowering the car. Form a new gasket from RTV sealant when installing the differential cover. See Chapter 1. On 1978 models, be sure the auxiliary horn does not interfere with the oil cooler lines.

7

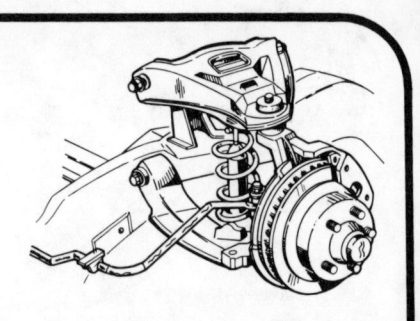

Suspension and Steering

FRONT SUSPENSION

A MacPherson type front suspension, with vertical shock absorbers attached to the upper fender reinforcement and the steering knuckle, is used. Lower control arms, attached inboard to a cross-member and outboard to the steering knuckle through a ball joint, provide lower steering knuckle position. During steering maneuvers, the upper strut and steering knuckle turn as an assembly.

Strut

REMOVAL AND INSTALLATION

NOTE: *A new bonded mount assembly is now used on late 1978 and later models, replacing the double nut, bearing retainer, isolator and strut retainer previously used. To remove the welded nut, grind the hex flats for proper wrench fit.*

1. Raise and support the vehicle.
2. Remove the wheel.
3. NOTE: *If the original strut is to be assembled to the original knuckle, mark the cam adjusting bolt.* Remove the cam adjusting bolt, through bolt and brake hose bracket retaining screw.
4. Remove the strut mounting screws and remove the strut.

5. Installation is the reverse of removal. Position the knuckle leg in the strut and install the upper (cam) and lower through-bolts. Index the cam bolt with the match marks. Torque the strut mounting screws to 27 ft lbs; the brake hose bracket screw to 10 ft lbs; the cam bolt to 85 ft lbs, and the wheel nuts to 80 ft lbs.

Spring

REMOVAL AND INSTALLATION

NOTE: *A spring compressor is required to remove the spring from the strut. A crow's foot adaptor and torque wrench are also required.*

1. Remove the struts.
2. Compress the spring, using a reliable coil spring compressor.
3. Hold the strut rod and remove the rod nut.
4. Remove the retainers and bushings.
5. Remove the spring.

NOTE: *Springs are not interchangeable from side to side.*

CAUTION: *When removing the spring from the compressor, open the compressor evenly and not more than 9¼ inches.*

6. Assembly is the reverse of disassembly in the following order:
Bumper dust shield

SUSPENSION AND STEERING 165

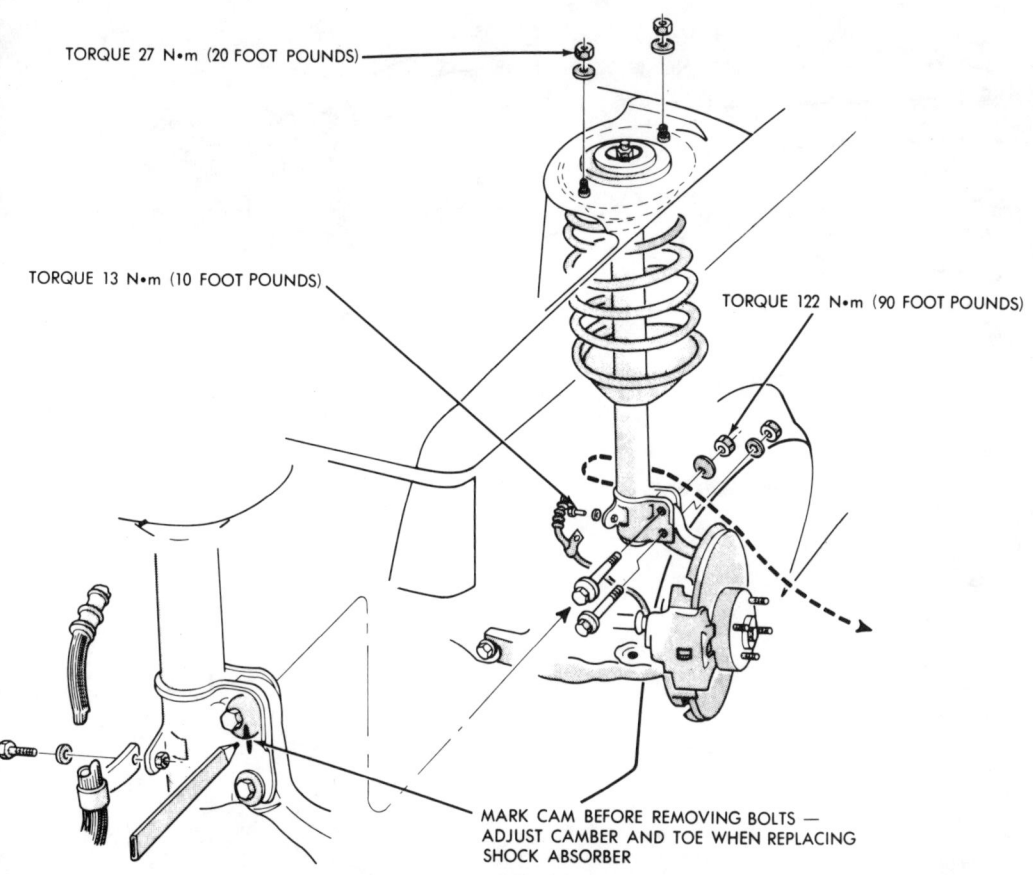

TORQUE 27 N•m (20 FOOT POUNDS)
TORQUE 13 N•m (10 FOOT POUNDS)
TORQUE 122 N•m (90 FOOT POUNDS)

MARK CAM BEFORE REMOVING BOLTS — ADJUST CAMBER AND TOE WHEN REPLACING SHOCK ABSORBER

Removing or installing strut damper

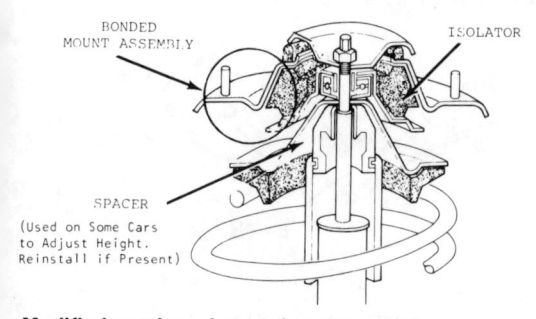

BONDED MOUNT ASSEMBLY
ISOLATOR
SPACER (Used on Some Cars to Adjust Height. Reinstall if Present)

Modified version of strut damper mount

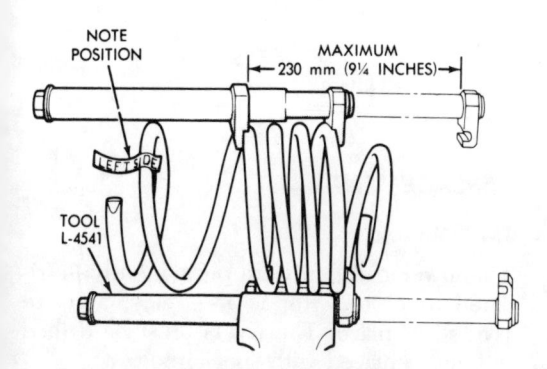

NOTE POSITION
MAXIMUM 230 mm (9¼ INCHES)
TOOL L-4541

Remove or install the coil spring

Spring seat
Upper spring retainer
Bearing and spacer
Mount assembly
Rebound bumper
Retainer
Rod nut

NOTE: *Torque rod nut to 55 ft lbs before removing the spring compressor. Use a crow's foot adaptor to tighten the nut while hodling the rod with an open end wrench.*
Be sure the lower coil end of the spring is seated in the seat recess.

Ball Joints
INSPECTION

1. Raise and support the vehicle.
2. With the suspension fully extended (at full travel) clamp a dial indicator to the lower control arm with the plunger indexed against the steering knuckle leg.
3. Zero the dial indicator.
4. Use a stout bar to pry on the top of the ball joint housing-to-lower control arm bolt

SUSPENSION AND STEERING

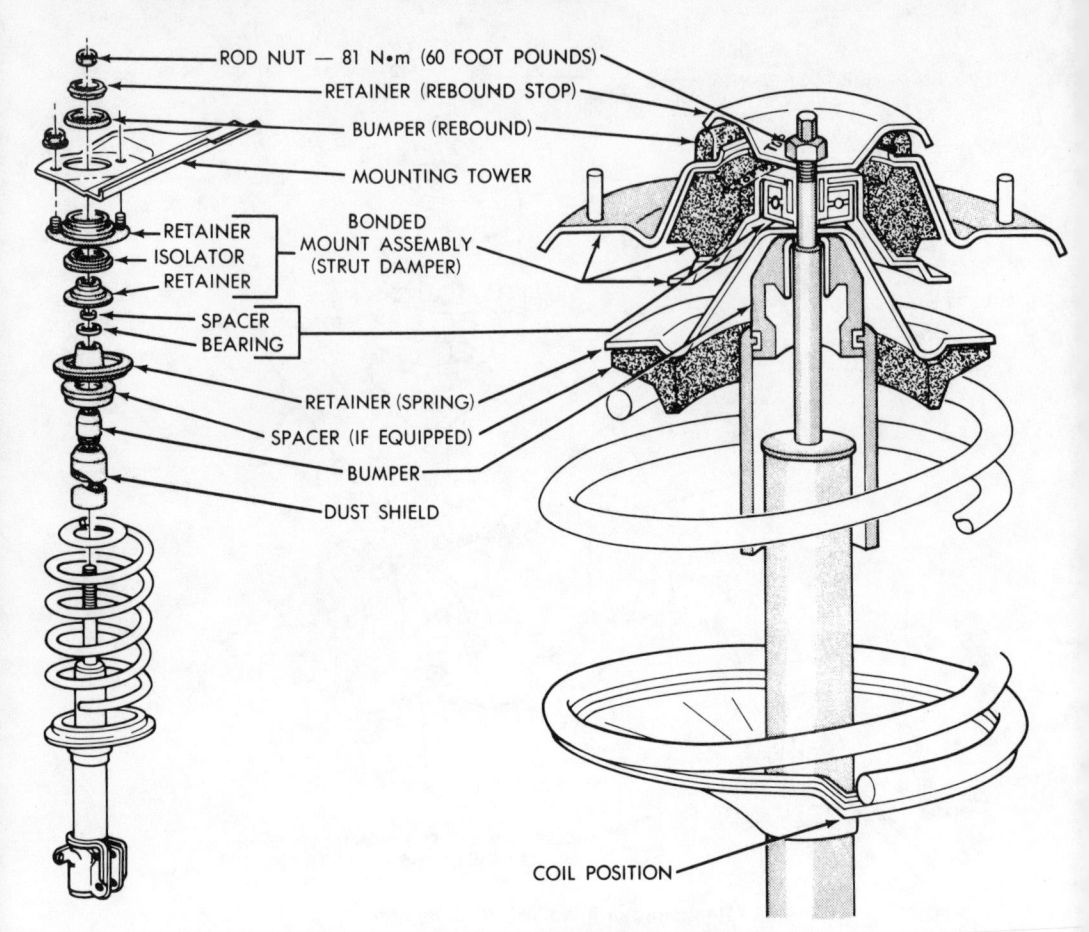

First version of strut damper mount

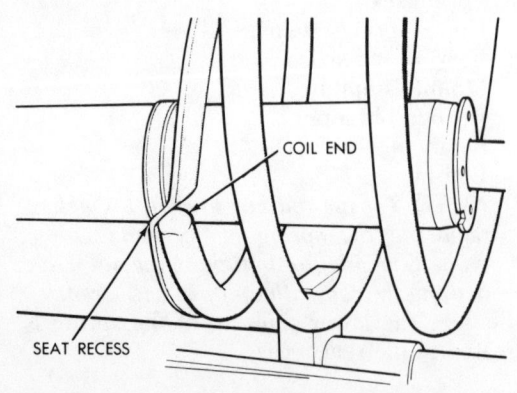

Be sure the lower coil end seats in the recess

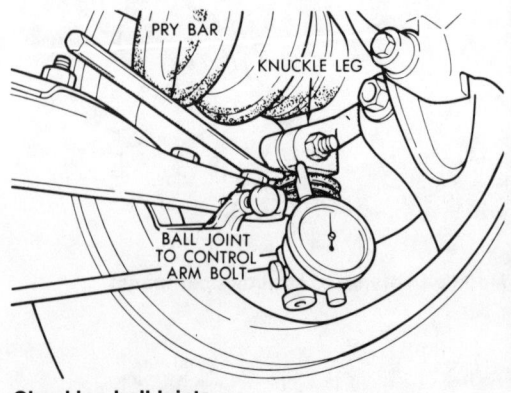

Checking ball joints

with the bar tip under the steering knuckle leg.

5. Measure the axial travel of the steering knuckle leg in relation to the control arm by raising and lowering the steering knuckle as in Step 4.

6. If the travel is more than 0.050 in., the ball joint should be replaced.

REPLACEMENT

1978 Models

The lower ball joints are permanently lubricated, operate with no free play, and are riveted in place. The rivets must be drilled out and replaced with special bolts.

NOTE: *To avoid damage to the control*

SUSPENSION AND STEERING

arm surface adjacent to the ball joint during drilling, the use of a center punch and a drill press are strongly recommended.

1. Remove the lower control arm.
2. Position the assembly with the ball joint up.
3. Center punch the rivets on the ball joint housing side.
4. Using a drill press with a ¼ inch bit, drill out the center of the rivet.
5. Using a ½ inch bit, drill the center of the rivet until the bit makes contact with the ball joint housing.
6. Using a ⅜ inch bit, drill the center of the rivet. Remove the remainder of the rivet with a punch.
7. Position the new ball joint on the control arm and tighten the bolts to 60 ft lbs.
8. Install the control arm and tighten the ball joint clamp bolt to 50 ft lbs; the pivot bolt to 105 ft lbs and the stub strut to 70 ft lbs.

1979 and Later Models

The ball joint housing is bolted to the lower control arm with the joint stud retained in the steering knuckle by a clamp bolt.

1. Raise and support the car.
2. Remove the steering knuckle-to-ball joint stud clamp bolt and separate the stud from the knuckle leg.
3. Remove the 2 bolts holding the ball joint housing to the lower control arm.
4. Remove the ball joint housing.
5. Install a new ball joint housing to the control arm. Torque the retaining bolts to 60 ft lbs.
6. Install the ball joint stud in the steering knuckle. Tighten the clamp bolt to 50 ft lbs.
7. Lower the car.

Lower Control Arm
REMOVAL AND INSTALLATION

1. Raise and support the vehicle.
2. Remove the front inner pivot through bolt, the rear stub strut nut, retainer and bushing, and the ball joint-to-steering knuckle clamp bolt.
3. Separate the ball joint stud from the steering knuckle by prying between the ball stud retainer on the knuckle and the lower control arm.
   CAUTION: *Pulling the steering knuckle out from the vehicle after releasing it from the ball joint can separate the inner C/V joint.*
4. Remove the sway bar-to-control arm

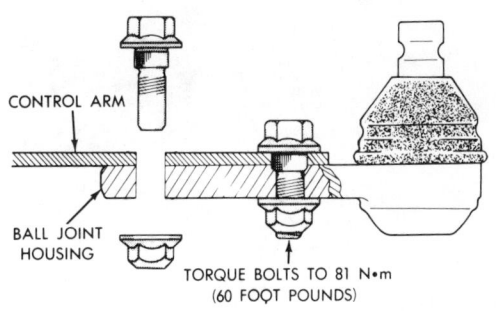

Ball joint bolted to lower control arm (1979 and later models)

nut and reinforcement and rotate the control arm over the sway bar. Remove the rear stub strut bushing, sleeve and retainer.
   NOTE: *The substitution of fasteners other than those of the grade originally used is not recommended.*
5. Install the retainer, bushing and sleeve on the stub strut.
6. Position the control arm over the sway bar and install the rear stub strut and front pivot into the crossmember.
7. Install the front pivot bolt and loosely install the nut.
8. Install the stub strut bushing and retainer and loosely assemble the nut.
9. Position the sway bar bracket and stud through the control arm and install the retainer and nut. Tighten the nut to 10 ft lb.
10. Install the ball joint stud into the steering knuckle and install the clamp bolt. Torque the clamp bolt to 50 ft lb.

Sway Bar
REMOVAL AND INSTALLATION

1. Raise and support the car.
2. Remove the nut from the control arm end bushing and reinforcement plates.
3. Remove the nut, retainers and insulator holding the sway bar to the crossmember linkage.
4. Remove the sway bar.
5. Inspect the sway bar for distortion or fatigue cracks in the metal. Replace any damaged or distorted bushings.
6. Installation is the reverse of removal.

Steering Knuckle
REMOVAL AND INSTALLATION

Service or repair to the bearing, hub, brake dust shield or the steering knuckle itself will require removal of the knuckle. Before attempting this operation, be aware that to re-

168 SUSPENSION AND STEERING

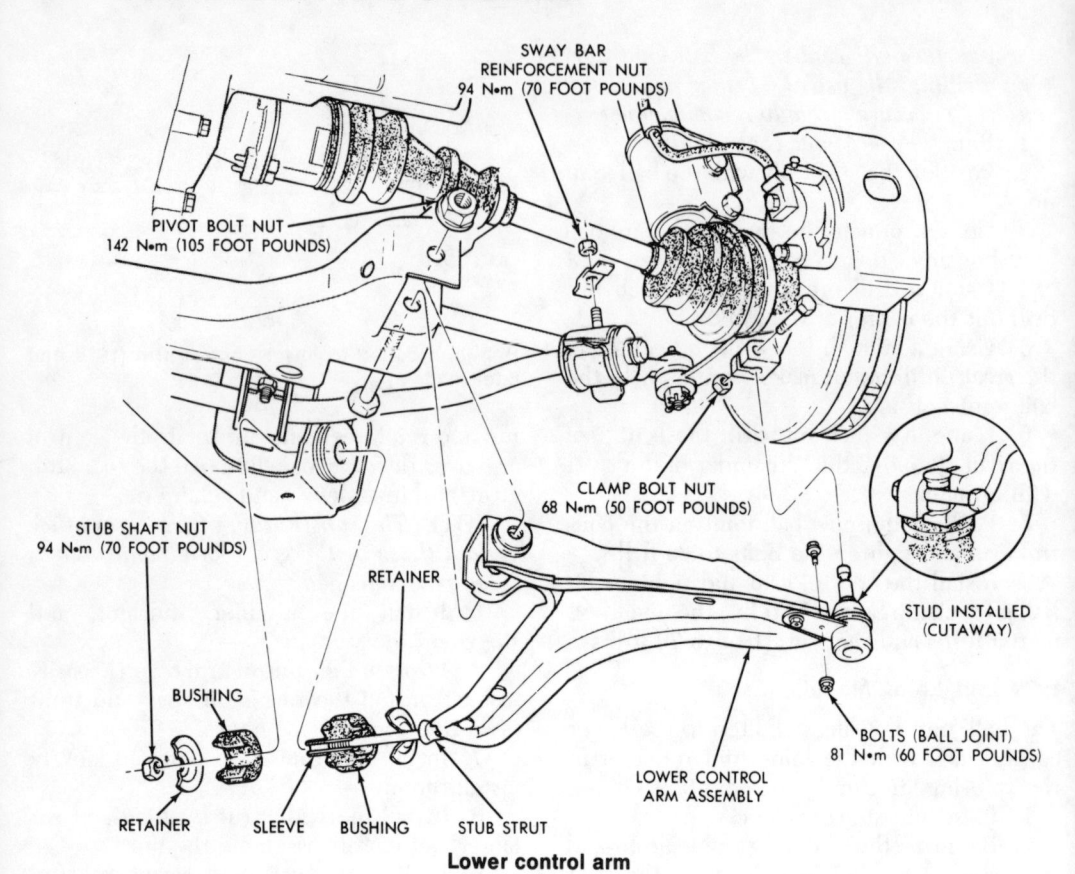

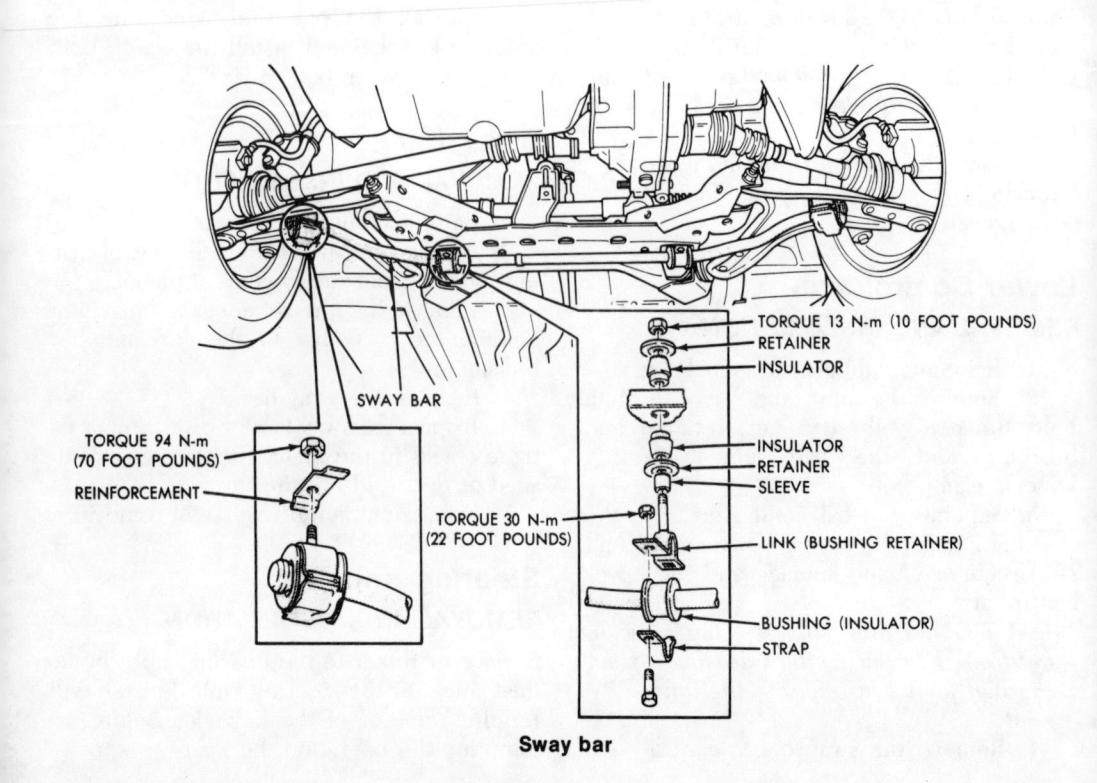

Lower control arm

- SWAY BAR REINFORCEMENT NUT 94 N•m (70 FOOT POUNDS)
- PIVOT BOLT NUT 142 N•m (105 FOOT POUNDS)
- CLAMP BOLT NUT 68 N•m (50 FOOT POUNDS)
- STUD INSTALLED (CUTAWAY)
- STUB SHAFT NUT 94 N•m (70 FOOT POUNDS)
- RETAINER
- BUSHING
- RETAINER
- SLEEVE
- BUSHING
- STUB STRUT
- LOWER CONTROL ARM ASSEMBLY
- BOLTS (BALL JOINT) 81 N•m (60 FOOT POUNDS)

Sway bar

- TORQUE 13 N•m (10 FOOT POUNDS)
- RETAINER
- INSULATOR
- INSULATOR
- RETAINER
- SLEEVE
- LINK (BUSHING RETAINER)
- BUSHING (INSULATOR)
- STRAP
- TORQUE 30 N•m (22 FOOT POUNDS)
- SWAY BAR
- TORQUE 94 N•m (70 FOOT POUNDS)
- REINFORCEMENT

SUSPENSION AND STEERING 169

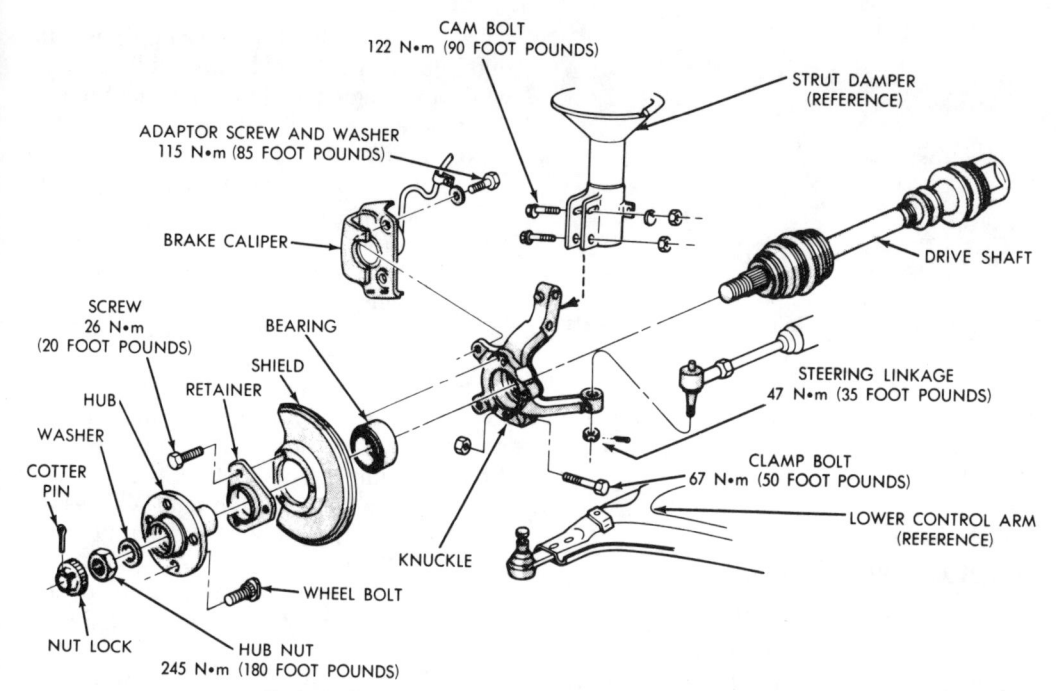

Exploded view of front suspension (steering knuckle)

assemble the components it is necessary to torque the front hub nut to at least 180 ft lbs. You will need a large torque wrench to read that high and a great deal of strength to attain that much torque on the nut.

1. Remove the cotter pin and nut-lock.
2. Loosen the hub nut while the car is resting on the wheels with the brakes applied.

NOTE: *The hub and driveshaft are splined together through the knuckle and retained by the hub nut.*

3. Raise and support the car.
4. Remove the wheel and tire.
5. Remove the hub nut. Be sure the splined driveshaft is free to separate from the spline in hub when the knuckle is removed.
6. Disconnect the tie rod end from the steering arm.
7. Disconnect the brake hose retainer from the strut.
8. Remove the slamp bolt holding the ball joint stud in the steering knuckle.
9. Remove the brake caliper adaptor screw and washers.
10. Support the caliper on a wire hook.
11. Remove the brake disc.
12. Matchmark the camber adjusting cams and loosen both bolts.
13. Support the steering knuckle and remove the cam adjusting and through-bolts. Remove the upper knuckle leg out of the strut bracket and lift the knuckle from the ball joint stud.

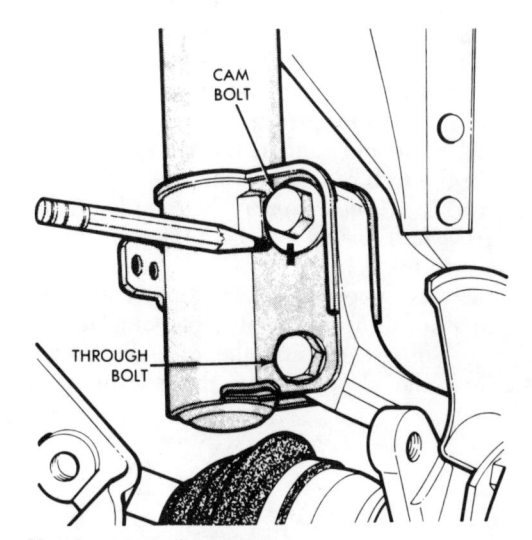

Matchmark the cam bolts

NOTE: *Do not allow the driveshaft to hang during this procedure.*

14. Service procedures requiring hub removal also require that a new bearing be installed.
15. Installation is the reverse of removal. A new hub nut is required. When the car is resting in the wheels, with the brakes applied, tighten the hub nut to:

200 ft lbs—1978 models

SUSPENSION AND STEERING

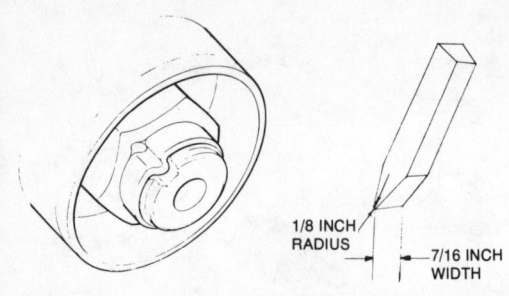

Staking the nut retainer in place in 1978 models

180 ft lbs—1979 and later models
On 1978 models, stake the hub nut in place. 1979 and later models use a cotter pin and nut-lock.

Driveshaft

REMOVAL AND INSTALLATION

Manual Transmission Models

NOTE: *Anytime the differential cover is removed, a new gasket should be formed from RTV sealant. See Chapter 1.*

1. With the vehicle on the floor and the brakes applied, loosen the hub nut.

NOTE: *The hub and driveshafts are splined together and retained by the hub nut which is torqued to at least 180 ft lbs.*

2. Raise and support the vehicle and remove the hub nut and washer.

NOTE: *Always support both ends of the driveshaft during removal to prevent damage to the boots.*

3. Disconnect the lower control arm ball joint stud nut from the steering knuckle.
4. Remove the Allenhead screws which secure the CV joint to the transmission flange.

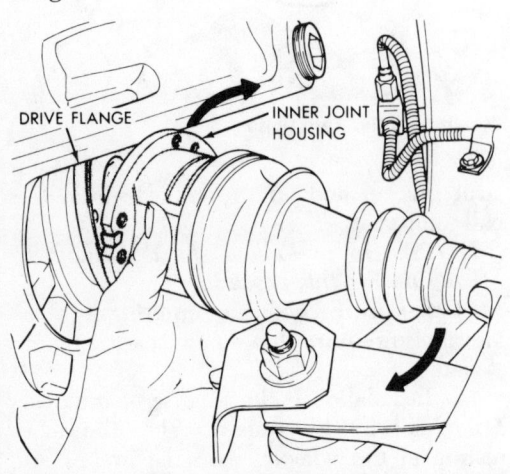

When removing the driveshaft, separate and tilt the joint housing to prevent leakage

5. Holding the CV housing, push the outer joint and knuckle assembly outward while disengaging the inner housing from the flange face.

NOTE: *The outer joint and shaft must be supported during disengagement of the inner joint.*

Quickly turn the open end of the joint upward to retain as much lubricant as possible, then carefully pull the outer joint spline out of the hub. Cover the joint with a clean towel to prevent dirt contamination.

6. Before installation, make sure that any lost lubricant is replaced. The only lubricant specified is Chrysler part number 4131389. No other lubricant of any type is to be used, as premature failure of the joint will result.
7. Clean the joint body and mating flange face.
8. Install the outer joint splined shaft into the hub. Do not secure with the nut and washer.
9. Early production vehicles were built with a cover plate between the hub and flange face. This cover is not necessary and should be discarded.
10. Position the inner joint in the transmission drive flange and secure it with *new* screws. Torque the screws to 37–40 ft lb.
11. Connect the lower control arm to the knuckle.
12. Install the outer joint and secure it with a *new* nut and washer. Torque the nut with the car on the ground and the brake set. Torque is:
   200 ft lbs—1978
   180 ft lbs—1979 and later
13. On 1978 models, stake the new nut to the joint spindle using a tool having a radiused end of .063 inch and approximately 7/16 inch wide. A sharp chisel should not be used since the collar will probably be split.

NOTE: *1979 and later models use a cotter pin and nut-lock to retain the nut. Staking is unnecessary.*

14. After attaching the driveshaft, if the inboard boot appears to be collapsed or deformed, vent the inner boot by inserting a round-tipped, small diameter rod between the boot and the shaft. As venting occurs, boot will return to its original shape.

Automatic Transmission Models

The inboard CV joints are retained by circlips in the differential side gears. The circlip tangs are located on a machined surface on the inner end of the stub shaft.

SUSPENSION AND STEERING 171

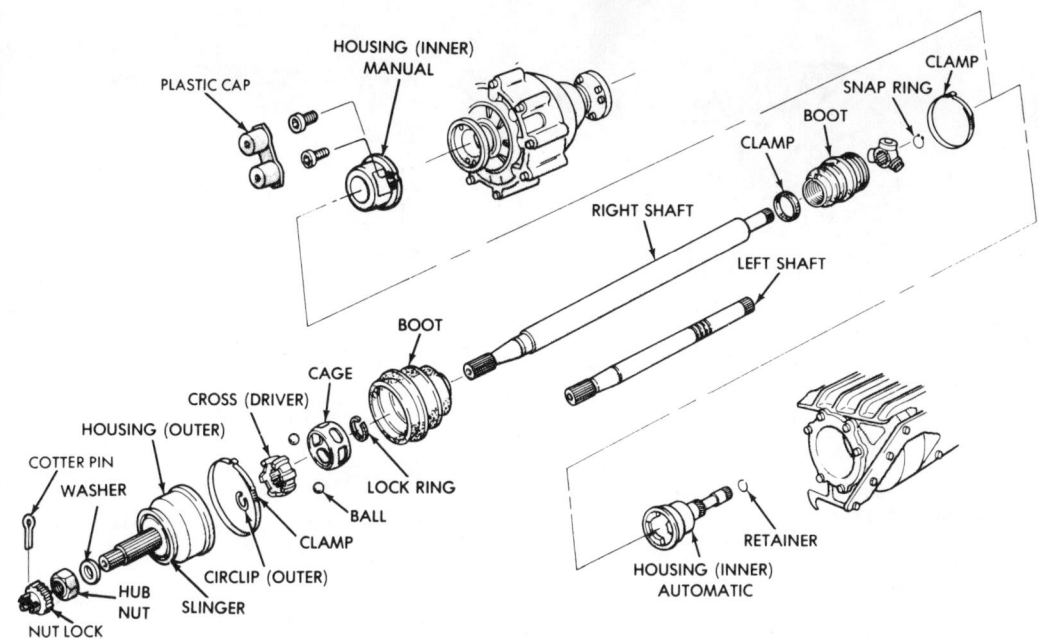

Exploded view of driveshafts

1. With the car on the ground, loosen the hub nut, which has been torqued to 200 ft lbs.

2. Drain the transaxle differential and remove the cover.

NOTE: *Anytime the transaxle differential cover is removed, a new gasket should be formed from RTV sealant. See Chapter 1.*

3. To remove the right-hand driveshaft, disconnect the speedometer cable and remove the cable and gear before removing the driveshaft.

4. Rotate the driveshaft to expose the circlip tangs.

5. Compress the circlip with needle nose pliers and push the shaft into the side gear cavity.

6. Remove the clamp bolt from the ball stud and steering knuckle.

7. Separate the ball joint stud from the steering knuckle, by prying against the knuckle leg and control arm.

8. Separate the outer CV joint splined shaft from the hub by hodling the CV housing and moving the hub away. Do not pry on the slinger or outer CV joint.

9. Support the shaft at the CV joints and remove the shaft. Do not pull on the shaft.

NOTE: *Removal of the left shaft may be made easier by inserting the blade of a thin prybar between the differential pinion shaft and prying against the end face of the shaft.*

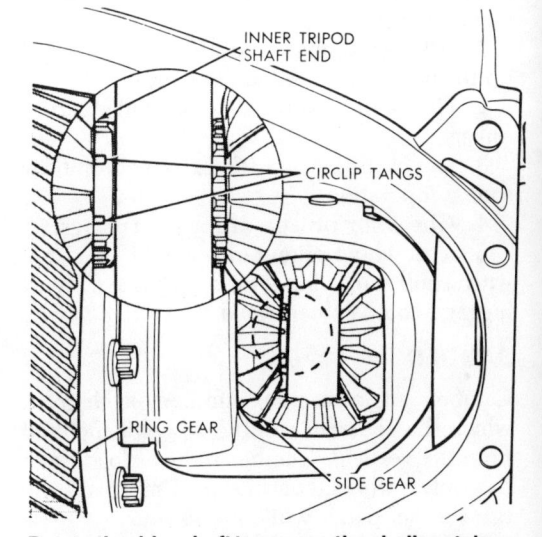

Rotate the driveshaft to expose the circlip retainer

10. Installation is the reverse of removal. Be sure the circlip tangs are positioned against the flattened end of the shaft before installing the shaft. A quick thrust will lock the circlip in the groove. Tighten the hub nut with the wheels on the ground to 180 ft lbs.

Wheel Alignment

Wheel alignment requires the use of fairly sophisticated equipment to accurately measure the geometry of the front end. The information is given here so that the owner will

SUSPENSION AND STEERING

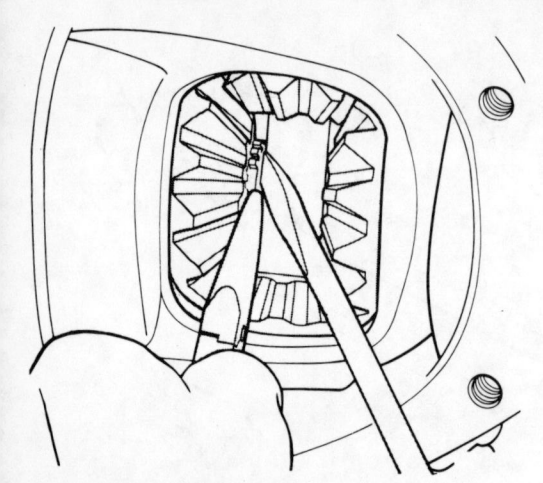

Compress the circlip tongs and push the shaft toward the side gear

be aware of what is involved, not so that he can do the work himself.

Before the wheels are aligned, the following checks should be made, since these are factors that will influence the wheel alignment settings.

1. All tires should be of the same size and up to the recommended pressures.
2. Check the lower ball joints and steering linkage.
3. Check the struts for extremely stiff or spongy operation.
4. Check for broken or sagged springs.
5. The wheel alignment should be made with a full tank of gas, and no passenger or luggage compartment load.

CAMBER

Camber angle is the number of degrees which the centerline of the wheel is inclined from the vertical. Camber reduces loading of the outer wheel bearing and improves the tire contact patch while cornering.

Camber is adjusted by loosening the cam and through-bolts on each side. Rotate the upper cam bolt to move the top of the wheel in or out to the specified camber.

CASTER

Caster angle is the number of degrees in which a line drawn through the steering knuckle pivots is inclined from the vertical, toward the front or rear of the car. Positive caster improves directional stability and decreases susceptibility to crosswinds or road surface deviations. Other than the replacement of damaged suspension components, caster is not adjustable.

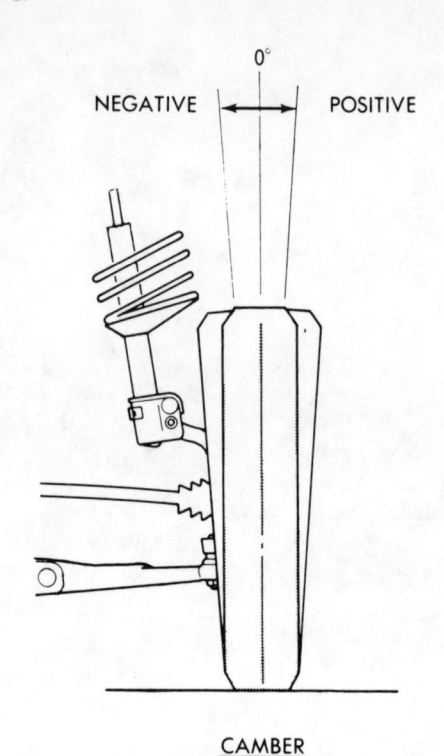

Front suspension camber

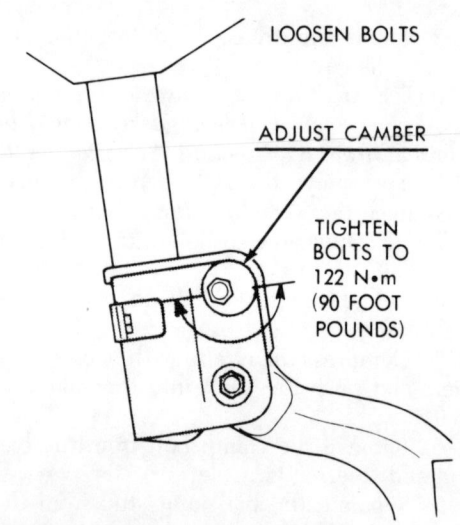

Camber adjusting location

TOE-OUT

The front wheels on the Omni and Horizon are set with a slight toe out, as on most front wheel drive cars, to counteract the tendency of the driving wheels to toe-in excessively. Toe out is the amount, measured in inches, that the wheels are closer together at the rear than at the front. Toe is checked with the wheels straight-ahead. The tie-rod linkage is adjustable. Loosen the nuts and clamps and

SUSPENSION AND STEERING 173

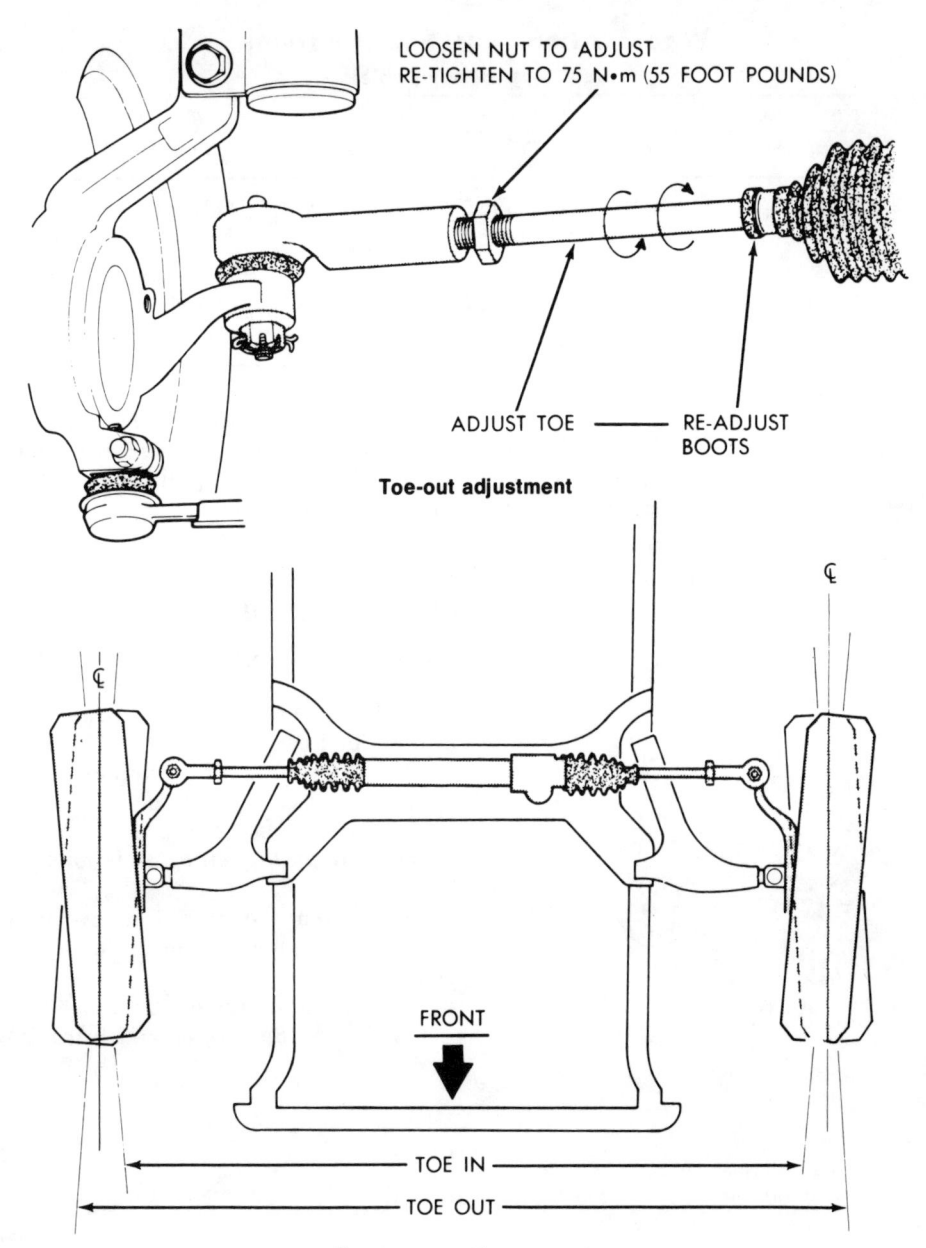

Toe-out adjustment

Front suspension geometry

adjust the length of the tie-rod for correct toe out.

REAR SUSPENSION

A trailing, independent arm assembly, with integral sway bar is used. The wheel spindles are attached to two trailing arms which extend rearward from mounting points on the body where they are attached with shock absorbing, oval bushings. A crossmember is welded to the trailing arms, just to the rear of the bushings. A coil spring over shock absorber strut assembly, similar to the front suspension, is used.

Shock Absorber Strut
REMOVAL AND INSTALLATION

1. Remove the protective cap from the upper mounting nut.
2. Remove the upper mounting nut, isolator retainer and isolator.
3. Raise and support the vehicle.
4. Remove the lower strut mounting bolt.

SUSPENSION AND STEERING

Wheel Alignment Specifications
(caster is not adjustable)

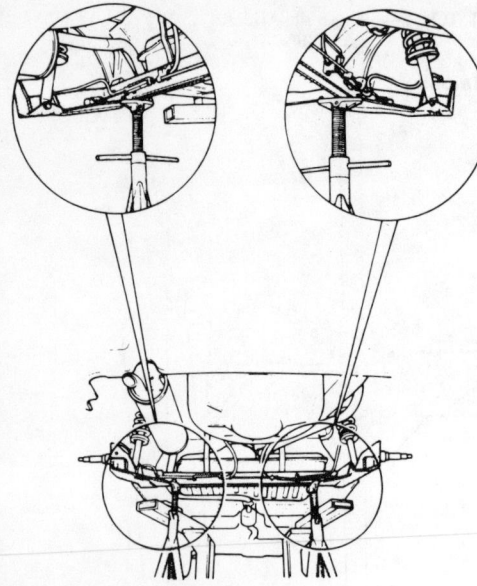

Year	Front Camber Range (deg)	Front Camber Preferred	Toe-Out (in.) Front	Toe-Out (in.) Rear	Rear Camber Range (deg)	Rear Camber Preferred
'78	¼N to ¾P	5/16 P	1/8 out to 0	5/32 out to 1/32 in	1½N to ½N	1N
'79–'80	¼N to ¾P	5/16 P	5/32 out to 1/8 in	5/32 out to 1/32 in	1½N to ½N	1N

Supporting the rear axle

5. Remove the strut and spring assembly.
6. Installation is the reverse of removal. Torque the lower mounting bolt to 40 ft lbs; the upper nut to 20 ft lbs.

Rear Spring
REMOVAL AND INSTALLATION

The use of a coil spring compressor, such as Chrysler part #L-4514, is necessary.

1. Remove the strut and spring assembly as described earlier.
2. Install the spring compressor on the spring and place it in a vise.

CAUTION: *Always grip 4 or 5 coils and never extend the retractors beyond 9¼ inches.*

3. Tighten the retractors evenly until pressure is removed from the upper spring seat.
4. Loosen the retaining nut.

CAUTION: *Be very careful when loosen-*

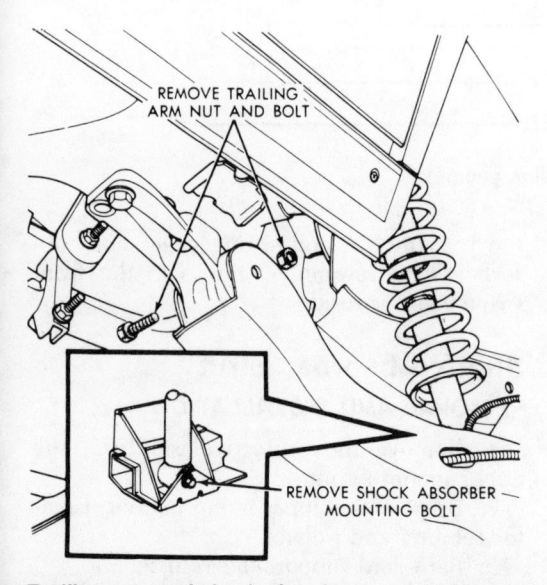

Trailing arm and shock absorber mounting bolts

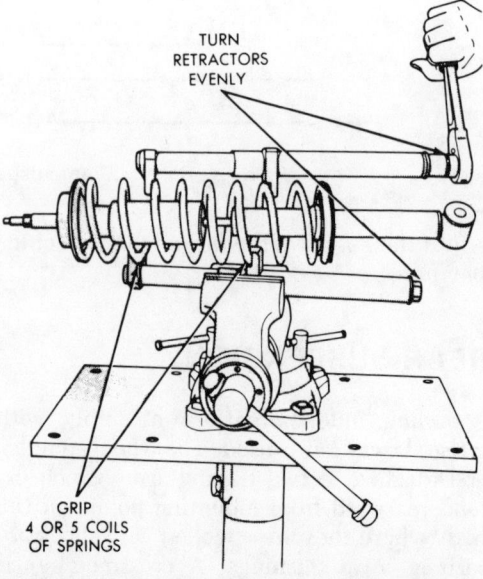

Removing coil spring from rear shock absorber

SUSPENSION AND STEERING 175

ing the retaining nut. If the spring is not properly compressed, serious injury could result.

5. Remove the lower isolator, pushrod sleeve, and upper spring seat.
6. Carefully slip the strut from the spring.
7. Remove the rebound bumper and dust shield from the strut.
8. Remove the lower spring seat.
9. Carefully and evenly, remove the compressor from the spring.
10. Install the compressor on the spring, gripping four or five coils.
11. Compress the spring.
12. Install the lower spring seat, dust shield and rebound bumper on the strut.
13. Slip the unit inside the coil spring and install the upper spring seat.
14. Make sure that the level surfaces on the seats are in position with the spring.
15. Install the sleeve on the pushrod and install the retaining nut. Torque the nut to 20 ft lbs.
16. Install the lower isolator.
17. Install the strut and spring assembly.

Rear Wheel Bearings

See Chapter 1.

Rear Wheel Alignment

Due to the design of the rear suspension, it is possible to adjust both the camber and toe-in of the rear wheels. Alignment is controlled by inserting 0.010 in. shim stock between the spindle mounting surface and the spindle mounting plate. Each 0.010 in. shim stock changes wheel alignment by approximately 0° 18′. Be sure to adjust the rear wheel bearings.

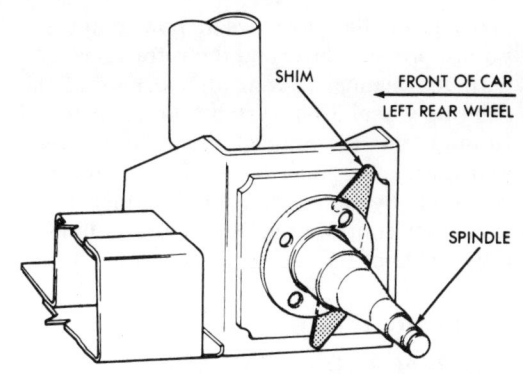

Shim installation for rear wheel toe-in

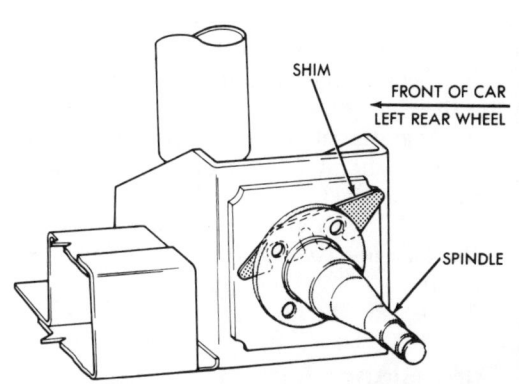

Shim installation for rear wheel positive camber

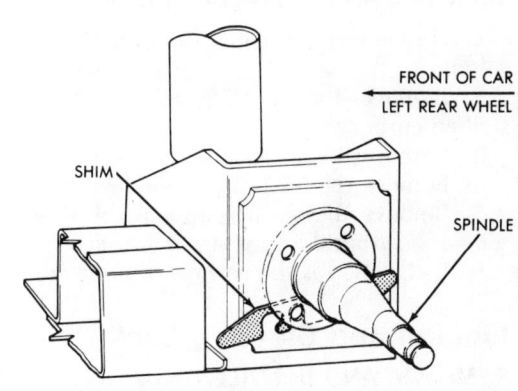

Shim installation for rear wheel negative camber

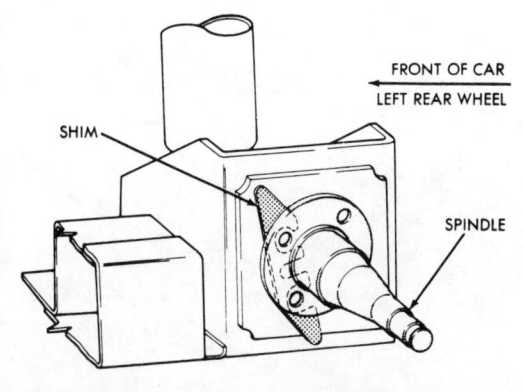

Shim installation for rear wheel toe-out

STEERING

The manual steering system consists of a tube which contains the toothed rack, a pinion, the rack slipper, and the rack slipper spring. Steering effort is transmitted to the steering arms by the tie rods which are coupled to the ends of the rack, and the tie rod ends. The connection between the ends of the rack and the tie rod is protected by a bellows type oil seal which retains the gear lubricant.

The power steering system consists of four

176 SUSPENSION AND STEERING

major parts: the power gear, power steering pump, pressure hose and the return hose. As with the manual system, the turning of the steering wheel is converted into linear travel through the meshing of the helical pinion teeth with the rack teeth. Power assist is provided by an open center, rotary type, three-way control valve which directs fluid to either side of the rack control piston.

Steering Wheel
REMOVAL AND INSTALLATION

1. Remove the horn button and horn switch.
2. Remove the steering wheel nut.
3. Using a steering wheel puller, remove the steering wheel.
4. Align the master serration in the wheel hub with the missing tooth on the shaft. Torque the shaft nut to 60 ft lbs.
   CAUTION: *Do not torque the nut against the steering column lock or damage will occur.*
5. Replace the horn switch and button.

Turn Signal Switch
REMOVAL AND INSTALLATION

1. Disconnect the electrical connector at column.
2. Remove the steering wheel as described earlier.
3. Remove the lower column cover.
4. Remove the wash/wipe switch.
5. Remove the wiring clip and the three screws securing the turn signal switch.
6. Installation is the reverse of removal.

Ignition and Steering Lock
REMOVAL AND INSTALLATION

1. Remove the steering wheel.
2. Remove the upper and lower column covers.
3. Using a hacksaw blade, cut the upper ¼

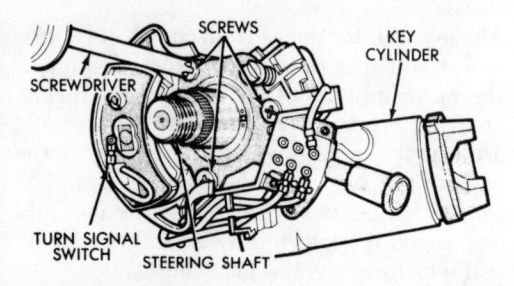

Turn signal switch

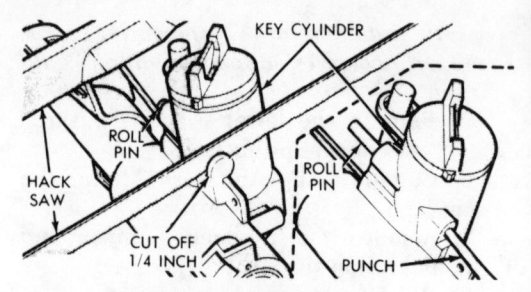

Remove the roll pin in key cylinder

inch from the key cylinder retainer pin boss.
4. Using a drift, drive the roll pin from the housing and remove the key cylinder.
5. Insert the new cylinder into the housing, making sure that it engages the lug on the ignition switch driver. Install the roll pin.

Ignition Switch
REMOVAL AND INSTALLATION

1. Remove the connector from the switch.
2. Place the key in the LOCK position.
3. Remove the key.
4. Remove the two mounting screws from the switch and pushrod to drop below the jacket.
5. Rotate the switch 90 degrees to permit removal of the switch from the pushrod.
6. To install the switch, position the switch in LOCK (second detent from the top).
7. Place the switch at right angles to the column and insert the pushrod.
8. Align the switch on the bracket and install the screws.
9. With a light rearward load on the switch, tighten the screws. Check for proper operation.

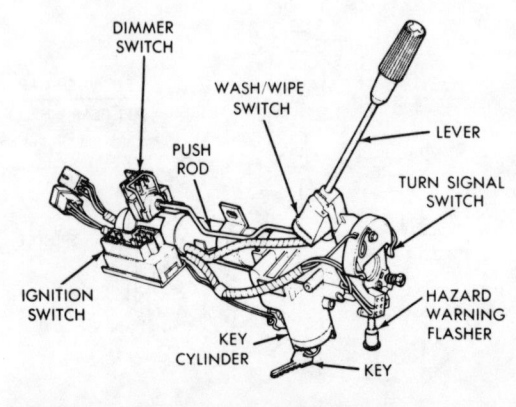

Steering column switch components

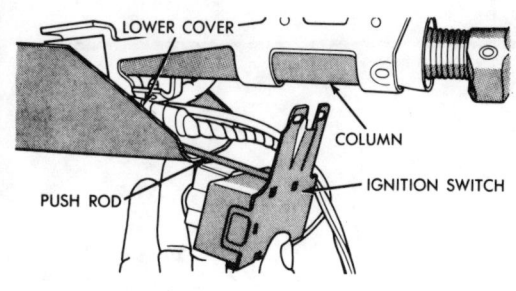

SUSPENSION AND STEERING 177

Ignition switch removal

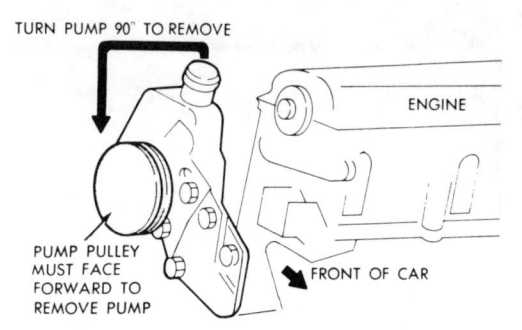

Power steering pump removal or installation

Tie Rod End
REPLACEMENT

1. Loosen the jam nut which connects the tie rod end to the knuckle. Mark the tie rod position on the threads.
2. Using a ball joint separator, remove the tie rod end from the knuckle.
3. Install a new tie rod end in reverse of removal. Torque the end nut to 50 ft lbs; the locknut to 65 ft lbs.
4. Check alignment.

Power Steering Pump
REMOVAL AND INSTALLATION

1. Disconnect the power steering hoses from the pump.
2. Remove the adjusting bolt and slip off the belt.
3. Support the pump, remove the mounting bolts and lift out the pump.
4. Installation is the reverse of removal. Adjust the belt to specifications. See Chapter 1.

8

Brakes

BRAKE SYSTEM

A conventional front disc/rear drum setup is used. The front discs are single piston caliper types; the rear drums are activated by a conventional top mounted wheel cylinder. Disc brakes require no adjustments, the drum brakes are self adjusting by means of the parking brake cable. The only variances in the system from those found on the majority of vehicles are that the system is diagonally balanced, that is, the front left and right rear are on one system and the front right and left rear on the other. No proportioning valve is used. Power brakes are optional.

Adjustment

All disc brakes are inherently self-adjusting. No adjustment is possible. Even though the drum brakes are self-adjusting in normal use, there are times when a manual adjustment is required, such as after installing new shoes or if it is required to back the shoes off the drum. A star wheel with screw type adjusters is provided for these occasions.

1. Remove the access slot plug from the backing plate.
2. Using a brake adjusting spoon pry downward (left side) or upward (right side) on the end of the tool (starwheel teeth moving up) to tighten the brakes. The opposite applies to loosen the brakes.

NOTE: *It will be necessary to use a small screwdriver to hold the adjusting lever away from the starwheel. Be careful not to bend the adjusting lever.*

3. When the brakes are tight almost to the point of being locked, back off on the starwheel 10 clicks. The starwheel on each set of brakes (front or rear) must be backed off the same number of turns to prevent brake pull from side to side.

Adjusting rear brakes

BRAKES

Brake Specifications
All measurements given are (in.) unless noted

Model	Lug Nut Torque (ft/lb)	Master Cylinder Bore	Brake Disc Minimum Thickness	Brake Disc Maximum Run-Out	Brake Drum Diameter	Brake Drum Max Machine O/S	Brake Drum Max Wear Limit	Minimum Lining Thickness Front	Minimum Lining Thickness Rear
1978	80–85	0.625	0.431 ②	①	7.87	7.927	7.927	③	5⁄16
1979	80–85	0.625	0.431 ②	①	7.87	7.927	7.927	③	5⁄16
1980	80–85	0.625	0.431 ②	①	7.87	7.927	7.927	③	5⁄16

NOTE: *Minimum lining thickness is as recommended by the manufacturer. Because of variations in state inspection regulations, the minimum allowable thickness may be different than recommended by the manufacturer.*

① Maximum 0.005 in. total combined run-out of disc and hub.
 Run-out of disc (installed on hub)—0.005 in.
 Run-out of hub (disc removed)—0.002 in.
② Thickness of new disc—0.490–0.505 in.
③ 0.3 in.—minimum thickness of lining and backing plate at any point.

4. When all brakes are adjusted, check brake pedal travel and then make several stops, while backing the car up, to equalize all the wheels.

TESTING ADJUSTER

1. Raise the vehicle on a hoist, with a helper in the car, to apply the brakes.
2. Loosen the brakes by holding the adjuster lever away from the starwheel and backing off the starwheel approximately 30 notches.
3. Spin the wheel and brake drum in reverse and apply the brakes. The movement of the secondary shoe should pull the adjuster lever up, and when the brakes are released the lever should snap down and turn the starwheel.
4. If the automatic adjuster doesn't work, the drum must be removed and the adjuster components inspected carefully for breakage, wear, or improper installation.

Hydraulic System
MASTER CYLINDER
Removal and Installation
WITH POWER BRAKES

1. Disconnect the primary and secondary brake lines from the master cylinder. Plug the openings.
2. Remove the nuts attaching the cylinder to the power brake booster.
3. Slide the master cylinder stright out, away from the booster.
4. Position the master cylinder over the studs on the booster, align the pushrod with the master cylinder piston and tighten the nuts to 16 ft lbs.
5. Connect the brake lines.
6. Bleed the brakes.

WITH NON-POWER BRAKES

1. Disconnect the primary and secondary brake lines and install plugs in the master cylinder openings.
2. Disconnect the stoplight switch mounting bracket from under the instrument panel.
3. Pull the brake pedal backward to disengage the pushrod from the master cylinder piston.
 NOTE: *This will destroy the grommet.*
4. Remove the master cylinder-to-firewall nuts.
5. Slide the master cylinder out and away from the firewall. Be sure to remove all pieces of the broken grommet.
6. Install the boot on the pushrod.
7. Install a new grommet on the pushrod.
8. Apply a soap and water solution to the

180 BRAKES

grommet and slide it firmly into position in the primary piston socket. Move the pushrod from side to side to make sure it's seated.

9. From the engine side, press the pushrod through the master cylinder mounting plate and align the mounting studs with the holes in the cylinder.

10. Install the nuts and torque them to 16 ft lbs.

11. From under the instrument panel, place the pushrod on the pin on the pedal and install a new retaining clip.

CAUTION: *Be sure to lubricate the pin.*

12. Install the brake lines on the master cylinder.

13. Bleed the system.

OVERHAUL

CAUTION: *Do not hone the master cylinder bore. Honing will remove the anodized finish.*

1. Clean the housing and reservoir.
2. Remove the reservoir caps and empty the fluid.
3. Clamp the master cylinder in a soft-jawed vise.
4. Pull the reservoir from the master cylinder housing.
5. Remove the reservoir grommets.
6. Use needle nosed pliers to remove the secondary piston pin from inside the housing.
7. Remove the snap-ring from the outer end of the housing.
8. Slide the primary piston out of the master cylinder bore.
9. Tap the open end of the cylinder on the bench to remove the secondary piston. If it sticks in the bore, it can be removed with light air pressure.

NOTE: *If air pressure is used to remove the piston, new cups must be installed.*

10. Note the position of the rubber cups and remove all except the primary cup.

NOTE: *Do not remove the primary cup from the primary piston. If the cup is worn, the entire primary piston assembly should be replaced.*

11. If the brass tube seats are not reusable, replace them using a suitable tool.
12. Wash the entire housing in clean brake fluid and inspect for pitting or scratches. If any are found, replace the housing. If the pistons are corroded, they should be replaced. Discard all used rubber parts and replace piston cups and seals.
13. Before assembly, dip all parts in clean brake fluid.
14. Install the check flow washer.
15. Install the secondary piston into the master cylinder bore. Be sure the cup lips enter the bore evenly. Keep well lubricated with brake fluid.
16. Center the primary piston spring retainer on the secondary piston and push the piston assemblies into the bore up to the primary piston cup.
17. Work the cup into the bore and push the piston in up to the secondary seal. Work the cup into the bore and push on the piston until fully seated.

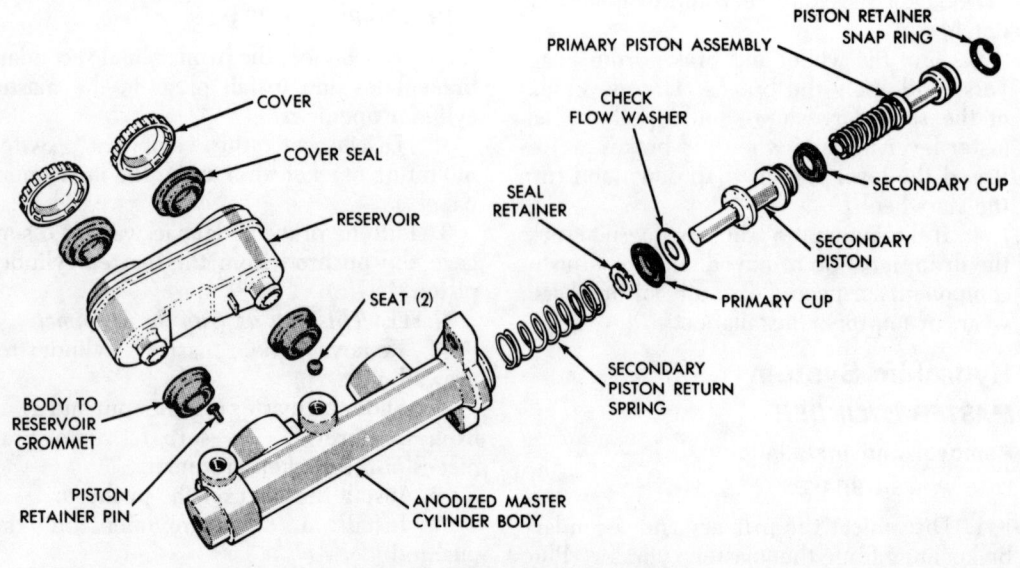

Master cylinder exploded view

18. Depress the piston and install the snap-ring.
19. Tap the secondary piston retainer pin into the housing.
20. Install new tube seats.
21. Install the reservoir grommets in the housing. Lubricate the area with clean brake fluid and install the reservoir. All the lettering should be properly read from the left side of the reservoir when it is properly installed. Make sure the bottom of the reservoir touches the top of the grommet.

PRESSURE DIFFERENTIAL VALVE AND WARNING LIGHT SWITCH

The brake system is split diagonally. That means that the right rear and left front brakes are connected to the same reservoir. Both systems are routed through, but separated by, the pressure differential valve, which also contains the warning switch. The function of the valve is to activate the switch in the event of brake system malfunction. The warning light switch is the latching type. It will automatically recenter itself after the repair is made and brake pedal depressed.

The bulb can be checked each time the ignition switch is turned to the ON position or each time the parking brake is set.

POWER BOOSTER

Removal and Installation

1. Remove the master cylinder; it can be pulled far enough out of the way to allow booster removal without disconnecting the brake lines.
2. Disconnect the vacuum hose from the booster.
3. Under the instrument panel, pry the retainer clip center tang over the end of the brake pedal pin and pull the retainer clip from the pin. Discard the clip.
4. Remove the four booster attaching nuts.
5. Remove the booster from the vehicle.
6. Position the booster on the firewall.
7. Torque the nuts to 20 ft lbs.
8. Carefully position the master cylinder on the booster.
9. Install the mounting nuts and torque them to 18 ft lbs.
10. Connect the vacuum hose to the booster.
11. Coat the bearing surface of the pedal pin with chassis lube.
12. Connect the pushrod to the pedal pin and install a new clip.
13. Check the stoplight operation. With vacuum applied to the power brake unit and pressure applied to the pedal, the master cylinder should vent (force a jet of fluid through the front chamber vent port).

CAUTION: *Do not attempt to disassemble the power brake unit, since the booster is serviced as a complete assembly only.*

BLEEDING THE BRAKE SYSTEM

Anytime a brake line has been disconnected the hydraulic system should be bled. The brakes should also be bled when the pedal travel becomes unusually long ("soft pedal") or the car pulls to one side during braking. The proper bleeding sequence is: right rear wheel, left rear wheel, right front caliper, and left front caliper. You'll need a helper to pump the brake pedal while you open the bleeder valves.

NOTE: *If the system has been drained, first refill it with fresh brake fluid. Following the above sequence, open each bleeder valve by ½ to ¾ of a turn and pump the brake pedal until fluid runs out of the valve. Proceed with the bleeding as outlined below.*

1. Remove the bleeder valve dust cover and install a rubber bleeder hose.
2. Insert the other end of the hose into a container about ⅓ full of brake fluid.
3. Have an assistant pump the brake pedal several times until the pedal pressure increases.
4. Hold the pedal under pressure and than start to open the bleeder valve about ½ to ¾ of a turn. At this point, have your assistant depress the pedal all the way and then quickly close the valve. The helper should allow the pedal to return slowly.

NOTE: *Keep a close check on the brake fluid in the reservoir and top it up as necessary throughout the bleeding process.*

5. Keep repeating this procedure until no more air bubbles can be seen coming from the hose in the brake fluid.
6. Remove the bleeder hose and install the dust cover.
7. Continue the bleeding at each wheel in sequence.

NOTE: *Don't splash any brake fluid on the paintwork. Brake fluid is very corrosive and will eat paint away. Any fluid accidentally spilled on the body should be immediately flushed off with water.*

182 BRAKES

Front Disc Brakes

Omni and Horizon's use a floating caliper front disc brake.

DISC BRAKE PADS

Inspection

Disc pads (lining and shoe assemblies) should be replaced in axle sets (both wheels) when the thickness of the shoe and lining is less than 0.3 inch.

NOTE: *State inspection specifications take precedence over these general recommendations.*

Note that disc pads in floating caliper type brakes may wear at an angle, and measurement should be made at the narrow end of the taper. Tapered linings should be replaced if the taper exceeds 1/8 in. from end to end (the difference between the thickest and thinnest points).

Always replace both sets on each wheel whenever one pad needs replacing.

NOTE: *Brake squeal is inherent in disc brakes. If the squeal is objectionable and constant it can be reduced by installing new brake pads (Chrysler (Chrysler Part No. 4176767). After 1000 miles of city driving these new compound pads should reduce noise, although a very low level of noise may be present under certain conditions.*

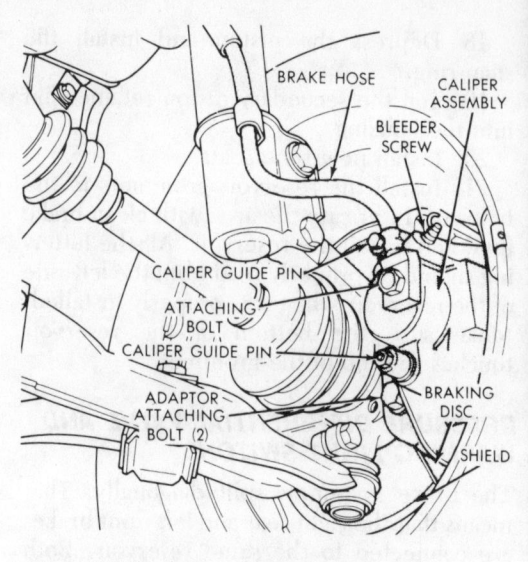

Front caliper attaching points

3. Remove the caliper guide pins and anti-rattle springs.
4. Remove the caliper by slowly sliding the caliper off the brake disc. Hang the caliper by a piece of stiff wire. Do not allow it to hang by the brake line.
5. Remove the outboard brake pad from the adaptor.
6. Slide the inboard pad out of the adaptor.
7. To install the pads, place new pads in the adaptor.
8. Loosen the rear cap of the master cylinder reservoir and slowly push the caliper pistons back into the housing.

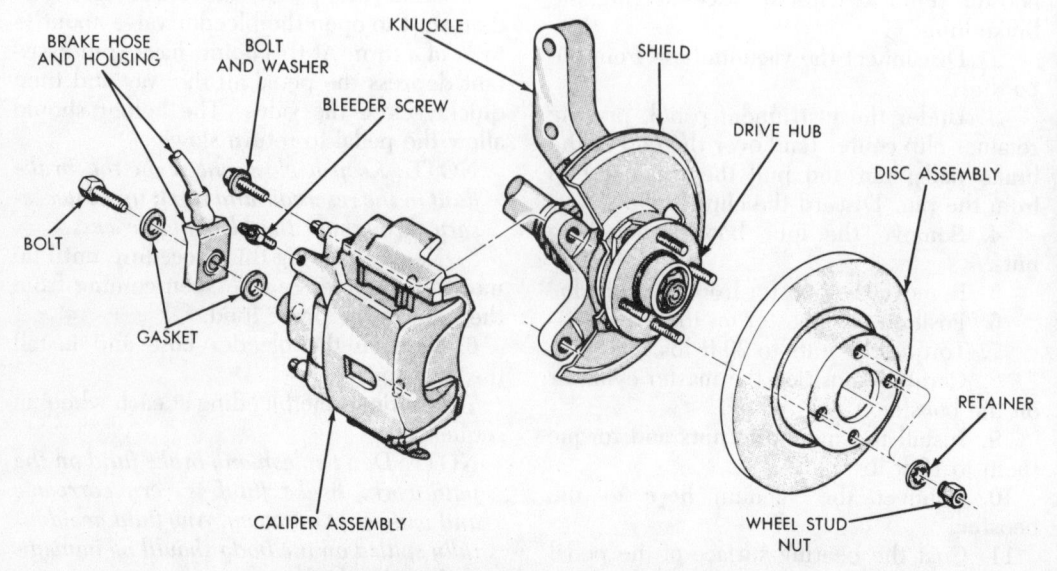

Removal and Installation

1. Raise and support the car.
2. Remove the wheels.

Exploded view of disc brake components

BRAKES 183

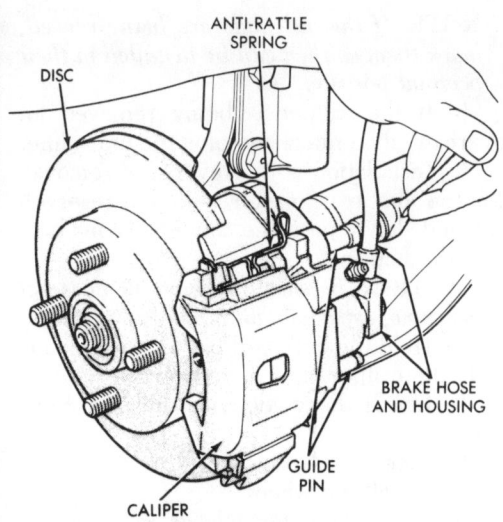

Remove or install the caliper guide pins

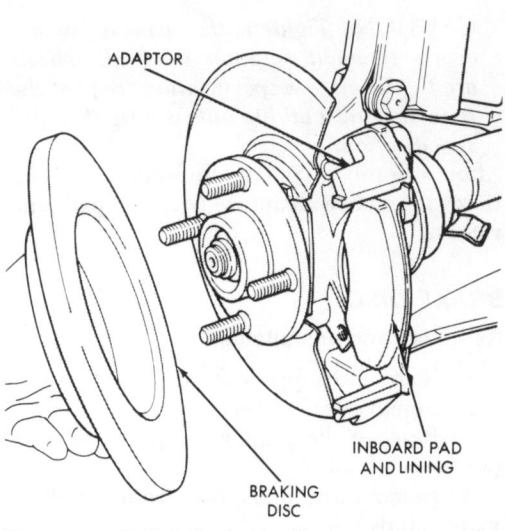

Remove or install the brake disc

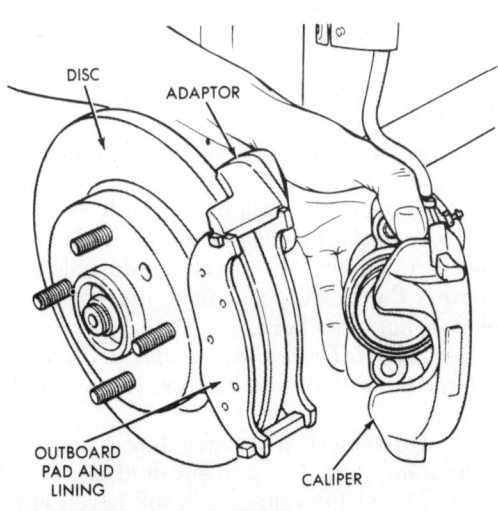

Remove or install the caliper

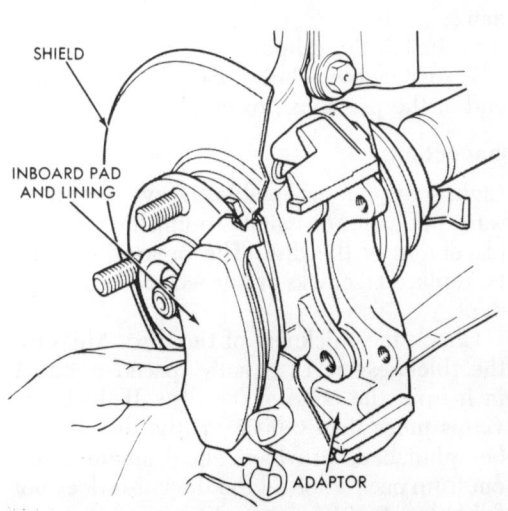

Remove or install the inboard brake pad

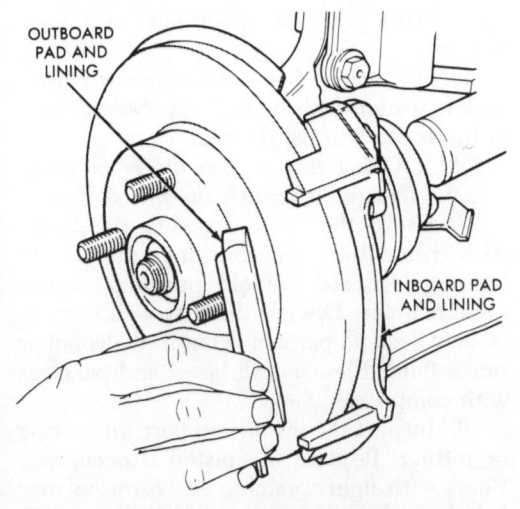

Remove or install the outboard brake pad

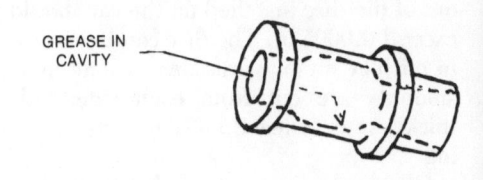

CAUTION: *Be sure the reservoir does not overflow, especially onto painted surfaces.*

9. Hold the outboard lining in position and carefully slide the caliper into position on the adaptor.

10. Install the guide pins (lightly lubricated with silicone grease) and anti-rattle springs. The anti-rattle spring clips are installed with the closed loop toward the center of the car.

11. Bleed the brakes.
12. Install the wheels.

184 BRAKES

CAUTION: *Tighten the wheels in an every-other-nut rotation until all wheels are tightened to ½ specification. Repeat the sequence until all lug nuts are tight to full specification.*

After assembly, pump the pedal several times to remove clearance between pads and rotors.

BRAKE DISC
Removal and Installation.

1. Raise and support the car.
2. Remove the wheels.
3. Remove the caliper. Suspend the caliper from a hook.
4. Remove the brake disc from the drive flange studs.
5. Install the brake disc on the drive flange studs.
6. Install the caliper.
7. Install the wheels. See NOTE at the end of the previous procedure.

Inspection

Light scoring is acceptable. Heavy scoring or warping will necessitate refinishing or replacement of the disc. The brake disc must be replaced if cracks or burned marks are evident.

Check the thickness of the disc. Measure the thickness at 12 equally spaced points 1 inch from the edge of the disc. If thickness varies more than 0.0005 in. the disc should be refinished, provided equal amounts are out from each side and the thickness does not fall below 0.431 in.

Check the run-out of the disc. Total run-out of the disc installed on the car should not exceed 0.0005 in. The disc can be resurfaced to correct minor variations as long as equal amounts are cut from each side and the thickness is at least 0.431 in. after resurfacing.

Check the run-out of the hub (disc removed). It should not be more than 0.002 in. If so, the hub should be replaced.

CALIPER
Removal and Installation

1. Raise and support the car.
2. Remove the wheels.
3. Remove the caliper guide pins and anti-rattle springs.
4. Remove the caliper by slowly sliding it off the adaptor.

NOTE: *If the old pads are being reused, mark them so they can be installed in their original position.*

5. If the caliper is being removed for overhaul, disconnect and plug the brake line.
6. Installation is the reverse of removal. Loosen the rear master cylinder reservoir cap and slowly push the caliper pistons back into the housing.

CAUTION: *Be sure the reservoir does not overflow, especially onto painted surfaces.*

7. Hold the outboard pad in position and slide the caliper onto the adaptor.
8. Install the guide pins and anti-rattle springs.
9. Bleed the brakes.
10. Install the wheels.

NOTE: *Tighten the wheels in an every-other-nut rotation until the nuts are tight to ½ specification. Repeat the sequence until all the lug nuts are tight to full specification.*

Overhaul

1. Remove the caliper assembly from the car *without* disconnecting the hydraulic line.
2. Support the caliper assembly on the upper control arm and surround it with shop towels to absorb any brake fluid. Slowly depress the brake pedal until the piston is pushed out of its bore.

CAUTION: *Do not use compressed air to force the piston from its bore; injury could result.*

3. Disconnect the brake line from the caliper and plug it to prevent fluid loss.
4. Mount the caliper in a soft-jawed vise and clamp lightly. Do not tighten the vise too much or the caliper will become distorted.
5. Work the dust boot out with your fingers.
6. Use a small pointed *wooden* or *plastic* stick to work the piston seal out of the groove in the bore. Discard the seal.

CAUTION: *Using a screwdriver or other metal tool could scratch the piston bore.*

7. Using the same wooden or plastic stick, press the outer bushings out of the housing. Discard the old bushings in the same manner. Discard them as well.
8. Clean all parts in denatured alcohol or brake fluid. Blow out all bores and passages with compressed air.
9. Inspect the piston and bore for scoring or pitting. Replace the piston if necessary. Bores with light scratches or corrosion may be cleaned with crocus cloth. Bores with

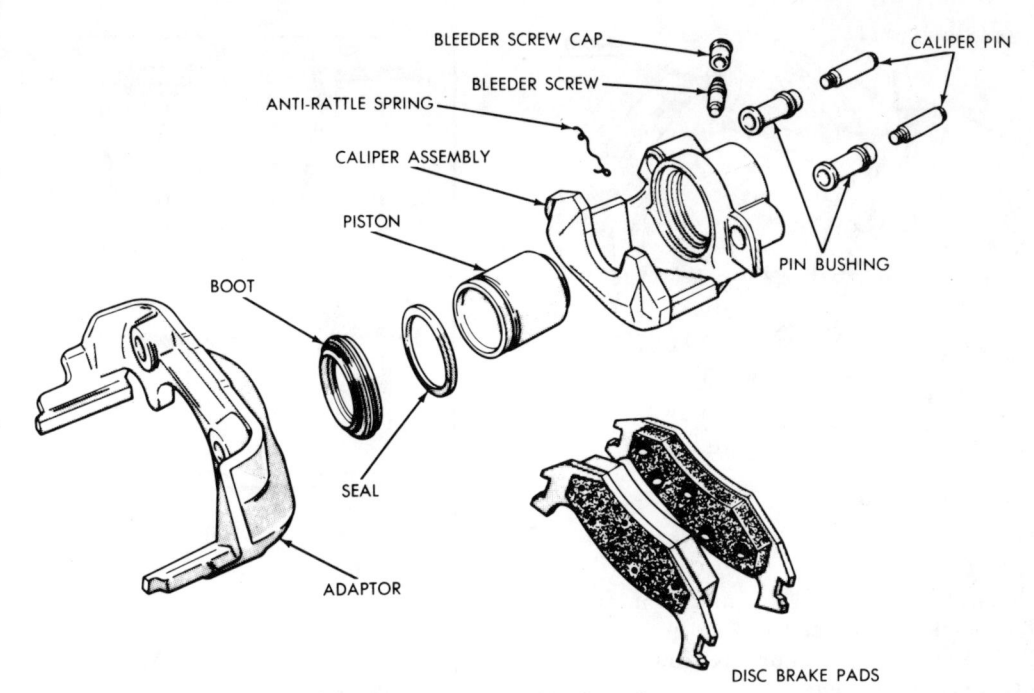

Exploded view of brake caliper

deep scratches may be honed if you do not increase the bore diameter more than 0.002 in. Replace the housing if the bore must be enlarged beyond this.

NOTE: *Black stains are caused by piston seals and are harmless.*

10. If the bore had to be honed, clean its grooves with a stiff, non-metallic rotary brush. Clean the bore twice by flushing it out with brake fluid and drying it with a soft, lint-free cloth.

Caliper assembly is as follows:

1. Clamp the caliper in a soft-jawed vise; do not overtighten.

2. Dip a new piston seal in brake fluid or the lubricant supplied with the rebuilding kit. Position the new seal in one area of its groove and gently work it into place with clean fingers, so that it is correctly seated. Do not use an old seal.

3. Coat a new boot with brake fluid or lubricant (as above), leaving a generous amount inside.

4. Insert the boot in the caliper and work it into the groove, using your fingers only. The boot will snap into place once it is correctly positioned. Run your forefinger around the inside of the boot to make sure that it is correctly seated.

5. Install the bleed screw in its hole and plug the fluid inlet on the caliper.

6. Coat the piston with brake fluid or lubricant. Spread the boot with your fingers and work the piston into the boot.

7. Depress the piston; this will force the boot into its groove on the piston. Remove the plug and bottom the piston in the bore.

8. Compress the flanges of new guide pin bushings and work them into place by pressing *in* on the bushings with your fingertips, until they are seated. Make sure that the flanges cover the housing evenly on all sides.

9. Install the caliper on the car as previously outlined.

Rear Drum Brakes
BRAKE DRUMS
Removal and Installation

1. Remove the plug from the brake shoe adjusting hole.

2. Using a brake spoon, release the brake shoes by moving the star wheel adjuster up (left side) or down (right side).

3. Remove the grease cap.

4. Remove the cotter pin, lock nut and washer.

5. Remove the brake drum and bearings.

6. Installation is the reverse of removal. Adjust the wheel bearings (see Chapter 1).

Inspection

Measure the drum run-out and diameter. If not according to specifications the drum

186 BRAKES

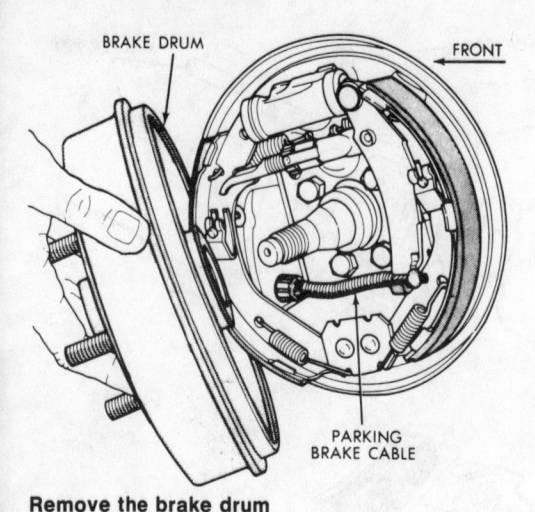

Remove the brake drum

should be replaced. The variation in diameter should not exceed 0.0025 in. in 30° or 0.0035 in. in 360°. All drums show markings of maximum diameter.

Once the drum is off, clean the shoes and springs with a stiff brush to remove the accumulated brake dust.

NOTE: *Avoid prolonged exposure to brake dust.*

Grease on the shoes can be removed with alcohol or fine sandpaper.

After cleaning, examine the brake shoes for glazed, oily, loose, cracked or improperly worn linings. Light glazing is common and can be removed with fine sandpaper. Linings that are worn improperly or below 1/16" above rivet heads or brake shoe should be replaced. The NHSTA advises states with inspection programs to fail vehicles with brake linings less than 1/32". A good "eyeball" test is to replace the linings when the thickness is the same as or less than the thickness of the metal backing plate (shoe).

Wheel cylinders are a vital part of the brake system and should be inspected carefully. Gently pull back the rubber boots; if any fluid is visible, it's time to replace or rebuild the wheel cylinders. Boots that are distorted, cracked or otherwise damaged, also point to the need for service. Check the flexible brake lines for cracks, chafing or wear.

Check the brake shoe retracting and hold-down springs; they should not be worn or distorted. Be sure that the adjuster mechanism moves freely. The points on the backing plate where the shoes slide should be shiny and free of rust. Rust in these areas suggests

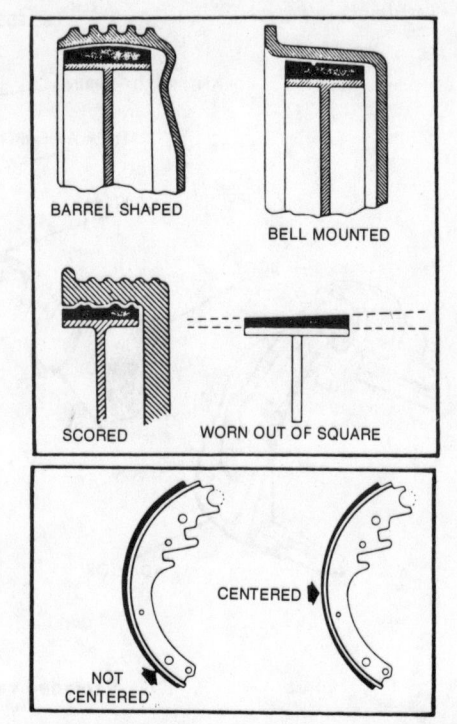

Improperly worn linings are cause for concern only if braking is unstable and noise is objectionable. Compare the lining and drum wear pattern, the drum being more important, since the drum shapes the wear of the shoe

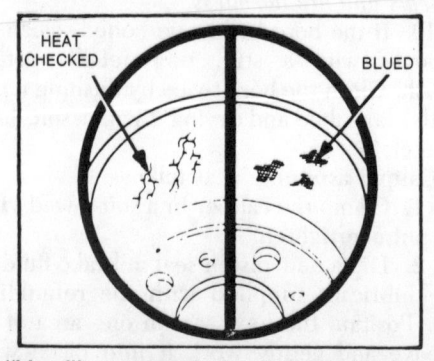

A "blued" or severely heat checked drum and "blued", charred or heavily glazed linings are the result of overheating. The brakes should be checked immediately

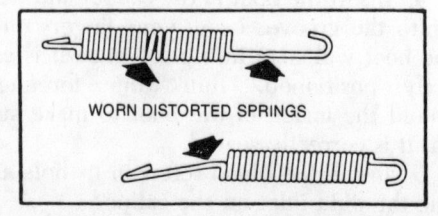

Check for weak or distorted retracting springs

BRAKES 187

Left rear brake

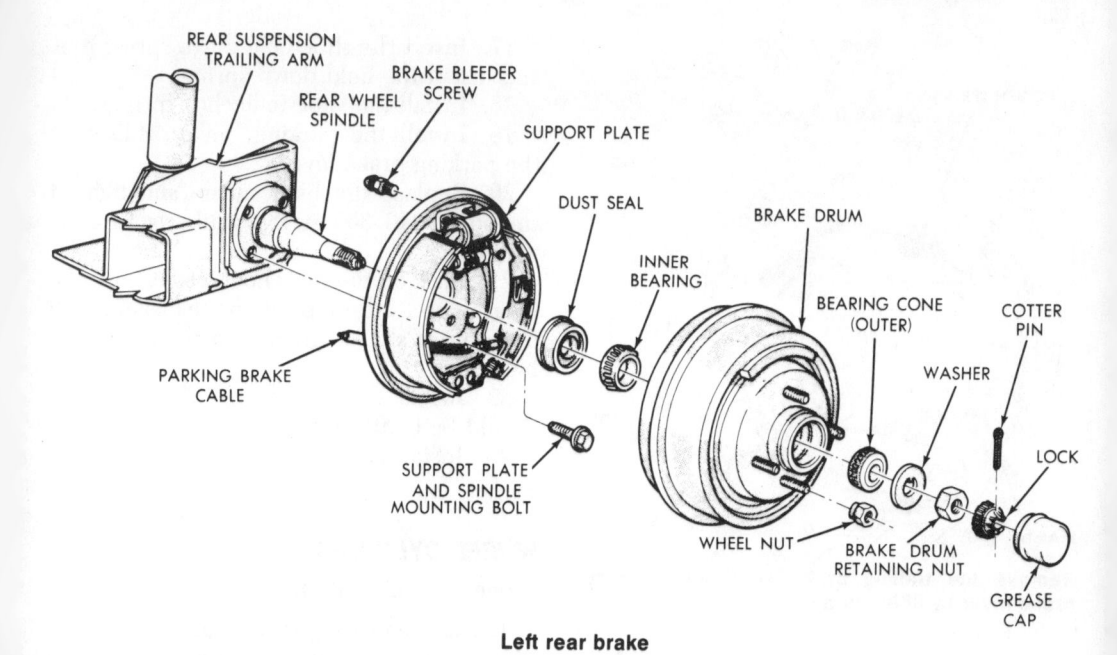

that the brake shoes are not moving properly.

BRAKE SHOES

Removal and Installation

NOTE: *If you are not thoroughly familiar with the procedures involved in brake replacement, disassemble and assemble one side at a time, leaving the other wheel intact, as a reference.*

1. Remove the brake drum. See the procedure earlier in this chapter.
2. Unhook the parking brake cable from the secondary (trailing) shoe.
3. Remove the shoe-to-anchor springs (retracting springs). They can be gripped and unhooked with a pair of pliers.
4. Remove the shoe hold down springs: compress them slightly and slide them off of the hold down pins.
5. Remove the adjuster screw assembly by spreading the shoes apart. The adjuster nut must be fully backed off.
6. Raise the parking brake lever. Pull the secondary (trailing) shoe away from the backing plate so pull-back spring tension is released.

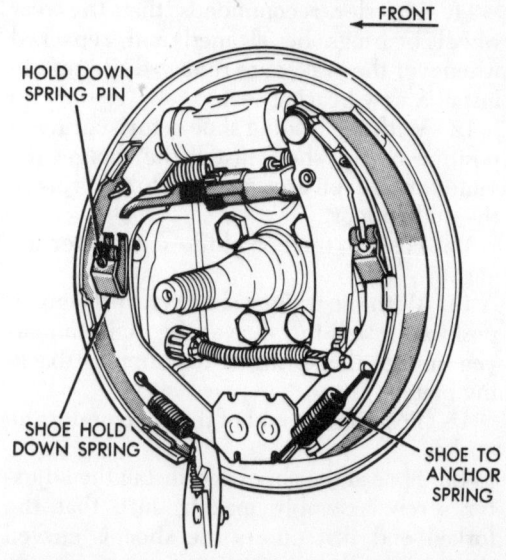

Left rear brake shoes and springs installed

The shoe-to-anchor springs can be removed with pliers

188 BRAKES

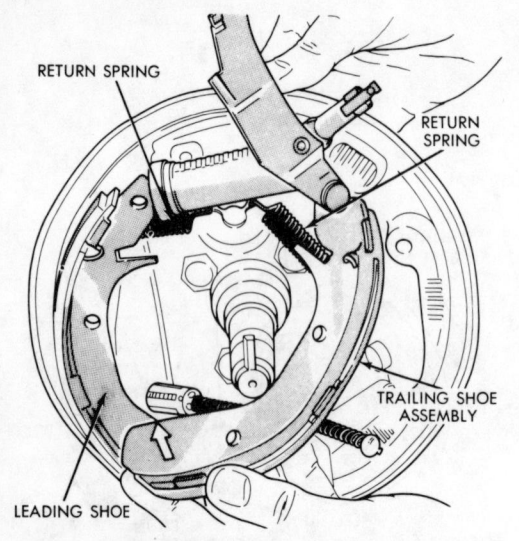

Remove the trailing brake shoe and parking brake lever by lifting upward

7. Remove the secondary (trailing) shoe and disengage the spring end from the backing plate.

8. Raise the primary (leading) shoe to release spring tension. Remove the shoe and disengage the spring end from the backing plate.

9. Inspect the brakes (see procedures under Brake Drum Inspection).

10. Lubricate the six shoe contact areas on the brake backing plate and the web end of the brake shoe which contacts the anchor plate. Use a multi-purpose lubricant or a high temperature brake grease made for the purpose.

11. Chrysler recommends that the rear wheel bearings be cleaned and repacked whenever the brakes are renewed. Be sure to install a new bearing seal.

12. With the leading shoe return spring in position on the shoe, install the shoe at the same time as you engage the return spring in the end support.

13. Position the end of the shoe under the anchor.

14. With the trailing shoe return spring in position, install the shoe at the same time as you engage the spring in the support (backing plate).

15. Position the end of the shoe under the anchor.

16. Spread the shoes and install the adjuster screw assembly making sure that the forked end that enters the shoe is curved down.

17. Insert the shoe hold down spring pins and install the hold down springs.

18. Install the shoe-to-anchor springs.

19. Install the parking brake cable onto the parking brake lever.

20. Replace the brake drum and tighten the nut to 240–300 in. lbs. while rotating the wheel.

21. Back off the nut enough to release the bearing preload and position the locknut with one pair of slots aligned with the cotter pin hole.

22. Install the cotter pin. The end play should be 0.001–0.003 in.

23. Install the grease cap.

WHEEL CYLINDERS

Removal and Installation

1. Raise and support the car.
2. Remove the brake drums.
3. Visually inspect the wheel cylinder boots for signs of excessive leakage. A slight amount of leakage is normal, but excessive leakage will necessitate boot replacement. Replace any boots that are torn or broken.
4. In case of a leak, also remove the brake shoes and check for contamination.
5. Disconnect and plug the brake line.
6. Unbolt and remove the wheel cylinder.
7. Installation is the reverse of removal. Bleed the brakes.

Overhaul

1. Pry the boots away from the cylinder and remove the boots and piston as an assembly.
2. Disengage the boot from the piston.
3. Slide the piston into the cylinder bore and press inward to remove the other boot and piston. Also remove the spring with it the cup expanders.

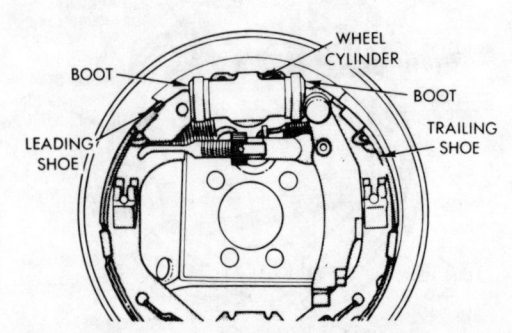

Wheel cylinder installed on backing plate.

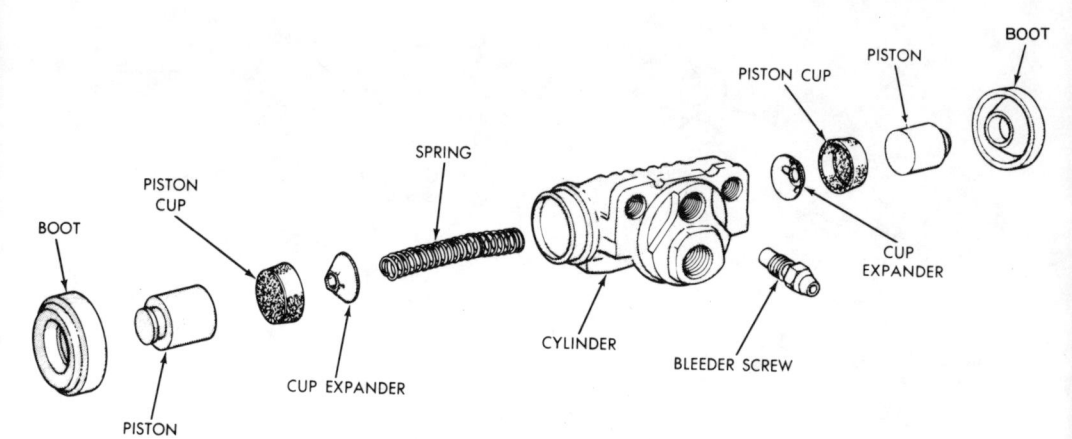

Exploded view of wheel cylinder

4. Wash all parts (except rubber parts) in clean brake bluid and fluid thoroughly. Do not use a rag; lint will adhere to the bore.

5. Inspect the cylinder bores. Light scoring can usually be cleaned up with crocus cloth. Black stains are caused by the piston cups and are no cause of concern. Bad scoring or pitting means that the wheel cylinder should be replaced.

6. Dip the pistons and new cups in clean brake fluid prior to assembly.

7. Coat the wheel cylinder bore with clean brake fluid.

8. Install the expansion spring with the cup expanders.

9. Install the cups in each end of the cylinder with the open ends facing each other.

10. Assemble new boots on the piston and slide them into the cylinder bore.

11. Press the boot over the wheel cylinder until seated.

12. Install the wheel cylinder.

Parking Brake

ADJUSTMENT

The cable operated parking brake is adjusted at the equalizer (connector) under the car.

1. Adjust the service brakes.
2. Release the parking brake lever and back off the parking brake cable until there is slack in the cable.
3. Clean and lubricate the adjuster threads.
4. Use a brake spoon to turn the starwheel adjuster until there is light shoe-to-drum contact. Back off the starwheel until the wheel rotates freely with no brake drag.
5. Tighten the parking brake adjustment until a slight drag is felt while rotating the wheels.
6. Loosen the cable adjusting nut until both rear wheels can be rotated freely, then back the cable adjuster nut off 2 full turns.
7. Test the parking brake. The rear wheels should rotate freely without dragging.

FRONT BRAKE CABLE

Removal and Installation

1. Raise and support the car.
2. Disconnect the brake cable from the connector.
3. Force the cable housing and attaching clip forward out of the body crossmember.
4. Fold back the left front edge of the floor covering and pry the rubber grommet out of the hole in the dash or from the floor pan.
5. Remove the cable-to-floor pan clip.
6. Engage the parking brake and work the cable out of the clevis linkage.
7. Force the upper end of the cable housing out of the pedal bracket.
8. Work the cable and housing assembly out of the floor pan.
9. Installation is the reverse of removal. Adjust the parking and service brakes and test the operation of both.

REAR BRAKE CABLE

Removal and Installation

1. Raise and support the car.
2. Remove the rear wheels.
3. Disconnect the brake cable from the connector.

190 BRAKES

Parking brake cables

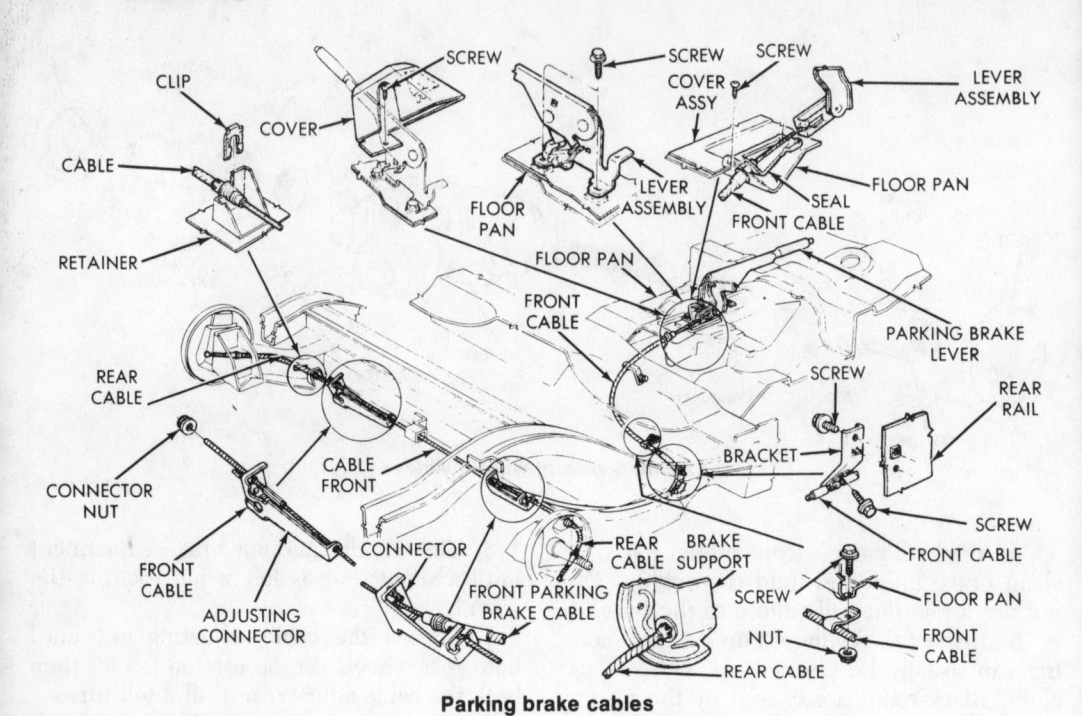

4. Remove the retaining clip from the rear cable bracket.
5. Remove the brake drum.
6. Remove the brake shoe return springs.
7. Remove the brake shoe retaining springs.
8. Remove the brake shoe strut and spring and disconnect the cable from the operating arm.
9. Compress the retainers on the end of the brake cable housing and remove the cable.
10. Installation is the reverse of removal. Adjust the service and parking brakes and test the operation of both.

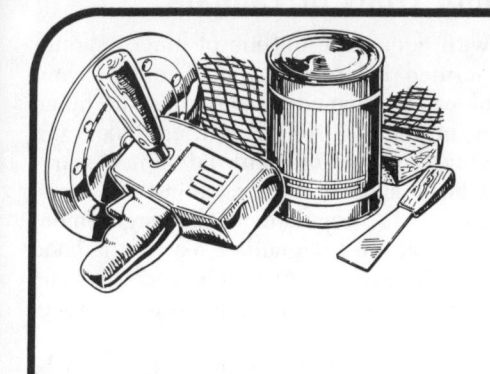

Body

The list of tools and equipment you may need to fix minor body damage ranges from very basic hand tools to a wide assortment of specialized body tools. Most minor scratches, dings and rust holes can be fixed using an electric drill, wire wheel or grinder attachment, half-round plastic file, sanding block, various grades of sandpaper (#120, which is coarse through #600, which is fine, in both wet and dry types), auto body plastic, primer, touch-up paint, spreaders, newspaper and masking tape. If you intend to try straightening any dents, you'll probably also need a slide hammer (dent puller).

Most auto body repair kits contain all the materials you need to do the job right in the kit. So, if you have a small rust spot or dent you want to fix, check the contents of the kit before you run out and buy any additional tools.

ALIGNING BODY PANELS

Doors

There are several methods of adjusting doors. Your vehicle will probably use one of those illustrated.

Whenever a door is removed and is to be reinstalled, you should matchmark the position of the hinges on the door pillars. The holes of the hinges and/or the hinge attaching points are usually oversize to permit alignment of doors. The striker plate is also moveable, through oversize holes, permitting up-and-down, in-and-out and fore-and-aft movement. Fore-and-aft movement is made by adding or subtracting shims from behind the striker and pillar post. The striker should be adjusted so that the door closes fully and remains closed, yet enters the lock freely.

DOOR HINGES

Don't try to cover up poor door adjustment with a striker plate adjustment. The gap on each side of the door should be equal and uniform and there should be no metal-to-metal contact as the door is opened or closed.

1. Determine which hinge bolts must be loosened to move the door in the desired direction.

2. Loosen the hinge bolt(s) just enough to allow the door to be moved with a padded pry bar.

3. Move the door a small amount and check the fit, after tightening the bolts. Be sure that there is no bind or interference with adjacent panels.

4. Repeat this until the door is properly positioned, and tighten all the bolts securely.

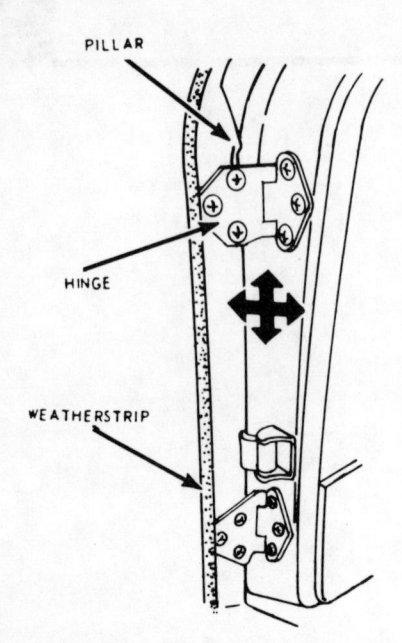

192 BODY

Hood, Trunk or Tailgate

As with doors, the outline of hinges should be scribed before removal. The hood and trunk can be aligned by loosening the hinge bolts in their slotted mounting holes and moving the hood or trunk lid as necessary. The hood and trunk have adjustable catch locations to regulate lock engagement bumpers at the front and/or rear of the hood provide a vertical adjustment and the hood lockpin can be adjusted for proper engagement.

The tailgate on the station wagon can be adjusted by loosening the hinge bolts in their slotted mounting holes and moving the tailgate on its hinges. The latchplate and

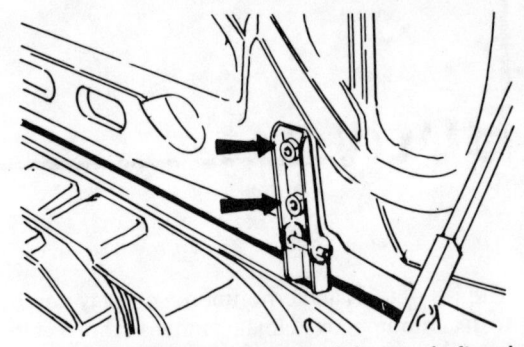

Door hinge adjustment

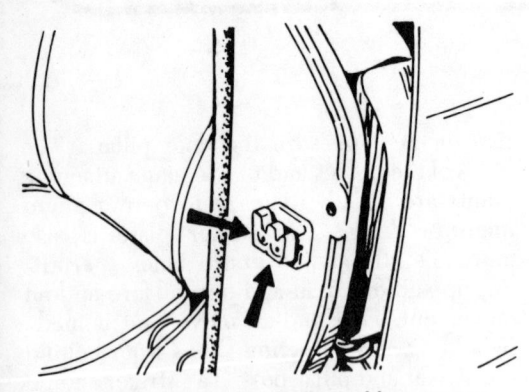

Move the door striker as indicated by arrows

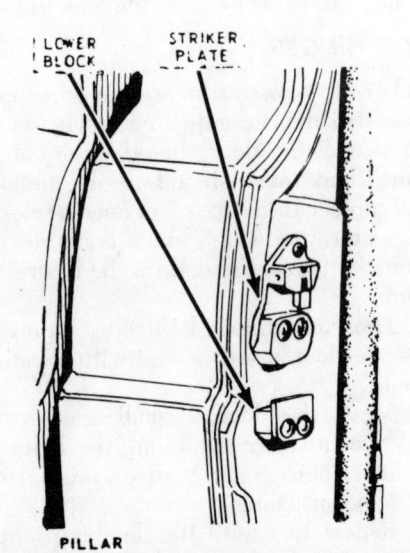

Striker plate and lower block

Loosen the hinge boots to permit fore-and-aft and horizontal adjustment

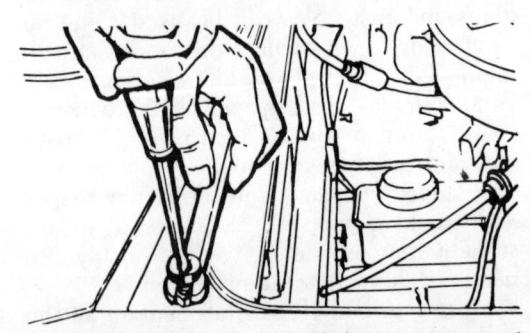

The hood is adjusted vertically by stop-screws at the front and/or rear

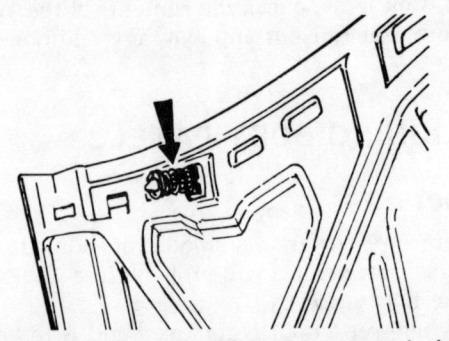

The hood pin can be adjusted for proper lock engagement

latch striker at the bottom of the tailgate opening can be adjusted to stop rattle. An adjustable bumper is located on each side.

RUST, UNDERCOATING, AND RUSTPROOFING

Rust

About the only technical information the average backyard mechanic needs to know about rust is that it is an electro-chemical process that works from **the inside out** on unprotected ferrous metals such as steel and iron. Salt, pollution, humidity—these things and more create and promote the formation of rust. You can't stop rust once it starts. Once rust has started on a fender or a body panel, the only sure way to stop it is to replace the part.

It's a lot easier to prevent rust than to remove it, especially if you have a new car and most late model cars are pretty well rustproofed when the leave the factory. In the early seventies, it seemed like cars were rusting out faster than you could pay them off and Detroit (and the imports) realized that this is not exactly the way you build customer loyalty.

Undercoating

Contrary to what most people think, the primary purpose of undercoating is not to prevent rust, but to deaden noise that might otherwise be transmitted to the car's interior. Since cars are pretty quiet these days anyway, dealers are only too willing to promote undercoating as a rust preventative. Undercoating will of course, prevent some rust, but only if applied when the car is brand- new. In any case, undercoating doesn't provide the protection that a good rustproofing does. If you do decide to undercoat your car and it's not brand-new, you have a big clean-up job ahead of you. It's a good idea to have the underside of the car professionally steam-cleaned and save yourself a lot of work. Spraying undercoat on dirty or rusty parts is only going to make things worse, since the undercoat will trap any rust causing agents.

Rustproofing

The best thing you can do for a new or nearly new car is to have it properly rust-proofed. There are two ways you can go about this. You can do it yourself, or you can have one of the big rustproofing companies do it for you. Naturally, it's going to cost you a lot more to have a big company do it, but it's worth it if your car is new or nearly new. If you own an older car that you plan to hang onto for a while, then doing it yourself might be the best idea. Professional rust-proofing isn't cheap ($100–$250), but it's definitely worth it if your car is new. The rustproofing companies won't guarantee their jobs on cars that are over three months old or have more than about 3000 miles on them because they feel the corrosion process may have already begun.

If you have an older car that hasn't started to rust yet, the best idea might be to purchase one of the do-it-yourself rustproofing kits that are available, and do the job yourself.

Drain Holes

Rusty rocker panels are a common problem on nearly every car, but they can be prevented by simply drilling some holes in your rocker panels to let the water out, or keeping the ones that are already there clean and unclogged. Most cars these days have a series of holes in the rocker panels to prevent moisture collection there, but they frequently become clogged up. Just use a small screwdriver or penknife to keep them clean. If your car doesn't have drain holes, it's a simple matter to drill a couple of holes in each panel.

Repairing Minor Body Damage

Unless your car just rolled off the showroom floor, chances are it has a few minor scratches or dings in it somewhere, or a small rust spot you've been meaning to fix. You just haven't been able to decide whether or not you can really do the job. Well, if the damage is anything like that presented here, there are a number of auto body repair kits that contain everything you need to repair minor scratches, dents, and rust spots. Even rust holes can be repaired if you use the correct kit. If you're unsure of your ability, start out with a small scratch. Once you've mastered small scratches and dings, you can work your way up to the more complicated repairs. When doing rust repairs, remember that unless all the rust is removed, it's going to come back in a year or less. Just sanding the rust down and applying some paint won't work.

Repairing Minor Surface Rust and Scratches

1. Just about everybody has a minor rust spot or scratches on their vehicle. Spots such as these can be easily repaired in an hour or two. You'll need some sandpaper, masking tape, primer, and a can of touch-up paint.

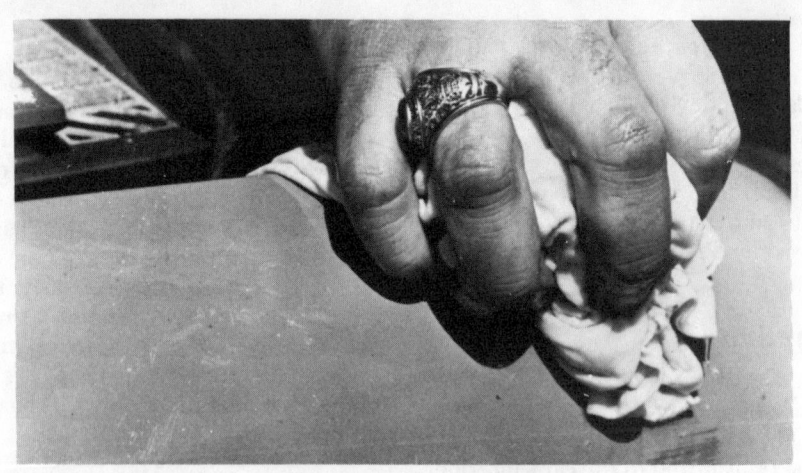

2. The first step is to wash the area down to remove all traces of dirt and road grime. If the vehicle has been frequently waxed, you should wipe it with thinner or some other wax remover so that the paint will stick.

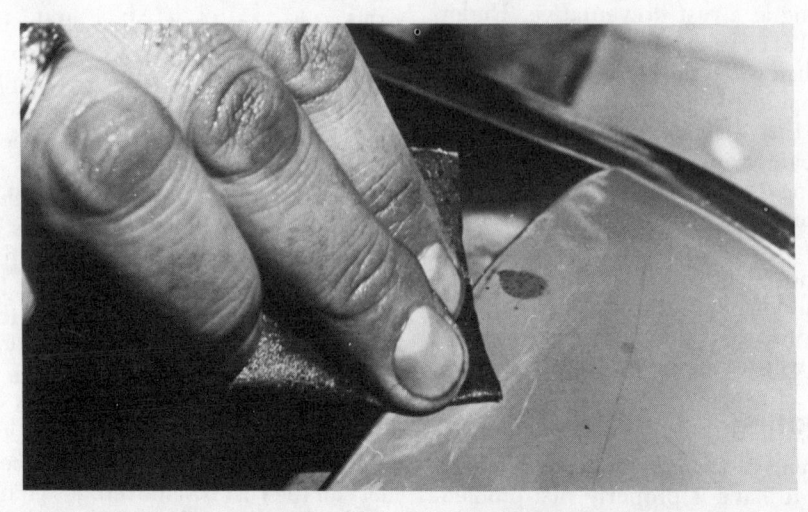

3. Small rust spots and scratches like these will only require light hand sanding. For a job like this, you can start with about grade 320 sandpaper and then use a 400 grit for the final sanding.

4. Once you've sanded the area with 320 paper, wet a piece of 400 paper and sand it lightly. Wet sanding will feather the edges of the surrounding paint into the area to be painted. For large areas, you could use a sanding block, but it's not really necessary for a small job like this.

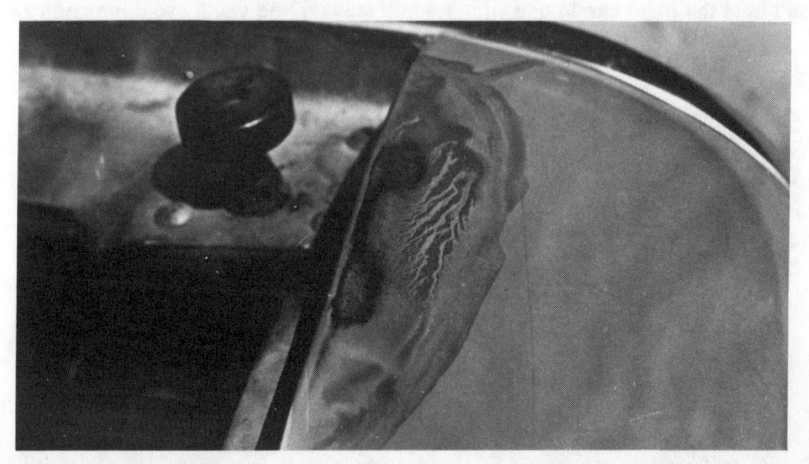

5. The area should look like this once you're finished sanding. Wipe off any water and run the palm of your hand over the sanded area with your eyes closed. You shouldn't be able to feel any bumps or ridges anywhere. Make sure you have sanded a couple of inches back in each direction so you'll get good paint adhesion.

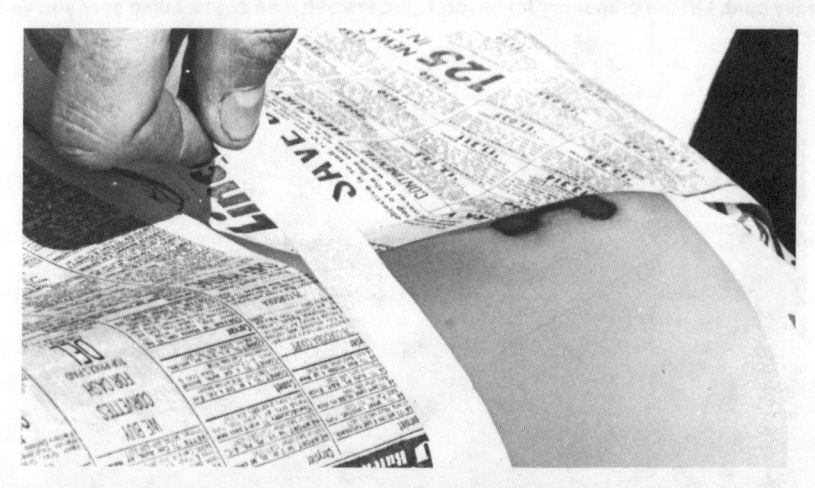

6. Once you have the area sanded to your satisfaction, mask the surrounding area with masking tape and newspaper. Be sure to cover any chrome or trim that might get sprayed. You'll have to mask far enough back from the damaged area to allow for overspray. If you mask right around the sanded spots, you'll end up with a series of lines marking the painted area.

196   BODY

7. You can avoid a lot of excess overspray by cutting a hole in a piece of cardboard that approximately matches the area you are going to paint. Hold the cardboard steady over the area as you spray the primer on. If you haven't painted before, it's a good idea to practice on something before you try painting your car. Don't hold the paint can in one spot. Keep it moving and you'll avoid runs and sags.

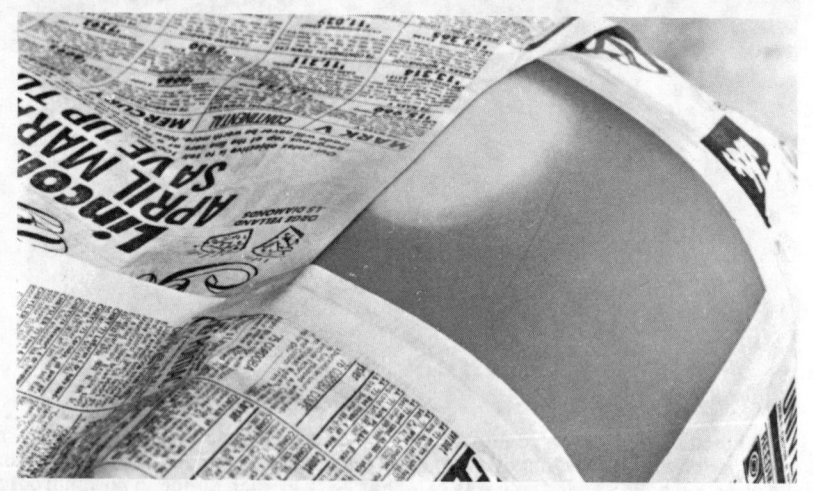

8. The primered area should look like this when you have finished. It's better to spray several light coats than one heavy coat. Let the primer dry for several minutes between coats. Make sure you've covered all the bare metal.

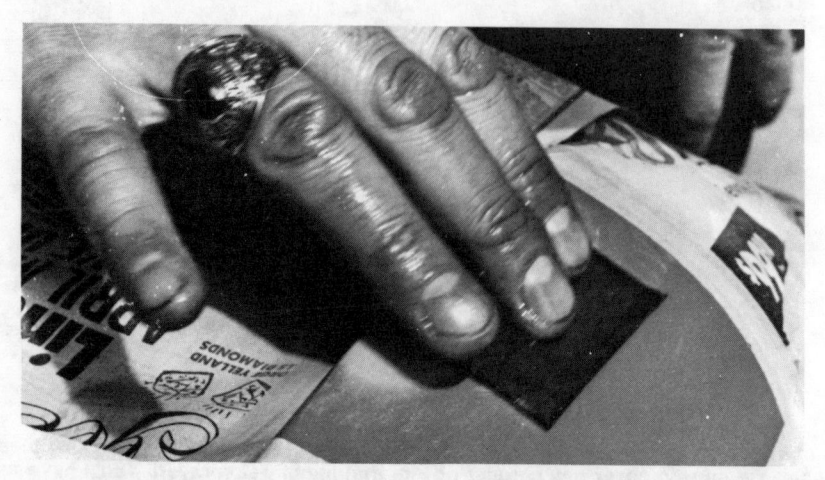

9. After the primer has dried, sand the area with wet 400 paper, wash it off and let it dry. Your final coat goes on next, so make sure the area is clean and dry.

10. Spray the touch-up paint on using the cardboard again. Make the first coat a very light coat (known as a fog coat). Remember to keep the paint can moving smoothly at about 8–12 inches from the surface.

11. Once you've finished painting, let the paint dry for about 15 minutes before you remove the masking tape and newspaper.

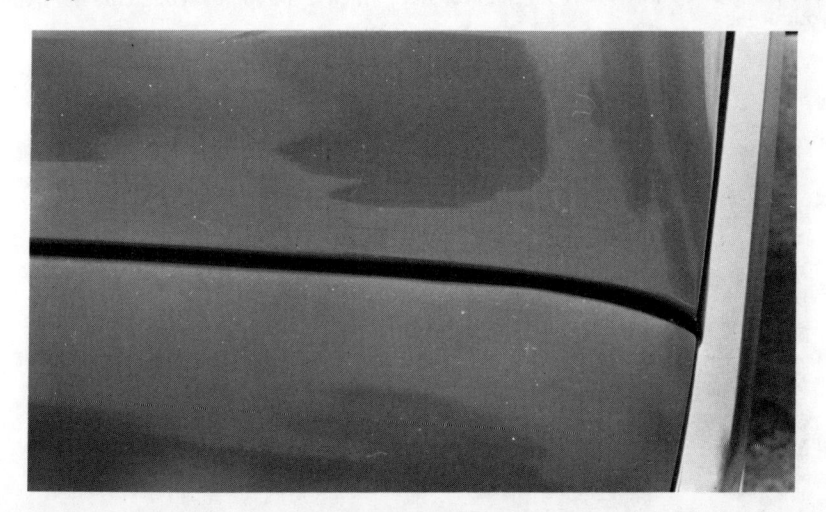

12. Let the paint dry for several days before you rub it out lightly with rubbing compound, and the finished job should be indistinguishable from the rest of the vehicle. Don't rub hard or you'll cut through the paint.

198 BODY

Repairing Rust Holes With Fiberglass

1. The job we've picked here isn't an easy one mainly because of the location. The compound curves make the work trickier than if the surface were flat.

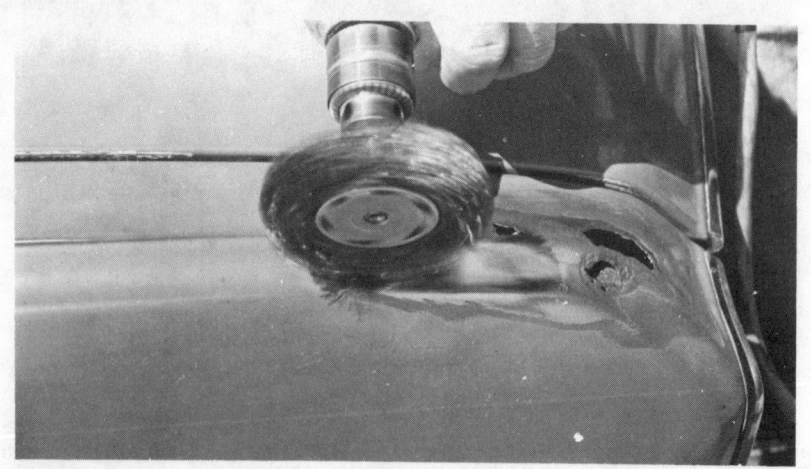

2. You'll need a drill and a wire brush for the first step, which is the removal of all the paint and rust from the rusted-out area.

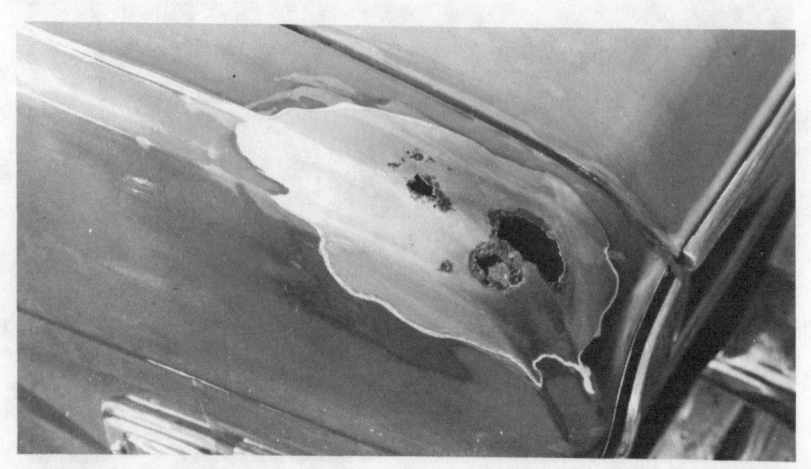

3. When you've finished grinding, the area to be repaired should look like this. Grind the paint back several inches in each direction to ensure that the patch will adhere to the metal. Remove all the damaged metal or the rust will return.

4. Tap the edges of the holes inward with a ballpeen hammer to allow for the thickness of the fiberglass material. Tap lightly so that you don't destroy any contours.

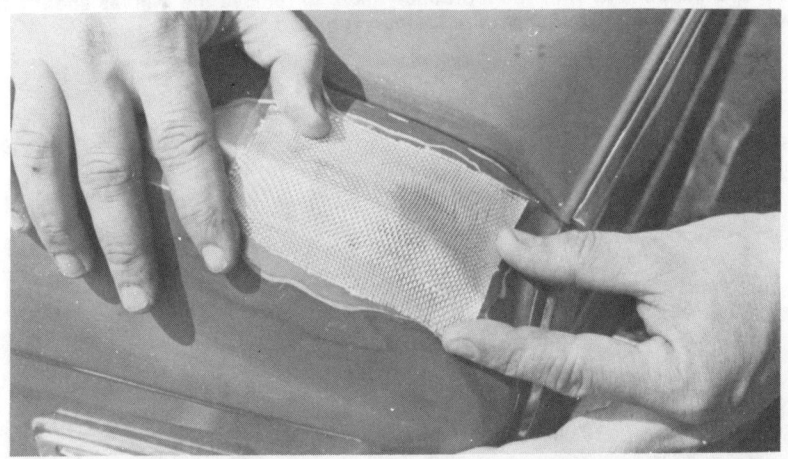

5. Follow the directions of the kit you purchase carefully. With fiberglass repair kits, the first step is generally to cut one or two pieces of fiberglass to cover the hole. Quite often, the procedure is to cut one patch the size of the prepared area and one patch the size of the hole.

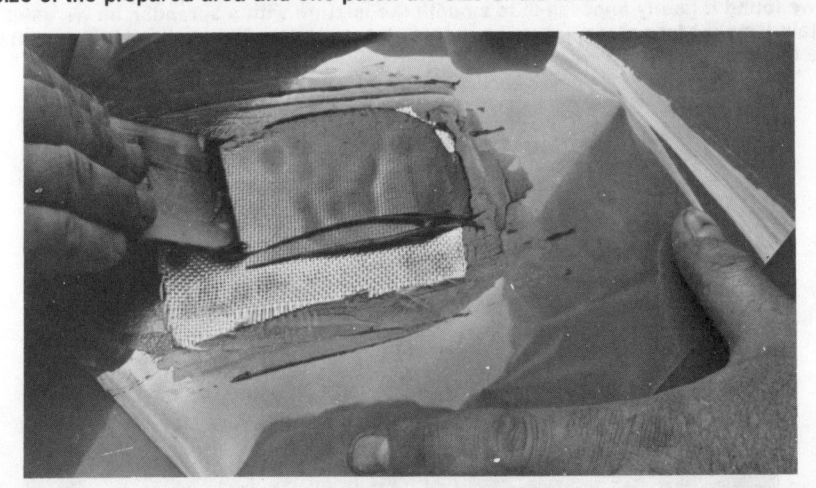

6. Mix the fiberglass material and the patching compound together following the directions supplied with the kit. With this particular kit, a layer type process is used, with the entire mixture being prepared on a piece of plastic film known as a release sheet. Keep in mind that not all kits work this way. Be careful when you mix the catalyst with the resin, as too much catalyst will harden the mixture before you can apply it.

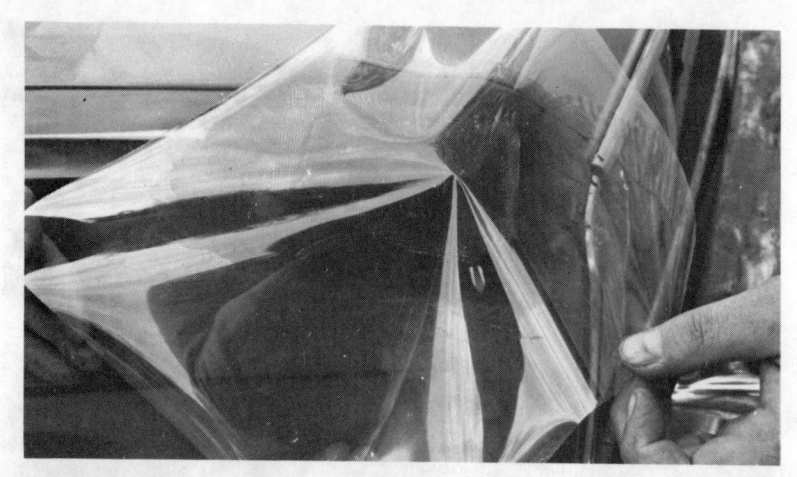

7. Spread the material on the damaged area using the release sheet. This process is essentially meant for smooth flat areas, and as a result, the release sheet would not adhere to the surface properly on our test vehicle. If this happens to you, you'll probably have to remove the release sheet and spread the fiberglass compound out with your fingers or a small spreader.

8. This is what the fiberglass mixture looked like on our vehicle after it had hardened. Because of the contours, we found it nearly impossible to smooth the mixture with a spreader, so we used our fingers. Unfortunately, it makes for a messy job that requires a lot of sanding. If you're working on a flat surface, you won't have this problem.

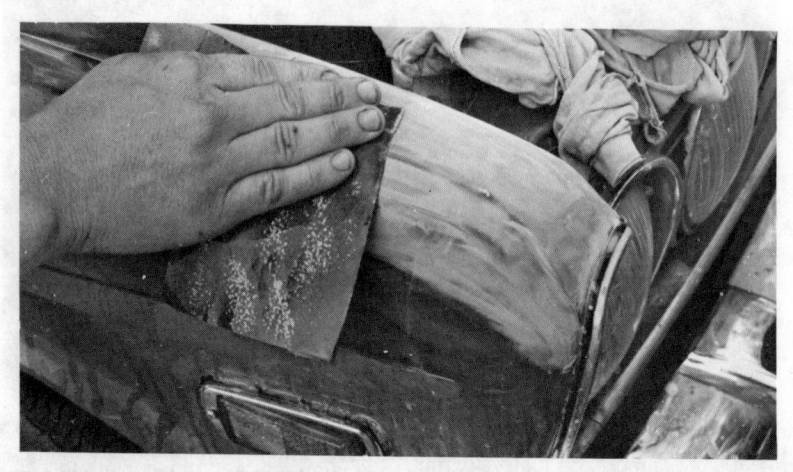

9. After the patch has hardened, sand it down to a smooth surface. You'll probably have to start with about grade 100 sandpaper and work your way up to 400 wet paper. If you have a particularly rough surface, you could start with a half-round plastic file.

BODY 201

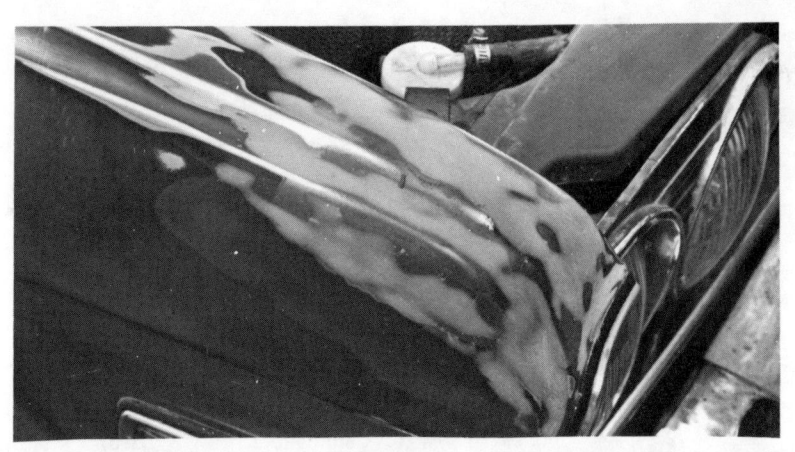

10. This is what the finished product should look like before you apply paint. Many of the kits come with glazing compound to fill in small imperfections left after the initial sanding. You'll probably need some. We did. The entire sanding operation took about an hour. Feather the edges of the repaired area into the surrounding paint carefully. As in any other body job, your hand is the best indicator of what's smooth and what isn't. It doesn't matter if it looks smooth. It's got to feel smooth. Take your time with this step and it will come out right.

11. Once you've smoothed out the repair, mask the entire area carefully, and spray the repair with primer. Keep the spray can moving in steady even strokes, overlap every stroke, and keep the spray can about 8–12 inches from the surface. Apply several coats of primer, letting the primer dry between coats.

12. The finished product (in primer) looks like this. If you were going to just spot paint this area, the next step would be to spray the correct color on the repaired area. This particular car is waiting for a complete paint job.

Appendix

General Conversion Table

Multiply by	To convert	To	
2.54	Inches	Centimeters	.3937
30.48	Feet	Centimeters	.0328
.914	Yards	Meters	1.094
1.609	Miles	Kilometers	.621
.645	Square inches	Square cm.	.155
.836	Square yards	Square meters	1.196
16.39	Cubic inches	Cubic cm.	.061
28.3	Cubic feet	Liters	.0353
.4536	Pounds	Kilograms	2.2045
4.226	Gallons	Liters	.264
.068	Lbs./sq. in. (psi)	Atmospheres	14.7
.138	Foot pounds	Kg. m.	7.23
1.014	H.P. (DIN)	H.P. (SAE)	.9861
—	To obtain	From	Multiply by

Note: 1 cm. equals 10 mm.; 1 mm. equals .0394".

Conversion—Common Fractions to Decimals and Millimeters

Common Fractions	Decimal Fractions	Millimeters (approx.)	Common Fractions	Decimal Fractions	Millimeters (approx.)	Common Fractions	Decimal Fractions	Millimeters (approx.)
1/128	.008	0.20	11/32	.344	8.73	43/64	.672	17.07
1/64	.016	0.40	23/64	.359	9.13	11/16	.688	17.46
1/32	.031	0.79	3/8	.375	9.53	45/64	.703	17.86
3/64	.047	1.19	25/64	.391	9.92	23/32	.719	18.26
1/16	.063	1.59	13/32	.406	10.32	47/64	.734	18.65
5/64	.078	1.98	27/64	.422	10.72	3/4	.750	19.05
3/32	.094	2.38	7/16	.438	11.11	49/64	.766	19.45
7/64	.109	2.78	29/64	.453	11.51	25/32	.781	19.84
1/8	.125	3.18	15/32	.469	11.91	51/64	.797	20.24
9/64	.141	3.57	31/64	.484	12.30	13/16	.813	20.64
5/32	.156	3.97	1/2	.500	12.70	53/64	.828	21.03
11/64	.172	4.37	33/64	.516	13.10	27/32	.844	21.43
3/16	.188	4.76	17/32	.531	13.49	55/64	.859	21.83
13/64	.203	5.16	35/64	.547	13.89	7/8	.875	22.23
7/32	.219	5.56	9/16	.563	14.29	57/64	.891	22.62
15/64	.234	5.95	37/64	.578	14.68	29/32	.906	23.02
1/4	.250	6.35	19/32	.594	15.08	59/64	.922	23.42
17/64	.266	6.75	39/64	.609	15.48	15/16	.938	23.81
9/32	.281	7.14	5/8	.625	15.88	61/64	.953	24.21
19/64	.297	7.54	41/64	.641	16.27	31/32	.969	24.61
5/16	.313	7.94	21/32	.656	16.67	63/64	.984	25.00
21/64	.328	8.33						

APPENDIX 203

Conversion—Millimeters to Decimal Inches

mm	inches	mm	inches	mm	inches	mm	inches	mm	inches
1	.039 370	31	1.220 470	61	2.401 570	91	3.582 670	210	8.267 700
2	.078 740	32	1.259 840	62	2.440 940	92	3.622 040	220	8.661 400
3	.118 110	33	1.299 210	63	2.480 310	93	3.661 410	230	9.055 100
4	.157 480	34	1.338 580	64	2.519 680	94	3.700 780	240	9.448 800
5	.196 850	35	1.377 949	65	2.559 050	95	3.740 150	250	9.842 500
6	.236 220	36	1.417 319	66	2.598 420	96	3.779 520	260	10.236 200
7	.275 590	37	1.456 689	67	2.637 790	97	3.818 890	270	10.629 900
8	.314 960	38	1.496 050	68	2.677 160	98	3.858 260	280	11.032 600
9	.354 330	39	1.535 430	69	2.716 530	99	3.897 630	290	11.417 300
10	.393 700	40	1.574 800	70	2.755 900	100	3.937 000	300	11.811 000
11	.433 070	41	1.614 170	71	2.795 270	105	4.133 848	310	12.204 700
12	.472 440	42	1.653 540	72	2.834 640	110	4.330 700	320	12.598 400
13	.511 810	43	1.692 910	73	2.874 010	115	4.527 550	330	12.992 100
14	.551 180	44	1.732 280	74	2.913 380	120	4.724 400	340	13.385 800
15	.590 550	45	1.771 650	75	2.952 750	125	4.921 250	350	13.779 500
16	.629 920	46	1.811 020	76	2.992 120	130	5.118 100	360	14.173 200
17	.669 290	47	1.850 390	77	3.031 490	135	5.314 950	370	14.566 900
18	.708 660	48	1.889 760	78	3.070 860	140	5.511 800	380	14.960 600
19	.748 030	49	1.929 130	79	3.110 230	145	5.708 650	390	15.354 300
20	.787 400	50	1.968 500	80	3.149 600	150	5.905 500	400	15.748 000
21	.826 770	51	2.007 870	81	3.188 970	155	6.102 350	500	19.685 000
22	.866 140	52	2.047 240	82	3.228 340	160	6.299 200	600	23.622 000
23	.905 510	53	2.086 610	83	3.267 710	165	6.496 050	700	27.559 000
24	.944 880	54	2.125 980	84	3.307 080	170	6.692 900	800	31.496 000
25	.984 250	55	2.165 350	85	3.346 450	175	6.889 750	900	35.433 000
26	1.023 620	56	2.204 720	86	3.385 820	180	7.086 600	1000	39.370 000
27	1.062 990	57	2.244 090	87	3.425 190	185	7.283 450	2000	78.740 000
28	1.102 360	58	2.283 460	88	3.464 560	190	7.480 300	3000	118.110 000
29	1.141 730	59	2.322 830	89	3.503 903	195	7.677 150	4000	157.480 000
30	1.181 100	60	2.362 200	90	3.543 300	200	7.874 000	5000	196.850 000

To change decimal millimeters to decimal inches, position the decimal point where desired on either side of the millimeter measurement shown and reset the inches decimal by the same number of digits in the same direction. For example, to convert 0.001 mm to decimal inches, reset the decimal behind the 1 mm (shown on the chart) to 0.001; change the decimal inch equivalent (0.039") shown) to 0.000039".

Tap Drill Sizes

National Fine or S.A.E.

Screw & Tap Size	Threads Per Inch	Use Drill Number
No. 5	44	37
No. 6	40	33
No. 8	36	29
No. 10	32	21
No. 12	28	15
1/4	28	3
5/16	24	1
3/8	24	Q
7/16	20	W
1/2	20	29/64
9/16	18	33/64
5/8	18	37/64
3/4	16	11/16
7/8	14	13/16
1 1/8	12	1 3/64
1 1/4	12	1 11/64
1 1/2	12	1 27/64

Tap Drill Sizes

National Coarse or U.S.S.

Screw & Tap Size	Threads Per Inch	Use Drill Number
No. 5	40	39
No. 6	32	36
No. 8	32	29
No. 10	24	25
No. 12	24	17
1/4	20	8
5/16	18	F
3/8	16	5/16
7/16	14	U
1/2	13	27/64
9/16	12	31/64
5/8	11	17/32
3/4	10	21/32
7/8	9	49/64
1	8	7/8
1 1/8	7	63/64
1 1/4	7	1 7/64
1 1/2	6	1 11/32

APPENDIX

Decimal Equivalent Size of the Number Drills

Drill No.	Decimal Equivalent	Drill No.	Decimal Equivalent	Drill No.	Decimal Equivalent
80	.0135	53	.0595	26	.1470
79	.0145	52	.0635	25	.1495
78	.0160	51	.0670	24	.1520
77	.0180	50	.0700	23	.1540
76	.0200	49	.0730	22	.1570
75	.0210	48	.0760	21	.1590
74	.0225	47	.0785	20	.1610
73	.0240	46	.0810	19	.1660
72	.0250	45	.0820	18	.1695
71	.0260	44	.0860	17	.1730
70	.0280	43	.0890	16	.1770
69	.0292	42	.0935	15	.1800
68	.0310	41	.0960	14	.1820
67	.0320	40	.0980	13	.1850
66	.0330	39	.0995	12	.1890
65	.0350	38	.1015	11	.1910
64	.0360	37	.1040	10	.1935
63	.0370	36	.1065	9	.1960
62	.0380	35	.1100	8	.1990
61	.0390	34	.1110	7	.2010
60	.0400	33	.1130	6	.2040
59	.0410	32	.1160	5	.2055
58	.0420	31	.1200	4	.2090
57	.0430	30	.1285	3	.2130
56	.0465	29	.1360	2	.2210
55	.0520	28	.1405	1	.2280
54	.0550	27	.1440		

Decimal Equivalent Size of the Letter Drills

Letter Drill	Decimal Equivalent	Letter Drill	Decimal Equivalent	Letter Drill	Decimal Equivalent
A	.234	J	.277	S	.348
B	.238	K	.281	T	.358
C	.242	L	.290	U	.368
D	.246	M	.295	V	.377
E	.250	N	.302	W	.386
F	.257	O	.316	X	.397
G	.261	P	.323	Y	.404
H	.266	Q	.332	Z	.413
I	.272	R	.339		

APPENDIX 205

Anti-Freeze Chart

Temperatures Shown in Degrees Fahrenheit +32 is Freezing

Cooling System Capacity Quarts	\multicolumn{14}{c}{Quarts of ETHYLENE GLYCOL Needed for Protection to Temperatures Shown Below}
	1	2	3	4	5	6	7	8	9	10	11	12	13	14
10	+24°	+16°	+ 4°	−12°	−34°	−62°								
11	+25	+18	+ 8	− 6	−23	−47								
12	+26	+19	+10	0	−15	−34	−57°							
13	+27	+21	+13	+ 3	− 9	−25	−45							
14			+15	+ 6	− 5	−18	−34							
15			+16	+ 8	0	−12	−26							
16			+17	+10	+ 2	− 8	−19	−34	−52°					
17			+18	+12	+ 5	− 4	−14	−27	−42					
18			+19	+14	+ 7	0	−10	−21	−34	−50°				
19			+20	+15	+ 9	+ 2	− 7	−16	−28	−42				
20				+16	+10	+ 4	− 3	−12	−22	−34	−48°			
21				+17	+12	+ 6	0	− 9	−17	−28	−41			
22				+18	+13	+ 8	+ 2	− 6	−14	−23	−34	−47°		
23				+19	+14	+ 9	+ 4	− 3	−10	−19	−29	−40		
24				+19	+15	+10	+ 5	0	− 8	−15	−23	−34	−46°	
25				+20	+16	+12	+ 7	+ 1	− 5	−12	−20	−29	−40	−50°
26				+17	+13	+ 8	+ 3	− 3	− 9	−16	−25	−34	−44
27				+18	+14	+ 9	+ 5	− 1	− 7	−13	−21	−29	−39
28				+18	+15	+10	+ 6	+ 1	− 5	−11	−18	−25	−34
29				+19	+16	+12	+ 7	+ 2	− 3	− 8	−15	−22	−29
30				+20	+17	+13	+ 8	+ 4	− 1	− 6	−12	−18	−25

For capacities over 30 quarts divide true capacity by 3. Find quarts Anti-Freeze for the ⅓ and multiply by 3 for quarts to add.

For capacities under 10 quarts multiply true capacity by 3. Find quarts Anti-Freeze for the tripled volume and divide by 3 for quarts to add.

To Increase the Freezing Protection of Anti-Freeze Solutions Already Installed

Cooling System Capacity Quarts	\multicolumn{5}{c}{From +20° F. to}	\multicolumn{5}{c}{From +10° F. to}	\multicolumn{4}{c}{From 0° F. to}
	0°	−10°	−20°	−30°	−40°	0°	−10°	−20°	−30°	−40°	−10°	−20°	−30°	−40°
10	1¾	2¼	3	3½	3¾	¾	1½	2¼	2¾	3¼	¾	1½	2	2½
12	2	2¾	3½	4	4½	1	1¾	2½	3¼	3¾	1	1¾	2½	3¼
14	2¼	3¼	4	4¾	5½	1¼	2	3	3¾	4½	1	2	3	3½
16	2½	3½	4½	5¼	6	1¼	2½	3½	4¼	5¼	1¼	2¼	3¼	4
18	3	4	5	6	7	1½	2¾	4	5	5¾	1½	2½	3¾	4¾
20	3¼	4½	5¾	6¾	7½	1¾	3	4¼	5½	6½	1½	2¾	4¼	5¼
22	3½	5	6¼	7¼	8¼	1¾	3¼	4¾	6	7¼	1¾	3¼	4½	5½
24	4	5½	7	8	9	2	3½	5	6½	7½	1¾	3½	5	6
26	4¼	6	7½	8¾	10	2	4	5½	7	8¼	2	3¾	5½	6¾
28	4½	6¼	8	9½	10½	2¼	4¼	6	7½	9	2	4	5¾	7¼
30	5	6¾	8½	10	11½	2½	4½	6½	8	9½	2¼	4¼	6¼	7¾

Test radiator solution with proper hydrometer. Determine from the table the number of quarts of solution to be drawn off from a full cooling system and replace with undiluted anti-freeze, to give the desired increased protection. For example, to increase protection of a 22-quart cooling system containing Ethylene Glycol (permanent type) anti-freeze, from +20° F. to −20° F. will require the replacement of 6¼ quarts of solution with undiluted anti-freeze.

Index

A

Air cleaner, 11
Air conditioning, 24
  Sight glass check, 24
Alternator, 77
Automatic transaxle, 160
  Adjustment, 160
  Filter service, 161
  Removal and Installation, 162
Axle shafts, 170

B

Back-up light switch, 161
Ball joints, 165
Battery, 17
  Jump starting, 41
  Maintenance, 17
Belt tension, 18
Body, 191
Brakes, 178
  Adjustment, 178
  Bleeding, 181
  Fluid level, 29
  Fluid recommendations, 30
  Front brakes, 182
  Master cylinder, 179
  Parking brake, 189
  Rear brakes, 185
Bulbs, 154

C

Camshaft and bearings, 92
Capacities, 31
Carburetor, 135
  Adjustment, 136
  Overhaul, 139
  Replacement, 135
Catalytic converter, 121
Charging system, 77
Chassis lubrication, 36
Clutch, 158
  Adjustment, 159
  Removal and installation, 158
Coil, ignition, 50
Compression, 62
Connecting rod and bearings, 94
Control Arm
  Lower, 167
Cooling system, 21
Crankcase ventilation (PCV), 11
Crankshaft, 96
Cylinder head torque sequence, 89

D

Distributor
  Removal and installation, 77
Driveshaft (axle shaft), 170

E

Electrical
  Chassis, 142
  Engine, 68
Electronic ignition, 68
Emission controls, 121
Engine
  Camshaft, 92
  Cylinder head, 88

INDEX

Cylinder head torque sequence, 89
Exhaust manifold, 91
Identification, 10
Intake manifold, 90
Oil recommendations, 33
Piston (positioning), 95
Rebuilding, 96
Removal and installation, 83
Specifications, 86
Timing belt, 91
Timing gears, 94
Tune-up, 43
Evaporative canister, 16

F

Firing order, 77
Fluid level checks, 27
  Battery, 30
  Coolant, 30
  Differential, 28
  Engine oil, 34
  Master cylinder, 29
  Power steering pump, 30
  Transmission, 27
Fluid recommendations, 33
Front suspension, 164
  Wheel alignment, 171
Front wheel bearing, 39
Fuel filter, 32
Fuel pump, 132
Fuel system, 132
Fuel tank, 141
Fuses and flashers, 155

H

Hazard flasher, 155
Headlights, 153
Heater, 144
History, 6

I

Identification
  Vehicle, 7
  Engine, 10
  Transmission, 10
Idle speed and mixture, 50
Ignition switch, 153
Ignition timing, 47
Instrument Panel, 151
Intake manifold, 90

J

Jump starting, 41

L

Light bulb specifications, 154
Lower control arm, 167

Lubrication
  Chassis, 36
  Engine, 33

M

Maintenance (routine) Intervals, 13
Manifolds, 90–91
Manual transaxle, 156
Master cylinder, 179
Model identification, 7

N

Neutral safety switch, 161

O

Oil and fuel recommendations, 33
Oil change, 34
Oil filter (engine), 34
Oil pan, 99
Oil pump, 99
Oil level (engine), 34

P

Parking brake, 189
Piston and rings, 94
  Installation, 94
  Positioning, 95
PCV valve, 11
Power steering pump, 177

R

Radiator, 99
Radio, 148
Rear axle, 173
Rear suspension, 173
Rear wheel bearing, 39
Regulator, 80
Rear main oil seal, 99
Rings (piston), 95
Routine maintenance, 11

S

Safety, 4
Serial Number Identification, 7
Shock absorber
  Front, 164
  Rear, 173
Spark plugs, 43
Specifications
  Brakes, 179
  Capacities, 31
  Carburetor, 140
  Crankshaft & connecting rod, 87
  Fuses, 155
  General engine, 86
  Light bulb, 154

INDEX

Specifications (*continued*)
    Piston and ring, 87
    Torque, 86
    Tune-up, 44
    Valve, 86
    Wheel alignment, 174
Speedometer cable, 153
Springs
    Front, 164
    Rear, 174
Starter, 80
Steering, 175
    Pump, 177
    Wheel, 176
Strut, 164
Sway Bar, 167

T

Thermostat, 102
Tie-rod, 177
Tires, 31
Tools and Equipment, 2
Towing, 40

Transaxle
    Automatic, 160
    Manual, 156
Troubleshooting, 52
Tune-up, 43
    Procedures, 43
    Specifications, 44
Turn signal switch, 176

V

Valves
    Adjustment, 47
    Service, 89
Vehicle identification, 7

W

Water pump, 101
Wheel alignment, 171
Wheel bearings, 39
Wheel cylinders, 188
Windshield wipers, 149
    Blade, 25
    Motor, 149

25 Ways
TO BETTER GAS MILEAGE

The Federal government's goal is to cut gasoline consumption 10% by 1985. In addition to intelligent purchase of a new vehicle and efficient driving habits, there are other ways to increase gas mileage with your present car or truck.

Tests have shown that almost ¾ of all vehicles on the road need maintenance in areas that directly affect fuel economy. Using this book for regular maintenance and tune-ups can increase fuel economy as much as 10%, depending on your vehicle.

1. **Replace spark plugs regularly.** New plugs alone can increase fuel economy by 3%.
2. **Be sure the plugs are the correct type and properly gapped.**
3. **Set the ignition timing to specifications.**
4. If your vehicle does not have electronic ignition, **check the points, rotor and cap as specified.**
5. **Replace the air filter regularly.** A dirty air filter richens the air/fuel mixture and can increase fuel consumption as much as 10%. Tests show ⅓ of all vehicles have air filters in need of replacement.
6. **Replace the fuel filter** at least as often as recommended.
7. **Be sure the idle speed and carburetor fuel mixture are set to specifications.**
8. **Check the automatic choke.** A sticking or malfunctioning choke wastes gas.
9. **Change the oil and filter as recommended.** Dirty oil is thick and causes extra friction between the moving parts, cutting efficiency and increasing wear.
10. **Replace the PCV valve** at regular intervals.
11. **Service the cooling system** at regular recommended intervals.
12. **Be sure the thermostat is operating properly.** A thermostat that is stuck open delays engine warm-up, and a cold engine uses twice as much fuel as a warm engine.
13. **Be sure the tires are properly inflated.** Under-inflated tires can cost as much as 1 mpg. Better mileage can be achieved by over-inflating the tires (never exceed the maximum inflation pressure on the side of the tire), but the tires will wear faster.
14. **Be sure the drive belts (especially the fan belt) are in good condition** and properly adjusted.
15. **Be sure the battery is fully charged** for fast starts.
16. **Use the recommended viscosity motor oil to reduce friction.**
17. **Use the recommended viscosity fluids in the rear axle and transmission.**
18. **Be sure the wheels are properly balanced.**
19. **Be sure the front end is correctly aligned.** A misaligned front end actually has wheels going in different directions, creating additional drag.
20. **Correctly adjust the wheel bearing.** Wheel bearings adjusted too tight increase rolling resistance.
21. **Be sure the brakes are properly adjusted and not dragging.**
22. **If possible, install radial tires.** Radial tires deliver as much as ½ mpg more than bias belted tires.
23. **Install a flex-type fan** if you don't have a clutch fan. Flex fans push more air at low speeds when more cooling is needed. At high speeds the blades flatten out for less resistance.
24. **Check the radiator cap for a cracked or worn gasket.** If the cap doesn't seal properly, the cooling system will not function properly.
25. **Check the spark plug wires for bad cracks, burned or broken insulation.** Cracked wires decrease fuel efficiency by failing to deliver full voltage to the spark plugs.

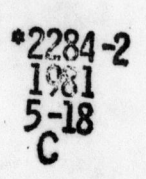